T0339084

# NORTH OF AMERICA

# NORTH
# OF
# AMERICA

Loyalists, Indigenous Nations, and the
Borders of the Long American Revolution

JEFFERS LENNOX

Yale

UNIVERSITY PRESS

New Haven and London

Published with assistance from the Annie Burr Lewis Fund.

Yale University Press books may be purchased in quantity for
educational, business, or promotional use. For information, please
e-mail sales.press@yale.edu (U.S. office) or sales@yaleup.co.uk
(U.K. office).

Set in Janson type by IDS Infotech Ltd., Chandigarh, India.
Printed in the United States of America.

Library of Congress Control Number: 2021952605
ISBN 978-0-300-22612-6 (hardcover : alk. paper)

A catalogue record for this book is available from the British Library.

This paper meets the requirements of ANSI/NISO Z39.48-1992
(Permanence of Paper).

10 9 8 7 6 5 4 3 2 1

*For my family on both sides of the border. But especially for Paul, who read every word and asked the best questions.*

# Contents

NORTH OF AMERICA

# Prologue

WHEN EZRA STILES FIRST learned of the Quebec Act, he recorded his sentiments in a diary. It was 23 August 1774, and he was upset. "The King has signed the Quebec Act," he wrote, "extending that Province to the Ohio & Mississippi and comprehending nearly two thirds of the territory of English America, and establishing the Romish Church & IDOLATRY over all that space." He was "astonished" that leading imperial figures "should expressly establish Popery over three Quarters of their Empire."[1] The act was "intolerable" not simply because Catholics could continue practicing their religion in Quebec—an accommodation provided by the Royal Proclamation of 1763—but because Quebec's territory now extended down the back of the American colonies.

While often listed among the other "intolerable acts" imposed on the American colonies after the Boston Tea Party, the Quebec Act (often called the "Canada Bill") was a unique piece of legislation. It did not spring fully formed from Parliament in the summer of 1774 but was years in the making and relied on established precedent for dealing with foreign subjects. In many ways it was the culmination of a string of proclamations and treaties dating from the fall of Quebec in 1763 at the end of the Seven Years' War, when France ceded its North American colonies to Great Britain. But its history went deeper than the capture of New France. British administrators had struggled to govern French subjects and their Indigenous allies since 1713, when French Acadia fell under de jure British control and was renamed Nova Scotia.[2] This experience provided British officials with lessons that could be applied in 1774.[3] When

Samuel King, *Ezra Stiles*, 1771. Oil on canvas, 34 × 28 in.
(86.4 × 71.1 cm). Bequest of Dr. Charles Jenkins Foote, B.A.
1883, M.D. 1890, 1995.3.1. Yale University Art Gallery.

American Patriots described the Quebec Act as despotic, they ignored
the fact that they themselves were responsible for many of its elements.[4]

When Quebec fell to the British in 1763, the British reduced its size.
French Quebec had extended into the Ohio River Valley, but British Que-

bec was limited to lands along the St. Lawrence River from just west of Montreal to the Gaspé Peninsula. Colonial officials faced the challenge of incorporating the French settlements, centered at Quebec but strung out along lakes and river systems that ran deep into the continent's interior, into a British American empire forged along the Atlantic littoral but increasingly influenced by agricultural and expansionist ideals.[5] Complicating this task was the need to appease powerful Indigenous groups that resisted English expansion and remained allied with French traders. In a perfect world, the former French subjects would have become loyal subjects of the Crown and, even better, Protestants. But British officials and settlers had spent the past century and a half demonizing their French neighbors for their "Romish" religion and Indigenous alliances. French traders more easily adopted Indigenous fashion and customs; their *courieurs du bois* traversed the geographic and cultural boundaries that separated settlements and homelands.[6] This tradition dated to the early seventeenth century, when Samuel Champlain sent the young Étienne Brûlé to live with Algonquian allies. Brûlé quickly adopted Algonquian dress and learned their languages, acting as a link between the Huron and the French.[7] For English settlers, such a transition was unimaginable; they often depicted English captives as martyrs who endured the "savage" lifestyle only by the grace of God while their loved ones prayed for their return.[8]

The Proclamation of 1763 was meant to regulate the governance of French and Indigenous territories, but it was an expedient measure that failed to recognize the realities on the ground. It created a border between British and Indigenous territory along the Appalachian Mountains, which separated water flowing into the Atlantic from that running toward the Mississippi. But in doing so, it ignored the regions west of the boundary where British settlers already resided and lands east of the boundary under Indigenous control. It was left to the superintendents for Indian Affairs—Sir William Johnson in the northern department and John Stuart in the southern—to craft acceptable boundaries between British and Indigenous lands.[9]

William Johnson was born in Smithtown, County Meath, Ireland, around 1715 and came to British America in 1738 to oversee his uncle's estate in the Mohawk Valley. Success in trade and good relations with the powerful Iroquois Confederacy quickly paved the road for official positions. Appointed superintendent for Indian Affairs for the northern department in 1756, he had a talent for using Indigenous ways for his own profit. According to one (likely apocryphal) story, Johnson was in a

Charles Spooner, after Thomas Adams, *Sir William Johnson*, 1756. Mezzotint,
36.3 × 26 cm (14 5/16 × 10 1/4 in.). Mabel Brady Garvan Collection,
1946.9.789. Yale University Art Gallery.

council with a group of Mohawks when one of the chiefs told him about a dream. He had dreamt that Johnson gave him a fine lace coat, the same coat Johnson was wearing. Johnson replied that if he had dreamt it, he must have the coat. The next time the two met, Johnson told the chief that *he* had recently had a dream: he dreamt that the chief had given him a large tract of land along the Mohawk River to build a house and settlement. The chief smiled and said he should have it, but cautioned that they must never dream together again, as a single coat was hardly worth what Johnson got in return.[10]

As land speculators pressured the British government to open the west, and Indigenous nations witnessed violence and enclosures on their traditional lands, Johnson worked to secure more realistic boundaries between colonies and homelands. At the Treaty of Fort Stanwix (1768), he negotiated a boundary four hundred miles farther west than the Proclamation line while also protecting Indigenous claims to the Ohio Valley.[11] This border gave hope to settlers who wished to expand, but with few British forces stationed at trading posts, the administration could not control the settlers' commercial interactions in Indigenous territory.[12] As Indigenous groups grew increasingly angry in the late 1760s about settler expansion, it fell to Johnson to balance imperial demands against Indigenous concerns.[13]

Johnson's ability to win Indigenous support while retaining the imperial administrators' trust secured his position, and he soon employed several deputies to assist him and keep him informed of regional issues.[14] Johnson and his agents often faced the complicated task of also governing French settlers, who had established trading posts and settlements on Indigenous lands throughout the eighteenth century. From the imperial perspective, then, reserving territory for Indigenous peoples also prevented the extension of British law to the French inhabitants south of the Great Lakes. In considering a new plan for governing the French subjects in Quebec, officials had to keep in mind French subjects living in the heart of the continent. After 1763, Johnson (who died unexpectedly in 1774), his deputies, and his nephew (who replaced him as superintendent) helped triangulate British-Indigenous-French relations in lands Britain claimed but could not control.

The Indigenous nations who worked to assert control over their territory did not forget the promises made in the 1760s. It fell to Daniel Claus, one of Johnson's deputies, to answer Indigenous concerns in Canada.[15] On a tour of Quebec in 1773, Claus recorded the concerns and complaints of many Indigenous peoples. In July, he attended a meeting with Hurons living at Lorette who reminded him of the promises made by the king. A common complaint was that even after they relocated under French encouragement in the seventeenth century, the Hurons were losing their traditional land. One speaker lamented that priests sold away land that had been reserved for Huron settlement and that warriors "were hemmed in by the white people with regard to their hunting grounds at Tadousack."[16] Claus offered the Hurons a response a few days later. Without a trace of irony, he simply informed them that when a group moves to a new place, they have to follow the laws established by those already living there.[17] The Hurons had moved from the Great Lakes to a region controlled by the French. The British now controlled that region, so new rules applied. That both the French *and* the British had settled on Indigenous land, with its own established laws and customs, appears never to have crossed Claus's mind.

In 1773, Lord Dartmouth, the secretary of state for the colonies, wrote to Théophile-Hector de Cramahé, the lieutenant governor of Quebec, and outlined his concerns for governing Quebec, particularly as they related to the province's boundary. "The Limits of the Colony will also in my Judgement make a necessary part of this very extensive Consideration," he wrote, adding, "There is no longer any Hope of perfecting that plan of Policy in respect to the interior Country, which was in Contemplation when the Proclamation of 1763 was issued."[18] The problem, wrote Dartmouth, was that in 1763, Parliament had known too little about the French settlements and had defined Quebec as a thin strip of land along the St. Lawrence. Extending the boundaries to encompass a greater number of inhabitants might also protect Indigenous territory. Cramahé had previously expressed to Dartmouth his opinions on how best to secure the allegiance of the Canadians. Religion was central. "It has ever been my Opinion," he argued, "that the only sure and effectual Method, of gaining the affections of His Majesty's Canadian Subjects to His Royal Person and Government, was, to grant them all possible Freedom and Indulgence in the Exercise of their Religion, to which they are exceedingly attached, and that any Restraint laid upon them in Regard to this, would only retard, instead of advancing, a Change of their Ideas respecting religious Matters."[19] He was more concerned about the Canadians who were promised their religion than about the Indigenous nations whose homelands were officially protected by the Royal Proclamation and later treaties.

In the decade after 1763, leading colonial officials, such as the governor of Quebec, Guy Carleton (later Lord Dorchester), and imperial bodies, including the Board of Trade and Privy Council, discussed, drafted, and redrafted what would eventually become the Quebec Act. Carleton believed that Quebec would be best governed if British officials agreed to restore the colony's pre-1763 boundaries, extending it into the Ohio Valley. Other government figures, including Wills Hill (Lord Hillsborough, the secretary of state for the colonies) and Francis Maseres (Quebec's attorney general) refused to relinquish the idea that Quebec would become a Protestant province, but Carleton believed loyalty would be best preserved if the Canadians could maintain their religion. To that end, he suggested to Hillsborough in 1768 that a coadjutor be appointed to guarantee the continued presence of a bishop in the province and thus fend off troublesome complaints from Rome. While Hillsborough disagreed, Carleton ignored him and, in 1770, named Canadian priest Louis-Philippe Mariauchau d'Esgly to the position.[20]

By 1773, few residents of Canada were happy with the state of affairs in the province and calls for addressing Quebec's boundaries came from a variety of groups. Indigenous nations were unhappy about land encroachment, and merchants were skeptical about the economic potential of the spatially restricted colony defined by the Royal Proclamation of 1763. In late December, a group of English merchants in Quebec drafted a memorial to Lord Dartmouth expressing concern about the colony's prosperity.[21] Looking both west to the Ohio Valley and east to Labrador, they argued that "if the province is not restored to its antient limits the morals of the Indians will be debauched, and the fur trade as well as the winter seal fishery forever lost."[22] The province's Roman Catholic inhabitants shared many of these sentiments. That same month, several French petitioners sent their own memorial to Dartmouth stating their pleasure that so many French institutions had been maintained after 1763 and promising that "this excess of kindness towards us we shall never forget." But they wanted confirmation that the allowances would continue: "vouchsafe, most illustrious and generous sovereign, to dissipate these fears and this uneasiness, by restoring to us our ancient laws, privileges, and customs, and to extend our province to its former boundaries."[23] A supporting memorial, attached to the original, dealt with the boundary issue in more detail, noting that the province's limits left fertile land and loyal subjects outside legal jurisdiction.[24]

There were differing opinions on whether Quebec required an assembly. Leading French inhabitants argued that the province was in no state to govern itself, but English merchants pushed for it.[25] These demands were at odds with the request for expanded boundaries, which would leave Quebec too big and too sparsely settled to provide for a functioning assembly.[26] But the calls for a more general reworking of colonial governance resonated in London. In late December 1773, Dartmouth informed the lieutenant governor of Quebec that plans were in the works to address the colony's demands.[27]

The means by which the Crown would do that was the product of much investigation and debate.[28] It was left to the first minister, Lord North, to commission the actual drafting of the Quebec Act and help marshal it through the parliamentary process. While the bill easily passed the House of Lords (where it originated), it faced stiffer but disorganized resistance when presented to the House of Commons in June 1774. Various ministers objected to different elements of the bill—the toleration of Catholicism, the proposed boundaries, or the lack of an assembly—but those in opposition could not combine their efforts effectively. The bill presented to the House of Commons represented an effort to balance these competing considerations of religion, law, and geography.[29]

Given that it arrived at the tail end of a legislative session largely dedicated to addressing the troubles in America, it is perhaps understandable that British Americans saw the Quebec Act as another "coercive" policy meant to punish them. But it wasn't, and in fact most of its main clauses were settled well before politicians in London learned of the American disturbances that followed the passage of the Tea Act. The major elements of the Quebec Act were already in place by the time of the Boston Tea Party in May 1773. But timing matters, and although the act was meant to be debated early in the 1774 session, it was pushed later into the calendar, and thus news of the act arrived at a time when many colonists were already furious at British administrators.

On the American side, much had happened between the summer of 1771, when the Privy Council first requested reports on Quebec to inform the act, and June 1774, when Parliament finally debated the legislation. Rhode Islanders burned the customs ship *Gaspée* after it ran aground in 1772, a demonstration of merchant and trader anger at the ship captain's heavy-handed patrol.[30] In 1773, British Americans read letters between Massachusetts governor Thomas Hutchinson and Thomas Whately, an assistant to Prime Minister George Grenville. The letters dated to the late 1760s but came to light only after Whately's death. In them Hutchinson

Le Roy le Veult.

Whereas his Majesty by his Royal
proclamation bearing date the seventh day
of October in the third year of his reign
thought fit to declare the provisions which
had been made in respect to certain countries
Territories and Islands in America ceded to
his Majesty by the definitive Treaty of
Peace concluded at Paris on the tenth day
of ffebruary One thousand seven hundred
and sixty three And whereas by the
Arrangements made by the said Royal
proclamation a very large _extent of country_
within which there were
several colonies and settlements of the
subjects of ffrance who claimed to remain
therein under the ffaith of the said Treaty
was left without any provision being made
for the Administration of Civil Government
therein and _certain_ parts of the _Territory of Canada_
where sedentary ffisheries had been established
and carried on by the subjects of ffrance
inhabitants of the said province of Canada
under Grants and Concessions from the
Government thereof were annexed to the
Government of Newfoundland and thereby
subjected to Regulations inconsistent with
the nature of such ffisheries May it
therefore please your most Excellent Majesty
That it may be Enacted And be it Enacted
by the King's most Excellent Majesty by and
with the Advice and Consent of the Lords
Spiritual and Temporal and Commons in
this present parliament assembled and by
the Authority of the same That all the
Territories Islands and Countries in North
America
bounded on the south by a Line from the
Bay of Chaleurs along the high Lands

The Quebec Act, 1774. British Parliamentary Archives,
HL/PO/PU/1/1774/14G3n226. Photo by Pierre5018 /
Licensed under CC0 1.0.

discussed colonial unrest, but his reference to the "abridged" liberty of the colonists in America stirred British Americans' fury and also put Benjamin Franklin in a delicate position. Franklin, in London as the agent for Massachusetts in December 1772, had received the letters from an unnamed source and sent them to Thomas Cushing, the speaker of the Massachusetts Assembly, with strict instructions that they not be published. When they appeared soon after in the American and British press, Franklin found himself in Lord Dartmouth's crosshairs and was nearly charged with treason.[31] All this happened even before imperial officials could fully address the Boston Tea Party, in which colonial leaders in Massachusetts dumped East India Company tea into Boston Harbor to protest imperial interference with trade.[32] By June 1774, when the Quebec Act came before Parliament, American affairs were on everyone's mind. What should have been an uncontroversial piece of legislation dealing with specific problems of governing a French province became entangled with colonial resistance and imperial assertions of authority.

The Quebec Act received royal assent on 22 June 1774. Its nuanced measures, intended to improve relations with French subjects, drew swift and disproportionate reactions in the British colonies. Ezra Stiles, in addition to documenting his own disapproval, also recorded how other British Americans responded. Often these protests were less about the Quebec Act than about the speaker's anger and frustration over the restrictions imposed by Parliament after the Boston Tea Party. In late fall, writing from his impressive house in Newport, Rhode Island, Stiles recorded, "This afternoon three popes &c. paraded thro' the streets, & in the evening they were consumed in a bonfire as usual—among others were Ld. North, Gov. Hutchinson, & Gen. Gage." Across the Atlantic, Lord North's supporters responded by tarring and feathering the effigies of leading American figures.[33]

The Americans' inclusion of effigy popes in their processions alongside leading British administrators shows that the guarantee of Catholic faith extended to Quebec was now joined with their other, more immediate grievances. Popular images encouraged their outrage. An engraving by Paul Revere published in October 1774 depicted Anglican bishops dancing around the "Quebec Bill" as Lord North, with the devil on his shoulder, looked on approvingly. Coming on the heels of the "intolerable" acts, the Canada Bill was seen as adding insult to injury. In early September, Frederick Haldimand, the second-in-command to British General Thomas Gage, reported from New York to General Jeffery Amherst that

Paul Revere, *The mitred minuet*, 1774. Four bishops dance around the
Quebec Bill, while royal officials (including Lord Bute and Lord North)
and the Devil look on approvingly. From *Royal American Magazine* 1, no. 10
[Boston], October 1774. Corcoran Collection (Museum Purchase, Mary E.
Maxwell Fund), National Gallery of Art / Licensed under CC0 1.0.

"they do not approve here of the Act that set (wisely) the government and
the boundaries of Canada. . . . The people here do not want to see a chain
pulled along the backs of their settlements."[34]

The bill's crafters might have hoped for a better reception. This was
not the first time Roman Catholicism had been tolerated or that French
subjects had been welcomed into political institutions. For much of the
eighteenth century, Catholic priests had operated openly and with tacit
British consent in Nova Scotia, serving both the Acadians and the
Mi'kmaq. Governance in Nova Scotia depended on the participation of
Acadian deputies who would, in an unofficial capacity, represent their settlements, bring complaints to the provincial council, and often enlist Acadian elders to help resolve disputes.[35] Elsewhere in the British Atlantic
world, accommodations with French inhabitants helped facilitate governance and incorporate new subjects into the British empire. In Grenada
after 1768, French Roman Catholics were allowed to sit in the Assembly
despite the Test Act, which required members to take a religious oath that

rejected transubstantiation and so prevented Catholic political participation in Great Britain.[36] As Pauline Maier argues, "In many ways, the government's efforts to establish regular government in Grenada by absorbing the old French settlers into public office, while making necessary alterations in traditional English procedure to accommodate them, forecast the Quebec Act of 1774, which became for many the strongest proof for despotism."[37] Accommodations, then, could be tolerated. What made the Quebec Act different was the province's new geography and the resulting proximity to older British colonies. Quebec's borders were the issue.

For opponents, maps were an excellent medium for demonstrating the Quebec Act's nefarious intent. Ezra Stiles's map of the new Quebec, titled "The Bloody Church" and presumably drawn around the time he documented public protests about the act, colored the province as a blood red pool threatening to engulf the light green Protestant colonies.[38] In case his religious aversions were not already clear, Stiles wrote across Quebec the legend "Idolatry and the Church of Rome established by Act of a Protestant Parliament and the Voice of the English Protestant Bishops to restrain and suppress the spreading of the damn Presbytians, as they are politely called." Then, as a devout Protestant, he dutifully crossed out the expletive. Across the southern colonies he wrote, "The Church of England established by the King & the provincial assemblies. For this the Bishops sold the imense northern territory to the Church of Rome." The new boundaries mattered because they expanded Catholic territory.[39] This outrage encouraged British Americans to challenge the empire.

The First Continental Congress, a meeting of colonial delegates assembled to address the coercive acts, convened on 5 September 1774, but business didn't begin in earnest until the seventeenth, when Congress received the Suffolk Resolves. Delivered by Paul Revere, who apparently had a knack for bringing important news, the Resolves were a list of suggested actions that might be taken in response to the "intolerable" acts. The tenth item on the list dealt with the enlarged Canada: "That the late act of parliament for establishing the Roman Catholic religion and the French laws in that extensive country, now called Canada, is dangerous in an extreme degree to the Protestant religion and to the civil rights and liberties of all America; and, therefore, as men and Protestant Christians, we are indispensably obliged to take all proper measures for our security."[40] Over the following month, Quebec remained on

*Map of Christian sects in British North America resulting from the Quebec Act, 1774* (MVP #627). An expansive Quebec, colored blood red and labeled "The Bloody Church," threatens the British American colonies on the Atlantic coast. Ezra Stiles Papers, General Collection, Beinecke Rare Book and Manuscript Library, Yale University.

members' minds. During a session in mid-October, John Adams jotted
notes for his speech on the Canada Bill, in which he compared the British Empire to late Rome. They read almost like a poem:

> Proof of Depth of Abilities, and Wickedness of Heart.
> Precedent. Lords refusal of perpetual imprisonment.
> Prerogative to give any Government to a conquered People.
> Romish Religion.
> Feudal Government.
> Union of feudal Law and Romish Superstition.
> Knights of Malta. Orders of military Monks.
> Goths and Vandals—overthrew the Roman Empire.
> Danger to us all. A House on Fire.[41]

The "house on fire" metaphor merged the internal dangers men like
Adams believed threatened their safety with the hellish imagery that
linked Roman Catholicism with the devil.

Adams's scribbles reflected sentiments shared by most of the Congress, whose members expressed these ideas in an open letter to the people of Great Britain issued on 21 October. Near the end, the letter turns
to the Quebec Act and the dangers of Catholicism. "And by another Act
the dominion of Canada is to be so extended, modelled, and governed, as
that by being disunited from us, detached from our interests" so that the
settlement itself posed a danger to the older English colonies.[42] This
claim, of course, was a complete fabrication. Congress imagined that an
extended Quebec would soon be filled with French Catholics, ardent
devotees of their faith and laws, who would become "instruments in the
hands of power, to reduce the ancient free Protestant Colonies to the
same state of slavery with themselves."[43] But Canada's population in 1774
was approximately 70,000, including enslaved African and Indigenous
peoples whose bondage was real, not rhetorical, versus almost 2.5 million
British Americans.[44] There was no chance of a Catholic invasion. Still,
having territory under French law and religion was concern enough, and
Congress expressed its dismay "that a British Parliament should ever
consent to establish in that country a religion that has deluged your island in blood, and dispersed impeity, bigotry, persecution, murder and
rebellion through every part of the world."[45] Congress hoped this language would stir up support among the British, but the letter only served
to distance British Americans from their French neighbors.[46]

By the time Congress sent its letter, publications in the colonies were discussing the impact of the Quebec Act in similar terms.[47] Newspapers were an important tool not just to circulate news, ideas, and opinions but to create a sense of belonging among people who lived at great distances from each other and from the site of action.[48] Once the *Pennsylvania Gazette* provided an abstract of the Quebec Act, in July 1774, it didn't take long for contributors to argue against it.[49] "As the spirit of liberty, in some of our colonies, has given so much trouble to the Government," one contributor noted, "it was resolved to cherish the spirit of slavery in others." French laws and popery would enslave the body and mind and so were "adopted by our state movers behind the curtain."[50] By the fall, there were calls to resist the act and rebalance the territorial adjustments. One writer demanded action not for "greediness to enlarge our territories, or to enrich ourselves with spoils, at the expense of innocent and peaceable neighbours," but to preserve "what encroachment and usurpation would draw away: to assist in adjusting such a balance of Power, as may prevent ourselves and sister colonies becoming a prey to an insatiable devourer."[51] Few literate colonists would have taken the "insatiable devourer" for anyone other than the devil, as represented by their new French Catholic neighbors.

Readers in South Carolina might have been surprised when Satan himself chimed in on the matter, predictably in favor of the Quebec Act. A letter signed "Devil on Two Sticks" praised Quebec's new borders for preventing Americans in that region from governing themselves and from "ruining themselves by their opposition to that power which protects them." What's more, an enlarged Quebec increased the value of land in the other colonies by preventing expansion. "Now this spirit of dispersion is confined, the happy consequences of which will be, that our fields will equal the well-cultivated Gardens of England."[52] In New England, opinions were rarely leavened with such humor. Reverend Ebenezer Baldwin, of Danbury, Connecticut, expressed the dangers of the Quebec Act in no uncertain terms. He thanked God that Americans had not "experienced the galling chains of slavery"—exempting, apparently, their experience as slavers and slave traders—and thus "few perhaps among us, realize the horrors of that slavery, which arbitrary and despotic government lays men under."[53] Now, however, a despotic government had been established at the back of the colonies. Most immediately affected, Baldwin wrote, would be those English settlers who had already moved to Quebec on the promise that English law would be established there.[54] But he was even more troubled by the colony's new size. Foreshadowing

the language of the Continental Congress, he described how easily thousands of French Canadians might pour into the Ohio Valley:

> And that this French arbitrary government may take in as much
> of America as possible, its limits are extended southward to the
> Ohio, and westward to the Mississippi: so that it comprehends
> an extent of territory almost as large as all the other provinces.
> When this vast extent of territory comes to be filled up with in-
> habitants, near half America will be under this arbitrary French
> government. So that upon the whole the Quebec Act doubtless
> wears as threatening an aspect upon Americans as any act that
> hath been passed by the British government.[55]

Tolerating Roman Catholics in specific places—Acadia, Grenada, Maryland, or a limited Quebec—was one thing. Reserving such a huge expanse for this "despotic" government was simply too much.[56]

As the situation grew more tense, Benjamin Franklin, in London act-
ing as a colonial agent, became involved in secret negotiations to resolve
American affairs. In December 1774 he was approached by Dr. John
Fothergill, formerly his physician, and a London banker named David
Barclay. The two men, both Quakers, assured Franklin that they had
Dartmouth's ear and hoped to broker a peace between Whitehall and the
colonies.[57] Shortly after this meeting, Franklin offered Barclay and
Fothergill his "Hints or Terms for a Durable Union," a list of suggestions
for measures that might ease tensions between Britain and the colonies.
It included returning duties paid and repealing certain acts (including
the Tea Act) after the destroyed tea was paid for. Number eleven on
Franklin's list was a suggestion for "the late Massachusetts and Quebec
Acts to be repeal'd, and a free Government granted to Canada."[58]
Fothergill and Barclay pushed these issues with Lord Dartmouth, but
the distance between Franklin's demands and the ministry's position was
simply too wide. Barclay tried to convince an increasingly pessimistic
Franklin that reconciliation was possible, even suggesting that one of
Franklin's more radical demands—amending the Quebec Act to reduce
the province's size—was under serious consideration. But Barclay could
not change the fact that Lord Dartmouth had no intention of giving
Franklin what he wanted.[59]

The fruitless negotiations lasted until February 1775, after which
Franklin returned to the colonies. During the voyage he organized his pa-

pers and wrote an account of his discussions in the form of a letter to his son. He believed Americans should have some say over the government of Quebec. "We having assisted in the Conquest of Canada," he wrote, "at a great Expence of Blood and Treasure, had some Right to be considered in the Settlement of it. That the Establishing an arbitrary Government on the back of our Settlements might be dangerous to us all; and that loving Liberty ourselves, we wish'd it to be extended among Mankind, and to have no Foundation for future Slavery laid in America."[60]

This book is about how the Indigenous homelands and British provinces that later became Canada shaped the progress of the American Revolution and the creation of the United States. In it I make two related arguments. First, the American Revolution was not only "American"; second, the early national period was hardly national at all. Both should be seen as regional and continental developments in which the paths taken and not taken had reverberations within and beyond what would become the United States.[61] The American Revolution eventually created two countries: the United States by 1789 and Canada nearly a century later, in 1867. What is overlooked, however, is that during the War for Independence and the decades that followed, the loyal British provinces were instrumental in the creation of the United States and the character of its citizens. From 1774 to the outbreak of the War of 1812, Americans living in the thirteen rebelling colonies and then in an independent country spent a great deal of time thinking, reading, and talking about the British colonies that remained loyal to the empire. Unlike these early Americans, and despite recent efforts by leading historians, citizens of the United States have not looked north with any regularity.[62] In this book I hope to encourage them to do so. To understand the United States and its citizens, we must explore how this country and its people were born of a relationship with people and places that refused the revolutionary path.

During the revolutionary era and into the nineteenth century, most places in North America were ideological borderlands. When they looked to Nova Scotia, New Brunswick, the Canadas, and the western expanse beyond settler towns and cities, early Americans saw alternate ways of framing governments, organizing societies, dealing with Indigenous peoples, and growing economies. Although the Canadian colonies were loyal to the Crown, they were far from apathetic. The revolution happened in every British province, but not all at once. The Loyalists who fled New York and Charleston left with their families, their luggage, and their revolutionary ideology. They fundamentally changed political and social life in Nova Scotia and Quebec, but they did so within the empire. American citizens from New England to Georgia, witnessing these changes, began to have a new view of the differences and similarities among states and provinces.

Taking a regional and continental approach to the creation of the United States shows us that Americans never lost sight of what was happening on the "other side" of the revolution.[63] They crossed the largely imaginary borders dividing states and provinces without necessarily thinking they were moving between worlds. Many moved back. Indigenous nations fought to remain independent and protect their ancestral homelands (which often straddled these invisible national borders) from Britain and the United States alike. Enslaved and free Blacks moved to British provinces after they were promised freedom, and many then returned to American states when those states outlawed slavery. Western expansion was less about nation building than about economic competition, and British and American firms learned from each other even as they competed for the same trade. Early Americans understood the differences between provinces and states, but they also knew that regional affiliations, kinship networks, and commercial ties could elide de jure national and colonial divisions. This broader concept of North America's development shaped Americans' self-image as well as the character of the new nation. In an era that was more connected than we tend to assume, the United States could never ignore what was happening to its north. Exploring how early Americans discussed, analyzed, and at times feared the British provinces and Indigenous homelands that are so often left out of the story, in this book I reframe the American founding as a continental event.

CHAPTER ONE

# Of Montreal

I N APRIL 1776, a weary Benjamin Franklin made his way from Philadelphia to New York, then to Albany, and finally Montreal. He was
traveling as part of a commission charged with persuading the Canadians to join the Patriot cause. Feeling unwell on his journey as a
result of persistent gout, he wrote to a few friends, perhaps with tongue
in cheek, offering his final goodbyes. A few weeks later, when he returned to Philadelphia tired and ill, he had little to show for his efforts
save a marten fur hat.[1] He didn't enjoy his time in Canada. Over eleven
days in Montreal in early May, he endured what were surely frustrating
diplomatic meetings with pro-rebel merchants and politicians. From his
lodgings at Thomas Walker's house on rue Notre Dame, he wandered
the narrow streets of what is now "old" Montreal, hoping through
planned meetings and chance encounters to spread the idea of "American" liberty. Franklin's Canadian mission reflected a trend: Patriot politicians, military leaders, and the general public were both interested in and
frustrated by the Canadian colonies.

Canada is perhaps one of the last things that comes to mind when we
consider the rebel colonies' decision to declare independence. The Declaration is a quintessentially American document, either born of practical necessity or the product of a divine plan, depending on whom you ask. But
the "American Revolution" is American only if we read the outcome back-
wards.[2] The "thirteen colonies" familiar to so many as the building blocks
of the United States existed in a continent without hard-and-fast borders,

and the revolutionary spirit could be found not only in Boston, Philadelphia, and Savannah but also in Halifax, Montreal, and many places in between. By shifting the focus of the revolution slightly north—past Loyalist New York, along the Hudson River to Albany, and beyond the Mohawk River and Iroquoia to Lake Champlain, the St. Lawrence, and Quebec—we can see how events in Canada influenced revolutionary ideas by encouraging Patriots to think about a future free from Great Britain.[3] In the early months of 1776, Thomas Paine's *Common Sense* and Patriot victories in the northeast helped shape the path toward independence.[4] But to the list of factors that culminated in Thomas Jefferson's most famous document, we must add the failed invasion of Quebec, a campaign that transformed the colonies' quarrel with the empire and further distanced the rebels from both the northern Indigenous nations and the inhabitants in Quebec. Patriot actions before the invasion of Quebec had been defined as demands for British rights, but the Canadian campaign created Patriot martyrs, intercolonial bonds, and the particularly "American" idea of spreading democracy and freedom. Leading revolutionaries hoped that social unrest in Boston and Philadelphia would catch fire in Montreal and Quebec.

Ultimately, colonial leaders and most of their subjects in Quebec rejected the idea of breaking away from the British, favoring social order and loyalty over unrest and violence. In return, British officials invested money and manpower to protect the loyal provinces.[5] This episode demonstrates Canada's wider influence on colonial independence, especially the broad territorial goals of the Patriot movement that helped crystallize the desire for independence.[6] A fuller understanding of this relationship requires an examination of the invasion of Quebec, the Canadian response, and the revolutionaries' reaction to failure. The Canadian theater put its stamp on the revolutionary movement both practically and ideologically. Ultimately, the "radicalism" of the revolution was hastened by its Canadian experiences.[7] The Patriots' inability to separate Canada from Great Britain invigorated their discussions about leaving the empire themselves. Failures in (and second thoughts about) Canada became entangled in discussions of independence, allowing military and diplomatic leaders to focus their efforts not on attacking British tyranny wherever they found it but on fighting for their liberty where it could be won.[8]

Shortly after shots were fired at Lexington and Concord, and months before he was dispatched to Montreal, Franklin considered how the Canadians might be attracted to the Patriot cause. His interest in Canada extended back to the early 1760s, when he published a pamphlet, *The Interests of Great Britain Considered*, extolling Quebec's importance to Britain and British American foreign policy.[9] As the revolution began, attempts to win Canadian support relied on propaganda and diplomacy. In June 1775, Charles-Guillaume-Frédéric Dumas, an American sympathizer who provided intelligence from Europe throughout the war, sent Franklin a letter from The Hague in which he recounted several recent publications. One item was a short overview of British-colonial relations after 1763.[10] Dumas didn't write it; he claimed he wasn't sufficiently educated to produce such a work.[11] Several months later, not long before Congress would send him to Montreal, Franklin sent a reply to Dumas in which he thanked his friend for the books and assured him that the pamphlet "being a very concise and clear statement of facts, will be reprinted here, for the use of our new friends in Canada."[12]

At the time of Franklin's reply, these "new friends" were responding with careful consideration to the invasion of Quebec. There can be no doubt that the Canadians were aware of Patriot intentions. In 1774, 1775, and 1776, Congress published addresses to the citizens of Quebec trying to persuade them to join the revolutionary cause. In the first letter, drafted in September and October 1774 and published in Philadelphia newspapers, Congress seemed to be working at cross purposes.[13] Their "Letter to the Inhabitants of the Province of Quebec" informed Canadians that they were being denied important British rights and encouraged them to send delegates to the next meeting of the Continental Congress. But it was sent at the same time as the "Address to the People of Great Britain," which complained about the Quebec Act generally and Catholics specifically, accusing them of spreading "impiety, bigotry, persecution, murder, and rebellion, through every part of the world."[14] It is perhaps no surprise that no delegates from Quebec arrived for Congress's next meeting. The second address, published on 29 May 1775, was shorter than the first but worked harder to inspire social upheaval. Coming shortly after Lexington and Concord, it invited Canadians "to join with us in resolving to be free, and in rejecting, with disdain, the fetters of slavery, however artfully polished." Slavery was the letter's central theme: "By the introduction of your present form of government, or rather present form of tyranny, you and your wives and your children are made slaves." Relying on the Canadians' sense of their past and the history of animosity between the French and the British, Congress explained that its members could not presume "that you are so lost to all sense of honor. We can

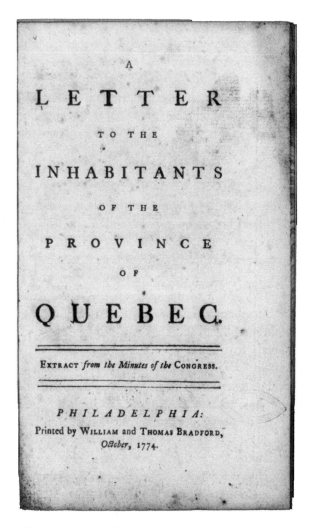

"A Letter to the Inhabitants of Quebec," the first
of three letters from the Continental Congress
urging the Canadians to join the rebel colonies.
Extract from the Minutes of the Continental
Congress, Philadelphia, October 1774. Library of
Congress, Prints and Photographs Division.

never believe that the present race of Canadians are so degenerated as to
possess neither the spirit, the gallantry, nor the courage of their ancestors."[15] For Patriots reading these letters (which were published in the
colonial press), Canadian recalcitrance would have been infuriating.

Within months of the second letter, the Patriot attack on Quebec signaled a shift in revolutionary ideology. Successful attacks on British forts near Canada, including Ticonderoga and Fort Saint-Jean in the late spring of 1775, provided spoils that included much-needed armaments for the siege of Boston. Yet the Quebec missions were not overtly conceived as offensive campaigns against a Loyalist colony. George Washington was concerned about how such an aggressive move would affect the Patriot cause. Writing to the Massachusetts General Court in August 1775 in response to a request from the people of Machias, a town in what is now coastal Maine, for an attack on Nova Scotia, Washington noted the difference between offensive and defensive measures. Because Nova Scotia had sent no representatives to Congress, the province was subject to the commercial restrictions imposed on British goods. But Nova Scotians had not launched hostilities against the United Colonies, and "to attack them therefore is a Step of Conquest rather than Defence, & may be attended with very dangerous Consequences."[16] Just weeks later, however, he changed his tune, complaining that the British were "constantly Cannonading & Bombarding" colonial towns, though doing little damage. They were also pillaging lands along the coast for supplies and taking ships indiscriminately in what Washington called a "Piratical War." Worse, they were threatening to unleash Russian and Hanoverian troops on their own colonists. King George III had refused Congress's July 1775 Olive Branch Petition (which asked him to cease hostilities against the colonies) and was securing German mercenaries to fight in America the following spring. Britons were themselves divided over the conflict, and Lord North, the prime minister, led an increasingly fractious cabinet. Opponents of the war were similarly divided and could not rally against the king and government. "Alas!" Washington lamented, "how is the dignity of great Britain fallen!"[17]

The perception of British perfidy made it easier for Washington to set aside his concerns about taking offensive measures. The British were refusing to attack Patriot positions around Boston once they were completed, and Washington knew that the British were so entrenched in that town "as to render our approaches almost impossible without great Slaughter." So he sent Benedict Arnold up the Kennebec River to attack the fortress of Quebec and, importantly, to divert attention from a second attack, on Montreal, led by Philip Schuyler and Richard Montgomery. "If these Expeditions succeed," Washington confided to his brother, "the Ministry will make a glorious figure with their Canada Bill, & the

Regiments which they proposed to raise in that Government for the purpose of Deluging our Frontier Settlements in Blood."[18] If Canadians
wouldn't come to the revolution, Patriots would take the revolution to
Canada.

Officials in Canada had reason to expect an attack. British agents operating among members of the Iroquois Confederacy, whose homeland
stretched across what is now upstate New York west of the Hudson
River, learned that colonists were moving north almost as soon as they
set out. In May 1775, Guy Johnson, who served as British superintendent
of Indian Affairs after the death of his uncle, William Johnson, received
word that a party of New Englanders had been dispatched to Iroquoia to
arrest him. He fortified his house but eventually fled to Montreal, where
he met with the governor of Quebec, Guy Carleton, and proposed organizing Indigenous forces to help attack the Patriots. According to his
journal, he told Carleton of accounts he "had received of the preparations making by the New Englanders at Ticonderoga, and that they considered Canada as an essential object," adding that it was necessary "to
put the Indians as soon as possible in motion." But Carleton, noting that
he hoped to assemble a good body of Canadian militia to join his dimin-
ished regular troops, replied that he didn't want to let Indigenous forces
go beyond the provincial border. Johnson tried to keep the Six Nations
engaged in the conflict, but being unable to launch attacks frustrated
them. They admitted to Johnson, using the metaphor of the war hatchet
raised and ready, that "they were afraid the Axe would cut them if they
kept it long without using it."[19]

British and American politicians had both been negotiating with Indigenous nations for months, with slightly different objectives. The British hoped to secure their alliance, while the Patriots, though apparently
open to alliances, seemed more focused on encouraging their Indigenous
neighbors to remain neutral. In mid-June 1775, Congress resolved to appoint a committee of five—Philip Schuyler, Patrick Henry, James Duane,
James Wilson, and Philip Livingston—to report on the best steps "to be
taken for securing and preserving the friendship of the Indian Nations."[20] Two weeks later, this committee began preparing for talks with
several nations about the colonies' "unhappy disputes with Great Britain."[21] Unless the British sent Indigenous allies to attack the colonies, in
which case the Americans would respond in kind, Congress preferred to
push for Indigenous neutrality.[22]

Sir Guy Carleton, Lord Dorchester, 1783. Library of
Congress, Prints and Photographs Division.

British officials were interested in Congress's overtures and soon
encouraged the use of Indigenous warriors against the Patriots. As hostilities increased, administrators in London struggled to keep their Indigenous allies satisfied without letting themselves be distracted from the
demands of colonial unrest. Lord Dartmouth, the secretary of state for
the northern department, tried to explain the ministerial demands to Guy
Johnson. Dartmouth admitted that colonial affairs took up much of the
government's time and energy, making it impossible to give due consideration to Indigenous demands and complaints. But in July 1775 he instructed Johnson to pass along, "in the strongest of terms," the king's
"firm resolution to protect and preserve them in all their rights." Johnson
was also to try to learn if the colonists were employing "any artifices" to

engage Indigenous nations in the rebellion against the king. Dartmouth knew that the British forces would need allies at some point, and he wanted them available.[23] Three weeks later, Dartmouth wrote again to ask that Johnson send Indigenous warriors into battle. "The unnatural rebellion now raging there," he wrote, "calls for every effort to suppress it, and the intelligence His Maj'ty has received of the Rebells having excited the Indians to take a part, and of their having actually engaged a body of them in arms to support their rebellion, justifies the resolution His Maj'ty has taken of requiring the assistance of his faithful adherents the six Nations." Just how the Six Nations should be induced to go to war was left to Johnson, but he was to make every effort toward this goal.[24]

Patriot efforts to win Indigenous support had met with only modest success.[25] At an August 1775 meeting with the Six Nations at a settlement along the Mohawk River called German Flatts (Herkimer) deep in the Mohawk homelands, Patriot commissioners invited the Six Nations delegates to meet in the near future at Albany for a "council fire" (the Indigenous term for a diplomatic meeting) to discuss the growing hostilities. Just as Dartmouth had raised concerns about Patriot influence among the Six Nations, the commissioners at German Flatts warned the Six Nations that "many mischievous and ill-disposed persons may attempt to raise up in your minds sentiments that are unfriendly to your brethren of the Twelve United Colonies." They asked the Iroquois to "shut your ears and fortify your minds against any such evil and false reports." The Six Nations were asked to spread the word about the council fire far and wide, but Kanaghquaesa, an Oneida sachem, replied that this would not be easy. "You have desired that all our confederates should receive this invitation," the sachem said, a day after receiving the request. "This cannot be done short of one year," he warned, "as we extend very far, and could not possibly call the extremities of our confederacy to this intended meeting. But possess your minds in peace. When this Congress is over, and the council-fire raked up, we shall acquaint all of our allies with what has passed." Part of the problem, Kanaghquaesa said, was that Guy Johnson had already moved north and was mobilizing the Iroquois along the St. Lawrence. Many of them were ready to fight but were being restrained by Carleton. "We are very much embarrassed for this reason," the sachem admitted, "the man is now there who will vex your minds, and never consent to their coming down, and will draw hard upon their minds another way." Kanaghquaesa assured the Patriot commissioners that he and his followers had been trusted with representing the wishes of those farther north, who had told them they hoped peace could be maintained. When pushed by the commissioners to name which man was influencing the northern nations, Teiorhéñhsere (Little Abraham), a Mohawk sachem, replied, "We take it for granted that you all know the very man we mean, as we said he was of your blood. We see no necessity of pointing him out more explicitly."[26]

Johnson had less influence in Canada than Kanaghquaesa and Little Abraham suggested. On his arrival at Montreal in 1775, he had faced a challenge to his authority from John Campbell, the superintendent of Indian Affairs for the province of Quebec. Campbell, a Scot, had enjoyed a military career in North America that began in the 1740s and lasted until 1765, when James Murray, then the governor of Quebec, appointed him "Inspector of Indian Affairs." He was an odd choice given that he spoke no Indigenous languages.[27] But Campbell had married the daughter of Luc de la Corne, a French officer, merchant, and interpreter in Quebec whose familiarity with Indigenous peoples apparently provided his *beau-fils* with the necessary credentials. Campbell's position in Quebec infringed on that of Daniel Claus, then William Johnson's deputy in the province. After Johnson complained about the overlapping responsibilities, the government acquiesced and allowed Claus to continue his activities. Shortly after he was appointed, Campbell was accused of attacking Thomas Walker, a magistrate who had used his position to restrict the benefits enjoyed by military officers billeting in Montreal. Campbell and a group of men were accused of breaking into Walker's house, destroying his belongings, and cropping one of his ears.[28] His brief imprisonment made it significantly easier for Claus to continue his work, and Campbell's regiment, the 27th Foot, left Quebec in 1767.[29] In 1773, after a year of petitioning government officials and with Governor Carleton's support, Campbell was appointed superintendent of Indian Affairs in Quebec.

This appointment was part of Carleton's larger plan to weaken the Johnson family's influence in Canada and the northern district; it also helps explain, in part, why Carleton was reluctant to heed Guy Johnson's advice to employ Indigenous warriors to attack the Patriots. Who would serve as superintendent to the various Indigenous nations in Canada and Iroquoia was not a simple question, so in November 1775 Guy Johnson and Daniel Claus traveled to London for answers. Their mission was complicated by imperial and colonial leaders with their own strategies to advance. As Johnson discovered after meeting with officials in London, the best resolution was a compromise. He returned to North America in the summer of 1776 with his jurisdiction reduced to the Six Nations.[30] Claus remained in London for an extra year, leaving Campbell responsible for non-Iroquois nations.

Accompanying Johnson and Claus on their trip to London were two members of the Iroquois Confederacy: The Mohawk leader Thayendanegea, better known as Joseph Brant, and Oteroughyanento, a Mohawk warrior. Brant's friendship with William Johnson had been strengthened when Johnson married Brant's sister, Molly, in 1759.[31] In Iroquois society, women held great political power, often appointing or at least approving the appointment of male chiefs. As a matrilineal and matrilocal culture, families took their lineage via their mother's family. Molly Brant, like many women in Indigenous nations, served as an important cultural and political connection between the Six Nations and the British.[32] Because Joseph Brant had followed Guy Johnson to Montreal, it made sense that he would travel with the superintendent and his deputy to London. When they arrived, Brant was shown around London and introduced to politicians and leading citizens, and he had his portrait painted. He also met with Lord George Germain, the secretary of state for the American colonies, whom he addressed on 14 March 1776. Calling Germain "Brother Gorah," or Great One, he told him, "We have cross'd the great Lake and come to this kingdom with our Superintendent Col. Johnson from our Confederacy the Six Nations and their Allies, that we might see our Father the Great King, and joyn in informing him, his Councillors and wise men, of the good intentions of the Indians our bretheren, and of their attachment to His Majesty and his Government." Brant reminded Germain that the Mohawk had long been loyal to the king. But despite their efforts on the king's behalf, the Mohawks "have been very badly treated by his people in that country, the City of Albany laying an unjust claim to the lands on which our Lower Castle is built." What troubled Brant most was that although the Mohawks had allowed the English to settle on their lands, the colonists wanted more and would not leave his people alone. "Indeed it is very hard," he lamented, "when we have let the Kings subjects have so much of our lands for so little value, they should want to cheat us in this manner of the small spots we have left for our women and children to live on. We are tired out in making complaints & getting no redress."[33] Germain assured Brant that his concerns had not fallen on deaf ears, but he asked the Mohawk leader for further patience. Nothing could be resolved until the troubles with the colonists were settled. These assurances satisfied

Brant and his companion, and the group prepared to return to North America.[34]

Johnson had gone to London partly because Carleton refused the Six Nations' offer to fight, which left Quebec in a precarious position as few Canadians were prepared to raise arms for the British. After the Continental Army's attacks on Ticonderoga and Saint-Jean, Carleton discovered just how difficult raising a local militia would be. He hoped he could rely on the upper classes of French inhabitants to rally the Canadians, but they were largely unsuccessful, and he managed to form only a small corps of volunteers.[35] In addition, the region itself was unprepared for a sustained attack. No more than six hundred regular soldiers were stationed along the entire St. Lawrence River, nor were there sufficient armed ships or fortifications.[36] The reasons for Canadian ambivalence varied, but colonial officials in Canada took a harsh view. Quebec's chief justice, William Hey, saw no prospects for persuading the Canadians to fight, and he hoped he could return to England and avoid what he predicted would be an easy American victory in Canada. He saw the Canadians as fearful, ignorant, and gullible and thus susceptible to agents of the American cause who circulated among them spreading rumors. "They are terrified or corrupted to a degree that your Lordship can have no Idea of," Hey informed Lord Apsley, the lord chancellor, "& are impressed with the strangest ideas that ever entered into the minds of men." Canadians, Hey asserted, could be convinced that Patriots were fighting simply to prevent the imposition of the Stamp Act or that the entire colony had been sold to Spain. Convinced that the rebel capture of Canada was only a matter of time, he told the lord chancellor, "In this situation I hold myself in readiness to embark for England where I possibly may be of some use your Lordship will I hope agree with me that I can be of none here."[37]

Other officials in Canada were equally skeptical of their militia but took a more positive view of their Indigenous allies. By the end of September 1775, while Benedict Arnold and his men were making their way along the Kennebec River to join Richard Montgomery's forces for an attack on the fortress at Quebec, Quebec's lieutenant governor wrote to the secretary of state to update him on "the disagreeable account of a disagreeable business." The Patriots were collecting their forces just south of Canada, and at least one attack had been repelled by Indigenous fighters. "In this Action," he wrote, "the Savages behaved with great Spirit and Resolution, and had they remained firm to our Interests, probably the Province would have been saved for this Year." But the Six Nations and their allies were not prepared to do all the work, and "finding the Canadians in General averse to the taking up Arms for the Defence of their Country, they withdrew, and made their Peace."[38] With the colony guarded only by a few British regulars, ambivalent Canadians, and restrained Indigenous warriors, Canada seemed to be an easy target for rebel forces intent on spreading their ideas of freedom and liberty into regions dominated by the British empire.

And it was easy, at first. Montgomery marched his forces to Montreal (General Schuyler remained at Albany), and the city fell without resistance on 13 November 1775.[39] Just days earlier, Patriot forces had captured the strategically important sites of Chambly and St. Johns. Washington and Congress received the news with great joy, and the rebels were optimistic that Montgomery and Arnold would work together effectively in Canada.[40] The two had a formidable task ahead of them. Governor Carleton, who barely escaped Montreal before Montgomery's arrival, fled to the city of Quebec. The Patriot general followed shortly after, meeting Benedict Arnold and his troops outside the fortified city. Their voyage from Cambridge via the Kennebec, Chaudière, and St. Lawrence Rivers had been hard, and reports filtered back to the colonies of men "subsisting upon dead dogs, devouring their shoes . . . to complet the grand work of the subduction of Canada."[41] Arnold's "Little Army" had completed a march "equal to Hanibals over the Alps."[42] The Patriot forces camped outside Quebec for several weeks before launching an attack. Members of Congress remained optimistic, but the bombardment of Quebec over several days in December brought only two Canadian casualties: a noncombatant and a turkey (also unarmed). The Patriot forces then launched an ill-fated attack during the stormy night of 30–31 December. Montgomery was killed quickly, and Arnold was badly wounded. Without the aid of the Canadians, most of whom refused to raise arms for the Patriots, Quebec remained in British hands. Word of the failed attempt caused violence and unrest in Montreal, but it was mostly committed by frustrated rebel troops, whose behavior did little to win over Canadian neutrals. News trickled slowly to Philadelphia. In a 12 January 1776 letter, John Hancock declared that "by the last advices from Canada we are flattered with the hopes of a fortunate issue of the Campaign in that quarter." Just five days later, a more somber Hancock reported, "we have this day rec'd disagreeable accotts. from Canada, poor Montgomery & severall officers kill'd, Arnold Wounded, &c."[43]

The failed attempt on Quebec prompted Congress's third letter to the Canadians. If the first letter was meant to educate and the second to scare, the last was a more humble plea. Congress had learned of Montgomery's death, and they reassured Canadians that "the best of causes are subject to vicissitudes; and disappointments have ever been inevitable. Such is the lot of human nature," but "we will never abandon you to the unrelenting fury of your and our enemies." To that end, the letter called upon Canadians to raise regiments and appoint delegates to Congress.[44] With Montgomery's defeat at Quebec and the lack of specie to pay Canadians for their supplies, what little support the Patriots enjoyed was waning. But many in Congress remained convinced of Canada's importance. "No Cost or pains must be Spared to Secure the important Province of Canada," blustered Josiah Bartlett, the New Hampshire delegate.[45] Several issues needed to be resolved, most importantly obtaining the Canadians' allegiance and increasing troops and supplies in the region. But Canadians were about as eager to fight for the Patriots as they had been to raise arms for Carleton. Brigadier General David Wooster wrote from Montreal to Colonel Seth Warner that the Canadians "are not to be depended upon, but, like the Savages, are very fond of chuseing the strongest party." His complaints echoed those leveled months earlier by Chief Justice Hey: the Canadians were too quick to believe rumors and false information. "Among other things," Wooster wrote, Patriot enemies were telling Canadians that "the United Colonies intend to abandon this country."[46] Though time would prove this argument true, Wooster was nonetheless troubled by how easy it was to discourage the Canadians from supporting the Patriot forces.

Despite the formidable challenges of Montgomery's death and Canadian ambivalence, Washington and Congress remained dedicated to the campaign. Washington called for more troops and reiterated that "no person can be more sensible of the importance of securing Canada than I am."[47] Congress agreed and did its best to keep troops and supplies marching north. In a letter to Washington, John Hancock argued that "the most vigorous Measures should be adopted, as well to defend our Troops against the Canadians themselves, as to ensure Success to the Expedition." Controlling Quebec was important "for Reasons too obvious to be mentioned," and Congress would do whatever it could to "quiet the Minds of the Canadians and to remove the Sources of their Uneasiness & Discontent."[48] John Adams thought these efforts might be too late. "That we have been a little tardy in providing for Canada is true—owing

John Trumbull, *The Death of General Montgomery in the Attack on Quebec, December 31, 1775*, 1786. Oil on canvas, 24 5/8 × 37 in. (62.5 × 94 cm). Trumbull Collection, 1832.2. Yale University Art Gallery.

to innumerable Difficulties," he wrote to Horatio Gates. "However We have been roused at last, and I hope have done pretty well."[49] Quebec was still in British hands, Patriot troops were tired and sick and wanted to return home, and the Canadians clung to their neutrality. It would take a small miracle for Canada to join the United Colonies.

No miracle could bring Richard Montgomery back from the dead, but he lived on in the pages of colonial newspapers and personal letters and signaled new ways of imagining intercolonial connections. He was also celebrated and lamented in England's increasingly vocal opposition press, which hailed the fallen general as a hero.[50] Montgomery's death shocked and saddened Patriots who had hoped he might prove instrumental in winning Canadian support, and it didn't take long before he acquired martyr status. "Never was any City so universally Struck with grief, as this was on hearing of the Loss of Montgomery," Thomas Lynch, writing from Philadelphia, informed Philip Schuyler. The delegate from South Carolina continued, "Every lady's Eye was filled with Tears. I happened to have Company at Dinner but none had Inclination for any other Food than sorrow or Resentment."[51] Some used the sorrow to craft new relationships that could give meaning to the sacrifices made at Quebec. Mercy Otis Warren, a playwright, satirist, and historian who would go on to write a history of the American Revolution, was in regular correspondence with such women as Abigail Adams and Catharine Macaulay. After news of Montgomery's death reached the colonies, Warren wrote to his widow, Janet Montgomery, reassuring her that "your friends are not confined to the limits of a province" but could be found throughout the United Colonies. In Warren's condolences, Richard Montgomery's death in Canada weakened colonial differences and hinted at a larger union. These letters, shared with other prominent women, helped form affectionate bonds through which the widow's grief became a shared burden and gave Montgomery's death a broader purpose. This network of letters gave women yet another way—beyond boycotts, wearing homespun, acting as caregivers, tending to homes and business while men were absent, and countless other efforts—to contribute to the Patriots' cause.[52]

Thousands of women read what became the defining tract of the Patriot cause, Thomas Paine's *Common Sense*. Published in January 1776, just as news of Montgomery's death was arriving in the colonies, *Common Sense* put into plain language the ideas that had helped drive the troops to Canada in the first place. Thus "Paine's work and the memory of Montgomery's sacrifice helped galvanize a national identity and an independence movement."[53] Paine allowed that his sentiments were "not yet sufficiently fashionable to procure them general favor," but he argued forcefully that the colonies should separate from Great Britain.[54] Many readers related Paine's calls for independence to the Patriot invasion of Canada. In February 1776, Joseph Hawley, a prominent associate of Samuel Adams and James Otis and a member of the Massachusetts Provincial Congress, wrote to Elbridge Gerry to warn him of a potential British attack from Quebec. He suggested that the American forces send their best-trained troops to Canada, warning that Britain would likely send "their land forces for the reduction of America . . . chiefly . . . by the way of Quebeck and New-York." Hawley followed this advice with an opinion on independence. "I beg leave to let you know that I have read the pamphlet, entitled, 'Common Sense, addressed to the Inhabitants of America,' and that every sentiment has sunk into my well prepared heart for good seed."[55] Others made more direct connections between *Common Sense* and Canada. In an open letter to Thomas Paine published just a week after Hawley wrote to Gerry, one colonial resident suggested, "Let it be the work of your Continental Conference to set the bounds to their claim as an associated Continent, which ought to include, at least, the thirteen at present associated Colonies, with those of Quebec and Nova-Scotia."[56] For some, including Canada (and Nova Scotia with its access to valuable fisheries) in American independence was the epitome of common sense.[57]

As reports of Montgomery's death circulated within the rebelling colonies, interested readers became aware of Canada's impact on the rebel colonies' relationship to Great Britain. In early May 1776, the *Virginia Gazette* published Thomas Paine's imagined dialogue between the ghost of General Montgomery and a delegate for Congress. Readers were likely unsurprised to learn that death had not dampened Montgomery's zeal for the Patriot cause. "I still love liberty and America," he told the delegate, "and the contemplation of the future greatness of this continent now forms a large share of my present happiness."[58] Yet the dead general was concerned that the rebelling colonies might consider some accommodation from Britain. The delegate voiced his worry that independence would bring "domestick wars without end." Montgomery replied that delaying independence by fifty years would not prevent "the supposed contensions between sister colonies," if they existed. The weakness of the colonies would preserve the union, because each needed the others. Canada served as an important example: "Had the colony of Massachusetts Bay been possessed of the military resources which it would probably have had fifty years hence, would she have held out the signal of distress to her sister colonies, upon the news of the Boston port bill? No; she would have withstood all the power of Britain alone, and afterwards the neutral colonies might have shared the fate of the colony of Canada." The only thing worse than dying in Canada would be living to see Britain's American colonies remain in the empire: "I would rather die in attempting to obtain permanent freedom for a handful of people than survive a conquest which would serve only to extend the empire of despotism."[59]

Military leaders, soldiers, and even revolutionary ghosts having failed to persuade Canada to join the American colonies, Congress turned to Benjamin Franklin. A pro-Patriot faction in Montreal had been telling Congress for months that more diplomatic efforts were required to persuade Canadians to support the rebels fully. In February 1776, Prudent Lajeunesse, a resident of Longueuil (just across the St. Lawrence River from Montreal) who had campaigned for the Patriot forces in the Richelieu Valley, appeared before Congress and requested that they send delegates to explain the Patriot position in the hope that Canadians might be more willing to take up the cause.[60] Congress agreed and named Benjamin Franklin, Samuel Chase, and Charles Carroll of Carrollton as the "Commissioners to Canada." Franklin was already an elder statesman and much respected. Samuel Chase was a member of the Maryland legislature and a future Supreme Court justice, and Charles Carroll (who added "of Carrollton" to his name to distinguish himself from his relatives) was a Roman Catholic planter, businessman, investor, and politician. Also invited was Charles's cousin John Carroll, a Catholic priest. The Carrolls knew only too well the challenges facing Catholics in the colonies.[61] John was not optimistic about the commission, though he fretted less about religion than about the proper process of revolution. He laid out his concerns over neutrality and social order in a letter begun (but never finished) shortly after he learned of his appointment:

> From all the information I have been able to collect concerning the State of Canada, it appears to me, that the inhabitants of that country are no wise disposed to molest the united colonies, or prevent their forces from taking & holding possession of the strong places in that province, or to assist in any manner the British arms. Now if it be proposed that the Canadians apprehend it will not be in my power to advise them to it. They have not the same motives for taking up arms against England, which render the resistance of the other colonies so justifiable. If an oppressive mode of government has been given them, it was what some of them chose, & the rest have acquiesced in. Or if they find themselves oppressed they have not tried the success of petitions & remonstrances, all of which ought, as I apprehend, to be ineffectual before it can be lawful to have recourse to arms & change of government.[62]

For John Carroll, any Canadian revolution, regardless of Patriot encouragement, was illegitimate until all other options were exhausted.

He wasn't the only one with reservations. Early in 1776, Robert R. Livingston of New York confided to Thomas Lynch that he had always opposed the expedition to Canada. Patriot success at Montreal did nothing to convince him, and the death of his dear friend Montgomery at Quebec only hardened his opinions. Canada, he argued, would drain precious funds from the United Colonies and weaken the rebel forces. Moreover, the Canadians couldn't be trusted: "Their perfidy may be the total destruction of any troops we have sent there." If the British returned to Canada, the Patriots would find themselves fighting not only the redcoats but also the Canadians and Indigenous nations, who would undoubtedly side with the strongest force. Taking a broad view of the imperial machinations driving British and French strategy, Livingston admitted, "I must own that I can not help entertaining a thought which may perhaps be too visionary to realize," but he submitted it to Lynch's judgment nonetheless. He noted that France had recently sent about seven thousand men to Hispaniola, a force whose commander surely had sizeable "discretionary power." Why not offer "the quiet possession of Canada" and assurances that Patriot forces would never aid Great Britain "in any designs that they may form against the French West Indies"? Such an exchange would cost Congress nothing and bring the French closer to the revolutionary cause. Livingston foresaw objections to this idea, most notably that such a deal would "not be treating the Canadians as we promised them." But any promises made to Canadians were contingent on their joining the union, which had not happened. Given that the British use of Hessian troops had "set us the example of calling in foreign aid," it made sense, wrote Livingston, to seek support from France.[63] France did eventually side with the rebel colonies, but not because they were promised territory in North America. The rebels were not yet ready to surrender the dream of pulling Canada to their cause.

In February 1776, as the Patriot forces stalled outside Quebec and endured disease, malnourishment, and short supplies, Samuel Ward, a delegate from Rhode Island whose son had been captured in the battle, wrote to his daughter, one of eleven children. Doing his best to comfort her, Ward reassured his daughter that her brother was serving an important purpose. He encouraged her to trust in Providence. "I do not wonder that you feel so much at the Recollection of what your dear Brother has suffered," he wrote. Perhaps to lift her spirits, he added, "From the large Reinforcements which We have ordered to Canada (some of which are there before now) & the favourable Disposition of the Canadians I doubt not but We shall soon get Quebec & that your Bror. if he escapes or recovers of the small Pox will soon be released." But it was important to remain realistic. While women played many roles during the revolution, Ward's sense of gender divisions fit his time: a soldier's job was to fight, and the duty of those left behind—including sisters, mothers, and wives—was to be brave and remain faithful. He cautioned his daughter: "Do not My dearest depend upon seeing him soon. The small Pox may open the Doors of eternal Bliss to him, if not He will probably make the next Campaign in Canada but in whatever Situation he may be, while you are satisfied that he is either reaping the Rewards of his Virtue or bravely fighting for his Country your Love of Liberty & your Country will notwithstanding your ardent affection for him make you support his Absence with Fortitude."[64]

After getting Congress's agreement to send a commission to Canada, Prudent Lajeunesse made his way back to Canada via Albany, with a little help from General Schuyler. Franklin hoped to set out for Montreal shortly after being appointed, but the commission's instructions were not approved until 20 March.[65] Meanwhile, members of Congress discussed the mission's prospects. John Adams wrote to his wife, Abigail, "I wish I understood French as well as you. I would have gone to Canada, if I had."[66] The same day Adams wrote to James Warren, president of the Massachusetts Provincial Congress and husband to Mercy Otis Warren, noting that "the Unanimous Voice of the Continent is Canada must be ours, Quebec must be taken." He was satisfied that Congress had done everything in its power to accomplish this goal, and if the mission fell short, "I shall be easy because I know of nothing more or better that We can do." Canada was important, according to Adams, because while under British control it could do so much damage to the Patriot cause. "In the Hands of our Enemies, it would enable them to inflame all the Indians upon the Continent, and perhaps induce them to take up the Hatchet, and commit their Robberies and Murders upon the Frontiers of all the southern Colonies as well as to pour down Regulars, Canadians and Indians together upon the Borders of the Northern."[67] It was this danger that Franklin, Chase, and the Carrolls undertook to prevent.

Once in Canada, the commissioners were instructed to "make known to the people of that country, the wishes and intentions of the Congress with respect to them," specifically the hopes that together they could reimagine a relationship with Great Britain. Canadians were to be informed that Patriot forces had been sent into their country "for the purpose of frustrating the designs of the British court against our common liberties" and that "we expect not only to defeat the hostile machinations of Governor Carleton against us, but that we shall put it into the power of our

Canadian brethren, to pursue such measures for securing their own freedom and happiness, as a generous love of liberty and sound policy shall
dictate to them."[68] The commissioners were encouraged to assure the
Canadians that they would be welcomed into the union and that they
would exist under the same types of laws and enjoy the same freedoms as
the United Colonies. They should also be put at ease concerning France,
as it was unlikely France would "take any part with Great Britain" but
rather would likely "cultivate a friendly intercourse with these colonies."
Nor would the Canadians have to worry about their religion. Congress
promised them the free practice of Catholicism, including the right of
the clergy to maintain their estates as long as all other denominations
had free exercise of their faith, and to remain exempt from denomina-
tional tithes or taxes. The commissioners were to establish a free press, a
responsibility that fell to Fleury Mesplet, a French-born printer who had
worked with Congress to translate the letters to Quebec and was subsequently named to travel with Franklin's group.[69] Additionally, the commissioners were to settle whatever disputes might arise between Patriot
soldiers and Canadian inhabitants, inquire about the imprisonment of
Continental soldiers and commanders, and promote and regulate trade
with the Indigenous nations.[70] With these instructions formalized and
approved, the commissioners and their printer left for Canada.

Piecing together the commissioners' actions is not easy.[71] Franklin,
whose diary and writings comprehend so much of his life, is largely silent
about his time in Montreal. David Ramsay's history of the revolution
notes only that Congress sent the commission "and signaled them to
promise on behalf of the united colonies, that Canada should be received
into their association on equal terms, and also that the inhabitants
thereof should enjoy the free exercise of their religion, and the peaceable
possession of all their ecclesiastical property."[72] The commission's failure
to win over the Canadians shouldn't negate its diplomatic, religious, and
civic importance. Franklin himself was fully dedicated to weakening British influence and retaliating for imperial misdeeds. Before leaving for
Montreal, he wrote to Anthony Todd, Britain's postmaster general, to
vent his frustration about England's behavior in the conflict. "How long
will the Insanity on your side of the Water continue?" he asked. "Every
Day's Plundering of our Property and Burning our Habitations, serves
but to exasperate and unite us the more." He concluded with a warning:
"Your Ministers may imagine that we shall soon be tired of this, and submit. But they are mistaken, as you may recollect they have been hitherto

in every Instance in which I told you at the time that they were mistaken. And I now venture to tell you, that tho' this War may be a long one, (and I think it will probably last beyond my Time) we shall with God's Help finally get the better of you. The Consequences I leave to your Imagination."[73] Within days Franklin was en route to Montreal, charged with convincing Canadians to abandon the empire.

It wasn't an easy voyage, but according to one traveler even the geography seemed to suggest that Canada should join the Patriots. The group left New York on 2 April 1776 and traveled along the Hudson, which Charles Carroll of Carrollton described as "intended by nature to open a communication between Canada and the province of New York by water."[74] Six days later the group had reached Albany, and on the sixteenth they left Saratoga after having enjoyed "a most pleasing séjour" with the Schuyler family. Franklin sent several letters from Saratoga, few of which indicate that he was enjoying his travels or foresaw much success in Montreal. To Josiah Quincy, he wrote, "I begin to apprehend that I have undertaken a Fatigue that at my Time of Life may prove too much for me, so I sit down to write to a few Friends by way of Farewell."[75] While his report to John Hancock two days earlier lacked this dark humor, it can hardly have inspired much hope. "We have been here some Days," he wrote, "waiting for General Schuyler's Orders to proceed, which we have just received, and shall accordingly leave this Place to morrow. Tho' by the Advices from Canada communicated by him to us, and as we suppose sent forward to you, I am afraid we shall be able to effect but little there."[76] Later in the month, voyaging through Lake George and along Lake Champlain, Charles Carroll mused about the region's potential and the purpose of the rebellion. "If America should succeed," he noted in his journal, "and establish liberty throughout this part of the continent, I have not the least doubt that the lands bordering on Lake Champlain will be very valuable in a short time, and that great trade will be carried on over Lake Champlain, between Canada and New York."[77] The party reached Montreal on 29 April and was met by Benedict Arnold and then feted in the Chateau de Ramezay, the impressive former residence of the governor of New France, "where a genteel company of ladies and gentlemen had assembled to welcome our arrival." After dining with the general, the men were escorted "by the general and other gentlemen" to the residence they would inhabit while in Montreal. They were hosted by Thomas Walker, who was up to his cropped ears in the Patriot cause and whose house was "the best built, and perhaps the

*Joseph Tayadaneega, called the Brant, the Great Captain of the Six Nation (Indian Chief)*, after George Romney, 1779. Mezzotint, platemark: 50 × 35.5 cm (19 11/16 × 14 in.), sheet: 63 × 43.7 cm (24 13/16 × 17 3/16 in.). Mabel Brady Garvan Collection, 1946.9.2090. Yale University Art Gallery.

best furnished in this town."[78] Their journey had not been easy, but the real difficult work had only begun.

As Franklin and the other commissioners were setting out for Montreal to win the Canadians to the Patriot cause, James Dean was enduring his own voyage to repair rifts in the Six Nations Confederacy in the hopes of securing a fruitful alliance. Dean was a graduate of Dartmouth College who had trained to serve as a missionary to the Indigenous peoples, but he preferred the less religious vocation of interpreter. Dartmouth College was founded by Eleazar Wheelock, a Congregationalist minister who had previously run schools in Lebanon, Connecticut, to educate Indigenous youth and settlers for missionary work. Joseph Brant, Samson Occom, and Samuel Kirkland were all products of Wheelock's schools or influence.[79] By the 1770s, Dean was working for the Continental Congress, which was desperate to secure Iroquois neutrality. The Oneida had adopted him as a young boy, and he took on Indigenous culture so well that one missionary referred to him as "a perfect Indian boy" and even cautioned Dean's father that he might require additional instruction in English language and manners.[80] Dean could, as Alan Taylor put it, "explain the Indians to the Americans—and the Americans to the Six Nations."[81] In 1774, he traveled to Montreal and impressed missionaries and Indigenous peoples alike with his fluent mastery of the Iroquois' use of tone, cadence, and metaphor.[82]

Dean's ability to cross cultures while remaining tied to the Patriot cause made him an important asset for the Continental Congress, though his strong ties to the Oneida put him in a dangerous position when the Six Nations began to split over which side to support in the revolt. While the commission members were in Albany in early spring 1776, Oneida and Tuscarora sachems presented them with the war belt taken up by the other Six Nations on behalf of the British. The sachems' action signaled real tensions within the confederacy.[83] Dean then traveled with the Oneidas and representatives from the Seven Nations of Canada (a collection of Indigenous nations living in Quebec) to attend a conference of the Six Nations at Onondaga meant to determine whether the nations could agree on neutrality as a common stance. Their first stop, about sixteen miles outside Albany, was at a small village inhabited by the Onondagas and Tuscaroras. It was during this rest that Dean learned of possible threats against his life. "The Mohawks, it seems, who came from Niagara to attend the Congress at Onondaga, in one of their

drunken frolicks, threatened to take my life if I presumed to appear at
the Council," he recorded in his journal. When they heard these rumors,
the sachems grew concerned and asked the Mohawks if the threat was legitimate. The Mohawks "assured the Chiefs it was, and that my life
should end upon my arrival at Onondaga."[84] Not wanting to risk any violence against the interpreter, the Oneidas waited for instructions. When
none came, they sent another message to the Onondagas to confirm that
it was their desire that Dean should not attend the council. While they
were waiting for a reply, Little Abraham, the Mohawk sachem who had
met with the Americans at German Flatts the previous August, arrived at
the village on his way to the meeting. He was traveling with another
Mohawk from Niagara, who was related to the group that apparently intended to kill Dean. Shortly after, a message arrived from the Onondagas
assuring Dean that the passage was safe and that those who had initiated
the plan to kill him "had laid aside their wicked design."[85]

The leading women of the town remained worried for Dean's safety
and suggested that he and the Oneida turn back. In a formal speech, the
women addressed their concerns: "We, the female Governesses, take this
opportunity to speak a word, and let you know our minds. In truth, our
hearts have trembled and our eyes have not known sleep since you have
been here, while we consider the danger that appears to us to threaten
you at Onondaga, and the dreadful consequences that must ensue,
should some fatal blow be given you. We desire you to consider well of
those things, and to return back from this place."

Dean, convinced of the importance of his mission, replied, "Sisters,
Female Governesses: I sincerely thank you for what you have said and
the concern you appear to have for my safety; but, Sisters, possess your
minds in peace, and let it not offend you if I do not comply with your request. I am sent by the great men upon important business, and must
proceed as far as directed."[86] He and his companions continued on to the
council house at Onondaga, and eventually the meetings began. The first
day was occupied by traditional Indigenous ceremonies: introductory
speeches emphasized the need to "wipe the tears from each other's eyes
mutually, to cleanse each other's seats from blood; and, lastly, quite to remove that load of grief which obstructed their utterance, that they might
freely disclose their minds to each other." Dean announced that he was
sent by the Continental Congress and outlined what he hoped the meeting would accomplish. After a short disagreement over who should provide the libations "to wash the taste of the tobacco out of their mouths"

(the Indigenous delegates hoped Dean would send for some, while Dean answered that it was always the host's duty), the day's proceedings were adjourned.[87]

The next two days revealed some of the divisions within the Six Nations. On the second day, a Seneca sachem told the Oneidas that he had heard they had promised General Schuyler that they would capture or kill John Butler, a British Indian agent working under Guy Carleton. The Oneidas responded that the report was false, and despite any previous actions, they were content to "let the white people conduct their own affairs as they pleased." On the third day of the meeting, Dean heard a recounting of five speeches that John Butler had given to the Six Nations several months earlier. Butler was an interpreter, familiar with Iroquois languages and diplomacy, who had traveled with Guy Johnson to Canada at the outbreak of the revolution. When Johnson went to Britain to complain about Governor Carleton's refusal to use Indigenous warriors, Butler became acting superintendent for the Six Nations.[88] His speeches to the Onondagas, Cayugas, and Senecas were meant to maintain their alliance with Britain and prepare them for war against the Americans. He focused on how unprepared the Americans were to conduct proper diplomacy, provide security, and offer presents.[89] Dean listened while those at the conference repeated what Butler had told them: that the king spoke most of peace; that the king was saddened by the internal divisions among the Six Nations; that the king would "cross the sea two months hence, to talk of peace with the Bostonians"; and that Butler "advised his brethren, the Six Nations, to observe a perfect neutrality in the present quarrel, and to mind nothing but peace."[90]

Before and after these speeches were recounted, Dean noted the fissures among the Six Nations. It was Sorighhowane, a Seneca sachem, who summarized Butler's speeches, but he did not recount everything Butler had said. Dean learned from a Mohawk friend that because Dean was present, Sorighhowane had omitted one of Butler's speeches. Ultimately the final speech was shared, and though Dean did not record its contents, Oneida chiefs later told Philip Schuyler that Butler had pushed the Six Nations to take stronger actions against the Patriots, and many agreed to do so.[91] The following day "was taken up in uniting the minds of the Confederated tribes, and in mutual assurances of their fixed determination to observe a strict neutrality in the present quarrel; and that they would invariably pursue the paths of peace." Though the individual nations within the Iroquois Confederacy agreed to refrain from battle, divisions remained. During the discussions, Dean received a letter from General Schuyler that detailed the British evacuation of Boston in March. As he read Schuyler's letter to the sachems, "a variety of passions appeared in the faces of the assembly . . . some seemed much elated with joy, and others as much depressed with vexation and disappointment."[92] The meeting at the council house gave Dean a firsthand look at the complicated tensions tearing at the Six Nations Confederacy. As were the Canadians waiting in Montreal for Franklin and the commissioners to arrive, the Iroquois were divided among those who supported the Patriots, those prepared to fight for the king, and those who wanted no part of the settlers' disputes.

Before Franklin and the commissioners reached Montreal, John Adams, George Washington, Philip Schuyler, and others circulated Dean's report of the council fire and dissected the complicated issue of Iroquois neutrality. Samuel Chase met with Dean and the delegates from the Seven Nations of Canada at Fort George, where he and the other commissioners to Canada were resting en route to Montreal. Dean and the group, on their way back from the meeting at Onondaga, stayed long enough to inform Chase of what had been discussed and resolved. The warriors were to stay home and await the result of future councils, and Chase was sure the Indigenous delegates would appear in Montreal expecting presents. He was worried that the commissioners had nothing to give them. Dean's report that the Indigenous congress had agreed to maintain neutrality came as a relief, as did the news that the Oneida, Tuscarora, and Canadian nations seemed friendly toward the rebels. But Seneca and Mohawk hostility remained a worrying prospect, and Chase blamed Butler for pitting these nations against the Patriots. He could only hope that the commissioners would greet these groups with "good Words and some presents," but he warned that they must also be "very firm and resolute."[93]

Washington, overseeing the army from New York, was less optimistic about the assurances of Indigenous neutrality; he compared the state of Patriot-Indigenous relations with the challenges of winning Canadian support. In a letter sent to Schuyler, Washington admitted that the general at Albany knew the temper of the Six Nations better than he, but he was sure Schuyler would agree that "it will be Impossible to keep them in a State of Neutrality." Washington saw Indigenous affairs as a zero-sum game, and he urged Congress to engage the Iroquois and other nations for the Patriot cause before the British set them against the colonies. Then, pivoting to Canadian affairs, Washington expressed his concern that Quebec inhabitants had not been given due respect. He instructed Schuyler to ensure that soldiers and officials try to avoid further damaging the colonies' reputation, knowing that "human Nature is such, that It will adhere to the Side from whence the best Treatment is received." Indigenous affairs and Canadian relations required complementary efforts. "I therefore Conjure You Sir," Washington wrote, "to recommend to the Officers & soldiers in the strongest Terms to treat all the Inhabitants, Canadians English & savages with Tenderness & Respect," because potential allies could hardly be expected to respond well to violence and mistreatment.[94] While Schuyler agreed with these sentiments, he connected Indigenous alliances and Canadian affairs more directly. "I am perfectly in Sentiment with you my dear General that we ought to engage the Indians to co-operate with us," he assured Washington, but he warned: "I fear it will be a difficult, if not an impossible Task to accomplish, unless Canada should be entirely in our possession—You will be able to form an Idea of their present Temper and Disposition from the inclosed Copy of a Journal of Mr Dean the Interpreter."[95] Conquering Canada was not only a step toward weakening Britain's empire but a way for Patriots to improve their relations with Indigenous nations and thus make possible a future that did not require British assistance in Indigenous affairs.

The commissioners to Canada faced the formidable task of winning Canadian support, lest the Canadians and the Indigenous nations both turn against the Patriot cause. Their job was made no easier by the situation they encountered on their arrival. In the 1770s, Montreal remained the center of the British fur trade. The city's merchants and traders were supported by artisans and rural farmers who increasingly followed seasonal work patterns, spending the warmer months farming and colder seasons working in the city or in the lumber trade. Outside the city, Indigenous settlements lined the St. Lawrence River in both directions, including Lorette, Kahnawake, and Odanak, to which members of the Huron, Iroquois, and Abenaki had migrated to become the Seven Nations of Canada.[96] Montreal also suffered from a military-civilian divide dating back to the British capture of New France in 1763, which caused a power struggle between military officers and civilian authorities that the earliest governors had to constantly negotiate. After 1763, the influx of British merchants created a prominent Anglophone elite; businessmen and merchants lived in fine stone houses along a waterfront dotted with church steeples. In these prominent houses could be found white, Black, and Indigenous servants in various forms of unfreedom: some were enslaved, some indentured, and some simply poor. Many in the settlement would have remembered when the city nearly burned to the ground in 1734, and they would have recalled Angelique, an enslaved woman who was tortured into confessing to having set the fire and then publicly executed.[97] Even before the Patriots captured Montreal, it was a divided settlement: English versus French, elite versus poor, military versus civilian, free versus enslaved. Perhaps these internal divisions are what made the city such an easy conquest in 1775.

When Franklin and the other commissioners arrived in the spring of 1776, however, the Patriots in Montreal faced dire economic realities. The first two letters the commissioners sent to Congress recounted just how grave the situation had become. The low opinion of rebel credit was leading Canadians to question whether Congress had much power, and the habit of soldiers manning the garrison simply taking what they wanted did not win the Patriots many supporters. The reason, of course, was lack of money: as their letter of 6 May noted, "It is very difficult to keep soldiers under proper discipline without paying them regularly."[98] The Canadians themselves, the commissioners added, had long since tired of the congressional scrip used after coins ran out, and unless there were an infusion of hard money, it would be best to withdraw the army from the city and fortify the surrounding lakes against possible attack from the British and, quite possibly, the Canadians themselves.[99] Though Congress surely welcomed the news of Indigenous neutrality, it hardly made up for the disappointing situation the commissioners found in Canada.[100]

The commissioners' third letter to Congress outlined just how desperate things had become: "The Tories will not trust Us a Farthing, and some who perhaps wish Us well, conceiving that We shall thro' our own poverty, or from superior Force be soon obliged to abandon the Country, are afraid to have any Dealings with Us, least they should hereafter be called to Account for Abetting our Cause." Whatever good will had existed among the Canadians was evaporating quickly in the face of the violence they endured from Patriot soldiers taking what they needed, "a Conduct towards a people, who suffered Us to enter their Country as Friends, that the most urgent Necessity can scarce excuse, since it has contributed much to the Changing their good Dispositions towards Us into Enmity, makes them wish our Departure."[101]

The mission to Canada was a failure. Unlike the British after 1763, the Patriots were unable to win the support of the Catholic clergy. A 1776 *mandement* from Bishop Jean-Olivier Briand outlined for French Catholics the dangers, both temporal and spiritual, of supporting the Patriots.[102] John Carroll's assurances that Patriots would welcome French Catholics were challenged by the fact that John McKenna, an Irish Catholic priest from the Mohawk Valley, was in Montreal because he had been chased out of the colonies; Franklin had no luck with merchants or politicians at Montreal; and Chase and Charles Carroll could do little to improve military prospects.[103] By 11 May, less than two weeks after their arrival, Franklin and John Carroll had left for Philadelphia. They took with them Thomas Walker's wife, who had hosted the commissioners. "The fear of cruel treatment from the enemy on account of the strong attachment to, and zeal of her husband in the cause of the united Colonies," the commissioners informed General Schuyler, "induces her to depart precipitately from her home; and to undergo the fatigues of a long and hazardous journey."[104] Mrs. Walker stopped in Albany to wait for her husband to join her while Franklin and John Carroll continued on, but the Walkers soon caught up with them and the group traveled together. Franklin, sick and tired, was hardly buoyed by the company. "They both gave themselves such Liberties in taunting at our Conduct in Canada, that it came almost to a Quarrel," he reported to Charles Carroll and Samuel Chase, who had stayed in Montreal to oversee military affairs. "I think they both have excellent Talents at making themselves Enemies, and I believe, live where they will, they will never be long without them."[105]

Smallpox and a lack of supplies devastated the rebel troops in Quebec. In a report to Schuyler, Chase and Charles Carroll emphasized the need for food. "The army here," they complained, "is suffering from want of Provisions particularly Pork. None, or next to none, is to be procured in Canada. . . . For God sake send off Pork."[106] With so little going well for the Patriots, it is hardly surprising that officials were worried. Washington fretted that holding on to Canada, a region he considered essential to the Patriot cause, was quickly becoming impossible.[107] The province was becoming, according to Brigadier General John Sullivan, who led a force stationed just outside Montreal, "the General Hospital of America."[108] News of military losses and smallpox spread almost as quickly as the disease itself. The *Virginia Gazette* offered regular updates on the Patriot forces in Canada. In early June, the paper republished a report that had appeared in London in January. Canadian merchants in London applied to the government to ask if additional troops would be sent to Canada, and the merchants were assured that plans were in the works to dispatch an armament in the spring.[109]

It was the arrival of those reinforcements that convinced Brigadier General Benedict Arnold to send Patriot troops, under the command of Isaac Butterfield and Henry Sherburne, to posts outside Montreal. Things did not go well. In mid-May the Patriots suffered an embarrassing defeat at Fort Cedars, just southwest of Montreal. Forty British soldiers, about as many Canadian Loyalists, and over two hundred Indigenous warriors marched on the Patriot-held fort. Following some brief firefights that caused few casualties, the American leadership surrendered after British forces threatened to unleash an Indigenous massacre.[110] In mid-June the *Virginia Gazette* published a letter from a Gentleman in Philadelphia recounting how American troops at Fort Cedars were overpowered by a force of one thousand—a great exaggeration. The author, however, remained optimistic that forces in Canada would be replenished to continue the campaign.[111] This report may temporarily have buoyed readers' spirits, but more bad news came the following day. "I am sorry there is so little prospect of our keeping possession of that province," read an extract of a letter from Philadelphia.[112] Slowly, it seems, reality was sinking in.

With Canada slipping away, so too were hopes of enlisting the Indigenous people as allies. "Our Situation respecting the Indians is rather delicate & Embarrassing," Washington confided to Schuyler in late May. So many of them were attached to Guy Johnson that the Patriot forces were reluctant to seize him for "Danger of Incurring their Resentment." Washington's only advice was that Schuyler should "conduct the Matter in the least Exceptionable Manner & in that Way, that shall most advance the Public Good."[113] The little good news that trickled in was fleeting. In June, General Sullivan wrote to Washington from his station outside Montreal and expressed surprise that "our Affairs here have taken a Strange turn Since our Arrival. The Canadians are Flocking by Hundreds to take a part with us . . . I really find most of them Exceeding friendly."[114] Whatever enthusiasm Sullivan thought he saw was ephemeral. Just a day later he urged Washington himself to come to Canada, promising that the province "would be ours from the moment of yr Excellenceys arrival." And if Washington could not visit, Sullivan asked to be relieved of his duties in Canada: "I am well Convinced that the Same disorder & Confusion which has almost Ruined our Army here would again Take place & Compleat its Destruction, which I Should not wish to See."[115] It was becoming clear that neither diplomatic nor military action could win Canada to the revolutionary cause, and as a result the hoped-for Indigenous alliances would never materialize. The Patriots could do nothing but determine what had gone wrong and how best to proceed.

Members of Congress spent May, June, and July of 1776 dissecting the Canadian debacle and convincing themselves that the failed invasion was a strategic victory that could be used to advance more radical revolutionary aims. They also assigned blame, and there was plenty to go around. John Adams pointed at gullible colonial politicians. "This Day has brought us the Dismals from Canada. Defeated most ignominiously," he fumed to James Warren. "Where shall We lay the blame? America duped and bubbled with the Phantom of Commissioners, has been fast asleep and left that important Post undefended, unsupported."[116] Adams was referring to rumors of a possible peace negotiation which, he argued, had distracted colonial leaders from the task at hand. "The Ministry have caught the Colonies, as I have often caught a Horse," he quipped, "by holding out an empty Hat, as if it was full of Corn." He was furious and sick of witnessing "knaves imposing on Fools."[117] Just a few days earlier, Richard Henry Lee had expressed nearly identical sentiments. "Some still continue to gape for Commissioners," he wrote to his brother Charles, "altho' there is no more reason to expect any than to look for virtue from a Tory, or wisdom from a fool." Yet delegates—of sorts—were coming: "I fancy the Hessian, Hanoverian, & Highland Commissioners, will shortly give us a different kind of treaty from the one that has been expected."[118]

Disorganization within the military remained a problem. The troops, those not struck down by smallpox, continued to misbehave and plunder Canadians for food. Even the Canadians who hoped the Patriot forces would stay, General Schuyler informed George Washington, "complain loudly and with too much Reason, of the ill Treatment they have received from many of our Troops."[119] Of course, the soldiers were malnourished, sick, and unpaid. Congress continued to struggle to finance the expedition and cover the debts incurred in Canada. The commissioners to Canada complained about the lack of credit and need for specie (metal currency). They estimated in early May that the Patriots already owed about £14,000, and an additional £6,000 would be required to restore credit.[120] Near the end of May, Hancock replied that he had raised and was dispatching £1,662. This paltry sum, which had required no small effort to collect, was "all that was in the Treasury."[121] Without sufficient funds and with troop morale so low, commanders on the ground reported discouraging prospects. Brigadier General William Thompson, reporting from the rebel camp at Sorel (on the St. Lawrence River between Montreal and Trois-Rivières), complained that had he arrived two weeks earlier (and with more men) the situation would have been brighter. As it stood, his New England troops were sick, or afraid of getting sick, and neglecting their duties. As for the Canadians who had supported the Patriots, Thompson worried that he wouldn't be able to protect them "from the Vengeance of Genl Carleton with which they are threatened."[122] Ultimately, Carleton behaved admirably after the Patriot retreat. Rebel stragglers, many too sick to flee, were allowed to recuperate before being sent back to their homes. Canadians who had refused to fight for the British came out of the woodwork, and though Carleton initiated commissions to investigate the inhabitants' behavior, most were allowed to admit their wrongs and then were forgiven.[123]

The Patriots had expected that revolutionary sentiment would sweep across Canada, but instead loyalty prevailed. In the face of the campaign's failure, members of Congress worked to recast the episode in a more favorable light. Their arguments generally fell into two categories: first, if the Patriots could control the waterways leading into the colonies, it was unnecessary to hold Canada; and second, even if the campaign had failed to win Canadian support, it had been useful for other purposes. In early June, Richard Henry Lee described how the Patriots could benefit from what they held, rather than lament not having taken Quebec. The Patriot forces had retreated from Quebec and were now fortifying a region about thirty miles upriver, at the falls of Richelieu. "If they can maintain that Post," Lee argued, "which commands 8 tenths of Canada, we shall do almost as well as if we had Quebec, as we [there]by effectively cut off all communication with the upper Country, or Western Indians, and prevent the West Indies receiving supplies from that fertile Province."[124] Richard Morris agreed, suggesting a few days later, "I dont think we have any occasion to hold that Country, if we maintain the passes on the Lakes it is sufficient for our purposes and the Garrison that defend those passes will always be ready to rush into Canada if the Enemy quit it."[125] Controlling the country itself was less important than controlling points of entrance and exit, which could be done by maintaining a few key posts.

This plan, however, required men with discipline, a trait in short supply among the Patriot army. Here again, Canada served the important purpose of illuminating military weaknesses and intercolonial tensions. The army's shortcomings were of grave concern. Passing along one of the commission to Canada's letters to Washington, Hancock lamented: "The Contents of it are truly alarming. Our Army in that Quarter is almost ruined for Want of Discipline, and every Thing else necessary to constitute an Army, or to keep Troops together."[126] As Hancock was writing to Washington, the general was writing to Schuyler with his own concerns. Increasingly disturbed by the bad news from Canada, he hoped Schuyler might find a way to improve Patriot prospects in the northern theater. "The most Vigorous Exertions are necessary to retrieve our Circumstances there, & I am hopeful that You will strain Every Nerve for that Purpose," he implored. "Unless It can be now done, Canada will most probably be lost for Ever, the fatal Consequences of Which Every one must feel."[127]

A plan working its way through Congress promised to secure at least enough new troops to hold the posts to which the Patriots had retreated after failing to take Quebec. While the operation in Canada continued to deteriorate, attempts at shoring up the Patriot forces provided a unique opportunity to rein in colonists who challenged the authority of state conventions and to promote the idea of a broader unity among the colonies. New York faced particular difficulty from settlers in the Green Mountain region (which would later become the independent Vermont Republic), who felt their land grants fell outside the colony's political reach. Robert R. Livingston addressed this challenge to New York's authority by attempting to include as many of these men as possible in New York's complement of soldiers for Canada. Livingston, whose fears concerning the dangers Canada posed to the United Colonies were quickly being realized, complained that "the attachment which some people have for Canada have left us very defenceless." Regardless, New York had to raise 3,750 men. He asked John Jay to "get volunteers for Canada if possible from the Green Mountain Boys by offering higher pay than the Continent allows, the expence of which will be very triffling to the Colony." Doing so would "frustrate the schemes of some people here who affect to consider them as no part of our Colony, & to assert that they never did nor ever will act under our convention."[128] Even if the army failed to control Canada, the northern theater would help the Patriots address issues—including military preparedness and intercolonial divisions—and ultimately benefit the revolutionary cause.

It was not only the members of Congress and military leaders who fretted about Canada and the direction of the rebellion. The press churned out letters, rumors, and reports on the fate of Patriot troops at Montreal, Quebec, and Chambly. Family members of those involved in the mission shared Congress's worries. Mercy Otis Warren wrote Abigail Adams to ask for information about the northern campaign. "I am Exceedingly Concernd at the accounts we hear from Canada," she wrote, "if you have any Late Inteligence do Let me know."[129] Warren's regular correspondents included not just the Adamses but Martha Washington and Hannah Winthrop, wife of John Winthrop.

Jane Mecom, Benjamin Franklin's younger sister, enjoyed none of his fame, wealth, or education and was not part of Warren's circle of correspondents. She was, however, the most frequent recipient of Franklin's letters and did her best to keep tabs on her brother's political writings and diplomatic endeavors. In early June 1776, Mecom sat down to write to Catherine Green, one of her closest friends, with an update that encapsulated much of her brother's Canadian trip and his frustrations. "My Dear Brother and the whol worlds friend is Returned; the cause and Circumstances are maloncholy but thank God he is again saif hear," she began. Mecom noted that Franklin felt ill throughout his trip to Montreal and "was taken sick in a Day or two after His arival and has never had a well Day since." While she could not diagnose his physical ailment, she felt sure of the cause: "The Raiseing the seige of Quebeck, the Ignorance of the Canadans, there Incapasity and Aversnes to have any thing to do in the war and his [?] Indisposition I beleve Affected His Spirets." But, she added, "He seems [a] little chearfull this morning."[130] Mecom was happy with her brother's safe return, even if his mission failed to bear fruit.

Ultimately, defeat in Canada helped refocus Patriot revolutionary efforts. In June 1776, John Adams painted a vivid picture of what might befall the rebelling colonies if the British reclaimed Canada. Should the British regulars secure full possession of the province, they could easily rebuild their communication with strategic points along major waterways, including Niagara, Detroit, and Michilimackinac. They would have open and easy communication with the Indigenous nations along the colonial boundaries, "and by their Trinketts and Bribes will induce them to take up the Hatchett, and Spread Blood and Fire among the Inhabitants by which Means, all the Frontier Inhabitants will be driven in upon the middle settlements, at a Time when the Inhabitants of the Seaports and Coasts, will be driven back by the British Navy." Adams asked, "Is this Picture too high coloured? . . . Perhaps it is, but surely We must maintain our Power, in Canada."[131] Some surely agreed, but many others did not.

For John Hancock, the simple act of completing a successful retreat was worth celebrating. While losing Canada was a "misfortune," he wrote to Washington, he was pleased that "our Army should make so prudent a Retreat, as to be able to save their Baggage, Cannon, Ammunition," and keep too many of their sick from falling into enemy hands. The British forces, after reinforcements arrived, were too strong and retreat was unavoidable. "In short, Sir," he explained, "I am extremely glad, our Army is likely to get safe out of Canada."[132] With Canada lost to the revolutionary cause, British Americans increasingly looked to their own colonies in considering what to do next.

The defeat also stifled Congress's push to expand the revolution northward and made simply challenging British imperial tyranny an insufficient revolutionary cause. Benedict Arnold, somewhat ironically given his later career path, seems to have realized that Americans needed to derive a strategy from within their own colonies. "Shall we sacrifice the few men we have, by endeavouring to keep possession of a small part of the country, which can be of little or no service to us?" he asked in a letter to General Sullivan. "The junction of the Canadians with the Colonies, an object which brought us into this country, is now at an end." But from this loss came opportunity: "Let us quit them," Arnold urged, "and secure our own country, before it is too late."[133] We should not misread his use of the word "country." Like Jefferson and others who spoke fondly of their "country" before independence or the ratification of the Constitution, Arnold was talking about his "native land" or colony. Yet he suitably crystallized what Canada meant for the revolution itself: if the British colony would not fall to the Patriots, they were better off focusing on securing their liberties within the thirteen colonies rather than fighting for British rights throughout North America.

The failure to take Canada suggested that independence was never at the root of the rebellion, though paradoxically independence made that failure easier to swallow. "Should the Army be compelled to evacuate Canada," Hancock wrote to the Massachusetts Council in April 1776, "it is impossible to say what will be the consequences, or where the mischief may end. It becomes us, therefore, as we regard our country and its best interests, to exert every nerve to guard against so fatal an event."

The inability to carry on such an offensive, he continued, "furnishes a most striking proof of the weakness or wickedness of those who charge [the colonists] with an original intention of withdrawing from the Government of Great Britain, and erecting an independent Empire. Had such a scheme been formed, the most warlike preparations would have been necessary to effect it."[134] Meshech Weare argued that independence was "a measure the British Administration have long and very unjustly charged the Americans with having in view, but now we conceive are driven thereto by them."[135] Weare's next sentence concerned how best to reinforce the army in Quebec. In the months after the failed attempt on Quebec, the Canadian campaign had become entangled in discussions of independence and the future of the colonies.

Even before the delegates to Congress discussed independence, they imagined a united future that would, they hoped, involve Canada. The Articles of Confederation, the governing document that served as a blueprint for uniting the thirteen rebelling colonies into a congress to oversee the war effort, make alliances, and organize opposition to Great Britain, left open the possibility that Quebec would at some point ask to join the cause.[136] In Jefferson's 1775 copy of a "plan of Confederation by Dr. Franklin," Article 13 stated that "any & every colony from Great Britain upon the continent of North America not at present engaged in our association may upon application and joining the said association be received into this Confederation, viz. Quebec, St. John's, Nova Scotia, Bermadas, & the East and West Floridas: and shall thereupon be entitled to all the advantages and obligations of our union, mutual assistance, & commerce."[137] A year later, as the Articles were revised while delegates debated independence, only Canada retained this option. Article 10 in the July 1776 version stated that "Canada acceding to this Confederation, and entirely joining in the Measures of the United Colonies, shall be admitted into and entitled to all the Advantages of this Union." This offer was now exclusive: the article added that "no other Colony shall be admitted into the same, unless such Admission be agreed to by the Delegates of nine Colonies."[138]

Canadian considerations were never far from the process of drafting the Declaration of Independence. In June 1776, Thomas Paine's *Common Sense* was in its third edition, and its arguments for independence had gained wide acceptance. To more clearly connect Canada to independence, this latest printing included the "Dialogue" between the ghost of Montgomery and a congressional delegate that Paine had earlier published in the press.[139] Richard Henry Lee's resolution of 7 June, which argued "that these United Colonies are, and of right ought to be, free and independent States," pushed Congress to consider seriously the ideas Paine was promoting.[140] On 10 June, Congress appointed a drafting committee, known as the Committee of Five, which included Thomas Jefferson, John Adams, Roger Sherman, Robert R. Livingston, and Benjamin Franklin. Franklin, still suffering from the gout that had plagued him during his voyage to Montreal, had returned from Canada less than two weeks earlier. All members of the committee considered Jefferson the best writer, so drafting the Declaration fell to him.

Given the document's importance, we might imagine that Jefferson would be afforded the time to retire and dedicate himself solely to the task of crystallizing the Patriots' decision to break from Great Britain, but this did not happen. Canadian issues kept him at his seat in Congress. On 15 June, he was named to a committee concerned with sorting out issues, complaints, and logistics related to the failed attack on Quebec. On 24 June, he joined yet another committee convened "to enquire into the causes of the miscarriages in Canada." Pauline Maier has suggested that Jefferson probably kept a draft of the Declaration on his desk while serving on these committees and took the opportunity to "poke at it in dull moments" when not fretting over prisoner exchanges, Montgomery's death, or the failed siege of Quebec.[141]

As the debate over independence intensified, the Canadian theater remained a primary concern for the delegates. News of the Patriot defeat at the Battle of the Cedars, in May 1776, was received with much horror in the colonies. Canada was linked to Indigenous "savagery" that put both Canadians and Indigenous peoples outside the Patriots' "common cause" and helped the rebels see themselves as something distinct from their northern neighbors. As Robert G. Parkinson has argued, published responses to accounts of the Battle of the Cedars, including one from Thomas Jefferson, contained "themes the Declaration would make famous just one month hence."[142]

John Dickinson, in notes that he took in preparation for a speech in Congress regarding independence, used Canada to triangulate the British-French-American relationship that might result from permanent separation from Great Britain. He opposed declaring independence until proper articles of confederation were drafted and foreign alliances secured. "Suppose on this Event," he mused, "G.B. should offer Canada to France & Florida to Spain with an Extension of the old Limits. Would not France & Spain accept them? Gentlemen say the Trade of all America is more valuable to France than Canada. I grant it but suppose she may get both." Adam Smith had made a similar argument to ministers in London, noting that returning the Floridas to Spain and Canada to France would leave the colonies surrounded by imperial enemies and force them to look to Great Britain for protection. Dickinson believed independence would put France in too powerful a position: it need only intimidate Great Britain (which would be occupied fighting in America) until Canada "is put into her hands," at which point France could then "intimidate Us into a most disadvantageous Grant of our Trade."[143] Dickinson's vision would not come to pass exactly as predicted—although Florida was returned to Spain—but he absented himself from voting on independence.

In a jubilant letter the day before Congress adopted the Declaration, John Adams recorded his excitement for the future of the United Colonies and connected their new status with future opportunities to conquer British territory. "This morning is assigned for the greatest debate of all," he wrote to Archibald Bulloch, "a Declaration, that these Colonies are free and independent States, has been reported by a Committee, appointed some weeks ago for that purpose, and this day or to-morrow is to determine its fate. May Heaven prosper the new-born Republick, and make it more glorious than any former Republicks have been!" Adams then turned to matters to the north: "The small-pox has ruined the American Army in Canada, and of consequence the American cause . . . the small-pox, which infected every man we sent there, completed our ruin, and compelled us to evacuate that important Province. We must, however, regain it some time or other."[144]

Future attempts on Canada, however, would be undertaken not by rebelling British colonies but by newly united states. "A little more wisdom, a little more activity, or a little more integrity," Adams believed, "would have preserved us Canada." But "irretrievable miscarriages ought to be lamented no further than to enable and stimulate us to do better in future."[145] As Adams saw it, the Canadian failure—a miscarriage insofar as Patriot aims were not extended north—was midwife to a future free of imperial oversight. John's cousin Samuel Adams was himself focused on how the independent colonies might approach Canada. "Our repeated Misfortunes in Canada have greatly chagrind every Man who wishes well to America," he fumed just a few days after signing the Declaration of Independence. "To be acting merely on the defensive at the Time when we should have been in full possession of that Country is mortifying indeed. The Subject is disgusting to me," he continued: "I will dismiss it."[146] He had little choice.

Hours after the debate on independence, John Adams wrote to Samuel Chase, who had been one of the commissioners to Canada, and again connected past failures with future opportunities. Congress, Adams reported, had debated and agreed to independence, though the vote had been postponed to the following day, 2 July. He immediately changed the subject to Quebec, lamenting, "Alas, Canada! We have found misfortune and disgrace in that quarter—evacuated at last." After a short assessment of what had gone wrong, he compared the Canadian failure and the Declaration of Independence to ancient Roman strategies surrounding peace and power. "The Romans," he noted, "made it a fixed rule never to send or receive Ambassadors to treat of peace with their enemies, while their affairs were in an adverse or disastrous situation." Independence seems to have buoyed the Americans after the Canadian debacle. "There was a generosity and magnanimity in this becoming freemen," Adams declared. "It flowed from that temper and those principles which alone can preserve the freedom of a people. It is a pleasure to find our Americans of the same temper. It is a good symptom, foreboding a good end."[147]

The Declaration of Independence itself shows how Canadian affairs influenced the rebels' decision to break free of Great Britain. For all it has come to represent, the bulk of the Declaration is a list of complaints leveled by Congress at the British king and Parliament. Two of those complaints, both found in the bottom third of the list, directly relate to Canada. First, Parliament was accused of "abolishing the free System of English Laws in a neighbouring Province, establishing therein an Arbitrary government, and enlarging its Boundaries so as to render it at once an example and fit instrument for introducing the same absolute rule into these Colonies." This was a specific reference to the Quebec Act. The second complaint was directed at Indigenous nations, many of which fought alongside the British in Canada and throughout the northern theater. The Americans had signed treaties with various Indigenous groups and had their own Indigenous allies, yet the Declaration painted them all with the same brush: the king "has excited domestic insurrections amongst us, and has endeavoured to bring on the inhabitants of our frontiers, the merciless Indian Savages, whose known rule of warfare, is an undistinguished destruction of all ages, sexes and conditions."[148] These two complaints encapsulated the problems Canada caused: it was a safe haven for French Catholics and Indigenous peoples, two groups long seen as enemies to the British colonies and, after 1776, the independent states.

John Adams believed that if independence had been adopted earlier, Canada would have fallen to the Patriot forces. In a letter to his wife, Adams celebrated the Declaration but lamented that it came too late. "Had a Declaration of Independency been made seven Months ago, it would have been attended with many great and glorious effects. We might before this Hour, have formed alliances with foreign States . . .; we should have mastered Quebec and been in Possession of Canada." Congress's execution of the Canadian campaign had been frustratingly slow and haphazard. Many leading figures, Adams felt sure, had been duped by the promise of an early peace with Britain and thus distracted from taking real measures to support and supply the Canadian mission. Those who were not distracted might have sincerely wished that the Patriot forces would be defeated because had they been successful perhaps it "should elevate the Minds of the People too much to hearken to those Terms of Reconciliation which they believed would be offered Us." The combination of these two positions, both of which would have been eliminated had independence been declared earlier, had in the end "lost Us the Province."[149]

The Declaration also did nothing to change the Patriots' military prospects, but it certainly boosted morale among those who wished for a more promising future.[150] As weary soldiers straggled south from their failed campaigns, members of Congress ensured that they were returning to colonies now focused on achieving full independence. Rather than join the independent future, Canada would serve as a reminder of the United Colonies' imperial past. This symbolism was not lost on Abraham Clark, one of the delegates for New Jersey. "At the Time our Forces in Canada were retreating before a Victorious Army, while Genl. Howe with a Large Armament is Advancing towards N. York, Our Congress Resolved to Declare the United Colonies Free and independent States," he informed Elias Dayton, who led the Third New Jersey Regiment. The colonies' anger toward Britain had "gone so far that we must now be a new independent State, or a Conquered Country."[151] Perhaps this new independent state would later do some conquering of its own. Benjamin Rush, the noted Philadelphia physician, believed this might happen. He thought Canada should have been won on the merits of Arnold's march and Montgomery's sacrifice alone, and he allowed himself to believe that "the banner of liberty will be planted on some future day by the States of America upon the walls of Quebec."[152]

The invasion of Canada and the challenges faced by Patriot troops outside Quebec brought these revolutionary ambitions into stark relief. Attacking a loyal British colony with the goal of extending Patriot ideals into a society of French-speaking Catholics was a risky venture. Patriots were driven not only by dreams of expanding their geography but by the hope that removing the British from Quebec would facilitate a more peaceful relationship with the continent's Indigenous nations. The failure of both the military campaign and the diplomatic commission helped revolutionary leaders reorient their efforts toward the more plausible—yet audacious—goal of breaking free from the British empire. The newly united states turned their backs on Indigenous peoples, who were cast as enemies rather than allies, even though some had supported the Patriot cause. When the military leaders and politicians who had planned and executed the failed campaign against Canada turned their attention toward an independent future, they helped to reframe the intent, outcome, and significance of the invasion of Quebec. In turn, Quebec and Canada became integrated into the many histories of the Declaration of Independence.

# CHAPTER TWO

# Sea Power

ENRY WADSWORTH LONGFELLOW's 1847 epic poem *Evangeline, A Tale of Acadie*, concerns the Acadian expulsion of 1755, during the Seven Years' War, when British soldiers rounded up the French settlers of Acadia, put them on ships, and drove them from the province. *Evangeline* tells of two lovers separated by the expulsion, a story Longfellow first heard at the dining table of his own house in Cambridge, Massachusetts, while enjoying a meal with his friend and fellow poet Nathaniel Hawthorne and a priest named Horace Conolly. Conolly, who heard the tale from his Acadian housekeeper, had told Hawthorne the story before, but the poet asked him to tell it again. Longfellow was enthralled. He made Hawthorne promise not to write about it and immediately set to work turning it into a poem.

Opening in "the forest primeval" of Acadia, the poem focuses on Evangeline Bellefontaine and Gabriel Lajeunesse, the separated lovers. In describing Evangeline's wanderings through the American colonies and early states in a lifelong search for Gabriel, Longfellow gives readers a tour of the new nation and transforms the Acadian expulsion into a specifically American story.[1] The couple eventually find each other in Philadelphia when both are old and gray. Evangeline, working for the Sisters of Mercy while an epidemic is ravaging the city, discovers Gabriel among those suffering from the disease. He dies in her arms. Longfellow's grandfather had his own stories about lands that had once been considered Acadia. During the War for Independence, General Peleg Wadsworth fought against the British in the northeast. Both grandfather and grandson were driven by a fiction: for Longfellow, it was Evangeline; for Wadsworth, it was New Ireland, a colony that the British hoped to establish along the Penobscot River in eastern Maine, itself little more than a province of Massachusetts. Comprising three administrative districts and situated within the homelands of the Abenaki, Maine was almost as imaginary as New Ireland. Wadsworth fought alongside other notable revolutionary figures—including Paul Revere, whose midnight ride Longfellow would memorialize in another poem—to keep the British at bay and secure the eastern parts of Massachusetts for the Patriot forces.

Though thinly settled and difficult to defend, what would become eastern Maine was an important site of Indigenous diplomacy and imperial envisioning, and it demanded Patriot attention. Here the revolution was less about an independent future than about a contested past. Settlers in the small villages between the Penobscot and St. John Rivers were oriented east toward Nova Scotia as much as toward Boston. They fought for survival and recognition against British naval ships, Patriot militiamen, and colonial promoters in roughly equal measure. They took this stand as invaders of the traditional homelands of the Wabanaki. Many hoped the revolution would pass them by. The British, for their part, hoped to superimpose the entirely new colony of New Ireland over a part of the northeast that the Boston colonial government often ignored. This territory had also once been called Acadia, the home of Evangeline.[2] The blurry borders and fluid loyalties that defined the northeast during the revolution demonstrate how easily the conflict could sweep up those who hoped to be left alone.

Nova Scotia straddled the Patriot-Loyalist divide. If Quebec was a constant threat to the rebeling colonies, Nova Scotia was a nagging concern throughout the revolution. During the eighteenth century, New Englanders attacked French Acadia whenever Britain and France were at war, and after British troops expelled the French settlers in 1755, New Englanders took up the vacated lands and soon made up over half of the province's population. New England and Nova Scotia, closely connected by geography and trade, were developing what many considered a shared colonial identity.[3] During the American War for Independence, Nova Scotia, like Quebec, was torn between patriotism, loyalty, and neutrality. Indigenous peoples in the northeast, including the Mi'kmaq, Wulstukwiuk,

Passamaquoddy, and Abenaki, found themselves in an unwanted war they could not stop from spilling into their homelands.

Acadia, or Nova Scotia (the province was known by both names until the late eighteenth century), was a complex region with a deep history. Well before Europeans set foot in North America, Indigenous peoples lived in what became Nova Scotia, New Brunswick, and Maine in homelands that still exist. The Mi'kmaq live in and move through Mi'kma'ki, a region that includes present-day Nova Scotia, Cape Breton, Prince Edward Island, the Gaspé Peninsula, and parts of Newfoundland. The Wulstuk-wiuk and Passamaquoddy, distinct but related groups, live along the St. John River and Passamaquoddy Bay and down the Maine coast as far as Machias, a territory they call Wulstuk. The Eastern Abenaki inhabit the Dawnland, the region from the Penobscot River to the Saco River inland as far as the Canadian border.[4] These groups, known collectively as the Wabanaki Confederacy, have lived in these homelands for at least twelve thousand years.[5] In that time they developed spiritual, maritime, and terrestrial geographies that fully incorporated the land into their worldview. They used the land and its resources, altered their physical surroundings as necessary, and created complex cultures, rituals, adaptations, and diplomatic protocols to govern their interactions.[6]

The vague boundary between Nova Scotia and Massachusetts took on increased importance as the Patriots moved toward open rebellion against the British. Settlements in eastern Maine were inhabited by farmers and fishermen who enjoyed the quasi-independence provided by their distance from Boston. Their proximity to Nova Scotia brought trade relationships and extended kinship networks and fostered a regional rather than specific colonial identity that had them monitoring developments throughout the northeastern borderland.[7] In 1775, when the residents of Machias complained about Nova Scotia and pushed for an invasion, George Washington considered their appeals but demurred. One problem was that Nova Scotia had already been excluded from commercial intercourse, and he presumably deemed this a suitable punishment for their loyalty to the empire. He reminded the Massachusetts authorities that the province had "not commenced Hostilities . . . nor are any to be apprehended." He also reminded the Massachusetts Provincial Congress of their military and naval limitations. They quite simply could not afford an expedition that called for one thousand troops and a fleet of four armed ships and eight transport vessels.[8] But that did not mean

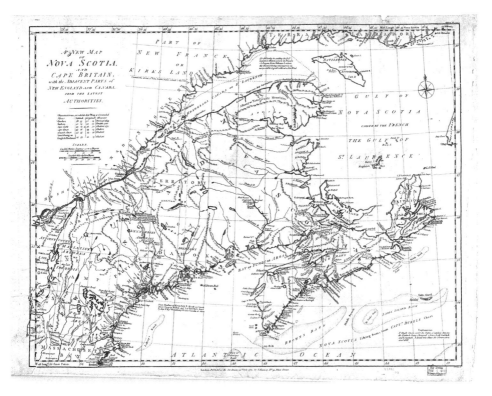

*A new map of Nova Scotia and Cape Britain*, 1785. John Murray,
cartographer and publisher, and John Lodge, engraver.
Library of Congress, Geography and Map Division.

they could not try to learn more about what was happening east of the
St. Croix.

Despite Washington's reluctance, the Continental Congress established a committee to consider the requests for attacks on Nova Scotia—
or warnings that the British were planning to attack *from* Nova Scotia.
Steady streams of both arrived in Philadelphia from the northeastern borderlands.[9] James Lyon of Machias sent a Christmas letter to Washington
offering to lead a charge from Maine. "The reduction of Nova Scotia," he
wrote, "is a matter of great importance, & lies near my heart, on account
of my many suffering friends in that Province, & on account of the many
advantages, that would arise from it, to this Colony, & to this place, in particular." Washington understood Lyon's desires but could not agree to the
proposal.[10] The committee charged with evaluating these requests issued a

report in November 1775. The report included two primary suggestions: first, five hundred men should be raised and prepared to fight if necessary; second, and more important, "a number of men" should be immediately dispatched to Nova Scotia to determine if the population was likely to support a Patriot invasion.[11] There could be no attack without first taking the inhabitants' temperature, and a diagnosis of revolutionary fever was no guarantee of an invasion.

Within days, Congress set the "number of men" at two: Aaron Willard and Moses Child. Perhaps they should have selected two women. Washington knew that women had an easier time getting behind enemy lines, but other members of Congress fretted that women provided the British with intelligence on Patriot movements.[12] Willard and Child were sent "at the Expence of these Colonies to Nova Scotia, to inquire into the state of that Colony, the disposition of the Inhabitants towards the American cause, & the Condition of the Fortifications, Docks, Yards, the Quantity of Artillery & Warlike stores, & the number of Soldiers, Sailors & Ships of War there, & Transmit the earliest Intelligence to General Washington."[13] There was hope that Nova Scotia harbored sufficient revolutionary spirit to facilitate a Patriot attack. Just a week before Congress decided to dispatch its spies, a broadsheet appeared in Salem with news from the province. Nova Scotia residents had learned of unrest in London, where a group of protesters demanded the repeal of imperial legislation allowing Parliament to tax the colonies. "The above news was joyfully received at Halifax and Liverpool, by the bulk of the people," the broadsheet noted, suggesting that perhaps Nova Scotia was not as loyal as many imagined. "Our friends are numerous," the account continued, "and are determined to make a bold stand for liberty, and shew their other American friends that they will not be behind-hand with the bravest and most resolute of them."[14]

Even if Congress's spies reported that Nova Scotia could be taken easily, Washington was not prepared to send troops, though he was not opposed to the Massachusetts government raising men for the purpose.[15] It was a moot point, however, because Willard and Child were terrible spies. Their report, delivered to Washington in February 1776, indicated that they had gotten no farther than Campobello, an island in Passamaquoddy Bay, just a few miles into Nova Scotia. In lieu of a proper investigation, they drew "from our own Knowledge and the Best Information from others." Their conclusions, apparently based on intuition and a few casual conversations with residents along the border, suggested that a good majority of the inhabitants would side with the Patriots if they could depend on protection as "there are no Fortifications in the Province only at Halifax and those much out of Repair."[16] This was not entirely accurate. A few forts, in various states of disrepair, remained scattered across Nova Scotia, most of them having been built in the 1750s during the lead-up to the Seven Years' War. The hapless spies, squinting at the province from across the Bay of Fundy, had little other intelligence to offer, correct or otherwise. Washington was unimpressed.[17]

Some within Nova Scotia asked the Patriots for help. Twelve Nova Scotians from Cumberland issued a petition in early February 1776 hoping Congress "would Cast an Eye of Pity towards this forlorn part."[18] They were responding to a memorial from the Nova Scotia assembly which argued that "no native of this province may ever be appointed a Governor or Lieut. Governor in this province," nor should Nova Scotians serve as judges. This presented a problem as colonists were already serving as judges, but the memorial suggested that as these men grew old and died off, they should be replaced by Englishmen appointed in England. Such a system was meant to provide a bulwark against factions and the ambitions of wealthy men, who, according to the assembly, were destroying the empire. "We can trace the present unhappy disorders in America," the memorial continued, "to the want of a regulation of this kind."[19] It was enough to make some inhabitants pray for an invasion.

The Cumberland rebels sent their petition via an Acadian, Isaiah Beaudreau, who would also answer any questions Washington or others might have. The Acadians, according to a letter accompanying the petition, were "to a man wholy Inclin'd to the Cause of America, I have oftend pityd them in their situation & the manner of proceedings Against them." The "Citizens of Nova Scotia" who wrote these documents complained that the British government in Halifax had passed a series of bills with the support of recent immigrants from England, who were used to paying taxes and following the dictates of Parliament. They also explained how settlement patterns and isolation prevented Nova Scotians from responding more robustly on behalf of the Patriot cause. News of Patriot actions and ideology was filtered and altered "to the disadvantage of the Americans," and residents of Nova Scotia were told that nearly all foreign powers supported Britain. Occasionally there would arrive "a flying Report that the Americans has Allies to help them," but such news was generally stifled. Despite these difficulties, "a Spirit of Sympathy I presume for our brethren on the Continent reigns in the breasts of the Generality of the Inhabitants." They needed only support from Patriot forces to participate more fully in their cause.[20]

There was little that Washington or Congress could do. Congress sent Washington proposals for an attack, and Washington sent Congress men from Nova Scotia who had come to lobby for an invasion, including the Acadian Isaiah Beaudreau and Jonathan Eddy, a New Englander living in the Chignecto region of Nova Scotia. But with Patriot troops stalled outside Quebec and no money available for additional campaigns, those hoping for an invasion of Nova Scotia would be disappointed.[21]

Many supporting the invasion and rebellion in Nova Scotia saw an opportunity to add another colony to the Patriot movement. Caught between the British and rebel forces, however, were the thousands of Indigenous peoples whose homelands stretched from what colonists called Maine to Gaspé. The polities of the Wabanaki Confederacy struggled to maintain their territorial rights while also keeping Patriot, Loyalist, and neutral demands at bay. Readers in the colonies would have known something about the Mi'kmaq as they were often described in pamphlets and tracts. They were sometimes depicted as bloodthirsty savages who must be exterminated and other times as a people mistreated and misunderstood by settlers who plied them with alcohol to gain the upper hand in trade.[22] In reality, they could be victims, warriors, and everything in between. The Wabanaki were no less multidimensional than the settlers who hoped to take their lands.

It was the warriors, however, who worried the settlers. If Congress was unwilling to attack Nova Scotia, it was certainly concerned with protecting eastern Massachusetts, and to do so, Patriot officials courted the region's Indigenous population. Wabanakia, the homelands of the Wabanaki Confederacy into which both British and Patriots hoped to expand, was thinly populated by settlers, who well knew how vulnerable they were to attacks from Indigenous peoples and British forces. Settlers had been trying to push east from Massachusetts Bay for over one hundred years, and they regularly met resistance from the Wabanaki.[23] A letter to the "Eastern Indians" from the Provincial Congress at Watertown in May 1775 attempted to alert the Indigenous nations to the "great wickedness" of the British. Addressing the Wabanaki as "Brothers," the letter claimed that "the ministry of great Britain, have laid deep plots to take away our liberty & your liberty." The British would deny colonists and Wabanaki alike the guns and powder necessary to kill game and collect skins for trade and would make colonists and Indigenous peoples their servants. "Our liberty & your liberty is the same," the letter concluded, "we are Brothers and what is for our good is for your good."[24] As they did with the Canadians, Patriot officials hoped to find common cause by identifying a shared threat.

The Wabanaki remained a formidable force in and around the Maine settlements. Like the Iroquois, however, many hoped to remain neutral and trade with either the British or the Patriots. Rebels tried to secure trade alliances that would prevent Indigenous attacks on their weak settlements.[25] These various interests—partly conflicting, partly aligned—came together in a flurry of activity in early July 1776. The workings of Congress, coupled with an unexpected visit from several Wabanaki chiefs, led to lengthy discussions about how the Wabanaki might participate in the revolution. The first step came when Congress authorized Washington, with assistance from the Massachusetts Bay General Court, to "call forth" Indigenous peoples from Penobscot, the St. John River, and Nova Scotia to join with the Patriots against the British.[26] Washington was thinking along similar lines. Four days before Congress's decision, he had written to John Hancock from New York, predicting a vigorous British attack that would include Indigenous forces. He hoped to counteract such designs as forcefully as possible. Although the "schemes for employing the Western Indians do not seem to be attended with any great prospect of success," he thought it might be possible to "engage those of the Eastward." He had heard that up to six hundred warriors might be ready to fight for the Patriots. The Wabanaki did not have to undertake offensive measures to be valuable allies. They could "prevent our Enemies from securing their friendship," which itself was beneficial, and "further they will be of Infinite service in annoying & harrassing them, should they ever attempt to penetrate the Country."[27]

In the same letter to Hancock, Washington outlined how best to bind the Wabanaki to the Patriot cause. He began by justifying the need for Indigenous allies, which in itself hints at the fractured nature of colonial and Indigenous relations. "At a crisis like the present," he argued, "when our Enemies are prosecuting a War with unexampled severity—When they have called upon foreign mercenaries, and have excited Slaves and Savages to arms against us, a regard to our own security & happiness calls upon us to adopt every possible expedient to avert the blow & prevent the meditated ruin." He thought the Indigenous nations were better as allies than as enemies, and since the British were employing mercenaries, the

Patriots could justify unleashing "savage" warriors. The British had made a similar argument to justify their own use of Indigenous warriors, because the first Indigenous peoples to participate in the revolution were men from the Mahican, Housatonic, and Wappinger nations that had resettled in Stockbridge, Massachusetts, and they fought alongside Washington's army.[28] Washington reinforced their ambiguous identity by referring to Indigenous peoples as "savages" when they were enemies but emphasizing that, as allies, they must be treated fairly. In a letter to the Massachusetts General Court in early July, Washington requested "friendly exertions" to engage as many Indigenous men as were willing to enlist "on the best terms you can." Some, he hoped, would join for less pay than the Continental troops, but if they demanded more, it "must be allowed."[29] They were needed for Washington's army in New York.

By coincidence, the process of negotiating with the Wabanaki to join in the American Revolution had begun the day before Washington's letter to the General Court. Ten delegates from the Wulstukwiuk, Passamaquoddy, and Mi'kmaw peoples had arrived in Boston on 10 July in response to letters they had received from Washington and the Massachusetts General Court the previous year. In late 1775 and early 1776, Washington had held meetings with Wabanaki and Iroquois delegates who wanted to know more about the war with Britain and offered their support in return for supplies.[30] When the Wabanaki chiefs returned to Watertown in the summer of 1776, they brought evidence of their relationships with both the British and the Patriots. The conference at Watertown, held at the Meeting House, included the Council of Massachusetts Bay; its president, James Bowdoin; and ten Indigenous delegates, including Wulstukwiuk chiefs Ambroise Saint-Aubin, who spoke for the delegates, and Pierre Tomah.

When the Indigenous delegates were asked at the beginning of the conference to prove that they represented others from the St. John River and Nova Scotia, Saint-Aubin presented a copy of the 1760 Treaty of Peace and Friendship between Great Britain and the Wulstukwiuk and Passamoquoddy.[31] He also presented a letter from General Washington, sent the previous February, and another from the Massachusetts General Court, sent the previous October.[32] These letters, he said, were the occasion for the chiefs' visit.[33] The Wabanaki had a treaty relationship with the British dating back to 1725 but had never surrendered their territorial or political sovereignty. The outbreak of the American Revolution offered them a possible new ally in the Americans, which some chiefs took as an opportunity to assert their economic and military independence.[34] After presenting his documents to the Council, Saint-Aubin, speaking through an interpreter and on behalf of the chiefs, made clear their desire to ally with the colonists: "The Captains that are come up with me, and all our people, are all one as Boston." While emphasizing their rejection of the British, Saint-Aubin also made a request. Having been converted to Catholicism over the seventeenth and eighteenth centuries, the Wabanaki wanted the Patriots to provide a French Catholic priest, which would allow the Passamaquoddy and Penobscot to end their regular travels to Nova Scotia for religious services. "We shall have nothing to do with Old England," the chief reassured the Council, adding, "All that we shall worship or obey will be Jesus Christ and General Washington." To demonstrate their fidelity, Saint-Aubin presented the president of the Council with a silver gorget and heart, on which were engraved the king's arms and busts of the king and queen. "All our Captains and Chiefs do pray," he continued, "that [Washington] and his brothers may be masters of this country. We are both one country. We are of their country and they are of our country."[35] The Wabanaki hoped to use a civil war among the settlers to realign the power structures in their favor in the northeast.[36]

Following Saint-Aubin's introductory statements, the conference became a forum for the Council president to collect as much information as possible about Nova Scotia. Given Willard and Chase's failure, the presence of friendly Indigenous delegates with intimate knowledge of the region was an opportunity too good to pass up. Bowdoin inquired about the disposition of the French in Nova Scotia and was told (in what was surely an exaggeration) that "they are all for you." What do the English in the province think about the disputes between England and America? Ambroise was not sure. How about the rest of the Mi'kmaq and St. John nations? "Both the Mickmac or Cape-Sable Indians and the St. John's Indians are all for helping Boston; we know their hearts, for we had a talk with them."[37] Ambroise was providing the answers Patriot officials wanted to hear, which pleased Bowdoin and the Council.

Bowdoin's response to the delegates demonstrated the importance of respecting Indigenous diplomatic protocol.[38] The president employed language, turns of phrase, and rhetorical structure that mimicked the Indigenous style of speech. He gave a history of the events that had led to the current crisis. "You have heard that the English people beyond the great water have taken up the hatchet, and made war against the United Colonies in America," he began. "We once looked upon them as our brothers, as children of the same family with ourselves, and not only loved them as brothers, but loved and respected them as our elder brothers." But the British had treacherously invaded and attacked the colonists, though "a number of our warriors assembled and drove them back." Leading the effort was General Washington, the "Great Warrior." Bowdoin had done well, all things considered, but a misstep at the end of the first day nearly derailed the conference. After warning Ambroise and the others not to be deceived by officials in Nova Scotia who would surely attempt to turn them against the Patriots, Bowdoin and the Council returned the silver pistol and silver gorget and heart that the delegates had presented to them earlier. "We thank you, and now return them to you," Bowdoin said, "in confidence that they will be employed by you only against your own enemies and our enemies." Returning a gift was highly insulting, and an Indigenous speaker "with great vehemence and displeasure" refused to take it. Hoping to make amends, Bowdoin suggested that his new allies should have a new gorget and heart, but with a bust of Washington and other "proper devices to represent the United Colonies."[39]

With the diplomatic blunder smoothed over, the two sides met the following day to continue their discussions. Bowdoin quickly addressed the request for a Catholic priest by applauding the Indigenous people's devotion but cautioning them that he might not be able to find a suitable French cleric. If the delegates were agreeable, he could send "one of our Priests," an English Protestant, and "take care he be a good man."[40] He then reminded the delegates that he was not asking them to enter the war unless they so desired. Ambroise reaffirmed his commitment, which led Bowdoin to ask how many warriors Ambroise could guarantee. Indigenous diplomacy differed from colonial governance in important ways, and Ambroise informed Bowdoin that "it is not in our power to answer for the whole of our Tribes." The delegates would have to return to their homelands, hold discussions with their kin, and see who wanted to go to war. There were also Wabanaki communities that had not received Washington's letter or that were away hunting and thus unaware that the conference was taking place.[41] For Indigenous nations, diplomacy was a continuous process, and treaties were always tentative agreements to be revisited as necessary to maintain an alliance. This thinking was foreign to most European officials, but in a region where Indigenous nations retained power and sovereignty, there was no way around it.[42] The treaty the two sides struck was about alliance, not surrender. The colonies and the Indigenous nations "shall henceforth be at peace with each other, and be considered as friends and brothers, united and allied together for their mutual defence, safety and happiness."[43] Bowdoin was confident it would last; yet friendships, even when solemnized in treaties, could fade away.[44]

In recounting the conference to Washington, Bowdoin told the general he expected the Wabanaki could provide 250 men but that it would take a few months to assemble them and transport them to New York, where they would join Washington's army. In the meantime, four delegates had enlisted on the spot and were en route to New York: Joseph Denaquara of Windsor, Nova Scotia, who spoke both English and French; Peter André of LaHave; Sabattis Netobcobuit of Gaspé; and Francis of St. John. Bowdoin hoped their participation "might not only secure the Fidelity of the Tribes to which they belonged, but induce many others of them to engage in the Service."[45] It was an auspicious beginning to the alliance, but these early volunteers suggested more than the delegates could ultimately deliver. Just a few weeks later, in late August 1776, the British under General Howe launched an amphibious attack against the Patriots at Brooklyn Heights on Long Island and pushed Washington and his troops across the river to Manhattan. It was a major victory for the British, but Howe did not follow the rebels into New York, where he might have crushed them and changed the course of the war.[46] The Patriots' narrow escape demonstrated that the Continental Army needed as much help as it could find. Any warriors who enlisted in the east were to be dispatched with all speed.

The Patriot negotiators at Watertown could not have known that in promising to secure warriors for the Continental Army, the Indigenous diplomats had gone well beyond their authority. Most Wabanaki tried to avoid being recruited by either side.[47] Their neutrality was on full display in the fall of 1776, when a small group of disaffected Nova Scotians and residents of Machias, led by Jonathan Eddy, attempted an attack on Fort Cumberland, a British post on the Isthmus of Chignecto. Eddy's previous attempts to secure support from the Massachusetts General Court for an attack on Nova Scotia had failed, but he asked them again in the summer of 1776. Although this proposal too was rejected, the Court promised to provide supplies and ammunition for whatever force he could raise on his own. Eddy moved quickly: he traveled to Machias and organized about twenty men, who then embarked for Nova Scotia. They made two stops en route, at Passamaquoddy and the Planter settlement of Maugerville, and managed to collect an additional fifty men. Of these, sixteen were Wabanaki, including Chief Saint-Aubin, who despite his promises at Watertown had persuaded very few Wabanaki to enlist. When Eddy and his men arrived at Cumberland, the town's pro-Patriot residents were rightfully disappointed at the size of the liberating force. The "siege" of the fort was an utter failure. Eddy demanded the fort's surrender on 12 November, was rebuked, and two days later his force attacked. They were easily repelled. A second charge met the same fate. By late November, British reinforcements had arrived from Halifax and easily forced Eddy's crew back to Machias.[48]

The failed attack demonstrated the paradox of eastern Maine: the region was isolated from the Massachusetts government and received little support, but it was an important center for organizing Indigenous alliances that helped defend Massachusetts from Nova Scotia. Coming on the heels of the British victory over the Patriots at White Plains at the end of October, at which General Howe finally pushed the Patriots out of New York for good, Eddy's failed campaign against Nova Scotia did little to boost Patriot morale. It was nearly impossible to raise a militia for defense, let alone organize a force to take the war to Nova Scotia. The weak economy of eastern Maine—mostly subsistence farming and fishing—meant that few families could afford to lose their men or their labor. Even when a militia was raised, there were not enough food and other supplies available to sustain it. A well-organized attacking force like the British regulars could gain control over the territory by controlling the food supply.[49]

In such a vulnerable region, Indigenous allies offered one of the best options for defense. Though the Treaty of Watertown had failed to gain the Patriots many Wabanaki warriors, officials remained hopeful that Indigenous nations would support the cause and perhaps help turn the tide against the British. John Allan, a member of the Nova Scotia assembly who had spent enough time in Massachusetts to acquire revolutionary sympathies and New England connections, traveled to Boston to meet with the Massachusetts Council and outline a plan for taking Nova Scotia. He recounted his dealings with the Mi'kmaq and explained to the Council on their behalf why the Mi'kmaq were not following the Watertown treaty. They had been courted by both the Patriots and the British and were now torn. They had attended a conference at Halifax on the invitation of Governor Legge of Nova Scotia, at which Legge demonized the Patriots and promised the Mi'kmaq whatever they needed should they support the British. The Mi'kmaq told Allan they had refused the British request but had accepted ammunition, provisions, and clothing. Patriot sympathizers who saw the Mi'kmaq after the conference worried that the British had in fact secured their alliance and would use them later in the spring.[50]

Allan knew how adept the Mi'kmaq were at playing one side against another, a skill they had honed over the past two centuries as various European factions laid claim to their homelands while hoping to secure their alliance. Allan told the Council that in June the Mi'kmaq had met at Fort Cumberland with a British official who, as Legge had done in Halifax, promised them whatever they needed should they fight for Britain. But if they would not fight for the king, the official expected they would not fight against him either. The Mi'kmaq left that meeting too with ammunition and provisions. When they told Allan about it, the Mi'kmaw delegates also expressed their reverence for George Washington. They showed him Washington's letter to the Wabanaki and praised him for wanting the Mi'kmaq "to be at peace, and if we want help he will grant it and defend us." The Mi'kmaw delegates mentioned that they had sent representatives to "their brothers the Boston men," referring to that summer's Watertown meeting, but they also expressed their confusion over the nature of the revolution. "We do not comprehend what all this quarreling is about," they admitted. "How comes it that Old England and New should quarrel and come to blows? The father and son to fight is terrible. Old France and Canada did not do so; we cannot think of fighting ourselves until we know who is right and who is wrong."[51]

What Allan reported next made clear to the Council that the Watertown treaty had done nothing to guarantee an alliance with the Wabanaki. During his recent travels, he had encountered a group of young Indigenous men who told him that John Baptist and Matua (both of whom attended the Watertown discussions) had returned with "a great packet . . . but that it much displeased the chiefs." They traveled together until they reached a large group of Mi'kmaq, who received Allan kindly but were obviously distressed. After a night's rest, Allan learned from one of his French guides that John Baptist and Matua had entered into the treaty without authority. The chiefs were so angry that when they confronted the Watertown delegates, both argued that the treaty had been forced on them and that they had not understood what they were signing. Allan then met with twenty-one chiefs, said to represent the entire nation. Though the Mi'kmaq were upset, Allan refused to discuss the treaty until he had made clear the root causes of the current war between

Britain and the colonies. He gave them a lengthy history, beginning with the earliest colonial settlements and ending with the current troubles. "They listened with the greatest attention," Allan reported, "and at the end of every sentence gave their assent."[52]

This assent signaled understanding, not agreement. When Allan pressed the chiefs to pick a side, they refused. He wanted to know their objections to the Watertown treaty, and they told him, "We never authorized those persons to do such a thing. Some of it we cannot perform . . . and these men say they were imposed on, and we are determined to return it." John Baptist clarified that he might not have been forced into the treaty, but he feared that neither side had fully understood the other, despite the interpreters' efforts. Allan offered to return the treaty rather than allow the Mi'kmaq to reveal its contents to the British at Fort Cumberland or Halifax. Before he did, however, he asked if the Mi'kmaq would help the Patriots in less formal ways. They could not, the chiefs responded, because they still depended on "Old England" for support. "We want not to molest any," they declared, "but to keep in friendship with all." Though the chiefs admitted they would rather trade with the colonists than with the British, Allan could not get them to promise assistance. When he asked if they would consider assisting the colonies if the other inhabitants of Nova Scotia joined with Massachusetts, the chiefs offered a pragmatic reply: "When we see a sufficient power in this country we will tell you what we will do. We know nothing certain about things. We know we must submit to the strongest power." They then showed him Washington's letter, affirming, "There is what we will stand to. George Washington wrote that we might continue in peace if we pleased, for which he must be a good man."[53]

Allan concluded his report to the Massachusetts Council by suggesting that the Mi'kmaq were easily swayed by authority and generally believed what they were told. What was required, he said, was someone with a deep understanding of their culture and an ability to communicate with them to serve as a superintendent. Such a person would "keep as constant as possible among them, acquainting them from time to time with the different news, and how things passes; by this, their different movements may be known."[54] Allan thought he was the man for the job and pressed his case to both George Washington and Congress, then meeting in Baltimore. On 11 January 1777, Congress resolved "That an Indian agent be appointed for transacting business between the United States and the several Indian nations and tribes in Nova Scotia, and the country to the northward and eastward thereof."[55] After two Patriot victories in New Jersey that demonstrated Washington's capabilities as a military general—his famous attack at Trenton on Christmas Day and the defeat of British troops at Princeton on 3 January 1777—Congress welcomed a revived effort to win Indigenous support in the northeast that might expand the theater of Patriot strength.

Four days later, Allan received his instructions to treat with the Indigenous nations of the northeast and "engage their friendship." If he could not persuade them to fight for the Patriots, he should work to prevent them from siding with the British and attempt to secure as much information from them as possible about Nova Scotia.[56] Allan was eager to use his new authority to gather Indigenous support and launch another attack on Nova Scotia, and on his way back from Baltimore he convinced the Massachusetts Council to support his invasion. After a few weeks of planning, Allan marched a modest and reluctant force of about one hundred ill-supplied men to the St. John River, where the campaign stalled.[57] When he attempted to rally Indigenous support, he learned that divisions within the Wabanaki were so deep that two of the delegates from Watertown were now against each other. Ambroise and a few of his warriors supported Allan, whereas Tomah remained suspicious and even hostile. When British reinforcements arrived at the mouth of the St. John, Allan and his Indigenous supporters had to abandon their invasion—yet another sign that Patriots lacked both the will and the alliances to attempt in Nova Scotia what they had tried in Quebec.[58]

To Allan's military failures were added the diplomatic competition he faced from Nova Scotia's governor, Michael Francklin, who was also working to win the support of the Mi'kmaq, Wulstukwiuk, and Passamaquoddy. A divisive figure who made lifelong friends and enemies, Francklin had arrived in Nova Scotia in 1752 and quickly became a wealthy merchant, a member of the Nova Scotia assembly, and, in 1766, lieutenant governor. During Governor William Campbell's frequent return trips to England from 1766 to 1772, Francklin served as Nova Scotia's acting governor. In 1777 he was appointed Nova Scotia's superintendent of Indian Affairs, which provided him with a fixed salary and funds to purchase gifts necessary to conduct Indigenous diplomacy. He was well suited to the job, having been kidnapped by the Mi'kmaq in 1754 and held for three months in Gaspé. During his captivity, Francklin had learned the Mi'kmaw language and enough about Indigenous culture to let him appreciate the Indigenous way of life.[59] His political connections, financial resources, and linguistic abilities gave him the upper hand in competition for alliances with the Mi'kmaq, Wulstukwiuk, and Passamaquoddy. At a conference with the Wabanaki at Fort Howe, a small fortress built at the mouth of the St. John River shortly after Allan's failed 1777 attack, Francklin offered the Wabanaki everything they desired: guns, supplies, and, most important, a French priest. It was a windfall for the Mi'kmaq and their neighbors, who promised not to fight for the Patriots and to tell the British if they heard of any rebel plans for an attack. They even handed over the letters from George Washington and presents sent them by the Massachusetts General Court.[60]

These promises, like those the Wabanaki offered the Patriots, weakened over time. The colonies' 1778 Treaty of Alliance—by which France recognized the independence of the United Colonies and agreed to provide naval support in their war against Great Britain—helped sway Indigenous alliances back toward the Patriots because France had a deep history of good relations with Indigenous peoples in the northeast dating back to the arrival of Champlain and the Acadians in 1604.[61] In addition, French ships brought French priests, who could be sent out to serve the Wabanaki as they had long desired, further cementing the alliance of some, such as the Passamaquoddy, to the Patriot cause and ensuring that settlements like Machias, near the Wulstukwik River, remained Patriot enclaves for the duration of the war.[62] The Wabanaki's shifting alliances maintained a perfect imbalance in the northeast that left the region susceptible to attack. Many Wabanaki, not unlike the Iroquois, had developed an active neutrality by which they supported either side at different times to ensure the survival of their people. There was no ambivalence to their actions.[63] The Wabanaki's grand strategy was to secure their position in the northeastern borderlands in such a way that if either British or Patriot forces hoped to control parts of the Dawnland, they would have to have Indigenous support.[64]

For the Patriots, eastern Maine and Wabanakia took on new importance in the war against Britain when administrators in Halifax attempted to create a new British colony in the northeast. Settlers and explorers had much practice imagining what might be created in this part of the world. In 1524, Giovanni da Verrazzano called the northeast "Norumbega," a name that stuck into the eighteenth century. Later in the sixteenth century, David Ingram, an illiterate English sailor, claimed to have walked from Florida to Cape Breton after being abandoned by his trading vessel. Upon returning to England (he was in fact rescued by a French ship somewhere between Florida and Nova Scotia, but it is unclear where), he would sit drinking in taverns, telling anyone who would listen of what he saw in Norumbega: Indigenous chiefs sitting on thrones made of jewels, fist-sized gold nuggets lying around for the taking, and immense dining halls with "pillers of massive silver and chrystall." His stories echoed from grog shops to Whitehall, and fifteen years after his voyage he was summoned by the secretary of state to describe his journey. Richard Hakluyt included Ingram's tale in the first (1589) edition of his *Principall Navigations*, though it was removed from future versions, likely because it was too outlandish even for those who peddled colonial fantasy.[65] As late as the 1730s, a London philanthropist, Thomas Coram, and a royal surveyor of the woods, David Dunbar, proposed a colony, to be called Georgia, that would extend from the Kennebec River to the St. Croix River.[66]

But for the Penobscot, Kennebec, Arosaguntacook, and Pigwacket, it was Maine that was imaginary. The Abenaki peoples defined their land by the waterways that cut through the northeast and the drainage basins that sustained forests of white pine, hemlock, and hardwoods along the coast ("the murmuring pines and the hemlocks" of Longfellow's *Evangeline*) and spruce and pine farther inland. Subsistence required seasonal patterns of hunting and gathering, with the family band serving as the political and economic unit. In the spring, the Abenaki fished for salmon, shad, and eel. In winter, using snowshoes, they hunted moose, deer, caribou, and bear. It was the homelands that were real; settlers' new names and maps could never replace these lived histories.[67]

The refusal of the Massachusetts General Court to support a full invasion of Nova Scotia left settlers between the Saco and St. John Rivers (in what is now Maine) vulnerable to British expansion, especially because Indigenous nations in the region would not fully support either the British or the Patriots. In the spring of 1778, after Patriot losses at Germantown and Brandywine and the horrid winter at Valley Forge, members of the Continental Congress reaffirmed their refusal to attack Nova Scotia. After several inhabitants of Nova Scotia petitioned for it, a committee appointed to consider the request found that "the wresting of Nova Scotia from the British power and uniting the same to these States is for many weighty reasons a very desirable object; but . . . the propriety of making this attempt at the present crisis seems doubtful." Congress, surely tired of fielding these appeals, resolved to wait and see whether war between France and Great Britain might provide a better opportunity for success.[68]

Meanwhile, British officials in London began developing their own plan for a new colony in the Maine borderlands.[69] A driving force behind this project was John Nutting, a carpenter and housewright from Cambridge, Massachusetts. His family had ties to the sea, outfitting ships at Marblehead and Gloucester. He did well in his trade and consequently took many trips along the coast from Boston to Maine for lumber. It was these trips that likely awakened Nutting to the Penobscot region's potential, and he began purchasing lands along Penobscot Bay and up the Bagaduce River. Just weeks before the British were pushed out of Boston in March 1776, he escaped to Halifax, where he was busier than ever as the garrison town struggled to accommodate fleeing soldiers and Loyalists.[70] He built houses and volunteered to pilot ships for British attacks on New England. After the British launched a failed attack on Machias in the fall of 1777, Nutting traveled to London carrying letters from the commanding officer concerning the failed attempt.[71] While there he began petitioning officials to support his proposal. He contacted Lord Germain, the secretary of state for the colonies, but received no reply. Eventually Nutting befriended William Knox, Germain's undersecretary. The two men had a shared interest in eastern Maine. Knox had long supported the idea of establishing a new colony between New England and Nova Scotia and had even roughed out some details. It would be called New Ireland (a nod to its location between New England and New Scotland); Thomas Hutchinson would serve as governor; and the settlement would protect the Bay of Fundy and St. John River while also offering a safe haven for Loyalist refugees from the colonies to the south.[72]

Hutchinson, the colony's suggested governor, thought the plan untenable. After meeting with Knox, he recorded in his diary that the proposed colony "put me in mind of Mr. Locke's story of Ld Shaftesbury's friend, who, after he was privately married, sent for his Ldship and another friend, to ask their advice: and I observed the same rule so far as to find no fault with the preposterous measure, because already carrying into execution. . . . However, I intend to make Mr. Knox acquainted . . . with my sentiments."[73] When imperial officials struggled to select a site for the new colony, Nutting volunteered his thoughts: Penobscot would be ideal. Perhaps this was because of its strategic location between Nova Scotia and New England, but more likely because it was where he owned land.[74] The imperial officials debating the matter accepted his counsel. He was named overseer of the construction of new forts at Penobscot and sailed for America in late 1778. After just a few days at sea, Nutting's vessel was attacked and ultimately captured by a Patriot privateer, but not before he tossed his letters and official documents overboard to avoid alerting the rebels to the plans for New Ireland. Nutting was injured and taken prisoner, but he was soon released and made his way back to London. By the time he arrived, it was too late in the year to attempt another transatlantic passage. After several weeks of waiting and recuperating, he set out again for Penobscot in early 1779.[75] Even before he arrived, however, British officials in New York and Halifax had learned of the New Ireland plan and organized an expedition. A fleet of ships led by Brigadier General Francis McLean left Halifax in late spring. Traveling with McLean as naval commander was Captain Henry Mowat, reviled in the Maine districts for his attack on Falmouth in 1775, in which he put the settlement to flames. Under orders from Sir Henry Clinton, McLean and Mowat sailed with about seven hundred men to Fort Majabigwaduce, later Fort George (at Castine, Maine), arriving in mid-June 1779.[76]

John Caleff was thrilled that the Penobscot plan had come to fruition. Caleff, whose Massachusetts roots went back four generations, had served as a surgeon on British military ships during the Seven Years' War, and in 1768 he had been one of only a handful of men in the Massachusetts General Court who supported the British right to tax the colonists, a position that brought him great harassment in his town of Ipswich. He had been interested in the settlements in Penobscot since the early 1770s, and in 1772, after the Massachusetts government issued a land grant for the region, settlers there had asked him to travel to London to try to procure royal assent for the grant. He wrote to Sir Francis Bernard, the former governor of Massachusetts Bay, and Bernard forwarded the letter to Lord Dartmouth, then the secretary of state for the colonies. When Dartmouth resigned in the fall of 1775, he may or may not have passed Caleff's plan to his successor, George Germain. The revolution interrupted Caleff's efforts in London, but he didn't forget about Penobscot. As tensions rose in Massachusetts and Caleff was forced to flee Ipswich for Penobscot in 1779, he once again attempted to secure a royal grant for the Penobscot inhabitants. He then traveled to Nova Scotia to encourage officials there to establish a post at Penobscot, but by then Nutting and Knox's plan was already in the works. William Knox, who had worked under both Dartmouth and Germain, certainly would have recalled Caleff's petition when Nutting came to him. The

Massachusetts men, Caleff and Nutting, were two ships sailing for the
same port but unable to see each other through the fog.[77]

When Francis McLean's fleet arrived off the Penobscot coast in mid-
June 1779, the men aboard had much to do. John Caleff, whose enthusiasm and knowledge of the region earned him a spot on the ships sailing
to Maine, kept a careful journal of British activities from the moment
they arrived. One of McLean's first tasks was to secure the loyalty of Penobscot residents, both white and Indigenous. On 15 June, aboard HMS
*Blonde*, he issued a proclamation announcing the arrival of the British
forces and assuring settlers that they would be allowed to keep their land
if they came and swore an oath.[78] In this borderland, claims and oaths
were stand-ins for authority. For the Penobscot, onto whose homelands
the British hoped to unfurl their New Ireland, imperial efforts to control
territory were nothing new. Some Penobscot who saw the arrival of
McLean and his ships would have remembered an earlier visit. In 1715,
British administrators, then located at Annapolis Royal, sent two delegates to the Penobscot to secure their recognition of the new imperial
power in the region. They were asked to swear an oath, and they refused:
"I do not like to be told that my land is under the authority of
Port Royal," one Penobscot representative declared. "I am the only master of this land given me by God, and I depend on no one."[79] More than
sixty years later, eastern Maine remained a region claimed but not controlled.

There were more practical concerns as well. "The time from this day
[of the fleet's arrival] to the 17th of July," Caleff wrote in his journal,
"was taken up in clearing a spot to erect a fort and building the same,
and a battery near the shore, with store-houses, etc." On 18 July, a month
after arriving, McLean and Mowat were informed that the Patriots had
learned of the British landing and were planning to dispatch vessels to
remove them. Washington and his army had endured another terrible
winter, this time at Morristown, New Jersey, where the Continental
Army was nearly eradicated by starvation. By the spring, however, matters had improved. This intelligence was corroborated by additional reports the following day, leading Mowat to suspend work on the
fortifications in favor of preparing the men for battle and putting ships
into position to defend the harbor.[80] Though the British landing faced no
local resistance, some settlers had fled the region. For those who stayed,
McLean offered amnesty in return for an oath of allegiance. Families

faced a difficult decision, and as they did throughout the colonies, many split over the issue. Thomas Goldthwait, a Loyalist with three sons, gave each one a choice. Two, Ben and Jo, fled immediately to join the Patriots, while Nat, the third, stayed to support the British. Ben would return, but not to rejoin his family. He was one of the first rebels off the boat when the Patriot forces arrived to dislodge McLean and his men.[81] A few Loyalists received appointments and commissions, and more worked to get the fortifications prepared.[82] Though he might have been satisfied that no settlers worked to push back the British landing and some were helping with preparations, McLean was not eager to do battle with the Americans because he thought he was unlikely to win.

Word of the British landing at Penobscot had reached Massachusetts officials within days. Messages of alarm were carried to Boston from many settlements in Maine, and at the end of the month the Navy Board of the Eastern Department proposed sending ships to remove the British.[83] Patriot officials might have hoped to keep their plan secret, but they could not. In mid-July, James Lovell complained about the publication of a letter received at the end of June, which mentioned that a rebel fleet would sail for Penobscot. "That fleet did not sail till the 8th or 9th of this Month," Lovell fumed, adding that "one capital Ship from New York or Halifax may ruin the whole Expedition."[84] Nathaniel Peabody, a delegate to Congress from New Hampshire, informed fellow delegate Josiah Bartlett that "the intended expedition to dislodge the Enemy from Penobscot not having been Conducted with that Secrecy the Nature thereof requir'd by which means the Enemy have got intelligence and Sent a reinforcement."[85] These were early signs that any altercation at Penobscot would not favor the Patriots.

A more covert operation might have helped, at least early on, but the Patriot effort to remove the British from eastern Maine ultimately fell victim to internal tensions and disorganization. The day that Lovell and Peabody complained of publications concerning the Patriot fleet's mission was the same day, 18 July, that John Caleff recorded that construction had halted on new fortifications on the Penobscot, which the British called Fort George. All hands were preparing "to receive the enemy." The following day brought a confirming report that a fleet of forty vessels (one more than the actual number) had left Boston.[86] Following the custom of the day, the Patriot forces had no unified command structure. Land forces fell under Solomon Lovell, a Massachusetts native who, as a child, had been educated by Reverend William Smith, the father of

Abigail Adams. His military career began during the Seven Years' War, after which he started life anew as a farmer and then as a colonial politician, all while remaining part of the militia. He participated as a field commander in the battle of Rhode Island (1778) and fought well in the attempt to push the British out of Newport. Command of the Penobscot campaign was the height of his career. His deputy commander, Brigadier Peleg Wadsworth, would be long associated with Maine and Nova Scotia as Henry Wadsworth Longfellow's grandfather.[87] Lovell's naval counterpart was Dudley Saltonstall, an officer from New London, Connecticut, and brother-in-law of Silas Deane, whose engagement in the Penobscot campaign was surely a low point in his naval career.[88] Command of the artillery train fell to another of Longfellow's muses, the Boston silversmith and engraver Lieutenant Colonel Paul Revere.

The Patriots sailed from Boston thirty-nine vessels strong, a hodge-podge of Continental navy, state navy, privateers, and supply ships. Some had intimidating names suitable for their task, such as the *Tyrannicide*, a fourteen-gun brig captained by John Cathcart. There were the *Vengeance*, a twenty-gun privateer, and the *Hunter*, with sixteen guns. Other vessels were named for loved ones or family, such as the *Charming Sally*, the *Abigail*, and two ships called *Nancy*.[89] The vessels carried two thousand sailors and one thousand militia, more than enough to overpower the seven hundred British troops and three ships of war at Fort George. But outfitting such an expedition was an expensive undertaking, costing £1,739,174 sterling at a time when Massachusetts could not afford to be reckless.[90] Anything less than a complete rout of the British would be a failure.

The outcome was worse than any Patriot sailor, soldier, or official could have imagined. The British forces at Fort George spotted the Patriot fleet on the afternoon of 24 July. The following morning, a brig appeared in the distance and by noon the full complement of Patriot vessels had arrived at Penobscot Bay. In the early afternoon the ships divided, took their position, and launched "a very brisk cannonade." Even from the shore, the British could tell that the rebels were disorganized. "The fire of the Enemy was random and irregular," noted John Caleff, "and their manoeuvres, as to backing and filling, bespoke confusion, particularly in the first division, which scarcely got from the line of fire when the second began to engage." During this first engagement the Patriots attempted to land troops on the Bagaduce River but were repelled.[91] And so it went for a fortnight: the rebels attacked and the

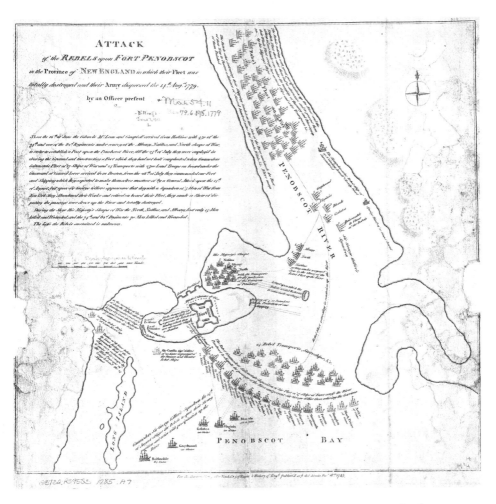

*Attack of the rebels upon Fort Penobscot in the province of New England in which their fleet was totally destroyed and their Army dispersed the 14th Augst. 1779, 1785.* Norman B. Leventhal Map Center Collection, Boston Public Library.

British repelled. The rebel troops secured a small island in the harbor from which they could launch cannon fire on Fort George, but the British were able to adjust their position and calibrate their guns. Surely the British troops were asking themselves when the big push would come, when the Patriot ships and troops would combine their efforts in a devastating amphibious attack. The rebels must have wondered the same thing, but Lovell and Saltonstall could not agree on a strategy. Lovell wanted the ships to push into the harbor and obliterate the royal vessels, which would allow Patriot troops to storm the shores and take the fort. Saltonstall refused, declaring, "I am not going to risk my shipping in that damned hole."[92] As the commanders bickered over strategy, the British waited. Outgunned and outmanned, McLean and Mowat needed time to organize an attack. The Patriots gave it to them.

No one in Massachusetts had any idea that their forces were faring so poorly. On 3 August, a cloudy and rainy day in Penobscot, the Patriots were regrouping after a failed attack that had taken place three days earlier. They had stormed the shore at 2 a.m. but were pushed back by the British. Things remained relatively quiet as the rebels repositioned their guns and the British fortified their defenses.[93] In Philadelphia, William Whipple expressed his sincere desire that the Penobscot expedition should succeed, and he saw only one possible obstacle: "the delays that have taken place in preparing which may give the Enemy opportunity to get reinforcements." His next sentence, however, described what a victory might look like. The Patriots could capitalize on their success by capturing a much more valuable British stronghold. "Should it succeed," Whipple wrote, "I can see no difficulty in crossing the Bay immediately & taking possession of Nova Scotia, this would be so Glorious an acquisition that it would surely be worth Hazarding much for. Pray let me know if such a plan is in contemplation."[94] An anonymous letter published in the *Pennsylvania Gazette* was equally optimistic. "Tis said their force is about 900 Highlanders," the account stated, "besides tories and sailors from their ships. We about 1200, besides sailors, and a fine fort within point blank shot of them, and expect every moment to receive orders to make one more bold attack, which I am confident must prove favourable."[95]

Within days, however, Patriot officials grew concerned about their Penobscot prospects, leading some to wish that the Gulf Stream might carry rebel successes from the Caribbean to the Maine coast. Charles Hector, comte d'Estaing, who commanded the first French fleet sent to support the United Colonies under the 1778 alliance, had won decisive victories in June and July against the British in the Sugar Islands. St. Vincent fell to the French without firing a shot. A week later, d'Estaing captured Grenada, Britain's second largest sugar-producing island after Jamaica. The British navy, commanded by Vice Admiral Byron, was poorly positioned to defend Grenada and arrived two days after the island fell. In the ensuing sea battle, the British fleet suffered heavy losses and retreated, leaving Grenada for America's allies.[96] "I never have had one single Moments real Hope of Success at Penobscot. I have now a Dread about that Expedition," Lovell admitted to Horatio Gates on 9 August 1779. But might Nova Scotia still fall? "I pray God," he continued, "to put you upon some Concert with D'Estaing either regarding Rh. Island or Nova Scotia. What shall I do . . . if you cannot gain me a quiet habitation up the Bay of Fundy?"[97] Nathaniel Peabody managed to distract himself from debates in Congress long enough to scribble a letter to Meshech Weare, who led New Hampshire's Committee of Safety and served as the colony's chief justice. Peabody had learned that the British were sending reinforcements from New York "with 7 arm'd Vessels, Several Transports, and two thousand Land forces put to Sea the 29 [July]. suppose! their object is Penobscott." But he was sure that events in the Caribbean would inspire victory in Maine: "The Success of Count D'Estang in the West Indies, the Singular advantage he has gained over Byron & the British fleet Cannot fail giving New life to our friends & Cause our Enimies to Stand agast. Hope You will give the Earliest intelligence of the Success of our Little Penobscott fleet."[98]

Those following the Penobscot campaign from afar allowed themselves to celebrate a Patriot victory before learning of their crushing defeat. The rebels at Penobscot were obliterated by British reinforcements that arrived from New York in mid-August. The nightmare began on the evening of 14 August, when the Patriots spotted British vessels and decided to retreat. It was an unmitigated disaster. Assuming all along that the campaign would succeed, none of the commanders had crafted an exit strategy. Not a single Patriot vessel made it back to Boston. Some were captured by the British, others were sunk in the ensuing battle, and the rest were run ashore, abandoned, and set aflame. The sailors and soldiers who escaped death or capture were left to make their way back home—haggard, hungry, and disorganized—through forests and fields that, they hoped, would eventually lead them to the Kennebec River, which they could then follow to Falmouth.[99] They surely would have preferred the outcome set out in *Pennsylvania Gazette*: "Yesterday we received an account that the business was compleatly done; that every man of the enemy, to the amount of 1000 (including sailors) fell into our hands, and among the rest master Mowatt, the firebrand that burnt Falmouth."[100] Virginians celebrated the same fictitious victory ten days later.[101]

Eventually word of the defeat reached Philadelphia and, later, the colonies more generally. "I fear the jig is up with Us," Henry Merchant wrote to Horatio Gates.[102] Samuel Holten, a congressional delegate from Massachusetts, recorded in his diary, "The Accts. this day by the Post are, that our fleet at Penobscot are all cut of[f] by the enemy."[103] Henry Laurens somberly informed Richard Henry Lee on 31 August, "News from Penobscot very unfavorable but no particulars. I would compound for the loss of all our Ships provided the Soldiers & Sailors escape Capture."[104] The accounts trickling south were almost too horrible to believe, leading one Pennsylvania newspaper to suggest that a British account of the victory must have been embellished.[105] As if it could have been.

There was plenty of blame to assign, and most of it fell on Saltonstall, who was accused of failing to provide Lovell with the naval support he needed to launch an effective land war. He was a useful scapegoat for two reasons. First, he was from Connecticut, so no one in the Massachusetts assembly was likely to defend him. Second and more important, he carried a Continental commission, which bolstered the argument that Congress, not Massachusetts, should pay for the disastrous campaign.[106] Even Paul Revere found himself threatened with an investigation into his alleged refusals to follow orders, "which tend to cowardice." During the failed retreat, Revere had only reluctantly helped Patriot crewmen because he had hoped to salvage his ship and personal belongings.[107] He was put under house arrest, and the committee charged with investigating the failures at Penobscot heard a litany of complaints against him: that he had his men stay on shore while he returned to dine, sleep, and take breakfast on his ship; that he was routinely absent from his men as they organized themselves; and, particularly damning for a lieutenant colonel of artillery, that he was a bad shot. Revere responded with a letter, more than three thousand words long, in which he detailed his past grievances against those now leveling charges against him. His defense failed to exonerate him, but neither did he suffer the further indignity of having the charges against him included in the committee's final report. He spent the next two years trying to clear his name. He requested a court martial, was denied, and repeated the request. This one was granted. Not until February 1782 was he acquitted of all charges and restored "with equal Honor as the other Officers in the Same Expedition."[108] Paul Revere's rough ride was over.

After the destruction of the Patriot fleet, and while Revere was fighting the charges against him, Alexander McNutt began imagining what New

Ireland might become. It was a delightfully impractical project, but its attempted execution demonstrated that eastern Maine was an ideological borderland, not just a geographical one. McNutt tried to co-opt an imperial idea and make it American. In so doing, he harkened to the region's contested past and the religious influence of Massachusetts's earliest European settlers. McNutt, who had attempted to settle new inhabitants in Nova Scotia earlier in the century, jumped on the scheme that Knox, Nutting, and Caleff had initiated. But where these imperial officials saw a colony for Loyalists, McNutt envisioned a theocracy for anyone willing to live by God's laws. Beginning in 1780, he undertook a promotional campaign that involved drafting an open letter to potential inhabitants, crafting a constitution and frame of government, and dispatching a treatise explaining the colony's sovereignty and independence to Congress's delegates, who were then negotiating the end of the war. Over several months, McNutt laid out his vision of a new colony in which British Americans could reinvent themselves as Patriot citizens and children of God.

Officials in Halifax had been warned to keep their eyes on McNutt. He was "a subtle, designing fellow, [who] has endeavoured to circulate several letters and dangerous pamphlets throughout the Province."[109] It is unclear exactly where McNutt was when he wrote his New Ireland pamphlets, all of which were printed in Philadelphia in 1780 and 1781, just as Washington and the Continental forces were turning their attention to the southern campaign, but he had left Nova Scotia around that time. In one of three pamphlets attributed to him, he outlined conspiracy theories in which British officials bribed Patriot merchants to circumvent nonimportation agreements and engaged in deliberate currency manipulation to ensure specie existed to pay British soldiers but not to circulate within the colonies. McNutt concluded his pamphlet with the promise of a second tract, which would tell Patriots how best to defeat British designs. If nothing came of his efforts, "I shall at least have the satisfaction that I have herein done my duty as a fellow citizen, and discharged my conscience, warning you of danger."[110]

McNutt did not follow up on his supposed conspiracy. Instead, his next pamphlet offered readers a constitution and frame of government for "the free and independent state and commonwealth of New Ireland." New Ireland thus joined eleven other states in drafting a new constitution after 1776, though McNutt's state was imaginary and his constitution a puritan's fever dream.[111] The state's religious foundation was made clear in McNutt's first sentence, which drew from Acts 6:3: "Chuse you out from amongst you Men fearing God." Such a call was "the divine Standard," and thus "the Fear of God is a Qualification absolutely necessary for every person, who may bear, or hold any Office, in a Christian State." Having established "the Truth of divine Revelation or Scriptures," McNutt proceeded to an overview of the government, which would be run by a council of seven members (presumably appointed by McNutt), including a governor, deputy governor, and secretary, each to be compensated by land proportional to the office.

New Ireland's constitution included a "Declaration of Rights" that drew heavily from the Declaration of Independence but offered a more progressive attitude toward racial equality, likely a result of McNutt's imperial connections.[112] Had New Ireland actually existed, it would have been the first state to abolish slavery. The first item in the Declaration of Rights asserted that "all Men are born equally free and independent" and that "Slavery is a gross Violation of the natural Rights of Mankind, and shall not be tolerated amongst us." What would be tolerated in McNutt's theocracy, somewhat paradoxically, was freedom of religion. The second enumerated right declared that "all Men have a natural and unalienable Right to worship almighty God, according to the Dictates of their own Consciences and Understanding; and no Man ought, or of Right can be compelled, to attend any religious Worship, or erect or support any Place of Worship, or maintain any Ministry, contrary to, or against, his own free Will and Consent." The rest of the individual rights would have been familiar to rebels in states with recently adopted constitutions, including that the government should serve the people, the right to a speedy trial, that warrants were needed for searches, and the right to bear arms.[113]

As a seasoned if not terribly successful colonial promoter, McNutt likely knew it was best to highlight the colony's most attractive elements. But his readers must have wondered where New Ireland was and who its people were. McNutt's cart was well ahead of his horse. New Ireland would be governed by the laws of nature and "by what Discoveries He has been pleased to make of his Will in the holy Scriptures." The state would be an asylum for all Christians, who would be able to worship however they wanted, there would be no established church to support, and no religion would be considered subordinate to any other. However, no one could hold office "who is not a regular Member of some Christian Society, acknowledging the Trinity of Persons and the Unity of Essence in the Godhead."[114]

Theocracies are seldom known for their jovial social atmospheres, and New Ireland would be no different: "no Stage Plays, Horse-Racing, Cock-Fighting, Balls and Assemblies, Prophane Swearing and Cursing, Sabbath-Breaking, Drunkeness, nocturnal Revelling, Whoredom, Cards." Engaging in these or similar activities rendered a citizen of New Ireland ineligible for public office. These fallen souls would enjoy the company of others barred from office, a list that included any person who "held any Office under the British Government since January 1775," enemies of religious liberty (as defined by the state), persons who had been involved in shedding Patriot blood, and lawyers.[115]

McNutt assumed that people would come for the government, as ordained by God, and for the land, which, apparently, God had made more fertile without informing the struggling settlers of eastern Maine. "We have said that the Climate is remarkably healthy," McNutt noted. It was an environment blessed with light, fertile soil, and waterways "crowded with the feathered and finny Tribes." There would be "no griping and racking Landlords to oppress you," and "no avaricious Priests to extort from you." McNutt wanted only those who sought a settlement that could marry their spiritual and independent selves:

> Are you ambitious? Come here, and be Proprietors of Lands. Have you any Regard for your Posterity? Bring them to a Country, where they may be forever free, and not be subject to the Scorn and Contumely of the Great.—Send here the Frugal and Industrious; no half Gentlemen with long Pedigrees from Nimrod and Cain, the first of their Order, nor any who expect to make Fortunes by any other Methods than the plain, beaten Paths of honest Industry; for idle, indolent People, unwilling to work, ought not to eat, but to live in all Places miserable.[116]

It would be impossible to be miserable in McNutt's New Ireland.

It was, however, quite possible to be miserable in the settlements around Fort George at Penobscot Bay. The real-life British province of New Ireland consisted of a few houses and was not a happy place. Most of those who moved to Penobscot before the British arrived had fled their old settlements after being threatened by rebels, who tolerated no neutrals and demanded active allegiance to the Patriot cause. Such harassment came in various forms, including general intimidation, confiscation of property, imprisonment, and death threats. John Carlton, a farmer from Woolwich who owned coasting vessels, found himself facing a mob that demanded his sworn allegiance to the rebel cause lest he be buried alive. Carlton refused and was forced to dig his own grave, but he escaped to Penobscot and joined other Loyalists. Arriving there was one thing, but leaving was another. As the situation in New Ireland deteriorated during and after the Patriot siege, some residents left the settlement and attempted to return to their former homes in eastern Maine. Many found themselves ostracized and treated as traitors. When they then returned to New Ireland they were charged with desertion and punished by lashings. Other settlers could be accosted by drunken soldiers looking for something to do and find themselves accused of vague wrongdoings that resulted in up to five hundred lashes. Residents were forced to watch.[117] Surely many of the settlers at Penobscot, considered Loyalists largely because they refused to fight for the Patriots, would have much preferred McNutt's New Ireland to McLean's.

McNutt had big expectations for his imagined colony. By co-opting the British plan for New Ireland and infusing it with religion and independence, he was not only working to derail Britain's plans for a new *loyal* colony but was also taking a shot at Nova Scotia itself. In April 1782 he wrote to Benjamin Franklin, then in Paris, sending him copies of his constitution and an essay meant for Franklin and the "Peace Makers" then negotiating with Britain.[118] The essay was included in a particularly delusional pamphlet McNutt published, entitled *Considerations on the Sovereignty, Independence, Trade and Fisheries of New-Ireland, Formerly known by the Name of Nova-Scotia and the Adjacent Islands.* Here, McNutt expanded his fictional colony of New Ireland to include Nova Scotia, St. John's (Prince Edward Island), Cape Breton, and Newfoundland. "By virtue of authority derived from the freemen of New-Ireland," the tract began, "these numbers are published and forwarded for the consideration of the European Courts: the preceding numbers more especially concern the people of New-Ireland and the United States. A person vested with full power to act in behalf of the people of New-Ireland, in the treaty of peace, when this shall take place, will soon be dispatched to Europe."[119] Perhaps Franklin had a good chuckle over this. If he bothered to read on, however, he might have found McNutt's ideas less far-fetched. McNutt argued that the existence of the Atlantic Ocean showed that "the God of nature" wanted Europe and America separated and intended "to have forbidden both to exercise rule or authority, except on their side of the ocean." To that end, Britain must not only recognize the thirteen colonies' independence but should "relinquish all claims of dominion over the part she yet holds on the continent, especially her northern possessions, and allow them to legislate for, and govern, themselves in the manner they may think best, either in union with the other states, or separate from them." During the peace negotiations to end the revolution Franklin himself would suggest that Britain voluntarily surrender Canada to the United Colonies.

The state of New Ireland remained a figment of McNutt's imagination. The British idea to reward Loyalists and thwart Patriot expansion stalled in the Penobscot harbor as soldiers and settlers failed to harness the idealism of William Knox, John Caleff, and John Nutting. Whereas Generals McLean and Mowatt employed shot and powder to claim territory, erect forts, and lay the groundwork for their New Ireland, Alexander McNutt used paper, ink, and ideology to co-opt the colony as an idea. The combination was never enough to forge any sort of common identity, and New Ireland remained little more than cannon smoke and worn parchment. For soldiers and settlers alike, the region was merely a refuge for castaways from the Royal Navy and settlements in eastern Maine. Most had been forced to go there, and few would have remained by choice.

"New Ireland" was little more than a name for a part of the northeast that had never really been controlled by any imperial or colonial power. The French, at various times, had called the region between the Kennebec and St. Croix both Acadia and Canada. The British had hoped the region was Nova Scotia, but their settlers at Massachusetts Bay challenged that position. Old maps often left the territory unnamed. New Ireland was only slightly less imaginary than Norumbega. In a measure of true power on the ground, Patriot settlers and British soldiers were attempting to push into the Dawnland, and the Wabanaki peoples, especially the Penobscot themselves, watched foreign forces kill each other and erect fortifications on Indigenous territory. That neither the British nor the Patriots could establish a permanent and lasting alliance with the Wabanaki helps explain why each side found the territory impossible to control.

With such a fluid geographic identity before the war—the Dawnland, Norumbega, Acadia, Nova Scotia, Maine—it is not surprising that the northeast coast between Massachusetts and Nova Scotia defied both categorization and colonization during the revolution itself. The attempts by both Patriots and the British to win Indigenous alliances and establish new settlements speak to the revolution's different course in the northeast. The battles at Penobscot Bay, the protracted negotiations at Watertown, and the calls for Patriot invasion by anxious settlers in Nova Scotia show that in this part of the world the war was about a contested past in which each side thought they could claim the territory as their own. Unlike the very real homeland of Wabanakia, New Ireland was a plan, a scheme, an aspiration. It could be an imperial colony or an American state, depending on who was doing the dreaming.

# CHAPTER THREE

# A Northern Chorus

BENJAMIN FRANKLIN ARRIVED IN Paris in early December 1776, cold, tired, and feeling older than his seventy years. His late autumn voyage across the Atlantic had been miserable, and he was forced to wait at anchor in Auray, Brittany, for four days before a local resident agreed to row him ashore. Franklin had been in France before—in 1767 and 1769—and had become famous there for his scientific experiments, his intellect, and his wit. This time was different. He was an ambassador from the thirteen British colonies that had just begun a new life after breaking away from Britain six months earlier. Years later, when tasked with negotiating a peace, he would be joined by his fellow negotiators; for now, however, he was a diplomat accompanied only by his two grandsons. Yet he carried with him the hopes of many Patriots, and he was eager to do what he could to secure an independent future for his fellow colonists.

It did not take long for Franklin to appear as an "American," an identity that had crept up on him over the years. Like many of his contemporaries, he had been a staunch Briton until he could no longer accept what his empire expected from the colonies. He brought to France a symbol of his new identity: a soft marten fur cap, bushy and brown in the style of a backwoods trapper. It fit snugly on his large head, and he pulled it down to his eyebrows. He wore it often, indoors and out, and even when he posed for a portrait.

Franklin wearing the marten fur cap he purchased in Canada. Johann
Martin Will, *Benjamin Franklin*, 1777. Mezzotint engraving, black and white,
38 × 25.2 cm (14 15/16 × 9 15/16 in.), Mabel Brady Garvan Collection,
1946.9.857. Yale University Art Gallery.

His appearance made waves. During previous visits he had con-
formed to French sartorial standards, powdered wig and all. But now he
was Franklin the American, and the fur cap announced his transformation. The funny thing about that cap, however, is that he got it in Canada. It was a souvenir of sorts from his 1776 trip to Montreal, which, as
one historian put it, "had the result of fixing Canada as a quest in Franklin's subtle mind."[1] Though the revolutionary cause drove Franklin's
heart, Canada, or at least a reminder of his time there, was never far from
his head. He now represented a weak collection of avowedly independent
states held together by little more than a shared desire to sever their imperial ties. His efforts in France from 1776 to 1783, instrumental to securing that independence, unfolded in two phases: first, he and other
representatives were dispatched to Europe to obtain loans from, and negotiate alliances with, European powers in the war against Great Britain;
second, Franklin, John Jay, John Adams, and Henry Laurens were later
charged with negotiating a peace to end the conflict. Two British provinces, Quebec and Nova Scotia, loomed large in both of these endeavors.

When the thirteen "united States" (a confederation of independent
colonies and not yet a coherent nation) entered into a treaty of alliance
with France in 1778, the two allies held conflicting ideas about Quebec's
future. Members of Congress were concerned that France might retake
Canada and thus replace one threatening imperial neighbor with another.
Many Patriots also believed (and hoped) that Quebec would ultimately
break free from Britain and join the union. French officials, on the other
hand, not only did not want to retake Quebec but firmly believed that
continued British possession of the province would strengthen the
Franco-American relationship.

During the peace negotiations, which began in April 1782, the fate
of the British provinces became entangled with the recognition of the
united States' independence. While Congress would never jeopardize its
separation from the British empire in order to acquire more British colonies, Benjamin Franklin worked steadily to add Quebec to the confederated states, while John Adams worked to ensure that fishing rights in the
St. Lawrence River and the Grand Banks off Newfoundland were included in the agreement. War and peace were overlapping projects, and
military actions affected the more pacific ventures underway in Europe.
Citizens of the united States followed the entire process—securing alliances, launching campaigns, and negotiating a peace—via news reports,
rumors, and editorials published in the press. Politicians and citizens

alike fretted over the fate of Quebec and Nova Scotia, debated their value and importance, and struggled to understand how British provinces and American states could coexist on the same continent.

From the earliest stages of negotiating an alliance between the united States and France, Britain's North American colonies were useful bargaining chips. In early 1777, just a few weeks after Franklin arrived in France, members of the Continental Congress met to discuss how best to secure allies for the war against Britain. In addition to Franklin, they also sent commissioners to Vienna, Spain, Prussia, and the Grand Duchy of Tuscany to inform those countries' royal courts that the united States were set on maintaining their independence and to ask what help might be on offer. But Louis XVI of France was of particular interest to Congress: he could help the revolutionary cause "by attacking the Electorate of Hanover," over which Britain's George III also ruled, "or any part of the dominions of Great Britain in Europe, the East or West Indies." Congress instructed its commissioners to Louis XVI (Franklin joined Arthur Lee and Silas Deane) to describe the conflict in terms that emphasized the danger to France should Britain succeed in North America: victory would leave Britain with a mass of well-trained troops that could be redirected against French possessions in the West Indies. But if the Patriots should triumph, France could expect increased trade, carried in French ships. To sweeten the offer, congressional officials were to inform their French counterparts that should French ships help reduce the British in Newfoundland, Cape Breton, and Nova Scotia, His Most Christian Majesty could claim half of Newfoundland, "provided, the province of Nova Scotia, island of Cape Breton, and the remaining part of Newfoundland, be annexed to the territory and government of the United States."[2]

Congress had long struggled to take the war to the sea, and naval assistance from France promised to redress perhaps the biggest imbalance between the British and Continental forces. Because it lacked ships of its own, Congress had to rely on privateer vessels, whose commanders were difficult to control. The privateers also competed for recruits—effectively, because they could pay higher wages than the Continental Army and offer a share of spoils. Patriot vessels were able to harass local fisheries in Nova Scotia, St. John's Island (Prince Edward Island), and Newfoundland, but Congress was unable to organize a sustained maritime attack on these important British sites.[3] The disaster at Penobscot

M.<sup>R</sup> DE VERGENNES,

*Ministre des affaires Etrangères*

*Sous Louis XVI.*

Charles Gravier, comte de Vergennes, ca. 1785. Library
of Congress, Prints and Photographs Division.

in 1779 demonstrated that Congress's maritime shortcomings were
not easily remedied. Needing something to offer the French in exchange
for maritime assistance, but wary that France might claim territories it
helped conquer, representatives from the united States took the position
that Congress would determine control over (and access to) any British
provinces that fell to the Franco-American alliance.

French officials used Canada as a pawn in their own way. When the
French government surrendered Canada in 1763 at the end of the Seven
Years' War, Étienne François, duc de Choiseul, foreign minister to Louis

XV, believed that British North Americans would eventually rebel against the empire.[4] Choiseul's successor, Charles Gravier, comte de Vergennes, who served as foreign minister to Louis XVI, shared that belief but had different ideas about the future of France in America. He had no hopes of reclaiming France's North American possessions or of rebuilding a colonial empire. Instead, he focused on weakening Britain to enhance France's position in Europe while maintaining its alliance with Spain.[5]

Vergennes got wind of the Patriot desire for an alliance around December 1774, after friends of the rebels approached a French official in London. A masterful tactician, Vergennes did not commit to either the Patriots or the British. But in September 1775 he sent Achard de Bonvouloir under the guise of an Antwerp merchant to begin conversations about France's position in the uprising. Bonvouloir's instructions specifically precluded him from making any official agreement, but upon his arrival in Philadelphia he informed congressional officials that France would accept the United Colonies' independence and, importantly, that French officials had no designs on Canada.[6] Both reassurances augured well for an official Franco-American alliance.

There had been some debate among French officials over whether to help the rebelling colonies. Some ministers were hesitant, so in the spring of 1776 Vergennes published (or had published) two pamphlets to rally support for the cause. The first, titled *Considérations*, outlined the possible outcomes France and Spain might face as a result of the colonial rebellion. In it, Vergennes suggested that France provide aid to the colonies but not establish an alliance. In the second pamphlet, entitled *Réflexions*, Vergennes's secretary Joseph Matthias Gérard de Rayneval outlined how France might aid the Patriots without openly intervening in the conflict.[7] These arguments for supporting the rebels were meant to play on France's ancient animosity toward Britain, though they warned against any notion that New France might be won back. "First," Vergennes argued in *Considérations*, assisting the rebels "will diminish the power of England, and increase in proportion that of France. . . . Second, it will cause irreparable loss to English trade, while it will considerably extend ours. Third, it presents to us as very probable the recovery of a part of the possessions which the English have taken from us in America, such as the fisheries of Newfoundland and of the Gulf of St. Lawrence, Isle Royale, etc." He concluded with a word of caution: "We do not speak of Canada." Persuaded by Vergennes, Louis XVI agreed furtively to supply funds and munitions to the Patriots. To ensure secrecy, aid was funneled through a fictitious enterprise, Roderigue Hortalez and Company, that was created for the purpose.[8]

Secret aid was helpful, but Congress longed for a more permanent and formal arrangement. The French, however, were less eager to establish an open alliance or recognize the colonies' independence. Many officials, including the finance minister, Anne-Robert-Jacques Turgot, worried that France simply could not afford to help the colonists. Vergennes thought it best to wait and see how successfully the rebels fought for their cause. The Patriot defeat on Long Island in August 1776 gave him pause, but the rebels fought on, and as the months passed and the Continental Army's prospects improved, it became increasingly obvious to French officials that with a little help, the united States could defeat the British. The process of securing an alliance was far from simple—involving intrigue, spies, and double agents working for both the British and the French—but the Patriot victory at Saratoga in the fall of 1777 pushed Vergennes to commit fully to an alliance.[9] In February 1778, France signed two treaties with Congress. In the first, the Treaty of Amity and Commerce, France recognized the united States as independent from Great Britain and promised to supply finances and munitions. In the second, the Treaty of Alliance, the confederated states and France agreed that should war break out between France and Britain—a virtual certainty—neither party would sign a separate peace, and neither would stop fighting until Britain recognized the states' independence. This treaty also formalized French promises to forgo any effort to recreate a North American empire. All lands east of the Mississippi, including the British colonies of Quebec and Nova Scotia, would belong to Congress should the states conquer them.[10]

While working to convince Vergennes to make an open alliance with the united States, Franklin also maintained a correspondence with British friends. From his home in the quiet suburb of Passy, he opined on matters significant and trivial—even establishing a press to circulate his writings—and rarely passed up an opportunity to remind his correspondents of Canada's strategic and symbolic importance. "A Peace you may undoubtedly obtain," he scolded a British friend in February 1778, "by dropping all your Pretensions to govern us. And by your superior Skill in huckstering Negotiation, you may possibly make such an apparently advantageous Treaty as shall be applauded in your Parliament." To make a peace that was lasting and meaningful, however, the British would have to demonstrate "a national Change of Disposition, and a Disapprobation of what had passed." Goodwill mattered, and Franklin had several suggestions for how British officials could win Patriot affections in peace. He admitted that Great Britain might retain Quebec, Nova Scotia, and the Floridas. "But," he added, "if you would have a real Friendly as well as able Ally in America, and avoid Occasions of future Discord, (which will otherwise be continually arising on your American Frontiers) you should throw in those Countries; and you may call it, if you please, an Indemnification for the needless and cruel Burning of their Towns; which Indemnification will otherwise be some time or other demanded."[11] The voluntary surrender of Quebec and Nova Scotia was a theme to which Franklin would return again and again.

Before Britain could give up Canada, however, the united States made another effort to take it by force. To lead the attacks, despite Vergennes's desire to distance France from any campaigns of conquest, the Continental Congress turned to a young French soldier. Marquis Marie-Joseph-Paul-Yves-Roch Gilbert du Motier Lafayette, who had as much ambition as name, was eager to serve the Patriot cause. He had inherited his title and wealth when only a teenager, at which point his social circle widened, his political connections grew, and his prospects improved. In 1774, at age seventeen, he married Adrienne de Noailles, the daughter of a prominent family with close ties to the king. Within the year he had set his sights on the colonists' war against Great Britain and worked his connections to find a way to participate. Silas Deane, in Paris as a diplomat to the French court, promised Lafayette a commission in the Continental Army. In early 1777 Lafayette and several other officers, including Baron de Kalb, were ready to sail to North America. He circumvented his government's hesitance to support such an endeavor by simply buying a ship. Arriving in South Carolina in June, he made his way to Philadelphia only to learn that Deane's promises were worthless. Undeterred, Lafayette offered to serve as a volunteer. Congress agreed—since the price was right—and placed him on George Washington's staff. The two quickly grew fond of each other, and within a year, the tall, red-haired teenager found himself overseeing a division of the Virginians.[12]

In early 1778, after France had formally allied with the United Colonies, Lafayette got wind of a plan to invade Canada.[13] A few months earlier a committee of Congress had suggested building a citadel near Lake Champlain that could house seven hundred soldiers and provisions enough for at least a year, and that would thus be capable of withstanding

*Gen. Lafayette's Departure from Mount Vernon 1784*, 1860s. Lithograph, 44 × 60.4 cm (17 5/16 × 23 3/4 in.), 1985.5.8. Yale University Art Gallery. Lafayette's doomed attempts at taking Canada caused him to worry about his reputation.

a siege. To prepare for the campaign, residents of Quebec were to be "instructed by Means of Emissaries and Papers dispersed in Canada to conciliate the Minds of the Canadians towards these States, and to prepare them for Effecting a Revolution, whenever the United States shall deem such a Measure Expedient."[14] Congress chose Lafayette to lead the campaign, which allowed the young Frenchman to dream of military glory despite the cautionary advice he received about the hazards of an invasion during winter.[15] Congress instructed him to keep the plans secret, make his way to Albany, and from there move on to Montreal, where he was to "publish a Declaration of your Intentions, to the Canadians; and invite them to join the Army of the United States" or at least remain neutral. The goal was to damage British forces, not to conquer the province. "The Consequences which may arise from Success," Washington warned Lafayette, "are to be viewed in a secondary Point of Light, and therefore the holding the Country or prevailing upon the Inhabitants to confederate with the States—is not to be undertaken but with the greatest Prudence, and with a Prospect of durable Success."[16] Given the Patriot failure at Quebec just two years earlier, it was a difficult task for even the most ambitious of military men.

Before long, Lafayette's optimism turned to doubt, and the campaign fell apart before it even began. As he pushed north toward Albany in the unforgiving February weather, he stopped regularly to update his friend and mentor, Washington. "I go on very slowly some times pierced by rain, sometimes covered with snow," he wrote from Albany, "and not thinking many handsome thoughts about the projected incursion into canada." He asked everyone he encountered about the prospects of an attack, and none thought an invasion was wise.[17] A failed mission, he confided to Washington, would "reflect on my reputation and I schall be laughed at." And that was the heart of it. Barely out of his teens, eager to make a name for himself, Lafayette trusted Washington to help make things right. "For you, dear general," he wrote, "I know very well that you will do every thing to procure me the only thing I am ambitious of: Glory."[18] Washington had never liked the renewed effort to invade Canada, calling it "the child of folly," but he offered reassurance.[19] Canada would not be his protégé's downfall. Lafayette would be applauded for having been selected to lead the campaign, and he could hardly "be chargeable with the invariable effects of natural causes" nor "be arraigned for not suspending the course of the Seasons."[20] In early March the plan was scrapped. Lafayette's fear of embarrassment was no doubt assuaged when he learned "that Congress entertain a high sense of his prudence, activity and zeal, and that they are fully persuaded nothing has, or would have been wanting on his part, or on the part of the officers who accompanied him, to give the expedition the utmost possible effect."[21] Still young, eager, and well connected, Lafayette's future remained his own to make.

Many Europeans were less worried about Lafayette's actions in war than about Canada's role in the peace. John Adams, stationed in France in the early summer of 1778, wondered if it was possible "to think of Peace, while G. Britain has Canada, Nova Scotia and the Floridas, or any of them? Such a Peace will be short." Any British foothold in North America would be an invitation to perpetual wars. Surely the belligerent powers would tire of fighting, and a time would come to deal with the possession—or at least the boundaries—of Britain's provinces.[22] Lord

North, Britain's prime minister, had made at least an attempt to win over the thirteen states currently at war with Great Britain. In 1778, after the Patriots had defeated the British at Saratoga and entered into an official alliance with France, he sent a commission led by Edward Howard, the fifth Earl of Carlisle, to woo the colonies back to the empire. If Congress surrendered its claims to independence, Great Britain would remove the taxes that had so angered the colonists, and North would negotiate directly with Congress, granting it quasi-legal status. Carlisle's commissioners wined and dined members of Congress, sent a packet of proposals to Congress for consideration, and used the press to try to sway public opinion, but they never stood a chance. There was simply no turning back the tides of independence.[23]

Adams was sure that Britain and the united States would remain enemies so long as they remained neighbors. This was partly the result of simple human nature, which Adams viewed pessimistically. "It is not much to the Honour of human Nature," he informed his bellicose second cousin Sam in late July, "but the Fact is certain that neighbouring Nations are never Friends in Reality." That was why France was an ideal ally. There was no reason "to expect her Enmity or her Jealousy" because she had surrendered all territorial claims in North America.[24] If Congress took possession of British Quebec, Nova Scotia, and Florida, it would eliminate the need for any borders at all.

Congress, like Adams, had not entirely given up on the idea of taking Quebec, even though the colonies' new French allies were wary of such an expedition. In the fall of 1778, Benjamin Franklin was given the title of minister plenipotentiary to the court of France, along with instructions from the Continental Congress. His new list of duties included promoting the "interest and honour" of the states and assuring the king of the united States' appreciation for all he had done. Also on the list was this item: to "constantly inculcate the certainty of ruining the British fisheries on the banks of Newfoundland, and consequently the British marine, by reducing Halifax and Quebec." Attached to the instructions was a proposal for such an undertaking.[25]

Coming after the failed 1775–76 campaign and the abandonment of Lafayette's efforts, this third plan was impossibly idealistic. But the fact that Congress initiated another effort shows that its members remained committed to reducing British provinces in the north. This new proposal required a perfectly timed and provisioned three-pronged attack leaving from Fort Pitt, the Wyoming Valley, and the upper Connecticut River to

LE DESTIN MOLESTANT LES ANGLOIS

Comte d'Estaing presenting a palm frond to America, [1779?]. An
Indigenous figure (representing America) sits on goods to be shipped to
France. Comte d'Estaing keeps three ferocious beasts (representing Great
Britain) on a leash. Library of Congress, Prints and Photographs Division.

attack Detroit, Fort Niagara, and Montreal, respectively, destroying Indigenous settlements along the way.[26] Congress resolved to communicate
the plan to Conrad Alexandre Gérard, Vergennes's minister plenipotentiary to the united States, who had arrived in Philadelphia in July with
firm orders to dissuade Congress of any attempt to take Canada.[27] Given
Vergennes's position that Britain should remain in North America so as
to keep the united States closely aligned with France, these instructions
required careful diplomacy.[28] Congress's hope that French forces would
help it "emancipate the province of Canada from its subjection to the
crown of Great Britain" was clearly at odds with the French position.
Without revealing his opposition, Gérard raised sufficient concerns
about the proposed invasion to cause Congress to send the proposal back
to committee.[29] French officials, not Congress, balked at the idea that
Canada should again be a target for a Patriot invasion.

Some French participants, however, were eager to push into Canada.
Charles Hector, comte d'Estaing, was sent by Louis XVI to serve in

North America shortly after the Franco-American alliance was signed. He participated in a brief and unsuccessful offensive against the British at Newport, Rhode Island, in late August 1778, after which he and his ships limped back to Boston.[30] That October, just as Gérard was discouraging Congress's latest plans for an invasion of Quebec, d'Estaing sat at anchor in Boston Harbor aboard the *Languedoc*, restless for the chance to do something meaningful. He got caught up in the idea of capturing Canada. Months before he would defeat the British fleet at the Battle of Grenada, he drafted "A declaration addressed in the name of the King of France to the antient French in Canada, and in every other part of North America." "You were born French," he wrote; "you never could cease to be French. . . . Can the Canadians, who saw the brave Montcalm fall in their defence, can they become the enemies of his nephews? Can they fight against their former leaders, and arm themselves against their kinsmen? At the bare mention of their names, the weapons would fall out of their hands." D'Estaing concluded by emphasizing the Franco-American alliance. The united States had aligned itself with a monarch who shared with the Canadians "the same religion, the same manners, the same language." The vice admiral reassured his audience that allying with the Patriots would gain them the protection of France.[31]

Congress read d'Estaing's letter in early December at Gérard's request. By that time it had made its way to Canada, where it was hammered to chapel doors and dutifully torn down by Catholic priests who remained loyal to the British government at Quebec. But those who read d'Estaing's words shared what they learned, just as they had shared news of Congress's earlier letters to the people of Quebec. In the minds of many French Canadians, Layfette's abandoned effort was combined with d'Estaing's projected one. Rumors spread that Lafayette was on his way, possibly supported by a French fleet. Even General Haldimand, now governor of Quebec and tasked with defending Canada from Patriot invasion, feared that his supposedly loyal priests secretly longed for reunion with France.[32] But there would be no invasion. In a long letter to Congress, Washington detailed the plan's many and significant faults: it was too ambitious, too complex, and depended too heavily on all elements succeeding in the proper order.[33] Though he understood that "the question of the Canadian expedition, in the form in which it now stands appears to me one of the most interesting that has hitherto agitated our national deliberations," he remained concerned that if Quebec fell to a Franco-American invasion, France would not relinquish its claim to the province.[34] Washington likely did not know that France strongly preferred for Quebec to remain British. His argument was nonetheless enough for Congress to cancel the proposed expedition. No doubt Gérard breathed a sigh of relief.[35]

In 1779, the British provinces north of the rebelling colonies remained objects of theorizing and speculation. Congress had planned and abandoned two invasions of Quebec after its failed campaign of 1775–76, and the British were meanwhile attempting to push into northern Maine. While much of the revolutionary action was migrating south, the northern theater served an important ideological role in revolutionary thinking. What did these provinces represent? What part might they play in the ebb and flow of revolution and counterrevolution? As fighting continued and the tides slowly turned in favor of the united States, some politicians allowed themselves to think of peace. In February 1779, William Whipple, a New Hampshire delegate, read in the press about possible peace negotiations in Europe and wondered whether Britain would surrender Canada and Nova Scotia. "That will stick in her stomach," he wrote from Philadelphia to John Langdon, "but she must swallow it."[36] Samuel Adams wondered, "Would it be safe for America to leave Canada, Nova Scotia & Florida in her hands?"[37] At that moment, however, Congress was not prepared to demand either Quebec or Nova Scotia in any future peace negotiation.[38]

British politicians in London were also discussing the war's progress and the prospects for peace. Parts of those discussions made their way into the Patriot press, where they were read by the public and officials alike. Of particular interest to readers in March 1779 was a speech given by George Johnstone, a naval officer and former governor of West Florida, who encouraged British officials to make known "for the encouragement of friends, and the terror of foes, that you will die in the last ditch." Surrendering the thirteen colonies, he claimed, would raise questions about defending Quebec, and then Nova Scotia, the Floridas, and the West Indies, "for they all hang together." Johnstone wanted to dig in and continue the fight to restore the colonies to Great Britain.[39]

Many in the states, however, were eager for peace. Writing as "AN AMERICAN" the same month, Gouverneur Morris, a New York delegate to Congress, refuted Johnstone's argument point by point in an editorial published in Pennsylvania.[40] What ditch, he wondered, would serve as Johnstone's final resting place? Would his blood "dash along the roaring

Susquehanna, swell the great Potowmac, or fill the bay of Chesapeak? Shall it empurple the Canadian snows, shall it fertilize the arid sands of Florida, or stain the rocks of Nova Scotia, hard and unpitying of the generous sacrifice?" The united States, as far as Morris was concerned, had seen the consequences of imperial aspirations and held none of their own. The Patriot desire for certain British provinces was practical and economic, not evidence of grander designs.[41] In mid-April, James Lovell imagined that the united States could secure peace by giving up "what we have no Claim to" (including Quebec, Nova Scotia, and the Floridas) as well as "what we have a right to" (including the cod and haddock fishery), but he could also imagine "writing the Treaty of Peace with the Bayonett."[42] Sam Adams, worried that the peace might undo all that had been accomplished during the war, cautioned against being timid in negotiating an end to the conflict. Independence required good trade, good trade required a strong navy, and a navy demanded a nursery for seamen. A fishery was a proven source of sailors, and "Nova Scotia & Canada would be a great & permanent Protection to the Fishery."[43] Acquiring Canada and Nova Scotia was crucial to a bigger strategy to ensure peace, trade, and independence once the Revolutionary War ended.

In the fall of 1779, Congress began sending additional representatives to European capitals to try to gain allies and financial support. John Jay sailed in October to plead the united States' case at the Spanish court. His wife, Sarah, accompanied him, and their friends sent gifts. George Washington sent Sarah a lock of his hair with a note wishing her calm seas and friendly winds.[44] A few weeks later, Congress sent John Adams to join Franklin in France to prepare for peace negotiations. Henry Laurens, a past president of the Continental Congress, received instructions to represent the united States in the United Provinces of the Netherlands. His voyage was delayed by an increased British presence in the southern colonies, and he could not depart from Philadelphia until August 1780. Waiting did not help: the British captured Laurens off the coast of Newfoundland in early September, and instead of currying favor in the Netherlands he took up residence in the Tower of London.[45] The others must have struggled with the contrast between war-torn North America and the relative luxury of Europe. Franklin certainly enjoyed Paris, where he was a famous man. He wrote to his sister, Jane, "My Face is now almost as well known as that of the Moon."[46] He enjoyed walking through the garden paths of his house in Passy, and when women paid him visits—as many regularly did—he employed soft diplomacy that resulted in coos and sighs. He practiced his French by flirting with all the language he could muster, and given his propensity to shower women with affection it is a wonder he never became truly fluent.[47]

The start of peace negotiations only inflamed speculation about what would become of the British colonies in North America after the war. Adams, writing from his home in Braintree some weeks before he sailed for Europe, suggested that "if Peace should unhappily be made, leaving Canada, Nova Scotia, the Floridas, or any of them, in [British] Hands, Jealousies, and Controversies will be perpetually arrising."[48] In April 1779, the *Pennsylvania Gazette* expressed its confidence that Great Britain would recognize American independence but leave the status of its loyal colonies undetermined.[49] A month later, a South Carolina paper speculated that "the whole extent of the country, comprized under the names of Canada, Nova-Scotia, and East and West-Florida, on the continent of America, shall be guaranteed to Great Britain."[50] Regardless of the status of these loyal colonies, most Patriots looked forward to the death—or at least the great reduction—of the British empire in North America. In a satirical last will and testament of "Old England" that appeared in the *South Carolina Gazette* in September 1779, Great Britain left its "stupidity and obstinacy" to the present ministry and its land and sea power to the king of France, and appointed "the United States of America, to the guardians of my said Colonies," including Quebec, Nova Scotia, and the Floridas.[51] It was wishful thinking, but official representatives and colonial citizens alike were eager to learn the fate of Canada and Nova Scotia.

Patriot leaders understood that between the states and the loyal provinces were thousands of Indigenous peoples who protected their homelands and resisted expansion from both their allies and enemies. The Patriots had struggled but largely failed to secure Indigenous allies, especially along the northern borderland. Of the Iroquois Confederacy, only the Oneida and Tuscarora had sided with the rebels. In March 1778, Lafayette had helped reassure these nations of the wisdom of their decision to side with Congress at a council hosted by General Philip Schuyler on the Mohawk River.[52] A year later, however, frustrated by the Patriot inability to defend against or counter Indigenous raids from Iroquoia, Washington decided simply to wipe out as much of Iroquoia as possible. He was determined "to carry the war into the Heart of the Country of the six nations; to cut off their settlements, destroy their next Year's crops, and do them every other mischief of which time and circumstances will

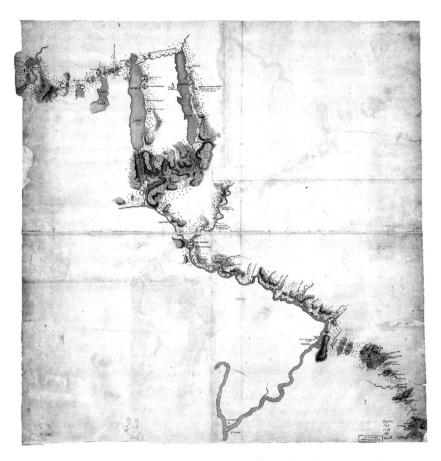

*Map of Gen. Sullivan's march from Easton to the Senaca & Cayuga countries,*
[1779]. General John Sullivan, along with General James Clinton, launched
an attack against Iroquoia on Washington's orders. This campaign earned
Washington the name "Town Destroyer" among the Iroquois. Library of
Congress, Geography and Map Division.

permit."[53] By ruining the Iroquois crops and preventing them from plant-
ing more, Washington, whom the Iroquois came to call "Town Destroyer," hoped to starve the Six Nations into submission.

Beginning in early August 1779, John Sullivan, James Clinton, and
Daniel Broadhead led a three-pronged attack of Patriot troops up the
Susquehanna and then from the western end of Iroquoia at the Genesee
River to Fort Stanwix on the Mohawk River. As Sullivan and his men

pushed east through Six Nations homelands, they spared neither people nor villages.[54] The Sullivan-Clinton expedition destroyed a total of forty towns, 160,000 bushels of corn, and whatever other sustenance they could find. In a cruel irony, the expedition was provisioned by the food-stuffs they found at the well-stocked Iroquois villages. Without these supplies, it is doubtful that the Patriot army could have been so destructive.[55]

As the war became more focused on the southern states, George Washington looked past Iroquoia and found a good use for Quebec. British forces captured Georgia over the winter of 1778–79, even managing to reinstate a British governor, and then reclaimed Charleston in South Carolina in May 1780.[56] Washington kept his army in the northern theater, suffering through the terrible winter of 1779–80 at Morristown, New Jersey. In late spring 1780, he proposed an imaginary invasion of Quebec, with details to be advertised by proclamations, as a ruse meant to fool the British into moving resources to the province's defense and perhaps provide an opening for an attack elsewhere. "We talked of a proclamation to the Canadians," he wrote to Lafayette. "If it is not already done, I think it ought not to be delayed." Washington suggested two proclamations. The first would hint at the imminent arrival of a French fleet and army that would land in Rhode Island and then make their way to the St. Lawrence; it would emphasize "the happy opportunity it will afford [the Canadians] to renew their ancient friendship with France." The second proclamation was to be drafted as though the fleet and army had already arrived and would encourage the Canadians to ally themselves under the Franco-American banner. It was imperative to shroud the entire fake campaign in mystery. "It will get out," Washington wrote, "and it ought to seem to be against our intention."[57] Lafayette needed only to copy the sentiments d'Estaing had expressed in his letter to the Canadians two years earlier.

Lafayette's proclamation—lengthy, written entirely in French, and signed by Lafayette himself—was of course not meant for the Canadians at all but for the British who would intercept it. Lafayette's phantom invasion may have served a purpose, but it is hard to tell. His documents made their way to Sir Henry Clinton, who wrote to George Germain in late August: "I have the honor to transmit to you the copy of a proclamation, which I have reason to believe the Marquis de Lafayette intended to have published in Canada, if the proposed expedition against that province had taken place." Perhaps Clinton was fooled for a time, but it is equally likely that Benedict Arnold told him of the proclamation's intent. Arnold, who had participated in the first invasion of Canada, had grown pessimistic about the Patriot cause and had been suspected since 1778 of selling sensitive information to the British. Washington had given Arnold several copies of the proclamation before Arnold turned his back on the Patriot cause for good in the fall of 1780.[58]

In the years that followed, the Patriots worked to strengthen Indigenous alliances in the northeast with the help of their French connection. In August 1780, in the wake of the destruction of Iroquoia, Schuyler again acted as liaison between their allied Iroquois and the French. King Louis XVI had that year charged the comte de Rochambeau, an experienced army officer who had served in the War of the Austrian Succession and the Seven Years' War, with organizing an expeditionary force to serve under George Washington.[59] In a letter to Washington, Schuyler asked whether Rochambeau might remind the Indigenous peoples in Canada of their attachment to France. "I do not know how far His Excellency Count De Rochambeau and Chevalier De Terney will conceive themselves authorized to address the Nations of which these people are a part, in his Majestys name," Schuyler wrote, "but If they could do It with propriety, I should not hesitate to recommend It persuaded that a variety of salutary consequences would flow from It, for both the Iroquois and the Indians of Canada still retain a strong and lively Attachment to the french nation." When the governor of Quebec surrendered the province to the British at the end of the Seven Years' War, Schuyler added, he had given his Indigenous allies a token of French recognition: a golden crucifix and a watch. Perhaps similar gifts might be dispatched now to invite "all the Canadian Indians" to send deputies to treat with the French representatives.[60] And so it was arranged. In 1780, a delegation of Tuscaroras and Oneidas traveled during summer's dying days to Rhode Island to meet with the comte de Rochambeau, who, as Lafayette had done, impressed them with platitudes, plates of food, gifts, and glasses of wine. The French connection had been extended to the Patriots' Indigenous northern allies.[61] As the war drew to a close and peace loomed, the Oneida and Tuscarora might have hoped the Patriots would value their contributions. As in previous imperial conflicts, however, Indigenous leaders were not invited to negotiate the peace that would drastically affect their homelands.

In Paris, the Six Nations and Iroquoia were far from the minds of Congress's representatives, but the British provinces remained a constant topic of discussion. Franklin made no secret of his desire to see Canada added to the united States, and for a while he found a kindred spirit in John Adams. In May 1780, Adams received a letter from Edmé-Jacques Genêt, a member of the French Foreign Office and thus a useful contact. He sent Adams an outline of a peace proposal that had appeared in the London *General Advertiser and Morning Intelligencer.* The article, written by Josiah Tucker, dean of Gloucester, was also published as "Proposals for a General Pacification" in the May issue of *Gentleman's Magazine.* Adams could hardly believe Tucker had written it. The same author had earlier argued in at least two pamphlets that it was in Great Britain's interest to grant the colonies independence and withdraw completely from North America.[62] But in the "Proposals for a General Pacification," Tucker suggested that Great Britain should retain Newfoundland, Canada, Nova Scotia, and lands along the Maine coast down to Penobscot (which Alexander McNutt was then imagining as New Ireland). Moreover, Tucker encouraged Britain to retain large swaths of land from the Connecticut to Delaware Rivers and from South Carolina to eastern Florida.[63] In a reply to Genêt, Adams scoffed, "As to the Propositions themselves it would be wasting time to consider them."[64] But as others echoed Tucker's ideas, he had to consider them.

Later that same month, Adams was inspired to write to Genêt after reading a bill introduced to the British Parliament by General Henry Seymour Conway. Conway believed reconciliation with the united States was possible for two reasons: first, it was ministerial blunders that had pushed the British colonies toward independence; and second, those colonies were tired of war and uncomfortable with their "unnatural alliance" with France. Adams's mind might have been working faster than his pen, as Genêt returned the letter with several words underlined as undecipherable. When corrected, Adams's letter, which was translated and published in several French newspapers, argued that despite their shared language, customs, and religion, there was more separating the states from England than from France. The war, and the prospects for peace, brought this fact into stark relief. Boundaries within North America, Adams warned, would further divide Great Britain from its former colonies. "If a Peace should unhappily be made leaving England in Possession of Canada, Nova Scotia, the Floridas or any one spot of Ground in America," he wrote, "they will be perpetually encroaching upon the states of America: whereas France, having renounced all territorial Jurisdiction in America, will have no room for Controversy."[65] In meaningful ways, the differences between the united States and France, and especially France's oath to surrender any claims to North American territory, made for a stronger alliance. It also helped that Adams did not know about Vergennes's preference for a British presence in North America.

In June, Adams returned to the topic of Conway's speech. In a letter to Edmund Jenings, a colonist living in Britain who had written pamphlets critical of the ministry, Adams argued that should the king surrender Britain's North American possessions, "the natural Cause of Avidity and Hostility, which arises from Territory, would be removed."[66] But he was unsure whether such a transaction could be accomplished.

Canada remained on Adams's mind for the rest of 1780. Not surprisingly, many of his correspondents had opinions on the Franco-American alliance and offered him advice or insights. Antoine-Marie Cerisier, a French historian and diplomat stationed at the French Embassy in Holland, wrote to assure him that France was not interested in recovering Canada, which "should be, according to my opinion, a very unpolitic step: they could lose the whole fruit of this war." Whereas Vergennes believed that British possession of Canada would keep the united States dependent on France for help, Cerisier feared that French possession of Canada would push the Patriots back into the arms of England. While encouraging Adams never to stop fighting until "your whole continent is free from European Yoke," he admitted that he would prefer an independent Canada "because it is a French settlement." He also dreamed of an Acadia "peopled, as before, with French colonists," that would be part of a country with French language and liberty, and as free as Massachusetts.[67]

As the names Lafayette, d'Estaing, and Rochambeau increasingly passed the lips of Patriots when they discussed the war's progress, some began to wonder how the revolutionaries—who were fighting to throw off the yoke of monarchy—had become allied with an absolutist king. Engaged citizens and Britons alike could hardly be faulted for questioning the colonies' dedication to liberty in the face of such an alliance.[68] For a primer on the Franco-American alliance, literate Americans needed to look no further than the pages of the *Pennsylvania Gazette*. In a series of articles running from August 1779 to February 1780, a contributor writing as "An Honest Politician" waded through the history of British and French interactions in North America to make sense of the united States' relationship with Louis XVI. To begin, the Honest Politician mused on what had drawn France to support the rebelling colonies. He understood, as many others did, that the united States had less to offer France than did Great Britain. "All that we can propose to her is a mere negative advantage, the ceasing to be connected with Great Britain," he argued. Britain, meanwhile, possessed a global empire from which it could draw gifts and baubles. The British could offer France settlements in the West or East Indies, on the coasts of Africa, "an enlargement of her right to the fisheries on the Banks of Newfoundland" or even "the restitution of Canada."[69] A week later, he returned to remind his readers that French officials had refused to side with the British in the war, and in negotiating an alliance with the united States "did not debate every article, and endeavour to extort from us the guarantee of Canada, of Nova Scotia, and the two Floridas." France wanted no more than "the happiness and peace of her Empire."[70] If that happiness came at the cost of British imperial suffering, all the better.

Undoing a century of British-American antipathy toward the French required a more nuanced history lesson. In February 1780, the Honest Politician asked his readers to think differently about the British "encroachment" into French territory during the eighteenth century. Because colonists had "taken all our ideas from the representations of Britain," they had been blind to the French perspective.[71] To illustrate his point, he turned to the Acadian boundary dispute. Acadia, the French colony established in 1604 that extended over present-day Nova Scotia, New Brunswick, and part of northern Maine, had long been an irritant to the English settlements of New England. The British "conquered" Acadia in 1710, which meant that they captured the poorly defended fort at Port Royal with no shots fired. When the French empire ceded the province "according to its ancient limits" under the Treaty of Utrecht (which ended the War of the Spanish Succession in 1713), the two sides could not agree what those ancient limits were.[72] The matter went unresolved until 1749, when the British established Halifax, a military town set on a steep hill fronting a large, commodious harbor.[73] The French responded by building their own forts in Nova Scotia, and soon the empires saw a new war approaching. To avert it, in 1750 British and French officials named commissioners to meet in Paris and settle the Acadian boundary once and for all.[74]

The Honest Politician noted just how wildly different were each empire's claims: the French argued that Acadia's "ancient limits" had never encompassed more than Port Royal (now Annapolis Royal) and a thin stretch of land along the peninsula's Atlantic coast. The British argued that Acadia comprised the entire Nova Scotia peninsula as well as lands stretching along the Bay of Fundy's western shore southwest toward New

England.[75] The chasm between the claims was simply unbridgeable. After years of back and forth, the Honest Politician informed his readers, French officials offered a concession to the British: they would surrender the peninsula. Still the British refused the offer. This disagreement led to a great conflagration that spread from squabbles over the Acadian boundary to shots in the Ohio Valley to a global war of unimagined proportions. The author might have cited Benjamin Franklin, who, when interviewed in 1766 regarding the repeal of the Stamp Act, had said of the Seven Years' War: "I know the last war is commonly spoke of here as entered into for the defence, or for the sake of the people of America. I think it is quite misunderstood. It began about the limits between Canada and Nova-Scotia, about territories to which the Crown indeed laid claim, but were not claimed by any British Colony."[76] But it was not the Honest Politician's intention to provide such a detailed analysis of Acadia's importance. Rather, he hoped to explain to his readers that "it is natural for all men to think their own cause just, and I have rarely met one who has been able to acknowledge the good qualities of his adversary." He closed his editorial by arguing that before the revolution, British Americans had held unjust attitudes towards the French.[77] The cure for these past transgressions was to recognize Britain's wrongdoing and value France's present friendship.

By the time the Honest Politician published his articles, in 1780, the American Revolution had become a nearly global war for Great Britain, and finding a path to peace grew increasingly appealing. Now fighting against France and Spain without any allies in Europe, and concerned with naval and military campaigns in England, the Continent, the Caribbean, and North America, many officials in London worried that the conflict might overwhelm the empire. John Montagu, the Earl of Sandwich and First Lord of the Admiralty, pressed members of Prime Minister Lord North's cabinet to withdraw from North America entirely. As early as 1778, when France allied with the United Colonies, the British navy had been surpassed by the combined navies of Spain and France, which had been building up maritime strength since the end of the Seven Years' War.[78] Those in the British cabinet who were unwilling to withdraw from North America also hoped that a peace negotiation might bring the colonies back into the imperial fold, allowing more rule at home without full home rule.[79]

Congress's delegates in Europe began preparing for peace negotiations in 1779. Because he was already stationed in Paris and had the best rapport with French officials, Franklin became the united States' most involved representative. John Adams had been in France since December 1777, when he arrived to help negotiate the Franco-American alliance, but he had never gotten along with Vergennes. In the summer of 1780, he was sent to the Netherlands to replace the imprisoned Henry Laurens and secure both a recognition of the united States' independence and much-needed financial support.[80] John Jay spent a frustrating time in Spain trying to persuade the Spanish court to recognize his position. Even at a distance, however, Jay and Adams maintained a steady correspondence with Franklin, and their input shaped the progress of the talks.

Each peace commissioner received the same instructions from Congress, which outlined six priorities. The first was that Great Britain recognize the independence of the united States, the second was that no agreement with Great Britain should infringe upon the Franco-American alliance, and the third outlined the desired boundaries between the united States and British colonies. The fourth item addressed Canada and Nova Scotia: "Although it is of the Utmost Importance to the Peace and Commerce of the United States, that Canada and Nova Scotia should be ceded and more particularly that their equal and common Right to the Fisheries should be guarantied to them, Yet a desire of terminating the War, hath induced Us not to make the Acquisition of these Objects an Ultimatum on the present Occasion." The fifth item granted the commissioners the authority to agree to a cessation of hostilities, and the sixth reminded them that in all other matters they should be governed by the Franco-American alliance.[81] Though desirable, possession of (or independence for) Canada and Nova Scotia was never a sine qua non.

The British defeat at Yorktown on 19 October 1781 accelerated the peace negotiations. For much of 1780 and 1781, Patriot newspapers had run reports and rumors about a French invasion of Canada, the likelihood that Congress would welcome Quebec, Nova Scotia, or both into the Confederation, or the possibility that the states might be forced to surrender claims to Canada and the Mississippi to France and Spain.[82] During those same years, British General Henry Clinton, the commander in chief of the British forces in North America, had focused on securing New York, not only because of the twenty-five thousand Loyalists who lived there but also because of its strategic position on the Hudson River and its access to Canada. But since 1776 the British government had also wanted a strong naval presence in the Chesapeake. As General Charles Cornwallis, who was second in command under Howe, launched attacks on the southern colonies, Clinton sent more men to fight with him. By the spring of 1781, more than nine thousand redcoats had been transferred from New York to Virginia. But the two commanders had conflicting views on how to fight the war. Cornwallis, after his victories in Georgia and South Carolina, argued that these regions could be defended only by pushing farther north into Virginia, which was a powerful insurgent colony, where his army would then join forces with Clinton's forces. Clinton believed Cornwallis should maintain his position until Georgia and South Carolina were fully subdued. The two men simply stopped communicating.[83] When Cornwallis marched his men north into Virginia, Clinton ordered him to take Yorktown and hold his position there. Cornwallis realized his forces were insufficient, and so did Washington, whose troops, supported by the French navy, launched a devastating attack on the isolated general. The British defeat in the Chesapeake resulted from the fact that both Clinton and Cornwallis believed that the British navy would defeat the French. Such was not the case. Cornwallis surrendered on 19 October 1781.[84]

Jean-Frédéric Phélypeaux, comte de Maurepas, Louis XVI's minister of state, learned of the British defeat on his deathbed and is said to have declared, "I die content." Lord North might have wished for such a fate. "O God! It is all over!" the first minister cried as he paced around 10 Downing Street.[85] North's resignation did not happen immediately. He lingered in the job for almost three months while the British government fretted over how, or whether, to proceed with the war. In addition to Yorktown, the British suffered losses elsewhere in the world, as the American War for Independence had become a truly global conflagration. French and Spanish ships also attacked the Mediterranean island of Minorca, forcing the British to surrender it in February 1782. At the same time, the French fleet that had defeated the British in Chesapeake Bay returned to the West Indies and added to the growing list of British defeats.[86] North, however, was in a difficult position because neither Lord Germain, the colonial secretary, nor King George III was ready to give up on the colonies. North made no public announcements, but his actions hinted at his sentiments. With his cabinet growing increasingly impatient with his inaction, North began to distance himself from Germain—both figuratively and literally. During one of Germain's speeches in Parliament urging renewed effort in the American war, the prime minister quietly removed himself from the front benches to those farther back. Not wanting to weaken Britain's negotiating position during the peace, he was reluctant to call for an end to the conflict. But on 20 March 1782, he composed his letter of resignation. He returned to the House of Commons that evening as the rain fell, quieted the members by announcing that he was stepping down, then quickly entered a waiting carriage. He paused only to invite a friend for dinner to "get the credit of having dined with a fallen minister on the day of his dismissal."[87]

North's resignation complicated King George's desire to maintain the war effort. He refused to offer the leading opposition ministers, Charles Fox and Lord Richmond, the chance to form a government and instead asked Lord Shelburne, who had always opposed independence, to serve as prime minister. Shelburne was unable to form a government, but Charles Watson-Wentworth, the second Marquess of Rockingham, could. Rockingham had been unhealthy for most of his life. He was a bad public speaker and often fortified himself with a strong drink before addressing in the House. He was also a Whig who questioned the royal prerogative and blamed the king for many of the country's woes. But he could maintain a cabinet.[88] George III at this point would have preferred to abdicate rather than surrender the colonies, and the short-lived Rockingham ministry operated only because Shelburne served as a go-between.[89] The governmental reorganization did, however, provide an opening for peace negotiations. To that end, Shelburne, in his capacity as colonial secretary, dispatched Richard Oswald in March 1782 to meet with Franklin and initiate discussions. Oswald was a Scottish merchant and trader whose fortune came from tobacco, slaves, and a good marriage. His wealth and connections led him to government contracting and eventually to land speculation. He acquired plantations in the Caribbean, thousands of acres in East Florida, and a sizeable holding in Scotland. During the revolution he had become increasingly interested in politics, and Shelburne persuaded Rockingham to make Oswald a peace emissary.[90] When he arrived on Franklin's doorstep in Passy, Oswald was introduced by Caleb Whitefoord, one of Franklin's old friends from London, and he came bearing complimentary letters of introduction from Shelburne and an old friend and business associate, Henry Laurens, whose release from the Tower of London Oswald had secured a few months earlier.[91]

The two men having been suitably introduced, Franklin and Oswald got to talking. Oswald admitted that the new ministry in England was eager for peace and would even agree to independence, while Franklin informed him that the united States would not enter a treaty while

*Benjamin Franklin and Richard Oswald Discussing the Treaty of
Peace at Paris,* halftone of drawing by Howard Pyle, 1898.
Library of Congress, Prints and Photographs Division.

France was still at war with Britain. He had gotten wind of British attempts to separate Patriot and French interests and suspected that
the British would offer Canada to France as incentive.[92] Oswald, who
had a talent for encouraging listeners to hear what they wanted, phrased

Shelburne's opinions in ways that did not always reflect their true intent. But he kept Franklin interested and earned his trust.[93] On 17 April 1782, a week after he arrived in Paris, Oswald left Passy for Versailles to meet with Vergennes, with a letter of introduction from Franklin in hand. They talked for an hour and parted feeling encouraged about the prospects for peace.[94]

The following morning, before setting off for London to confer with Shelburne, Oswald had an enlightening talk with Franklin about Canada. During their conversation, Franklin periodically stole a glance at a sheet of paper he was holding. He wrote later that he had "in view the entering into a conversation, which might draw out something of the Mind of his Court on the Subject of Canada and Nova Scotia" and so he had "thrown some loose thoughts on paper." The two men agreed that for peace to last, the war's end should be accompanied by reconciliation and reparations. Franklin, echoing what he had earlier shared with friends in England, slyly suggested that "perhaps there were things, which America might demand by way of Reparation, and which England might yield, and that the Effect would be vastly greater, if they appeared to be voluntary, and to spring from returning Good will."[95] It was around this point that Oswald realized that Franklin was glancing at his paper, and he asked to see what the old man had scribbled down. Franklin showed the Scot his notes: concerns over the American-Canadian border ("settlers on frontiers generally disorderly, removed from authority, more bold in committing offenses against neighbours"); arguments against Britain holding its northern provinces ("Her Expences in governing and defending that Settlement must be considerable"); and concerns about embarrassing Britain at the treaty table ("It might be humiliating to her to give it up on the Demands of America"). One item on the list Franklin would come to regret. He suggested that the vacant lands ceded to the united States might be sold, and the profits used to "indemnify the Royalists for the Confiscation of their Estates." The disposition of Loyalist lands would become a prickly issue during and after the negotiations, and Franklin's recommendation left the united States vulnerable on the subject.[96]

Oswald said that he agreed with Franklin's suggestions and would try to convince Shelburne. To that end, he asked if he might take Franklin's notes back to London. Franklin, perhaps too eager, agreed.[97] Oswald thus returned to Whitehall with incontrovertible evidence that Franklin had a plan to compensate Loyalists whose lands had been taken by the Patriots.[98] Oswald's possession of the page also made clear just how quickly Franklin had grown to trust him. Along with his notes, Franklin provided Oswald with a letter for Shelburne, in which he expressed how pleased he was with the emissary, reminded the minister that he and his co-commissioners were not empowered to treat separately from France, and suggested that official meetings be opened in Paris or Vienna. He hoped that Oswald might soon return with the authority to treat for peace.[99]

While Franklin and Oswald were getting to know each other, Henry Laurens and John Adams were in Holland discussing American affairs. Laurens, released from the Tower of London in December 1781, found himself in the crosshairs of British Whigs, who hoped that his past expressions of friendship to the British Crown might lead him to push for a separate peace with Britain. Shelburne himself attempted to convince Laurens, while he was still in London, that John Adams had told a British agent that the united States would enter into a separate peace. When Laurens remained skeptical, Shelburne encouraged him to go to Holland and discuss the matter with Adams in person. Laurens left London just as Oswald, his old friend and liberator, was setting out for Paris.[100] Upon arriving in Leyden, Laurens took a room in the Golden Lion Inn, where he later met with John Adams. Adams was relieved to hear that Laurens had told Shelburne and his ministers that the united States demanded independence and would not treat separately from France. Laurens, for his part, was reassured to learn that Adams had never hinted that a separate peace was possible. Adams then asked Laurens "between him and me, to consider, without saying any thing of it to the Ministry, whether we could ever have a Real Peace, with Canada or Nova Scotia in the hands of the English; and whether we ought not to insist at least upon a Stipulation, that they should keep no standing Army, or regular Troops, nor erect any Fortifications, upon the Frontiers of either." Laurens noted with some derision that Shelburne was still "flattering the King with ideas of conciliation and a separate peace." Shelburne was right on both accounts, but while peace was only a few months away, conciliation (between nations, not within the empire) would take longer. Nevertheless, Laurens assured Adams that most in England were hoping for a universal peace, "and many of the best are for giving up Canada and Nova Scotia."[101]

In late April and early May 1782, Franklin remained optimistic about adding Canada to the united States, the task he had failed to accomplish on his trip to Montreal six years earlier. He wrote to John Adams about his meeting with Oswald, telling Adams about his suggestion that Great

Britain surrender its British provinces but not mentioning that he had given Oswald his notes, or that the notes proposed selling vacant lands to compensate the Loyalists.[102] In a second letter, Franklin expressed satisfaction that Laurens agreed on the benefits of Britain's surrendering Canada and Nova Scotia.[103] Adams replied that Canada seemed to be a linchpin in the entire affair. "If there is a real Disposition to permit Canada to accede to the American Association," he wrote, "I should think there would be no great difficulty in adjusting all things between England and America, provided our Allies are contented too."[104] Franklin was surely pleased to hear that another emissary shared his desire to transform British provinces into American states.

Franklin also had Oswald to help smooth over Shelburne's more intemperate demands. In late April, Oswald returned to Paris with the authority only to name that city as the site of the peace negotiations. Franklin had wanted him to have the authority to enter into the negotiations themselves, but that was a stickier issue. Shelburne and Charles Fox were competing for the power to direct negotiations in Rockingham's ministry.[105] Each time Oswald crossed the Channel, he brought Franklin some useful information. Aside from naming Paris as the seat of negotiations, on this visit he told Franklin that the British government was considering its terms for recognition of American independence. The opening offer was likely to be independence in exchange for a return to Britain's 1763 North American boundaries.[106] Franklin, assuming this meant France would have to surrender the islands it had taken from Britain in the Caribbean, was not impressed. In a letter to Adams outlining this development, he quipped, "This seems to me a Proposition of selling to us a Thing that is already our own, and making France pay the Price they are pleas'd to ask for it."[107] Franklin's spirits were likely buoyed by Oswald's other news: he had given Shelburne Franklin's notes on the cession of Canada and had even let Shelburne keep them for a night. Oswald assured Franklin that the "matter might be settled to our Satisfaction towards the end of the Treaty" but asked him not to broach the subject in the negotiations' early stages.[108] These vague remarks allowed Franklin to believe that Canada remained on the table, thus keeping Franklin and Oswald on good terms. Shelburne never intended to give up such a vast part of Britain's North American possessions.[109] Oswald was using Canada as a carrot with which imperial officials would lead Franklin through the peace process.

Oswald also brought a third piece of news: an additional emissary, Thomas Grenville, would arrive shortly from London. Grenville, then twenty-seven years old, was to Charles Fox what Oswald was to Shelburne: a proxy for a minister jostling for power in a fractured cabinet.[110] Grenville met first with Franklin, who then took him to see Vergennes. Right away, Grenville launched into a discussion of possible peace terms. Should Britain recognize American independence, he suggested, France would be expected to return whatever conquests it had made in the British islands in return for Saint-Pierre and Miquelon, two small islands just south of Newfoundland. As far as Grenville was concerned, this arrangement satisfied the original objects of the war. Vergennes, who took a longer view of events, paraphrased Thomas Paine and replied that the Patriot states did not need their independence recognized. It had been claimed and earned.[111] As for Grenville's arguments regarding the original objects of the war, Vergennes answered with a history lesson. The Seven Years' War, he said, had started over the rights to "some waste Lands on the Ohio and to Frontiers of Nova Scotia," but Britain had not contented itself with the recovery of those lands.[112] At the peace of 1763, Britain retained Canada, Louisiana, Florida, and Grenada and other islands in the West Indies, as well as the lion's share of the northern fisheries and conquests in Africa. The French minister argued that the nation responsible for starting the war should hardly be made whole at the peace. Grenville, perhaps misguided by youthful confidence, remarked that the war had begun because France encouraged the colonies to revolt. Franklin, who had been observing the exchange, noted that Vergennes "grew a little warm, and declar'd firmly, that the Breach was made, and our Independence declar'd, long before we receiv'd the least Encouragement from France; and he defy'd the World to give the smallest Proof of the contrary."[113]

Grenville left Versailles with much to think about, including the Newfoundland fishery. He wrote Charles Fox to outline the challenges Britain would face in the coming negotiations, and his letter clearly shows that Vergennes's arguments had sunk in. "I must not forget," he wrote, "that tho' the last war began only upon the subject of Nova Scotia, we had not confined ourselves to that at the peace." Four days later, Grenville wrote again, lamenting that imperial rivalries would prohibit an easy peace. "Everything that I have hitherto seen and heard leads me to believe that the demands of France and Spain will be found such as it will be difficult, perhaps impossible for England to comply with, as they are presently conceived." Though Franklin had pushed the Canada issue on Oswald, Grenville was focused on another matter. The French, he reported to Fox, wanted "very essential alterations in the state of the Newfoundland fishery."[114] Nova Scotia and the Grand Banks would increasingly come to bear on the peace talks.

As a New Englander, John Adams kept one eye on the seas and all they contained. He argued for the states' rights to fish in the Grand Banks off Newfoundland, a region visited by Norse sailors in the tenth century and which had drawn European fishing ships across the Atlantic in regular numbers before Columbus's time. Adams had not fished since he was a boy, nor did he come from a seafaring family. But thousands of men from his state participated in the fishery, if only seasonally or for a few years before they settled on shore.[115] He was convinced that Americans had a right to fish in the northeast Atlantic. If he or other politicians in Massachusetts needed a reminder, they needed only to look up while in the State House in Boston. Hanging from the ceiling was the Sacred Cod, a painted pine carving that symbolized the fisheries' importance.[116] "Is there, or can there be, a clearer right?" he argued. "When God Almighty made the banks of Newfoundland, at three hundred leagues distance from the people of America, and at six hundred leagues distance from those of France and England, did he not give as good a right to the former as to the latter?"[117] The fishery mattered more than Canada, and thus Newfoundland and Nova Scotia loomed larger than Quebec in Adams's mind.

The competing interests of the Patriot, French, and British negotiators ran through a web of representatives and superiors. The Rockingham ministry was internally divided, suspicious, and impossibly dysfunctional. In early June, Charles Fox was increasingly desperate to wrest control of the negotiations from Shelburne, and despite objections from the cabinet, he was prepared to grant American independence ahead of the peace negotiations. Doing so would make each of the states a foreign power, not a collection of colonies, and thereby subject to his portfolio and not Shelburne's. Though Rockingham likely would not have condoned such a move, he was far too ill to intervene in the machinations of his ministers. On July 1 he ended the internal strife the only way he could: by dying. Shelburne, by this time, had secured enough influence to form his own government, which George III asked him to do. Fox and his man Grenville were out.[118] Oswald was put in sole charge of the talks in Paris.

Still very much alive were American concerns over the British provinces in North America, particularly Nova Scotia and its undefined boundaries. In late May 1782, Adams wrote Franklin about Britain's demand to reinstate the 1763 boundaries. Although Adams recognized that this was an imperial concern to be addressed by France and Spain, it would clearly affect the united States. If the British ministry was suggesting "that Britain shall remain in Possession of Nova Scotia, Canada and the Floridas as ceded to them by the Peace of 1763," then "it is a very Serious affair for Us, and for G. Britain too, for the foundation would be laid by it for her final Ruin." Adams, not unlike the duc de Choiseul twenty years earlier, foresaw such an agreement as leading to endless war with the states. Great Britain would have to maintain innumerable posts and fortifications. It could no more hold that territory "than her Navy can rule the Moon."[119] But just how much territory Britain would have to control remained an unresolved question. Francis Dana, who had sailed from Boston with Adams in 1779 and had been named minister to Russia (for which he engaged Adams's teenage son, John Quincy, as secretary), wrote John Adams and explained the difficulties of determining Nova Scotia's boundaries. Dana compared King James's 1621 Nova Scotia grant to William Alexander with a map of the province by Thomas Jefferys, one of Britain's most famous mapmakers. The boundaries did not match, and confusion remained over which river, the St. Croix or the St. John, defined the province's limits. "But perhaps you will meet with something to clear up this point among the papers I received just before my last departure from Paris, and left with you," Dana suggested, admitting, "I did not peruse them."[120] The peace would not resolve the question of which river separated Nova Scotia (or, later, New Brunswick) from Massachusetts (or, later, Maine), and the boundary remained a constant concern.[121]

As August dragged on and Oswald shuttled between London and Paris, he was unable to shake Franklin's insistence on adding at least one British province to the confederated states. Oswald recorded these conversations in his journal throughout the negotiations. Part of his entry for 11 August, for instance, reads: "The Doctor at last touched upon Canada, as he generally does upon the like occasions, and said there could be no dependence on peace and good neighborhood, while that country continued under a different government, as it touched their States in so great a stretch of frontier. I told him I was sensible of that inconvenience; but, having no orders, the consideration of that matter might possibly be taken up at some future time."[122]

Politicians in the states also hoped to have this matter resolved. Edmund Pendleton, chief justice of Virginia's High Court of Chancery, wrote to James Madison in late August 1782 outlining his desire that

Canada become the fourteenth member of the union but noted his reservations about demanding the province from Britain. The way Franklin had been hinting at this request had "a deep, insideous intention on our Integrity." Though it would be wise for Britain to yield Canada, a better solution "would seem to be to leave it to the Canadians to choose the party they would be annexed to."[123] Though the united States wanted Quebec, how it was acquired mattered.

Thomas Paine also believed Quebec would eventually become an American state. In 1782 he issued a response to a pamphlet entitled *The Revolution of America*, published by Abbé Guillaume Thomas François Raynal in 1781. Paine took issue with several of Raynal's conclusions, including that the revolution had been largely about taxes imposed by Britain after 1763, and argued that Raynal put too much emphasis on political theory and ignored the practicality of independence.[124] He also commented on the British provinces that remained in North America. It was probable, Paine wrote, that at the peace talks Britain would attempt to retain Quebec, Nova Scotia, or possibly both, but it would not be able to keep these colonies. The descendants of any settlers sent to Canada would become American in nature, and "they will look round and see the neighbouring States sovereign and free" and move south.[125] As for Halifax, Paine believed that its harbor would be useless to Britain after the peace. "A harbour," he argued, "when the dominion is gone, for the purpose of which only it was wanted, can be attended only with expence."[126] For Paine, the British provinces in North America were an imperial folly, and to hold them would do the empire more harm than good.

As Paine's ideas circulated throughout the united States, some began to consider whether peace might increase their territory, and Britons wondered if that would be such a bad thing.[127] In late August 1782, the *Independent Gazetteer* of Philadelphia printed reports from London in which British subjects expressed concern over keeping their North American colonies. "The expenses that we are obliged to undergo for the maintenance of our government in Canada," read one account, "must be very heavy; and perhaps the province is scarcely worth the keeping."[128] A couple of weeks later, a paper in New York alerted its readers that "late accounts from Europe mention, That the negotiation for a peace goes on rapidly, and that France urges, in the strongest manner, the ceding of Canada to these United States."[129] In mid-October, papers reported that France was pushing for independent united States that could trade freely and also that the French ministry was working toward securing independence for Nova Scotia and Canada, "which, it is thought, will by no means be complied with on the part of the British Ministry."[130] Some even thought Great Britain would trade Canada for valuable islands in the Caribbean, as the French had done in 1763.[131] To the average reader, the Canadian question was far from resolved. Britain could not afford to lose its North American possessions, many argued, yet it could hardly afford to keep them.

For the negotiators in Paris, September and October were busy months. Boundaries became the focus of intense debates. In early September, a fellow New Englander implored John Adams to "take care of the fishery, that the limits of Canada are reduced to what they were by the claims of G B before it was conquered and that Nova Scotia reaches no further than the river St Croix."[132] A few days later, Richard Oswald reported to Shelburne that Canada might serve as a northern boundary not only for the American states but also for Spanish territories running north from the Mississippi. The problem with this arrangement, however, was Spain's desire to maintain control over both sides of the great river.[133] Boundaries occupied Oswald's mind for much of September and October. He reported on 2 October to Thomas Townshend, secretary of state for the Home Department, that he hoped within a few days to reach agreement on the principal articles of the peace. These included independence, settling the boundaries between American states and British colonies, and "giving up the additional lands of Canada."[134] By the end of that month, John Adams and John Jay were considering entering a separate peace with Britain, despite the promises made to France. Franklin, who Adams had always thought was too close to Vergennes and too concerned about French demands, acquiesced.[135]

By then, Franklin had faded from the negotiations. His gout rendered him unable to participate in late September and early October, allowing John Jay and John Adams, who had arrived in Paris from Spain and Holland, respectively, to take a leading role. Franklin's ill health foiled his attempts to win Canada, just as it had in Montreal in 1776.

His negotiating partner, Oswald, faded for a different reason: his inexperience as a diplomat and negotiator worried some in Shelburne's cabinet, and in the fall of 1782 he was demoted and made to report to Henry Strachey, an undersecretary in the colonial office. Strachey arrived with specific instructions that contradicted Oswald's assurances to Franklin. Rather than cede Canada or grant it independence, the British negotiators now asked to retain the province within the extended boundaries defined by the 1774 Quebec Act, which had helped drive British colonists to rebel in the first place.[136] The proceedings were, if not friendly, at least cordial, and they often resulted in all parties dining together.[137] When these dinner conversations turned to boundaries and borders, and the negotiators spent many hours poring over maps, the possession of Canada came up less often, and the focus shifted to the united States' northeastern and southwestern limits.[138] The first draft of the articles of peace, composed from 5 to 7 October, did not mention the possession of Canada at all.[139]

The second draft of the treaty, finished in early November, reflected a tougher stance by the British. Shelburne had spent much of the intervening time chastising Oswald for being too accommodating to the Americans, and he sent Oswald and Strachey stern instructions to adjust Britain's demands to better reflect the ministry's desires. Nova Scotia's boundaries were to extend as far south as possible, ideally to include all of the territory of Maine or at least to the Penobscot, where the British still clung to their military outpost at Fort George in what would never become New Ireland. The two negotiators were also to challenge the Americans on their desire to catch and dry fish onshore along the Gulf of St. Lawrence.[140] Adams was adamant about the American fishery, arguing, "If Occupation, Use, and Possession give a Right, We have it as clearly as you. If War and Blood and Treasure give a Right, ours is as good as yours. We have been constantly fighting in Canada, Cape Breton and Nova Scotia for the Defense of this Fishery, and have expended beyond all Proportion more than you."[141] Oswald, who knew what the Americans wanted more than anyone in Britain, persuaded Strachey to relent on this question because any prohibition on the right to cure and dry fish on shore would only anger Congress and require money to enforce. The Americans secured fishing rights off the Grand Banks, thus providing the united States with a resource like the one that had facilitated Britain's rise as a global superpower: a nursery for seamen. The boundary question, however, was less easily settled. Though the British ultimately surrendered their claim to the extended boundaries of Quebec in favor of older limits (north of the St. Lawrence River and Great Lakes), the question of Nova Scotia remained unresolved.[142]

October and November 1782 witnessed a flurry of negotiations that sent Oswald back and forth to London as the preliminary articles of peace were hammered out. Jay, Franklin, Adams, and Laurens agreed to terms on 30 November. They had gone against Congress's instructions by negotiating separately with Great Britain. Since the treaty would not come into effect until France and Britain signed their own agreement, however, the Franco-American alliance of 1778 had not been broken. The Americans did well by the treaty. Most important, Great Britain recognized the united States' independence. In addition to setting northern and southern limits favorable to the states' demands (though the northern boundary would require attention in the future due to geographic misunderstandings), the treaty allowed the united States to fish as they had along the Grand Banks and to dry and cure their catch in "unsettled" bays and harbors in Nova Scotia. British and American creditors were allowed to collect their debts without impediment (a provision more important to the British than the Americans), and, in what would become a toothless article, Congress was to request that states reimburse Loyalists who had lost property.[143] Britain neither surrendered Canada and Nova Scotia to the united States nor made those provinces independent. Charles Carroll, who had traveled with Franklin to Montreal as one of the commissioners to Canada, was disappointed. He wished "that the Canadians were confederated with us." Yet he, like many other Americans, had not given up hope: "perhaps this must be the work of some future day."[144]

As the final draft of the peace treaty embarked across the Atlantic in the winter of 1782, to be read and ratified by Congress before returning to be signed in Paris, Franklin had time to think. He and Adams met in early December and discussed additional articles that might find their way into the final treaty. They created a short list, whose seventh article was a final effort to steal British provinces: "The concession of Canada & Nova scotia, to join the Confederation."[145] It was a long shot. Franklin modified his stance several months later, however, in a "sketch" of the proposed articles to be added to the definitive treaty. Rather than demand a fourteenth and fifteenth state, Franklin suggested "that all [the king's] Troops shall be withdrawn from the Continent, and the Provinces of Canada and Nova Scotia declared free and Independent States, and at Liberty to join the Confederacy or remain separate."[146] For Franklin, divorcing Quebec and Nova Scotia from the British empire, either by making them American or securing their independence, was a personal obsession. But the peace process had taught him that if Canada was to become an American state, it would not be because Britain gave it willingly.

News took weeks to cross the Atlantic, so readers of the colonial press had much time to consider the continent's future before accurate information regarding the discussions was widely published. In early December

1782, readers in New York were treated to a bitingly sarcastic report from London about just how much the empire would save once peace was concluded. Britain could remove from its accounts the "barren sandbanks of East Florida (which I would with all my heart give to the Devil), the frozen deserts of Nova Scotia, the extensive regions of Canada, Newfoundland, and St. John's."[147] Not everyone agreed. Writing under the name Lycurgus (the lawgiver of Sparta who helped give rise to a military society), one hawkish Briton argued that surrendering Canada or weakening the British presence in its remaining North American colonies would bring disaster because the government had planted its colonies "with so much difficulty, danger and expense." Troops in the maritime colonies were needed "to awe" the Americans against an attack on Canada, and a weakened Canada "must fall a prey to the revolted Colonies."[148] Others suspected betrayal by the great powers. One Boston paper published a rumor that British negotiators suggested partitioning the states and giving New England to France in return for Louis's help in bringing the southern colonies back to the British empire.[149]

While awaiting these reports from England and the Continent, Americans expressed their own opinions on Canada and Nova Scotia. In a March 1783 letter addressed to George III, a contributor to Philadelphia's *Freeman's Journal* offered a biblical analogy. "PHARAOH!," the letter began, before advising the king to "be wise, and immediately generously grant Canada their independence, and let them confederate with the other sovereign states of America." Echoing Thomas Paine's arguments in his response to Abbé Raynal, the letter warned King George that granting Canada its independence was the only way to prevent yet another rebellion: "'Tis but natural to expect that when [the Canadians] are told that ships from all nations resort to the harbours of independent America, bringing gold, frankincense, and myrrh, that they will . . . embrace the first favourable opportunity to make themselves free, and they will not want for assistance to bring it about."[150] But some wondered whether the debate about Canada was imperiling the peace process. Two weeks later, a Pennsylvania paper reported, "One of the great obstacles of peace is the restitution of Canada, which our ministers insist upon, and the court of London absolutely refuse; so that we fear the negotiation for peace will meet with long delays."[151] Those with opinions on the peace remained ambivalent. Canada should (and, according to most, *would*) be free, but there was a danger in allowing the question to delay recognition of American independence.

James Gillray, *The Times, Anno 1783*. John Bull, surrounded by a Dutchman, Frenchman, and Spaniard, surrenders a map of America to the Devil. Library of Congress, Prints and Photographs Division.

Unbeknownst to the general public, Great Britain had already recognized American independence, and Canada was not included. Congress ratified the treaty, which was sent back to Paris and signed on 3 September 1783. The process of getting to the treaty, however, illustrated that Congress and its French allies had nearly opposite views of where the British colonies fit into both the war and the peace. For French officials, particularly Vergennes, British control of Quebec and Nova Scotia served as security for the Franco-American alliance; as long as Congress worried about a British invasion from the north, it would need French military and financial assistance. France had no interest in retaking Quebec or Acadia, but the Americans did not believe this. The view within the united States was that an imperial power that had lost its North American possessions only twenty years earlier must be eager to reclaim them. The eagerness with which men like Lafayette and d'Estaing joined the war seemed to confirm this fear. Yet as the war drew to a close, Congress only flirted with another invasion of Quebec, while

Washington's pretense at a plan to attack the British province was only as a ruse to distract imperial officials while his army planned to move south.

The American negotiators in Paris seem to have been more eager for the northern provinces than either Congress or Washington. Franklin wanted Canada, and John Adams wanted access to the Grand Banks fishery. The British negotiators hoped to stymie both proposals. The internal divisions in the Rockingham ministry afforded some latitude for men like Richard Oswald, who humored Franklin's regular requests that Great Britain surrender its North American possessions. But the final treaty left many important details unresolved. Great Britain retained Quebec and Nova Scotia, but the latter's borders remained undefined until well into the nineteenth century. The independent united States would have to negotiate their post-revolutionary world as a junior player among more powerful nations—British, French, and Indigenous.

# CHAPTER FOUR

# The National

I N LATE 1783, before the sting of failing to gain Canada's independence had worn off, Benjamin Franklin encountered Pierre du Calvet. Du Calvet, then forty-eight, was a truly Atlantic citizen. Born in France, he sailed for Quebec in 1758 in search of fortune. Upon arrival in Quebec the ship he was on sank, carrying his merchandise and his dreams of a quick profit to the bottom of the St. Lawrence. Du Calvet found government work and eventually became a successful Montreal merchant. Like many others in his situation, he provisioned the Patriot invaders at Montreal during its occupation in 1775 and was owed a great deal of money when the Continental forces retreated in 1776.[1] The British, suspicious of his loyalties, kept him in prison in Montreal for two years, after which he returned to Paris.

After the end of the war, du Calvet somehow made Franklin's acquaintance and asked for his help securing the 56,394 livres he was owed. He presented Franklin with congressional scrip that, as Franklin wrote to Elias Boudinot in 1783, "appeared to me of our first Emissions, and yet all fresh and clean, as having passed thro' no other hands."[2] Franklin encouraged the merchant to find passage to the united States and appeal to Congress, which he did two years later, securing roughly half of what he was owed.

Du Calvet was part of a trend that emerged in the postwar years: subjects and officials in the British provinces who exerted pressure on the young confederacy as it transitioned to a peacetime government. The

1780s were a tumultuous decade, and many of the era's pressing issues had connections to the northern British provinces. In the period between the surrender of Yorktown in 1781 and the ratification of the Constitution in 1788, citizens from Massachusetts to Georgia struggled with their new reality. The Peace of Paris was a monumental achievement, but it would take some time before many of the promises and obligations laid out in the agreement were felt in the newly independent states. The treaty did not create a country ready to find its feet and exert its influence in the world; it only recognized a collection of independent states, bound by a feeble Congress and vulnerable to internal divisions and external advances. Worries about internal turmoil and government organization were exacerbated by the constant presence of Canadians and Nova Scotians who offered opportunities to, and made demands against, individual states and Congress. Congress had secured its imperial separation from Great Britain, but its geographical connection to British colonies raised issues that could not be resolved at a Paris negotiating table. The relevance of the peace and of the states' independence rested on how the postwar period would either bring the states together or, quite possibly, tear them apart. The very existence of British colonies to the north forced the young states to think about their futures.

Three primary concerns in the immediate postwar era kept Americans cautiously glancing north. First, citizens of the independent Vermont Republic, which sat along a strategically important waterway linking the states and British provinces, engaged in a troubling flirtation with British officials in Canada. The Green Mountain Boys, especially the brothers Ethan and Ira Allen, were willing to consider joining British Canada if Britain recognized Vermont's independence—something that Congress refused to do. Second, the movement of people—Loyalists fleeing to Canada and Nova Scotia (often bringing enslaved peoples with them) and "Canadian refugees" leaving these provinces for the states—forced Americans to think about how former enemies and far-flung allies fit into the new union. Third, Shays's Rebellion—an uprising of western Massachusetts farmers who were angry about debt and government tax collection—became entangled both with Vermont's questionable loyalty and with the Canadian government's desire to use the states' disorganization to its political advantage. These episodes of social and political upheaval culminated in the desire among leading officials to reimagine how the states were organized.

The process by which the united States, a collection of independent entities loosely aligned under a weak and cash-starved Congress, reorganized themselves into the United States—an independent nation with three branches of government—makes clear that the Treaty of Paris (1783) was the end of a global conflagration and the beginning of a continental process of nation making. The men and women who crossed from the united States into the British provinces—most voluntarily, but many against their will—forced residents of the united States to consider just what the war had wrought. British subjects in Nova Scotia and Canada participated in the founding of the United States because the peace envisioned boundaries that did not exist. The British provinces were too alluring, too powerful, and too close to ignore.

Before the Continental Army and its allies defeated Cornwallis at Yorktown, and before Franklin pushed for the surrender of Canada in Paris, British officials hoped to add Vermont to their list of loyal colonies. The independent Republic of Vermont was something of a test for Congress, as it represented the revolutionary ideals of American independence turned against itself. From 1779 until 1783, British agents operating in Canada tried to persuade Vermont's leaders to turn their backs to Congress and unite with the empire. The negotiations between the Allen brothers and representatives of General Haldimand demonstrate how Vermont, which declared itself an independent republic in 1777, could play the empire against the states in an attempt to secure legitimacy in an increasingly fractured North America. Though Vermont would ultimately find a home in the United States, the republic's close relationship with Quebec caused great concern during the final years of the revolution and the early years of the Confederation.

Vermont's very existence was a topic of debate from the time British American settlers pushed west from crowded settlements in New Hampshire and east from New York into the fertile upper Connecticut Valley where they could clear land and establish farms. The region was cut through with rivers: those east of the Green Mountains flowed into the Connecticut, and those to the west ended at Lake Champlain. Vermont was hilly but fertile, evidenced by the thick woods of elm, birch, and maple throughout the state, with white pine and oak growing along the riverbanks. Clearing the trees opened land for raising wheat, rye, barley, oats, and corn, adding to the flax, hemp, potatoes, pumpkins, and, of course, maple sugar.[3] For ambitious farmers, the region offered boundless opportunity.

Both New York and New Hampshire laid claim to the territory between the Connecticut River and Lake Champlain, and both offered grants to their settlers to move there. In 1764 Great Britain's Privy Council settled the matter by declaring the Connecticut River as New York's eastern boundary, and therefore all settlements within the contested region fell under the de jure authority of New York. That did not end the conflict between New Hampshire and New York speculators. The wording of the Privy Council's decision seemed to suggest that New York's eastern boundary had always been the Connecticut River, which authorities in the state took to indicate that all grants issued from New Hampshire were null and void. Speculators who purchased tracts from the New Hampshire government, and settlers who bought grants from those speculators, were not about to surrender their titles, and very few were willing (or could afford) to undertake the expensive legal process necessary to have their grants approved by officials in New York.[4] So they stayed and farmed.

The competition over the New Hampshire Grants only increased the region's importance in the revolutionary era. The years between 1764 and 1777 witnessed a continued conflict between small landholders (most famously the Green Mountain Boys led by Ethan Allen), who were reluctant to surrender their grants, and "Yorkers," speculators holding grants from New York who hoped their state would secure control of the region. Settlements derived from the New Hampshire Grants developed into towns, and in 1777, with jurisdiction yet unsettled, approximately twenty-eight of those towns adopted a constitution, declared a new republic named Vermont, and separated from New York.[5] It was independence within independence.

Vermont residents immediately found themselves navigating treacherous waters between the independent states and the loyal British provinces. Congress refused to recognize Vermont's independence for fear of alienating the powerful New York delegates, but it also had to protect Lake Champlain and monitor British advances. For British officials, a self-styled republic carved from two so-called states was the perfect target to disrupt revolutionary sentiment in northern North America. Vermont could be attacked, lured into the British orbit, or both.[6] But while delegates in Congress could air their grievances over Vermont and coordinate strategy with relative ease, the British had to negotiate local command structures and transatlantic communications. Throughout the war, the British army in North America was headquartered at New York under the command of Sir Henry Clinton, but most of the negotiations with Vermont went through General Frederick Haldimand at Montreal.

## To the Inhabitants of the State of VERMONT.

FRIENDS AND FELLOW CITIZENS,

PURSUANT to Appointment by the Legislature, and Instructions from the Governor and Council of this State, I waited on the General Court of New-Hampshire, at their Sessions in June last, and delivered the public Writings intrusted me by the Governor of this State, to the President, which were read in Council; and sent to the House for their Inspection: The House, after reading and considering the same, resolved into a Committee, to take into Consideration the whole Matter respecting Vermont, which was concurred in by the Hon. Board; and Thursday the 24th of June, the Committee met in the Assembly Chamber, and the Resolves of Congress of the 1st and 2d of June, respecting the Premises, and several other Papers were read; among which was the Appointments of Mr. Peter Olcott, and Bezaleel Woodward, Esq; impowering them as a Committee from the Committee of the Cornish Convention, to ...

Ira Allen to the Inhabitants of Vermont, 1779, a leaflet in which Ira Allen explains his meetings with New Hampshire officials over the status of Vermont. Library of Congress, Rare Book and Special Collections Division.

Lord George Germain, secretary of state for the colonies, authorized Haldimand to oversee the discussion because he and his army had readier access to Vermont.[7] Neither Haldimand nor Germain took up the cause with alacrity. Not until January 1779, two years after Vermont's independence, did Haldimand write Germain to inform him, with a mixture of glee and disdain, that "the Insurgents of Vermont under Allen continue to give umbrage to what is called the New York Government."[8] More than two months later, Germain's reply arrived: "The separation of the inhabitants of the country they style Vermont from the provinces in which it was formerly included is a circumstance from which much advantage might be derived." He saw no objection "to giving them reason to expect the King will erect their country into a separate Province."[9]

A year after this exchange, Ethan Allen was stopped on the streets of Arlington, Vermont's first capital, by a man dressed as a farmer who was looking for the governor. Allen's rise to prominence in Vermont had taken a circuitous route. Born in Litchfield, Connecticut, to a farming family, Allen served in the Seven Years' War, was married in 1762, opened an iron forge in Salisbury, Connecticut, and settled down to domestic life. It was not to be. Within three years, his aggressive nature and Deist beliefs had gotten him evicted from Salisbury and later from Northampton, Massachusetts. By 1770, he and his small family had relocated to the Green Mountains, then officially part of New York, where he quickly sided with the men and women working lands granted them by New Hampshire. His philosophy followed an idea of John Locke's that settlers elsewhere in North America would find familiar: to work the land was to own it. Allen and his supporters chipped away at New York's authority, but the war interrupted their efforts to transform the settlements into a republic.[10]

Allen was an overly eager participant in the revolution's early years. In May 1775, he and his Green Mountain Boys helped capture Fort Ticonderoga, a star-shaped fort at the south end of Lake Champlain, which made him something of a hero. That September, as part of Richard Montgomery's invasion of Canada, he launched an early and ill-advised attack on Montreal and was captured.[11] He was held captive for three years, taken to New York, and finally released in May 1778. Upon his release and return to Vermont, which had meanwhile declared its independence, Allen wasted little time before throwing himself back into politics as a vociferous promoter of Vermont rights. Though he did not hold the republic's top political post, he may not have been surprised to be stopped in Arlington in March 1780 by a farmer with a letter addressed to "Governor Allen."[12]

The letter came from Colonel Beverly Robinson, a Loyalist and member of the King's American Regiment.[13] Perhaps Vermont's actual governor, Thomas Chittenden, was offended that British officials assumed Allen led the government. The barely literate Chittenden might never have learned of the slight had Allen not rushed to his house to share the letter's contents.[14]

At the time he wrote to Allen, Robinson was a principal actor in the plan to turn Benedict Arnold. Apparently he had a talent for persuading Patriots to return to the Crown.[15] He began his letter, "Sir: I am now undertaking a task which I hope you will receive with the same good intentions that inclines me to make it." He had heard that Allen and "most of the inhabitants of Vermont" opposed the Patriot attempts to separate from Great Britain. Robinson described the proposal Haldimand and Germain had discussed a year earlier, hinting to Allen that, should he fight for the British cause, "you may obtain a separate government under the king and constitution of England . . . and be on the same footing as all the provincial camps are here." As if to reassure him, Robinson added that "I am an American myself, feel much for the distressed situation my poor country is in at present, and anxious to be serviceable toward restoring it to peace, and that mild and good government we have lost." The colonel concluded that if Allen should propose anything to which Haldimand did not agree, "the matter shall be buried in oblivion between us."[16]

Allen and Chittenden found themselves in a favorable position: they had in hand a British offer of allegiance that they could use in their negotiations with Congress. They were in no rush to respond: by delaying, they could begin to play Canada and Congress against each other. The Congress in Philadelphia could not simply recognize Vermont's independence because that would alienate the delegates from New York and, as James Madison noted, set a precedent that new states could erect themselves within the boundaries of old ones.[17] British officials in Canada, though hopeful that Allen would accept Robinson's carrot, also showed the stick. During the last two weeks of October 1780, they launched two attacks on Vermont. Combined British, Indigenous, and Hessian forces raided towns, killed settlers, and destroyed property. The second raid was followed by a visit, under flag of truce, by Lieutenant Colonel Justus Sherwood, a former Green Mountain Boy who represented General Haldimand. If Allen and Chittenden were ready to talk, Sherwood was ready to listen. So began two years of secret negotiations between Vermont and Canada.[18]

Allen and Chittenden wanted to be discreet, but it was also important that Congress know about Vermont's options. Philip Schuyler, informed right away of Sherwood's arrival, wrote to George Washington from Saratoga: "Sending a flag to Vermont for the purpose of exchanging prisoners appears to me only as a cover to some design of the enemy, and gives me much uneasiness." Schuyler was particularly concerned about rumors that "the person whom Your Excellency was informed to have been in New York in July last is negotiating with the enemy."[19] Ethan Allen was already on Schuyler's radar. In late November, John Adams received a letter from his friend James Warren expressing similar concerns and outlining the Green Mountain Boys' strategy. "The State of Vermont as they stile themselves grow troublesome," Warren warned. He informed Adams of the truce with Canada and suggested that it would be an occasion for "making peremptory demands on Congress, to Acknowledge their Independence, within a certain time."[20] For the Patriots, especially military officials and delegates at Congress, the arrival of British forces in and around Vermont was a troubling development.

At first, Allen and Chittenden were careful to keep both the British and Congress interested in Vermont. Haldimand, keeping his superiors informed of his correspondence with Allen, reassured Lord Germain that the "offers you made to the Chief of that district some time since, have been, or may be accepted."[21] A few days later, he dispatched instructions to Justus Sherwood and Dr. George Smythe (the commissioners charged with negotiating with Allen) expressing sympathy for Vermont residents, who he said had suffered at the hands of the New York government. "It is therefore with great cheerfulness," he wrote, "that I authorise you to give these people the most positive assurances that their Country will be erected into a separate province independent and unconnected with every Government in America." At least at this point, Haldimand believed the people of Vermont were "sincere and candid in their propositions," and he knew that "their situation is delicate," surrounded as they were by "powerful enemies." But he reminded them "that this negotiation should cease, and any step that leads to it be forgotten, provided the Congress shall grant the State of Vermont a seat in their assembly and acknowledge its independency."[22]

These cordial negotiations stood in stark contrast to Governor Chittenden's relations with Congress and Washington. Chittenden, Allen, and their supporters considered Vermont an independent republic. Whereas Haldimand seemed willing to recognize that independence, members of Congress were only willing to debate whether an entity such as Vermont had the right to exist at all, let alone claim independence. Vermonters had three options for asserting that their independence was legitimate: they could argue that Vermont had existed as a colony prior to 1776 and thus inherited its statehood; they could declare that revolutionaries had the right to create their own governments; or they could reason that a state within a community of other states gained legitimacy by the mutual recognition of its right to independence.[23] Congress could challenge each of these arguments. In a long letter to Washington, Chittenden bristled at the need for Congress even to debate the issue. "Vermont," he wrote, "being a free and Independant State, have denied the Authority of Congress to judge of their Jurisdiction." He compared the delegates from New Hampshire and New York to the king of Prussia and the empress of Russia, with Vermont as an American Poland. But there was a difference: "the former are not in possession of Vermont."[24]

Patriots considered Vermont's geographic position too strategic for it to be allowed to fall under British authority, yet the question of its independence prevented any coherent action. The region was "the only door into Canada, and one of the most important parts of the country, and ought to be under the best regulations."[25] Yet Congress continued to drag its feet. In March 1781 Ethan Allen wrote to Samuel Huntington, the president of Congress, outlining Vermont's position. He forwarded the letters he had received from Beverly Robinson and assured Huntington that his government had decided not to act. Allen was frustrated that the people of Vermont were made to suffer the competing claims of New York, New Hampshire, and Massachusetts, which had the effect of "weakening this government and exposing its inhabitants to the incursions of the British troops and their savage allies from the Province of Quebec." He made clear his attachment to the cause of liberty but pointed out the irony of having Congress deny that same liberty to Vermont. His letter ended with the ominous declaration that "I am as resolutely determined to defend the Independence of Vermont as Congress are that of the United States, and rather than fail, will retire with hardy Green Mountain Boys into the desolate Caverns of the Mountains, and wage war with Human nature at large."[26]

Both Allen brothers had a flair for peppering their diplomatic niceties with otherworldly threats of violence. While Ethan was dealing with

Congress, Ira held meetings with the British. Over several days in March, he met with British representatives, including Justus Sherwood, to discuss Vermont's position, the possibility of a truce and prisoner exchange, and the conditions for Vermont becoming a British province. Ira Allen was fairly straightforward about Vermonters' desires: the republic's council wanted to secure neutrality in the conflict to prevent attacks on its settlers. But he and others in Vermont knew that Congress did not intend to welcome them as a state. A report, most likely written by Justus Sherwood, summarizing the commissioners' discussions with Allen described him as "very cautious and intricate," but he was hardly reserved in his demand that Vermont have complete independence to choose its path. Upon being encouraged to make some proposals and receiving assurance that "it is now in the power of Vermont to become a Glorious Government under Great Britain," Allen replied that any agreement must state that Vermont could select its own governor (which, at this stage, Haldimand had not promised). On this Allen would not bend. The Vermont council preferred to stay neutral in the war and then align with the victor, so long as that power offered it a free charter. "If not," Allen told the commissioners, echoing his brother, "they would return to the Mountains, turn Savages and fight the Devil, Hell, and Human Nature at large."[27]

Sherwood was not impressed. "I told him Vermont could not accomplish those extravagant flights," he recorded in the report to Haldimand, adding, "I did not pretend to know how far these Chimeras might intimidate congress, but I could assure him General Haldimand had too much experience and good sense to take any further notice of them than by the contempt they merited." Chastised, Ira Allen calmed down and "the conversation again became warm and spirited." Yet a cordial discussion is not necessarily a productive one. Over the next several days, Ira Allen assured the British agents that he was interested in Haldimand's offer but that Vermonters were not yet ready to accept it. Many who supported the initial cause of the war, he wrote, now realized that "Congress has learned to play the Tyrant." The discussion ended with both sides resolving that a secret correspondence would continue, complete with instructions that messengers should swallow letters if they were in danger of being captured.[28]

After these meetings, Patriots grew increasingly worried about Vermont's relationship with Britain, while imperial officials grew concerned that the Allen brothers were playing each side against the other. At the end of April 1781, Washington received a letter reporting the rumor that

Haldimand had promised to make Vermont a separate province and that there was "some reason to suspect it to be true."[29] Around the same time, Haldimand sent Lord Germain a memorandum in which he noted "his suspicion that Ethan Allen is endeavouring to deceive both the Congress and Us."[30] Beverly Robinson echoed Haldimand's concerns, telling Germain that the Allens could be hoping their conversations with the British would push Congress to admit Vermont as the fourteenth state. But he added that such double-dealing was not necessarily a bad thing: "It may be well enough to suffer Vermont to play a double game in appearance till She can be aided by us, or form internal dispositions within her own limits to be able to act offensively with us." If the Allens were working within Vermont's political circles to win support for a British reunion, they needed time to do so.[31]

The matter dragged on through the spring and summer of 1781. Members of Congress expressed concern over Vermont's not-so-secret meetings with British officials, and British officials worried that they were being duped. In August, James Madison wrote to Edmund Pendleton that the controversy had been "at length put into a train of speedy decision" in Congress. "There is no question but they will soon be established into a separate & federal state," he argued.[32] Haldimand himself seemed increasingly convinced that Vermont would rather join the rebelling colonies than become a British province. But in a letter to Daniel Fay, a Vermont agent who was ostensibly negotiating the prisoner exchange, Haldimand offered words of caution. "Were that people [of Vermont] but half as desirous of a Union with Great Britain as with the Congress," he lamented, "they would now be a happy people, independent of every power on Earth except the parent one. The Congress has repeatedly denied them the Territory they contend for, and by temporizing they may fatally become the dupe of both parties; for should America prevail, they cannot suppose Congress will, in prosperity, grant what they have so repeatedly refused when their alliance would have been serviceable."[33] Vermont, he warned, might well negotiate itself out of options.

By fall, Haldimand had changed his tune, but time had run out. Acting on the advice of his commissioners, he informed General Clinton that he now believed the Vermont council was sincere in its desire to join the British. In early October, he issued an official proclamation announcing that he would negotiate with Vermont to become a British province, and he hoped this proclamation might serve to rally more support in the republic. But even the British commissioners disagreed over whether there was enough support for such a measure.[34] Matters grew more complicated after Cornwallis's defeat at Yorktown.[35] As it grew increasingly unlikely that Vermont would join the British, reports of the Haldimand discussions became widespread in Congress. Robert Livingston suggested that Vermonters had "tampered" with the government in Canada only to ensure that Britain did not attack them, and that "this has had the effect they intended."[36] But there was no immediate offer from Congress to join the union.

By March 1783 the jig was up. The peace treaty that ended the war considered Vermont part of New York (as King George III had declared in 1764). After Vermont was yet again denied recognition as either a state or an independent republic, Haldimand sent a weary letter to the Allens via his negotiators. He wrote, "While his Excellency sincerely regrets the happy moment, which it is much to be feared, cannot be recalled, of restoring to you the blessings of the British Government, and views with concern the fatal consequences approaching, which he has so long, and so frequently predicted, from your procrastination, he derives some satisfaction from a consciousness of not having omitted a circumstance, which could tend to your persuasion, and adoption of his desired purpose."[37] The British had done everything they could, but the Allens had been either unable or unwilling to convince enough members of their council to take up the offer of British independence. As Peter Onuf has argued, "Vermont was the only true American republic, for it alone had truly created itself."[38] But its self-creation mattered to many Patriots only because the independent republic fell along an imperial fault line, and there was a risk that the fourteenth American state might instead have become one more British province.

Peace with Great Britain in 1783, and the full recognition of American independence that came with it, did not mean that Americans suddenly turned their backs on the British colonies in North America. Interest in places north of the united States actually increased as these colonies were seen as the home of dastardly Loyalists and "Tories." Having secured independence, Americans now had to fashion it as preferable to the lot of those who remained British subjects. Even before the British began their official evacuation of New York in August 1783, newspaper reports and letters from congressional delegates lamented or celebrated their fate, depending on the author's disposition. In January 1783, the *Pennsylvania Gazette* reported on the travails of British subjects in Nova Scotia. "It is also reported," one article noted, "that the Indians have destroyed several of the Royal refugees, who went to form a settlement in Nova Scotia."[39] Other reports gleefully announced that ships were leaving New York, "and those who chuse to go to the wilds of Nova Scotia, or to the mountainous, barren island of Newfoundland, where for five or six months in a year the earth is covered with snow, will have vessels provided for them."[40] Oliver Ellsworth, a delegate from Connecticut, wrote to his wife, Abigail, to express both affection for his children and sympathy for the Tories. He hoped his daughter Nabby "will be a good girl while Daddy comes home" and imagined his "poor little boy stubbing about & finding Daddy's old Shooks." Either child was better off than the Loyalists, who "are gone from New York to the cold region of Nova Scotia which their royal master has provided for them."[41] In a letter to Oliver Wolcott, a fellow Connecticut delegate, Ellsworth noted that "the Tories are mostly gone from [New York] to Nova-Scotia, cursing their King all the way."[42]

Some might have been cursing, but others, especially free Blacks and the formerly enslaved, hoped to find a new beginning in British North America. Guy Carleton, who organized the evacuation of New York, kept a list of escaped enslaved people who left on British ships for the provinces in order to indemnify their owners should the final peace treaty demand it. He would not return them because Britain had promised them freedom.[43] Freedom was hardly equality, however, and free Blacks found themselves segregated into communities and churches, harassed and attacked, and left with few paths to prosperity. While prominent leaders emerged, including Boston King and David George, and Black communities did their best to support themselves and each other, many found life in Nova Scotia a promise unfulfilled. In the 1790s, hundreds left the province for Sierra Leone.[44]

While some Americans took delight in the terrible fate presumably awaiting the Loyalists, others were apprehensive about losing population and considered what might be done to attract or retain settlers. George Washington was thinking along such lines when he set down his sentiments on the peace in May 1783. He suggested that Congress consider seriously the benefits to be derived from treating settlers in Detroit and Illinois fairly. Washington was sure they could become good citizens, and such a gesture "would probably make deep and conciliatory impressions on their friends in the British settlements, and prove a means of drawing thither great numbers of Canadian Emigrants."[45] In regions where an imaginary line was all that separated citizens from subjects, crossing over to the better deal was always an option.[46] Given how hard the Patriots had worked to win Canadian favor—by means both military and diplomatic—the peace offered new ways to encourage migration south from Quebec.

A greater concern was preventing settlers within the states from relocating to British America. Fair treatment of Loyalists, set out in the fifth article of the peace, might help. "It is agreed that Congress shall earnestly recommend it to the legislatures of the respective states," the article read, "to provide for the restitution of all estates, rights, and properties, which have been confiscated belonging to real British subjects."[47] In a letter to Samuel Adams, one concerned Patriot argued that any delay in implementing such recommendations would result in the loss of "many good subjects & give the British great advantages by peopling Nova Scotia for them."[48] For those considering such a move, the publication in June of a letter from Nova Scotia offered encouragement: "The situation is abundantly provided by nature with one of the finest harbours on the continent of America, and the soil is by far the most preferable of any in the province; and the emulation and chearfulness with which every individual is providing comfort and convenience for the approaching winter, is truly laudable and pleasing."[49] Such reports posed a danger, especially in New England, with its history of emigration to Nova Scotia.[50]

In New York, Alexander Hamilton was similarly concerned about the treatment of those whose support of the Patriot cause might be questioned. Not surprisingly, Hamilton was worried about how such poor treatment would affect trade and the economy. In a June 1783 letter to George Clinton, the governor of New York, he noted "the impolicy of inducing by our severity a great number of useful citizens, whose situations do not make them a proper object of resentment to abandon the country" and establish themselves elsewhere to "become our rivals animated with a hatred to us" that would be passed along to their descendants. Settlers frustrated by poor treatment in New York would become economic rivals, and nothing could be more "unwise than to contribute as we are doing to people the shores and wilderness of Nova-scotia, a colony which by its position will become a competitor" in the fishery.[51]

Those considering a move to Nova Scotia would have to convince themselves that newspaper reports, most of which expressed staunchly anti-imperial views, were false. It was clear that the British would try to encourage migration to Canada and Nova Scotia by offering cheap lands and favorable trade. "These are Dreams, to be sure," scoffed John

Adams.[52] Many Americans, however, took the threat seriously and thus counted on the news reports to dissuade potential emigrants. Stories of settlers being attacked by Indigenous groups surely helped. Americans read of an account "lately received in New York, that a party of Indians had lately paid a visit to the loyal refugees settled in Nova Scotia, and had committed great outrages on the persons and property of those wretched people."[53] These reports were doubly effective since they outlined the dangers posed by the Mi'kmaq and Wulstukwiuk—whose efforts to protect their homelands from additional invasions relied on violence—while describing those already in the province as "wretched." At least one commentator suggested that those who moved to Nova Scotia got exactly what they deserved. A "curious anecdote" appearing in early July 1783 detailed the geographic and intellectual wanderings of an "honest and very religious man" from West Jersey. Several years earlier, this man had traveled to Nova Scotia and was detained there for over a year. He grew to hate the province so much that he could not help wondering why on earth it had been created. He was sure, however, that the good Lord had a plan, and thus Nova Scotia must serve a purpose. Time, "the great revealer of secrets," eventually answered his question: "Nova Scotia was created and specially designed, by an overruling Providence, for the dismal habitation of those pests of Society, the Tories, Refugees and Ingrates of America, where, on ground as rocky as their hearts, may they long continue."[54] Readers might have taken solace in learning that Nova Scotia, according to this pious man from West Jersey, was a horrible place designed by God for horrible people.

Neither Nova Scotia nor Quebec was godforsaken, even if those who knew little about northern North America tended to describe them as barren and worthless. For Voltaire, Canada was little more than "quelques arpents de neige" (several acres of snow). Jacques Cartier described the shores of the St. Lawrence as "the land God gave to Cain."[55] Some residents of the British provinces were genuinely miserable, and thus there was a steady trickle of settlers wandering south in the hope of securing land in the united States. In July 1783, a group of these weary settlers and soldiers, particularly those who had helped the Patriots during the invasion of Quebec, wrote to Washington and begged "leave to lay before your Excellency their sad situation," largely abandoned by Congress after having been promised "that all the Citizens of Canada who would join them should be protected and receive satisfaction for their trouble." To assist the Patriots, they had left "our little property"

and been "reduced to live like beggars." Having suffered for their support of the revolutionary cause, these French-speaking Patriot sympathizers lamented that they were now "likely to lose the small advances we
made to assist the army in Canada in 1776."[56] Washington was more than
sympathetic, but he could do little. In a letter to Congress, he urged the
delegates to remember "the Encouragements, the promises & assurances, which were published by them and their Orders, in Canada, in the
years 1775 & 6." If there were insufficient funds to support these "refugees from Canada," surely they could be given land.[57] The Patriots had
hoped to take Canada, but now Canadians were coming to them.

During the months after the peace of 1783, united States officials
were simultaneously wary that poor treatment of the Tories could send
them fleeing to British provinces, hopeful that Canada would still join
the union, and stymied over how to accommodate refugees from Canada
seeking aid from Congress. These concerns, left largely unaddressed by
the peace treaty, layered onto each other. The first concern, over the
treatment of Tories and Loyalists, was a constant theme in the post-
revolutionary era. The danger for Americans was that persecuting those
whose support for the revolution had been questionable would be, as Arthur Lee wrote James Madison, playing "Guy Carleton's game, since he
must wish to increase the Colony of Nova Scotia & diminish the people
of the U.S." Not only Carleton but the king of England himself would
have been pleased by the united States' "taking such measures as will add
to the number of his subjects & diminish ours."[58] At the same time, however, the press continued to report that Canada was suffering from poor
harvests and that Nova Scotia was a "land of misery."[59] One account, in
the summer of 1784, went so far as to suggest that the Canadians were
contemplating "a revolt from their present usurped masters and seem determined to add another STAR in the American collection."[60] But James
Monroe was less enthusiastic about taking Canada. He thought the best
policy was to weaken the British provinces by restricting their access to
the states' navigation systems and trade. Canada, he was convinced, stood
"upon a different ground in regard to us from any other part of the British Dominions." Free trade with Canada would only help Canada and
"defeat any political arrangement we can adopt respecting them."[61] In
Monroe's mind, Canada had transitioned from a desired colony to a site
of commercial negotiation.

In Canada, meanwhile, Frederick Haldimand hoped to strengthen
British resolve by denigrating the experiences of those living in the

united States. According to a report published in a Massachusetts news-paper in December 1784, Haldimand had "been very industrious in ca-lumniating the national character of the Americans." He described the independent states "as an enfeebled, petite nation, likely very soon to crumble to annihilation," a characterization, according to the article, meant to "dissipate the general disaffection to the British government which prevails in the province."[62] Clearly some of the province's inhabi-tants were frustrated, and not just French Catholics. Just a few weeks after news of Haldimand's disparagement of the American character, news broke of demands within Quebec itself for a change in government. A group of 230 inhabitants had submitted a petition based on three re-quests: the repeal of the Quebec Act, the establishment of an assembly ("in the manner as Nova Scotia"), and general improvements in the province's governance. The signers were mostly British, but the petition "is said to contain the sentiments of" the entire province. French Cana-dians had also signed, and their representatives declared that their pri-mary request was that Roman Catholics be admitted to the privileges of whatever government was formed.[63] In both the united States and Can-ada, there were grumblings about national character and government that would require significant attention in the years that followed.

A more pressing task, however, was how to handle the Canadian "refugees." John Adams, drawing on his understanding of British-American relations, had some suggestions. In 1785 Adams was serving as the confederated states' representative at the court of King George III, though he had been pressing for Congress to appoint a minister to Lon-don. It was an unenviable position, Adams observed; in a letter to John Jay in April 1785, he warned that whoever served "will probably find himself entangled in a thicket of briars, from which he will hardly get free without tearing his flesh." The issues requiring attention mainly re-volved around the terms of peace. In the immediate aftermath of the 1783 treaty, British merchants and officials claimed that the Americans were breaking these terms by refusing to repay debts, and Americans claimed the British were breaking them by not surrendering the western military posts from which they conducted Indigenous diplomacy and trade. Adams was adamant that the states should not break a single arti-cle of the treaty simply because they believed Britain had. Such a game would quickly spiral out of control. Moreover, good treatment of the Ca-nadian refugees would pay dividends in both local and international af-fairs. "If we have any thing to fear," he argued in his letter to Jay, "from

Canada and Nova Scotia, or for our whale fishery, it arises and will arise from our own severity to these people."[64] The peace treaty had made no mention of the Canadian refugees, who were now largely stateless and looked to Congress for help. Congress took steps to aid them, first by providing back pay to soldiers (or, in most cases, to speculators who had bought the soldiers' IOUs), and second by adopting the Ordinance for the Sale of Western Lands in May 1785. After a lengthy debate over how best to dispense lands northwest of the Ohio River that had been surrendered by Virginia and subsequently "purchased" from Indigenous nations to facilitate settlement, Congress adopted the resolution and published it as a broadside. Any migrants from Quebec or Nova Scotia would have been pleased to read that "three townships adjacent to lake Erie, be reserved to be hereafter disposed of by Congress, for the use of the officers, men, and others, refugees from Canada, and the refugees from Nova-Scotia."[65] In the race to people Indigenous homelands with American settlers, Congress more than welcomed immigrants from Canada and Nova Scotia.

The promise of land grants did not settle the matter. Nearly two years after the 1785 ordinance, Congress continued to receive requests for help from men who had fought for the Patriots in Canada. One such plea came from Moses Hazen, an army officer from Massachusetts whose life reflected the past decades' shifting attitudes toward Britain and its colonies. He had fought for the British army during the Seven Years' War, serving under Colonel Robert Monckton in Nova Scotia and General James Wolfe at Louisbourg. In 1759 he participated in the capture of Quebec, and after the war he settled in Montreal. His Canadian experience included several questionable business dealings and charges against his personal character. In 1766 there were public allegations that he seduced his neighbor's wife, and in 1770 he was accused of cutting trees that didn't belong to him in order to fulfill a naval contract. When war between the colonies and Britain broke out in 1775, Hazen, who by then owned property along the American invasion route, was arrested and imprisoned by both the Patriots and the British. Eventually he sided firmly with the rebelling colonies, and Congress created the Second Canadian Regiments, in which Hazen served as colonel. When the Patriots retreated from Quebec in 1776, Hazen and his regiment of Patriots and French Canadians joined them, their families in tow.[66]

Given that Congress, and not a state, had created Hazen's regiment, it made sense for Hazen to petition delegates in Philadelphia for relief.

He did so in 1787 with a simple request: "that Congress will please to recommend to the several independent states; the adoption of the unfortunate Canadian refugees from the time they left Canada, as Citizens of the States in which they reside or are settled."[67] Letters from other Canadian refugees also arrived at Congress. Five months after Hazen sent his letter, two army majors wrote to thank Congress for "the signal favours we have received" as refugees. Now naturalized citizens of New York, they were grateful that the state had granted them land at Lake Champlain. But upon surveying the property, they learned that part of it fell within a trading post not yet surrendered by the British, who would not let them take possession. They thus found themselves without a firm grant and requested additional assistance.[68] Within a few months, Congress granted "to the Canadian Refugees settled on Lake Champlain adjoining your posts one year's rations, to the aged & infirm who are incapable of providing for themselves, except rum, soap, & candles."[69] And so it went for years. Congress hoped that the states would help settle and support the "Canadian refugees," and the states (primarily New York, where so many of them took up residence) argued that Congress should do the heavy lifting. For decades after the peace of 1783, the "Canadian Refugees" in New York and other states, much like the Loyalists in the British provinces, petitioned the government to recognize their service, provision them until they got back on their feet, and grant them lands to make up for what they had lost when they fled across the border.[70]

After the war, Patriots found themselves struggling to keep the promises made at the peace. One challenge for the newly independent states was enforcing the requirement that Britain surrender forts located within what was now putatively territory of the united States. This task fell to Frederick William von Steuben, the Prussian inspector general of the Continental Army who in winter 1777–78 had whipped the forces into shape at Valley Forge. His trip to Canada in 1783 was his last official service for Congress. Washington, who assigned Steuben the task, hoped that the Prussian would secure promises from Haldimand to surrender the British forts and then tour the country from Montreal to Detroit, inspecting fort sites and other strategic places that would soon lie within state boundaries.[71]

Steuben made his way to Montreal in early August 1783, but his exchange with General Haldimand was fruitless. By month's end he was back in Saratoga, explaining his predicament in a letter to Washington:

"I esteem myself very unfortunate that I could not succeed in the business with which I was charged." He had met Haldimand, he reported, and "open'd the business on which I was sent." Haldimand informed Steuben he had no orders on surrendering any posts and had been instructed only to cease hostilities, which he had done. Haldimand would not permit Steuben to tour the forts, nor would he agree to any negotiations between the united States and the Indigenous nations "if in his power to prevent it." Steuben, obviously concerned that he not be assigned blame for a failure to complete his assignment, asked Haldimand to put his answer in writing, which he forwarded to Washington.[72]

When members of Congress learned that Haldimand had refused Steuben entrance into Quebec, they were by turns angry at the governor and skeptical of the British government's commitment to the articles of peace. "The purposes of his mission have been totally frustrated," delegates from Virginia reported, complaining that even if Haldimand received orders now, the forts could not be evacuated until the spring.[73] Even a season's delay was optimistic; others worried that Haldimand could delay any transfer of the posts for at least a year or two. Given that the peace treaty had only just been signed in Paris in September, it would take time for news of the finalized peace to reach North America. The treaty's articles on boundaries and western posts were "really a matter of much more importance in this country than it is in Europe," and given Haldimand's inaction, Americans had little reason to be optimistic about their new boundaries or their freedom to exploit trade opportunities within them.[74]

To gain a fuller sense of what was happening in Canada, members of Congress could turn to James Monroe. During the summer of 1784, Monroe traveled from New York to Montreal and got a sense of Canada's people, economy, and geography. He thought Canada held economic promise, but any benefit to Britain would have to be spent administering such a far-flung province. He reported to Thomas Jefferson that even the richness of the land from Cataraqui (now Kingston, Ontario) to Montreal and the wealth of good timber lining the St. Lawrence would not repay the costs of transporting goods down the St. Lawrence and across the Atlantic. The economics did not make sense. "If they keep up a military establishment in supporting it," he wrote, "I should think Britain would act a politic part in relinquishing it; and the not doing it satisfyes me [Britain] either has or will have other objects."[75] Monroe noted the difficulties in store for Canadian merchants given that the new boundary left important trading posts—and the valuable trade they administered—on the states' side. The people of Canada were not so unlike Americans, and yet the British were preventing free trade with the united States "lest the sweets of those rights which we enjoy might invite them to us." As a strategic matter, however, Monroe supported limiting trade with Canada. He viewed Canada "as standing upon different ground in regard to us from any other part of the British dominions; a free intercourse between us and the people of Canada can in my opinion only be advantageous to them." By denying them access to open trade, "we occasion them great difficulty." The more the British merchants in Canada saw the bounties and opportunities that lay inaccessibly on the states' side of the border, the more they would desire to join the confederation. "In the mean time," Monroe cautioned, "the acquisition of Canada is not an object with us, we must make valuable what we have already acquired and at the same time take such measures as to weaken [Quebec] as a British province."[76]

On the east coast, similar concerns about Nova Scotia's close economic relationship with Massachusetts began shaping official responses to the peace. The thousands of Loyalists who settled in Nova Scotia set about transforming its few English settlements and rapidly expanded into the former Acadian farms and Mi'kmaw homelands. They spread throughout the peninsula and down the coast, eventually demanding the creation of a new province, New Brunswick, which was carved out of Nova Scotia's southern limits in 1784.[77] In spring 1785, news of trade regulations between Nova Scotia and the state of Massachusetts circulated in the public press. Nova Scotian governor John Parr's proclamation, issued that April, complained of "frauds and impositions" and "clandestine trade" carried on by American vessels. Consequently, the governor "strictly forbid the importation of all kinds of provisions into this province" unless in ships owned by subjects of his Majesty.[78] This ban on non-British vessels was particularly infuriating for some in the united States, especially when they read stories of people fleeing Nova Scotia and settling in eastern Massachusetts. "The refugees in Nova Scotia," noted an editorial in the *Pennsylvania Gazette*, had made encroachments in the province of Maine, whose residents were "panting for a separate independence and cession of territory."[79] But as Nova Scotians pushed into state territory and Parr's trade restrictions limited the goods arriving in Nova Scotia, Americans noted the irony of these men and women "being obliged to return to the country they have injured, or starve." As more settlers arrived, the editorial noted, a simple question arose: "What true American can think of paying freight to foreigners for that relief which he would wish to send to any of his unhappy connections, while our vessels are not permitted to enter their ports?"[80] Whatever was happening in the British provinces, the arrival of refugees from Canada and Nova Scotia strained the states and raised questions about how to govern trade and migration between states and provinces.

Concerns over these refugees revealed some of the weaknesses of the Confederated Congress. With only limited authority under the Articles of Confederation, Congress could do little more than encourage individual states to welcome them and grant them land. Congress was also dealing with pressing issues that would eventually lead James Madison to call a convention to revise the Articles; the convention would scrap them entirely and produce a new constitution instead. The issues that drove these actions had, at first blush, little to do with Canada. In fact, however, the decision to revisit the Articles of Confederation was entangled within a matrix of concerns regarding the British provinces.

In the spring of 1786, farmers and poor workers in Massachusetts were reaching the end of their rope. The excitement of independence had given way to despondency about the system the revolution had installed.[81] The war had been expensive. James Otis's call for "No Taxation without Representation" helped bring forth a little of the latter and a lot of the former, and while Americans celebrated representation, they cursed the taxes that their delegates levied to pay off what Congress owed. Farmers who had raised glasses to celebrate George Washington's exploits were now drowning sorrows brought on by crushing debt, which, coupled with inflation and the role played by speculators, led to mass foreclosures. Appeals to the state for help—that it print more currency, lower taxes, or adjust regulations to help debtors—had largely fallen on deaf ears.[82] Many in Massachusetts began to organize, and their peaceful meetings in Worcester and Hatfield caused alarm among the ascendant "natural aristocracy."[83] In September, when a group of regulators (local militias formed to resist what they saw as government abuses) tried to prevent future foreclosures and debt collection by forcibly closing the courts at Springfield, Governor James Bowdoin sent in troops to disperse the crowds.[84] By December, the regulators had rallied around Daniel Shays, a former Continental Army officer whose bravery at Saratoga had earned him a commemorative sword presented by the Marquis de Lafayette. In his financial desperation after the war, Shays had to sell the for either.                                          JAMES BRYSON.

PENNSYLVANIA, ſſ.

## By the *Preſident* and the *Supreme Ex ecutive Council* of the Common-wealth of *Pennſylvania,*
## A PROCLAMATION.

WHEREAS the General Aſſembly of this Common wealth, by a law entituled 'An act for co-operating with " the ſtate of Maſſachuſetts bay, agreeable to the articles of " confederation, in the apprehending of the proclaimed rebels " DANIEL SHAYS, LUKE DAY, ADAM WHEELER " and ELI PARSONS," have enacted, " that rewards ad- " ditional to thoſe offered and promiſed to be paid by the ſtate " of Maſſachuſetts Bay, for the apprehending the aforeſaid " rebels, be offered by this ſtate ;" WE do hereby offer the following rewards to any perſon or perſons who ſhall, within the limits of this ſtate, apprehend the rebels aforeſaid, and ecure them in the gaol of the city and county of Philadelphia, ----- viz For the apprehending of the ſaid Daniel Shays, and ſecuring him as aforeſaid, the reward of *One hundred and Fifty Pounds* lawful money of the ſtate of Maſſachuſetts Bay, and *One Hundred Pounds* lawful money of this ſtate ; and for the apprehending the ſaid Luke Day, Adam Wheeler and Eli Parſons, and ſecuring them as aforeſaid, the reward (reſpec- tively) of *One Hundred Pounds* lawful money of Maſſachuſetts Bay and *Fifty Pounds* lawful money of this ſtate : And all judges, juſtices, ſheriffs and conſtables are hereby ſtrictly en- joined and required to make diligent ſearch and enquiry after, and to uſe their utmoſt endeavours to apprehend and ſecure the ſaid Daniel Shays, Luke Day, Adam Wheeler and Eli Par- ſons, their aiders, abettors and comforters, and every of them, ſo that they may be dealt with according to law.

GIVEN in Council, under the hand of the Preſident, and the Seal of the State, at Philadelphia, this tenth day of March, in the year of our Lord one thouſand ſeven hundred and eighty-ſeven.

BENJAMIN FRANKLIN.

ATTEST
JOHN ARMSTRONG, jun. Secretary.

Proclamation by the State of Pennsylvania offering reward for Daniel Shays and three other rebellion ringleaders, signed by Benjamin Franklin, 1787. Library of Congress, Prints and Photographs Division.

sword.[85] As the insurgency swelled that winter, Governor Bowdoin called in more men to put it down. Finally, in January 1787 the regulators tried to capture the Springfield armory and overthrow the state government but were repulsed. By February, volunteers led by General Benjamin

Lincoln had scattered the rebels. Shays and his followers fled to New Hampshire and Vermont.[86]

Shays's Rebellion became linked in both official correspondence and the popular press with Vermont's questionable loyalty and Canadian political influence. In the fall of 1786, as the regulators in western Massachusetts grew increasingly agitated, a now-retired General Washington—who wished only to live a quiet gentleman's life at Mount Vernon—received letters that triangulated the triple threat facing the feeble Confederated Congress. Henry Lee Jr. wrote him to say that Knox's report on the uprisings was "replete with melancholy information." Most people in the state, Lee wrote, were opposed to the government, and leaders of the regulators were seeking "the abolition of debts, the division of property and re-union with G. Britain." These "malcontents" were in "close connexion with Vermont," and, as Washington and others were well aware, "that district it is believed is in negotiation with the Governor of Canada." Put plainly, the situation was "dire."[87] Shays's connection to Vermont, and Vermont's to Canada, created the possibility of British support for insurgents. Three days later, Lee wrote to St. George Tucker: "I believe no American can entertain any doubt of the conduct which the British King would pursue was a civil war to take place among us."[88] Having just ended one war, the united States were in no position to begin another.

Concerns about a renewed conflict rippled through the northeast. In October 1786, a Massachusetts newspaper pleaded that "heaven avert the calamities of a civil war" and warned that "the recent scenes of British hostility would bear but a faint resemblance to the horrours of those that would quickly open upon us."[89] A few days later, an even more alarming report emerged from New Hampshire. "Troops are pouring into Nova Scotia and Canada," claimed the author of a letter published in the *New Hampshire Spy*, warning, "Commissioners from Vermont are, at this moment, in treaty with the British Commissioners at Montreal, to bring about a union. . . . A storm is gathering over your Republicks, more terrible than [those places] have ever experienced."[90]

Politicians were also aware of Shays's possible linkage to Vermont and thence to Canada. John Jay hoped that John Adams might pursue the matter in England. "There is reason to believe that the People of Vermont are in Correspondence with Canada," he wrote, noting that he raised the issue only so that Adams could ask questions "on your side of the water." Though less alarmist than the reports circulating in the press,

Jay nevertheless informed Adams that "some suppose that the eastern Insurgents are encouraged if not moved by Expectations from the same
Quarter," though he added, "but this is as yet mere Suspicion."[91] It was a
suspicion, however, worth investigating.

John Jay was not alone in his concerns: Shays's connection to Canada
through Vermont was a growing worry. William Grayson was "sorry to
inform" Madison that, according to rumors, Vermont was in league with
those threatening insurrection, "and that they are secretly supported by
emissaries of a certain nation."[92] In February 1787, shortly after Knox's
army scattered the Massachusetts regulators, John Jay sent Thomas Jefferson a collection of papers regarding the Massachusetts "troubles." Jay
was concerned that the uprising might not be over and even more troubled that it remained unclear just how far the Shaysites were "encouraged by our Neighbours."[93] Despite the lack of evidence of Canadian
involvement, Jay and other politicians employed loyal British colonies as
a bogeyman to explain agrarian rebellions that had more to do with the
rising debts, increasing foreclosures, and bankruptcies that plagued farmers in the 1780s.

Although politicians were cautious when discussing the likelihood of
British involvement in Shays's Rebellion, the public press freely un-
leashed accusations and stoked fears of an invasion. Many of these stories
were fanciful and included third- or fourth-hand accounts. In February
1787 the *Pennsylvania Gazette* ran an extract from a letter written in
Worcester. It told of a Captain Smith who had been told by a Captain
Rice that earlier in the week Rice had visited Mr. Dolittle, an innkeeper.
While there, Rice learned from members of Dolittle's family that the attorney general of Canada had lodged with them a few nights earlier. He
had on his person a "considerable quantity of cash, and . . . he had by
oblique enquiries endeavoured to find out the direct way to Daniel
Shays."[94] Such reports made lively reading but little else. Other accounts
published in early 1787 suggested that Shays and his men had left Vermont for Canada. "All accounts agree in this important point," exclaimed
the *Gazette*, "that Shays, with the greatest part of his leading men, are
fled—perhaps, say they, to the protection of Sir GUY!"[95]

With time, concern over Shays's whereabouts transformed into a
more general worry about how to stop Shaysism in all its forms. "Where
is Shays? —Is he in Canada, Vermont, or White-Creek?" pondered the
*Albany Gazette*. There was no ready answer. "But what in the name of
common sense is this Shays?" the author continued, for "it is Shayism (if

I may use the term) and not Shays, that is the object of my apprehen-
sions." The many-headed hydra of Shaysism took on a more expansive
geographic significance but maintained its connection to a Canadian
threat. Shaysism "is not alone, my dear sir, at the head of an armed ban-
ditti in Berkshire, in the forests of Canada or Vermont. . . . Where there
is the mock of semblance of government, without its energy—there is
Shays."[96] While British officials in Canada were often depicted as sympathetic to (if not complicit in) the Massachusetts regulation, some argued
that even the British would recognize the illegality of such behavior. In
an address to the General Court of Massachusetts published in the *Pennsylvania Packet* in June 1787, the author (writing under the pseudonym
PHILANTHROPOS) argued strenuously that the rule of law would prevail. If
Shays and his men "are fled to Canada, be assured, that on a just representation, Lord Dorchester will deliver them up. . . . No civilized nation
will protect robbers, pirates, and man-stealers."[97] At least one report
seemed to confirm that Canada was no haven for Shaysites. "How are
the mighty fallen!—poor Shays is at this instant cracking chestnuts in the
vicinity of Lake Champlain," read a letter in the *Philadelphia Freeman's
Journal.* Most of the men, the letter said, had returned home and "as far
as we can learn behave with decency and good order." For those still
"lurking on the borders of Canada, they are literally 'so warn, so wasted,
so despis'd a crew, As e'en Guy Carleton might with pity view.' "[98] Many
regulators suffered from their participation in the movement. They lost
their farms, their status, in some cases their lives. The rebellion was a
wake-up call for Congress that led Alexander Hamilton to propose a way
for Vermont to join the union and thus reduce the threat that it would
harbor disaffected farmers or reinvent itself as a British province.[99]

Shays's Rebellion and the general concern over local insurgencies illuminated one of the challenges facing the united States: its weak central government had difficulty controlling internal dissension. This fact led many
American political thinkers to consider altering or replacing the Articles
of Confederation. As Linda Colley has recently argued, violence—
warfare, uprisings, and insurgencies—are entangled with constitution
making.[100] As a war measure meant to facilitate colonial cooperation
against Britain, the Articles had helped Congress organize a coherent
campaign. In the postwar era, however, as independent states competed
with each other for commercial contracts and territory, Congress's inability to guide the direction of those states was a great cause of concern

for men like James Madison and Alexander Hamilton.[101] While much of the debate around a constitution focused on how power should be allocated between the federal and state governments, there was an undercurrent of concern over the young republic's proximity to British provinces, a tacit threat that those provinces might expand, and a worry that citizens might satisfy economic or political desires by moving to a British province or encouraging British provinces to annex territories.

Shortly after the peace of 1783, a plea "to the Public" appeared in the *Pennsylvania Journal.* "Turn your eyes, my fellow citizens! to those powers, who are your neighbours on this continent," the editorial implored. The British colonies stretched across the northern boundary of the united States, and it was unlikely that the British would soon forget their former colonies. American states "are poor, it will be long 'ere they recover from the deep wounds." If any Americans hoped that a dose of winter would transform Tories settled in Quebec or Nova Scotia into a gentler sort of beast, they were dangerously mistaken. "Will the frigid clime of Nova Scotia cool the glowing rancour of these men? No, every Tory is a torch to re-kindle the expiring flames of war," the editors argued.[102] Readers learned it was essential for the states to work together to protect themselves from the threat of British expansion.

This reasoning fueled desires for new states carved from older ones. Writing in October 1785 from Washington County, Virginia, Arthur Campbell hoped to persuade James Madison that a new state to be named Washington, "with a necessary cession from Pennsylvania, would soon become a firm barrier against any attempts from the Western parts of Canada."[103] There seemed little doubt that Great Britain "would not have many scruples of conscience about disturbing our peace," and they might go to great lengths "in order that she might get back but an inch of our territory."[104] New and old states, bound together with a common purpose, could help prevent British provinces from encroaching on American territory.

Arguments in support of uniting for protection against an avaricious northern neighbor became more prominent through the 1780s. State governments and delegates to the Confederated Congress were well aware of their precarious position, constantly reminded of what an anonymous writer from Halifax called "the unsettled, unhinged situation of the states (for which you are deservedly ridiculed)."[105] There was no guarantee that independence would succeed, and it was not uncommon for editors, pamphleteers, and politicians to remind citizens that British provinces had influence not just to the north but also along the backs of the American states. Critics of Congress could ask with a certain schadenfreude, quoting none other than Thomas Paine, "Pray, where are the men, the soldiers and patriots, who gained so much honor throughout the world—by their gallantry and wisdom—in the days of the war, 'the time to try men's souls.' "[106] To this ridicule was added the voice of a contributor writing as Americanus, who foresaw greatness for the independent states, but only if they could ward off the machinations of British officials in Quebec and other competitors. Americanus warned Americans to "be ye not too credulous; distrust the politics of your sister nations, and be industrious to pry into their cabinet secrets." Neatly foreshadowing events that would lead to the War of 1812, the author claimed that Great Britain and its provinces could "send forth hirelings, spies, and pimps ... with orders to spread sedition and sow the seeds of rebellion" while also buying the support of Indigenous nations to force the Americans "to submit to the tyrannical government that we will set over them." If they were not able to counteract such evil ploys to undermine independence, Americanus warned, then "VERMONT, CANADA, the INDIAN NATIONS &c. Will join their forces to the monster REBELLION, and drive you head-long, into the pit of POLITICAL DAMNATION."[107] The specter of Canada, the ghost of Shays, and the legacy of the Green Mountain Boys combined to great effect in the minds of those who desired a stronger federal government.

In addition to these fears was the insulting prospect of Americans choosing to move to the British provinces, or even encouraging the British government to move into neglected regions. Part of the problem was that many places within the united States fell outside the effective reach of Congress, and residents in those places were motivated more by concerns for safety and security than by any sense of political belonging. As people pushed west into Indigenous homelands that settlers called the backcountry, especially in the southern regions of Kentucky and the putative state of Franklin, they found themselves competing with Spanish settlements for access to the Mississippi. In Congress, most southern delegates pushed for full access to the river and its port at New Orleans, but opinion among New Englanders was split. Some considered access to the Mississippi less important than favorable trade relations with Spain, while others worried that backcountry settlers might surrender to the British in order to secure protections Congress could not provide.[108]

John Jay, Congress's unofficial representative in Spain, negotiated an agreement in 1786 with the Spanish crown (the Jay-Gardoqui Treaty) that favored New Englander merchants over backcountry settlers and traders. He surrendered American claims to the Mississippi in return for American access to Spanish ports. When Congress learned of the deal, however, southern delegates refused to ratify, leaving land and water rights around the Mississippi unresolved. In a letter to the comte de Montmorin, his superior in France, Louis-Guillaume Otto, the French representative to the united States, quoted a moderate New England delegate as claiming, "It would be better that an earthquake had swallowed this territory, the inhabitants of which, friends or enemies, will always raise obstacles to the political measures of the United States."[109]

Not even an earthquake could resolve the geographic and economic issues separating backcountry settlers from their eastern counterparts. "It appears that since the revolt of a County in Massachusetts," Otto continued, "all minds are struck with the apprehension that the interior regions would be joined to Canada." It seemed entirely likely that settlers in Kentucky, pulled between Spanish Louisiana and British Canada, might side with either power. To emphasize his point, Otto quoted the residents themselves: " 'It is not in vain,' say the Kentuckians, 'that nature has raised immense ranges of mountains between us and the United States; its intention was to separate us forever; our interests differ as much from theirs as our fertile plains differ from the sands of the Chesapeake; even our rivers, by flowing toward the Mississippi or the St. Lawrence, indicate the route we should take to make our commerce flourish.' "[110] If mountains and waterways divided backcountry settlers from the Atlantic states and guided them to British and Spanish territory, what could Congress do to forge meaningful connections?

Nothing guaranteed that these settlers would decide their interests were best represented by Congress. James Madison was concerned that "by degrees the people may be led to set up for themselves, that they will slide like Vermont insensibly into a communication and latent connection with their British Neighbours," which would in time inspire the British to do all they could to attract emigrants from "all parts of the Union."[111] Madison's concerns were echoed by members of the New York Assembly, meeting to discuss the possible independence of Vermont. "Great Britain," the delegates noted, "cannot but perceive that our governments are feeble and distracted, that the union wants energy; the nation concert." They feared not only Vermont's connection to Canada but the British government's plans to attract "discontents" to the dominion. "She may hope to see in this country a counterpart of the restoration of Charles the second," especially given that "the government lately established in Canada—the splendid title of viceroy—seem to look beyond the dreary regions of Canada and Nova Scotia."[112] It was a concerning prospect: perhaps Quebec's relationship with Vermont was but a stalking horse for a broader plan to retake American territories that had grown weary of independence.

Judging from letters sent from along the Ohio River, such a fear was not unfounded. One resident, writing in July 1787 from Louisville, at the Falls of the Ohio, vented his frustration over Congress's "late commercial treaty with Spain, in shutting up (as it is said) the navigation of the Mississippi River for the term of twenty-five years." This agreement had thrust politics, "which a few months ago were scarcely thought of," into the daily lives of settlers in the area. It was a subject presently "discussed by almost every person." The writer's driving complaint was the danger of forcing residents along the Ohio to depend on Spanish vessels to move their goods. In this fertile and plentiful place, where wheat production "will view with the Island of Sicily," it was unfathomable that such cultivation should be pursued for the benefit of Spaniards. "Shall we be their bondmen," the writer demanded, "as the Children of Israel were to the Egyptians?" Overwhelmed by the plight of the white settler forced to work for Spain (and without detectable irony), he went on, "Shall one part of the United States be slaves, while the other is free?—Human nature shudders at the thought, and despises those who would be so mean as to even contemplate such a vile subject." Echoing the actual enslaved people who fled when offered British protection during the Revolutionary War, the writer suggested that "in case we are not countenanced and succoured by the United States (if we need it) our allegiance will be thrown off, and some other power applied to." Great Britain stood ready "with open arms," and upon reunification with the king, the settlers would bid " 'farewell—a long farewell to all your boasted greatness'—The province of Canada and the inhabitants of these waters, of themselves, in time, will be able to conquer you." To ensure that the historical symmetry was not lost on his audience, the author concluded, "You are as ignorant of this country as Great-Britain was of America."[113]

The threat of losing settlers to British provinces—or, worse, losing settlers and land to the British empire—contributed to the decision to overhaul the Articles of Confederation. When the Connecticut legislature debated whether to send delegates to the proposed Constitutional Convention in Philadelphia, Thomas Seymour declared his support for the project because the states found themselves beset by interrelated issues. He was "fully of that opinion—that the state of Vermont was balancing between Canada and the United States," that settlements in the Ohio region were expanding rapidly, and that affairs in Massachusetts remained unsettled.[114] In each case, the British provinces lurked in the background, threatening to weaken or sever the frayed connections that united the states.

The heated debates that took place at the Constitutional Convention in Philadelphia over the spring and summer of 1787 focused on crafting a new governing document. The British provinces to the north did not feature meaningfully in these debates; instead, delegates to the convention proposed visions of how a national government would work, what shape it would take, and how the people would either accept or reject the proposed document. The Constitution contained no clause like the one in the Articles of Confederation that offered Canada immediate entry into the union. At the end of the sessions, the convention had a proposed Constitution that was presented to the individual states for ratification.

Only then did Canada reemerge, once again depicted as a threat to the independent states that could best be faced by a stronger, more centralized federation. By December 1787, Federalists (as the proponents of the Constitution came to be called) were employing the fear of a Canadian invasion to argue that only a government with the power to levy taxes and raise an army could protect the states. "Judge candidly what a wretched figure the American empire will exhibit in the eye of other nations," one pamphlet read, "without a power to array and support a military force for its own protection. Half a dozen regiments from Canada or New Spain might lay whole provinces under contribution, while we were disputing who has power to pay and raise an army."[115] Similar arguments in New York newspapers were read by citizens only too aware of their proximity to a powerful British government. Rejecting the Constitution would bring disunion, which would invite civil war and leave the state open to British invasion. "Turn our eyes to the north," warned one editorial, and "we shall find ourselves in the neighbourhood of an extensive military province of our most inveterate enemies, who are in close friendship and alliance with numerous tribes of warlike savages, whose hatchets are yet stained with the blood of our women and children."[116] Fear of "warlike savages," of British provinces, and of the return of imperial rule, was a Federalist talking point. The Constitution would not only transform a collection of states into a unified country, it would offer protection from what lay beyond that new nation's borders.

This rhetoric increased as the debates over ratification stretched into 1788, and even the southern states found themselves threatened by British Canada. A letter addressed "To the VIRGINIANS" warned readers that unlike during the American Revolution, the British were no longer fighting battles on numerous fronts. To dissolve the union, or to pursue "your own jarring interests" above those of the broader confederation, would "tempt and invite your own destruction." And who would be the author of that fate? The answer was clear: "The vast, investing province of Canada, loaded with foreign troops."[117] Anxiety over a Canadian invasion increased as one moved north from Virginia. Residents of Hartford or New Haven, casting their eyes over a March issue of the *Connecticut Courant*, were likely reassured that their state and Massachusetts had chosen wisely to adopt the Constitution. A letter from The Landholder, aimed at readers in New Hampshire, whose ratification convention had not yet taken a vote, castigated the state for not following the example of its neighbors, who had "decidedly judged the new government well calculated not only for the whole, but for the northern states." Either Connecticut and Massachusetts were wrong, or New Hampshire was. As far as The Landholder was concerned, New Hampshire faced an unenviable future should it reject the Constitution. "To prophesy evil is an ungrateful business," he cautioned, "but forgive me when I predict, that the adoption of this Constitution, is the only probable means of saving the greatest part of your state from becoming an appendage of Canada or Nova-Scotia."[118] From Virginia to New Hampshire, Americans were told that only the Constitution could prevent their being swallowed up or attacked by British forces to the north.

Those who opposed the new Constitution could invoke both the past and the future to argue against it. In either case, the Canadian experience was a useful weapon. De Witt Clinton, nephew of New York governor George Clinton, had just graduated from the recently renamed Columbia University (formerly King's College) in New York when he decided to issue a series of pamphlets under the pseudonym "A Countryman."[119] He was eager to illustrate the proposed Constitution's flaws, though he admitted "I really have not had much time to read it, or the papers about it." Like many men of privilege, he did not let this lack of information prevent him from sharing his opinion. He reminded his readers of the letters Congress had sent to Quebec in 1774, 1775, and 1776 in which Congress complained "grievously of the conduct of the rulers of our former government." Clinton was now "very much afraid, that this is the case with the new constitution men." The president under the Constitution was too much like a king, the Senate like a House of Lords, and there would inevitably be a standing army. He added, "There is another thing, our Congress told the people of Canada, that the trial by jury, was one of the best securities in the world, for the life, liberty and property of the people."[120] Yet there were rumors, he claimed, that the new Constitution might remove the trial by jury. How could Americans ignore warnings they themselves had issued to Canadians? The very threat of such an abrogation of rights was enough reason to oppose the new Constitution.

If reminders of the past were insufficient, perhaps warnings of the future could awaken Americans to the Constitution's dangers. In early 1788, a letter appeared in the *American Herald* from someone living in 1796. This kind of news from the future, as a setting for dire prediction, was popular among both Federalist and anti-Federalist propagandists. In 1796, readers learned, the president had become "KING OF ALL AMERICA," and Congress had surrendered sovereignty and government. The cause of these unfortunate events was the Constitution, whose adoption had enabled those in power to strip citizens of their rights, most notably the right to trial by jury, "the sacred Palladium of Liberty." The author lamented that "though now white with age," he was "at the time, in the vigour of manhood" and had fought to remind Congress of the importance of trial by jury. He had "produced former complaints of Congress in their addresses to the King, of his taking away the trial by jury, and of his establishing on these principles a Government in Canada."[121] Readers of this article would likely have missed the author's distortion of the Quebec Act. Trial by jury had not been revoked; it was simply not granted to a province that had never employed it in the first place. But they would have noticed that Canada was again an important foil against which to measure what a suitably American government should look like.

Many issues raised during the Revolutionary War remained unresolved when peace came in 1783. The Treaty of Paris ended the war and recognized the independence of the thirteen rebel colonies, but implementing the peace in North America and understanding how that peace would affect the future raised as many questions as it answered. People remained most connected to their state, but they also crossed borders from states to provinces. Uncertainty over boundaries and allegiances led Americans to castigate and mistrust those who chose loyalty to empire over state, but it also raised concerns about a population drain. The public press allowed American citizens to assure themselves that Loyalists would lead miserable lives in Quebec and Nova Scotia, but others worried that such places were benefiting from the arrival of subjects who, if treated more kindly in the states, might have remained and contributed to the growth of the United Colonies.

The most frustrated citizens in the united States, those who not only complained about their situation but dared to organize and push for change, were felt by many to have been corrupted by the British. Shays and those who followed the movement that took his name were desperate men impoverished by taxes, debts, land speculation, and foreclosures. Many observers, however, ignored the local causes of their grievances and tried to connect Shaysites with Vermont, and Vermont with Canada. Even if the British had failed to turn Vermont into a province, the argument went, that did not mean officials in Quebec would not help pull the union apart from within.

By the late 1780s, partly in response to the union's internal tensions, many leading citizens wanted to revisit the way the states were governed. The constitutional debates allowed delegates to focus on what they thought was necessary to ensure internal cohesion. There was no more talk of Quebec's becoming a state; instead, Canada and Nova Scotia became external threats used during the ratification debates to persuade independent states to join in a more permanent union that could unite and protect the people. The transition from united States to the United States created a country capable of policing its citizens and crafting its borders from within while protecting itself from threatening provinces without. Having created a nation, officials and citizens of the United States worked to gain international respect and recognition. While they looked to Europe, the real work began much closer to home.

# CHAPTER FIVE

# Oneida

RITING IN THE FALL of 1784 from the ruins of Fort Schuyler (formerly Fort Stanwix), deep in Oneida territory on the Mohawk River, Francois Barbé de Marbois recounted his dealings with the Iroquois chiefs who had arrived to treat with commissioners of the united States. This was not a meeting of conqueror and vanquished but a negotiation between allies who were former enemies. Breaking with the Six Nations Confederacy, the Oneida (and Tuscarora) had fought alongside the Patriots during the American War for Independence. Their chiefs were thrilled to once again see the Marquis de Lafayette, who, according to Marbois, was as popular among the Oneida as he was among Americans.

The meeting followed many of the diplomatic rituals that mattered to the Six Nations.[1] Despite the cold winds from Lake Oneida, the delegates met outside and sat on campstools or crouched as pipes were passed around. Marbois himself behaved "after the custom of the Savages" by taking "the hand of each of them" and receiving their compliments. General Oliver Wolcott, a commissioner of Indian Affairs and future lieutenant governor of Connecticut, opened the conference with a speech and then gave the Great Grasshopper, chief of the Oneidas, a "white chain of china beads" as a symbol of peace. After the Great Grasshopper repeated Wolcott's speech in their language (it had been translated by an interpreter), the chiefs conferred amongst themselves, and many "expressed their approbation by a faint grunt." What worried Marbois, however, was that the Seneca and Mohawk delegates remained silent. Even more troublesome was that they had come dressed for war: "They had their faces painted in a manner suitable to render their aspect horrible ... their chests were covered by silver plates bearing the arms of England and besides their clubs they carried bows." Also in attendance was a representative of one of the Seven Nations of Canada, who had come from Kahnawake, just outside Montreal. Marbois noted that though these Iroquois lived in British territory, they believed they were entitled to attend these meetings with the united States because "despite this dismemberment, they persist in garding as forming only one Nation." The delegate from Kahnawake complained about a lack of Catholic priests and asked the American delegates to bring him to France to discuss the matter with the French king.[2]

The entangled relationships among British, American, Indigenous, and French interests that would shape American diplomacy until the end of the century were all present in the meeting. Congressional delegates told the Iroquois Confederacy how things would go: the Indigenous nations had lost the war and thus would lose their lands. The Indigenous delegates were presented with a treaty and forced to sign it. This became known as the Treaty of Fort Stanwix, though the Iroquois refused to ratify it. Just a month earlier, a separate delegation, this one from the state of New York, had argued to the Iroquois that they were now subjects of the state and thus must treat with the governor. The battle for sovereignty—over land and over people—was triangulated among Indigenous nations, American states, congressional delegates, and Great Britain. The Iroquois were not about to abandon their diplomatic practices simply because New York or Congress told them to. Ultimately, Joseph Brant and communities from each nation of the Iroquois Confederacy would relocate to Upper Canada, where Governor Frederick Haldimand offered them lands along the Grand River.[3]

"The affairs with the Savages," Marbois wrote, "and those of the boundaries will for some time be the causes of misunderstanding between the united States and Great Britain, and the interests of the fur Trade will be a cause that will last as long as the dependence of Canada." The only outcome he could imagine was the removal of Indigenous peoples: "The Savages will serve one or the other as an instrument of jealousy between the two Nations, until politics and the natural consequences of the cultivation and the Settlements of the Europeans have entirely extirpated these unfortunate Nations from the country which they inhabit today."[4] On this point he was not entirely correct: the Indigenous powers in North America were never "entirely extirpated." American diplomacy after the peace of 1783 consisted in great measure of triangulating Indigenous, British American, and European desires and balancing them against the needs of a weak collection of independent states and, after 1789, a weak nation.

Before the United States could take its position among the "powers of the earth," Congress had to establish relations and develop diplomacy with the Indigenous nations and British colonies that encircled the American hearth.[5] Representatives from Congress cut their diplomatic teeth not only at the negotiating tables of London and Paris but also at the council fires of Indigenous homelands, where Indigenous diplomats were prepared to employ concepts of international law to defend their rights and resist settler claims.[6] In the years between the 1783 peace and the Jay Treaty (1794), Congress faced two connected challenges requiring delicate diplomacy: it had to persuade British administrators to surrender their western trade posts, as required by the Treaty of Paris, and it had to negotiate alliances with the Indigenous nations in whose homelands those posts stood. Confident after their victory over the British, congressional representatives attempted to dictate the terms of Indigenous land surrender and treat Indigenous nations as conquered peoples who had chosen the wrong side in the war.[7] This approach jeopardized the United States' chances of benefiting from the trade at the western posts. In both Europe and North America, diplomacy required a careful understanding of how Indigenous nations would continue to play the British against the Americans, how British colonies worked to influence Indigenous relations with the United States, and how these connections shaped both political boundaries and trade. Despite what American officials told themselves, Indigenous nations had territorial sovereignty and the military capabilities to defend their claims. As this reality dawned on congressional officials, they would be forced to change course and adopt the British style of negotiation and diplomacy, which treated the Indigenous peoples as the owners of the land who might be persuaded to part with it if their needs were met.[8] For the United States to define itself as a country, it first had to master the art of making peace with its Indigenous and British neighbors. Violence in this era did not signal the growing strength of the American military but failures of United States diplomacy.

In late 1784, Congress was in a shambles. Without the focus of the war effort, there were few issues around which the independent states could rally. The "common cause" that forced the colonies to coordinate their efforts during war did not extend beyond the Treaty of Paris, and members of Congress often found themselves at odds. Many simply went home. While the domestic implications of the situation did not cause immediate concern, there was fear, wrote Charles Thomson to Thomas Jefferson, that "it will have an ill aspect in the eyes of European Nations & give them unfavourable impressions."[9] These impressions mattered because so many Anglo-American issues remained unresolved. Of primary importance to American officials were the western posts, which remained under the control of British officers and traders. Despite the ostensibly definitive terms of the 1783 treaty, no British official had yet been charged with organizing their surrender.[10] Only by controlling these posts could the Americans hope to control the lucrative fur trade.

In a February 1785 letter to Patrick Henry, the Virginia delegates to Congress noted that "the province of Canada is at present in possession of the furr-trade. Our first exertion should be to draw it within the States."[11] British officials, however, claimed that the united States had abrogated the peace because laws in certain states prevented the payment of debts to British creditors, as demanded by the treaty's Article 4. American officials offered a counterclaim: why should creditors collect debts while the British retained possession of the forts south of the British-American border that they had promised to surrender in the same treaty? The entire affair, according to John Jay, was "more problematical than it has lately appeared to be."[12] This was an understatement: Jay would still be working on the problem a decade later.

The issue over possession of forts and payment of debts was communicated via John Adams, in London. In October 1785, as news circulated that the British were reinforcing their forts in Canada and enlarging their frontier posts, Adams wrote to John Jay that the surrender of any posts—if it ever happened—would likely be linked to questions of British debt collection, and possibly additional conditions.[13] Two weeks later, after an awkward conversation with Francis Osborne, Marquess of Carmarthen, who served as Prime Minister William Pitt's foreign secretary, Adams received confirmation that nothing would be done about the posts until British merchants collected their American debts. The condition left him dumbfounded. The British had first abrogated the 1783 peace agreement, he argued, when emigrating Loyalists took their enslaved peoples (or formerly enslaved peoples) to Nova Scotia and Quebec. "As the English had been first in the wrong," he wrote to Jay, "it was

Antoine Le Loup, *Vue du cataracte de Niagara, au pais des Iroquois.* The Niagara River was a strategic waterway. British forts on the American side caused concern after the Treaty of Paris. Here, the falls are noted as "Iroquois Country." Library of Congress, Prints and Photographs Division.

natural and reasonable to expect that they should be first to get right."[14] There was no separating debates over the western posts from broken promises stemming from the end of the war.

In some British circles, the 1783 treaty was only a promise of peace, whose full realization required dealing not only with the western posts but with British provinces and their connections to the united States. Adams, for his part, pushed for commercial interactions among the united States, Quebec, and Nova Scotia. In a discussion with Lord

Carmarthen, Adams warned that "those colonies, especially N. Scotia would find it difficult to subsist" without American trade. Whether those provinces remained British, however, seemed to be up for debate. Some British officials, Adams wrote to John Jay, would go so far as to "embarrass Mr. Pitt" by precipitating a war with the American states, "well knowing that it would be his ruin." He speculated that their reasoning was that such a war might bring a more lasting peace, because these officials thought "that Canada & Nova Scotia must soon be ours. There must be a war for it. They know how it will end, but the sooner the better. This done, we shall be forever at peace—till then never."[15] Franklin's argument still had legs.

American concerns about the possession of the western posts, the importance of the fur trade, and even the possible future of British colonies were only aspects of a much larger issue: how to convince the Indigenous nations that Congress had claims to territory beyond the states' boundaries. It was an issue that many officials did not know how to express without compromising the delicate world that independence had created. David Howell, a congressional delegate from Rhode Island, simply stated the reality as he saw it. "While these posts are held by the British," he wrote from New York to William Green, "the Indians will hardly be prevailed upon, by seeing only paper & parchments, to believe that the U. States are in fact the Sovereigns of that country."[16] Negotiations with Britain over evacuating the western posts were part of a series of international discussions that moved from the drawing rooms of London aristocrats to pitched tents along interior waterways. While men like Howell liked to think that Congress could gain sovereignty over territory simply by securing possession of trade outposts, the reality was that Americans would simply replace British traders at thinly scattered sites within Indigenous homelands.

In the years following the peace of 1783, most Indigenous nations viewed settlers with suspicion, and many Americans viewed Indigenous people with disgust. Opinions varied on how best to deal with "our savage neighbors."[17] At a series of meetings, delegates representing Congress imposed land surrenders on the Iroquois (1784), Delawares, Wyandots, Chippewas, and Ottawas (1785), the Shawnees (1786), and the Cherokees, Choctaws, and Chickasaws (1785–86). Each of these treaties made a radical departure from the British tradition. Rather than negotiating with Indigenous representatives to determine what lands they might sell or surrender, agents of Congress (at times in direct competition with delegates from individual states) informed Indigenous nations how much of their homelands they could keep as reserves.[18] The Treaty of Paris did little to ease American concerns about their Indigenous neighbors, none of whom had been included in the negotiations to end the war. To these nations, the idea that Britain could surrender Indigenous homelands was unfathomable.

Congress had to monitor British actions among Indigenous peoples closely, and British agents who informed their Indigenous allies of the peace of 1783 had to choose their words carefully. Guy Johnson, the British superintendent of Indian Affairs and nephew of Sir William Johnson, broke the news to the Iroquois, while Alexander McKee, representing Britain as a deputy Indian agent, traveled to tell the western confederacy, a loose organization of Indigenous nations around the Great Lakes that included members of the Wyandot, Miami, Shawnee, Lenape, and others. Both men assured their former allies that Congress would recognize Indigenous homelands in Iroquoia and north of the Ohio River.[19] There was certainly a lack of trust between Indigenous nations and Congress; American representatives grew concerned that rather than surrender to the united States, Indigenous nations would work together to challenge American authority in North America.

For the Iroquois diplomat Joseph Brant, land was a paramount concern. In late October 1784, just days after the Americans forced the Treaty of Fort Stanwix on the Six Nations, he secured from Governor Haldimand a tract of land "between the Lakes Ontario, Huron, and Erie" along the Grand River for the exclusive use of the Six Nations. Brant also intended to travel to London and ask British ministers how they might address Iroquois land losses and whether they would support the Iroquois should a new war break out between the Indigenous nations and the united States.[20] Peace without Indigenous participants was apparently not peace at all.

A worried John Adams noted Brant's arrival in London in 1785 and surmised that his presence "confirms and increases" reports that the Indigenous nations of North America were establishing a "general confederation" against the united States. Adams also suggested that Brant, along with other leading officials from Quebec, including Guy Carleton and Frederick Haldimand, had been summoned to help the British ministry decide a number of important issues, such as "who shall be governor, what form the government shall have[,] whether to give up the frontier posts," and "whether to treat with the Indians, for neutrality or alliance."[21] Local reports echoed Adams's concerns, noting a general movement of Indigenous peoples to meet with British officials either at Quebec or Niagara.[22] Rumors swirled "in conversation & print" that the British government had dispatched emissaries "to scatter the seeds of discord among the citizens of the United States." Even if this was not British policy, it was not hard for some Americans to imagine individual actors doing just that.[23] On both sides of the Atlantic, American officials viewed British-Indigenous relations with distrust and began strategizing how to win Indigenous support and weaken British influence.

American politicians could not simply wave their hands to turn the tide of Indigenous sentiment, and the government in British Quebec was not about to voluntarily surrender its alliance with the Iroquois and other Indigenous nations. When Carleton (who by then had been raised to the peerage of Great Britain and assumed the title Lord Dorchester) and Brant left England in the summer of 1786, many wondered if Adams's assumptions regarding their instructions and intentions were correct. Through diplomatic back channels, Thomas Jefferson, in Paris at the time, learned that Brant returned to Canada "loaded with Presents both for himself and for several chiefs of tribes which border on Canada." What Jefferson considered presents Brant understood as payments, both for Indigenous contributions to the war and to acknowledge all they had lost. Congress was weak, and, according to Jefferson's sources, American officials should expect "that quarrels will be fomented against them on purpose to derange their system of government." Settlers living beyond the borders of the united States risked finding themselves again under English rule or else attacked by Indigenous nations. The presence of such threats, made widely known by Joseph Brant and his Indigenous allies, damaged any effort to extend Congress's authority into the western homelands.[24]

When the Constitution created a new nation, the terms of the peace of 1783 transferred to the country as a whole. Congress now looked west with a more unified purpose, but the same obstacles to expansion remained. British soldiers and Indigenous "savagery" terrified many Americans. Congress was forced to negotiate with Britain over the fate of the western posts while also dealing with Indigenous resistance to American encroachment. By the late 1780s, leading American political and military figures were pushing to change how the country dealt with Indigenous nations. The forced treaty era of 1784–86 had only increased the likelihood of settler-Indigenous violence. Secretary of War Henry Knox and George Washington, among others, believed the United States should follow the British model of Indigenous diplomacy in an effort to avoid conflict. In a letter to Samuel Kirkland, a missionary living among the Oneida in Iroquoia, Knox noted that the practice of dictating treaties could no longer be supported. Joseph Brant had made that point to Kirkland, and Knox agreed. "Colonel Brant is right as to the principle of the boundaries," Knox argued, adding, "the idea in future of conquest ought to be relinquished, and fair purchase and optional sale take place."[25] Striking agreements that could be recognized internationally would elevate the United States' status and help bind Indigenous nations to the federal state. The Northwest Ordinance (1787) enacted this new style of diplomacy by recognizing Indigenous sovereignty and promising that the government would purchase rather than take lands.[26] In the next few years, the treaties struck after the war would be renegotiated in ways that reflected the United States' new policy. In dealing with expansion into western lands, the federal government exerted power on the margins of the nation that helped reify its authority within the states themselves.[27]

It was difficult for the Americans to understand the complex relationships between Indigenous nations and their territory, but when violence erupted it was easy to blame the British in Quebec. The Iroquois and the western confederacy, wrote comte de Moustier, the French ambassador to the united States, seemed "more disposed than ever to defend their possessions," and it was not uncommon for American traders, explorers, or scientists to find themselves under attack if they roamed too far from established settlements. Blame for many of these attacks was placed at the feet of Lord Dorchester, the governor of British North America. "It is feared," he reported to his superior in France, that Indigenous attacks "are being excited by the Government of Canada. The Americans are very inclined to think that the Savages could not form combinations to attack or to resist without foreign help."[28] The idea that Indigenous nations operated primarily as pawns for the British in Quebec colored American-Indigenous relations and elided the long history of Indigenous resistance to European expansion as well as the enmities among Indigenous nations that had complicated Euro-Indigenous alliances for much of the seventeenth and eighteenth centuries.[29] Alliances, in the Indigenous worldview, were living agreements that required constant attention and consultation and were not transferrable from one group to another.[30] British officials and Indian agents, for example, maintained their alliance with the Iroquois, known as the Covenant Chain, in the years after 1760, but British officials mistakenly assumed that Iroquois political influence extended over the western confederacy. Governor Haldimand thus assumed that his diplomacy with the Six Nations extended into the Ohio Valley. As Iroquois status declined among western nations during and after the revolution—two of the Six Nations had sided with the Patriots, causing members of the western confederacy to question Iroquois allegiance—British officials were forced to engage in more meaningful diplomacy with the Miamis, Ottawas, Delawares, and Shawnees.[31] Put simply, the British had less influence over the Indigenous groups resisting American expansion than Congress assumed. If delegates from the United States could offer attractive terms, Indigenous nations would certainly consider new alliances.

When American officials looked west, it was in anticipation of transforming Indigenous homelands into tidy settler states. Congress passed ordinances in 1784, 1785, and 1787 that established rules for territories to become states. Lands were divided and sold to speculators who could pay Congress in cash and then resell to settlers.[32] The United States government recognized, however, that these parcels were already occupied. Despite its title, Alexander Hamilton's 1790 *Report on Vacant Lands* noted that western lands would have to be purchased from Indigenous nations before they could be sold to speculators.[33] The plan to secure title from Indigenous nations in a manner that would advance "the dignity and interest of the nation" was not without flaws: squatters ignored the new legislation and simply moved in, fought Indigenous peoples, and disregarded the speculators' claims.[34] Desperate to assert its authority and finding that the Indigenous nations in the lands Congress claimed as the Northwest Territory were growing increasingly confederated against the Americans, Congress planned to launch assaults against them. To avoid alarming the British in Canada, Washington suggested sending letters to Quebec informing officials of the American plans and assuring the British that their quarrel was only with Indigenous nations.[35] These American attempts to secure the northwest were defeated twice— General Josiah Harmar's forces were pushed out in the fall of 1790, and General Arthur St. Clair suffered a similar fate in early November 1791—embarrassing the young nation but also solidifying the notion in many Americans' minds that Indigenous warriors were fighting a British campaign.[36]

In the months following the American defeats, officials fretted about British aid to Indigenous groups while citizens wondered why it was so difficult to secure the near west. After the first retreat, Washington wrote Jefferson from Mount Vernon to exclaim that "the best interests of the United States require such an intimation to be made to the Governor of Canada, either directly or indirectly, as may produce instructions to prevent the Indians receiving military aid or supplies from the british posts or garrisons—The notoriety of this assistance has already been such as renders enquiry into particulars unnecessary."[37] Jefferson, as secretary of state, began a long correspondence with George Hammond, the recently appointed British minister to the United States, in which he laid out these complaints. Hammond offered a full-throated denial: "I have it in express command from my superiors, to disclaim, in the most unequivocal manner the imputation that the King's government in Canada has encouraged or supported the measure of hostility, taken by the Indians in the western country."[38] This failed to settle the matter.

Jefferson, in reply, succinctly outlined the challenge facing Congress: the British retention of posts cut off American traders from Indigenous supplies and prevented them from establishing a peaceful relationship with western nations. Though his letter listed challenges facing the British provinces and United States—challenges shaped in no small part by the power of the Indigenous nations, which operated under their own strategies—he ended with a wish that such matters should "never be obstacles to friendship and harmony."[39] Yet there were obstacles to this friendship, particularly the American insistence—in official circles and the public press—that the government of Canada was supporting Indigenous raids and supplying chiefs with strategic information that might help their cause. Hammond answered in frustration that he had "passed over in silent disregard many malevolent insinuations upon the subject of the Indian war, which have been repeatedly thrown out against my Country, in the public prints, and have suffered their futility and falsehood to defeat the purposes, for which they might have been fabricated." But he could only hold his tongue for so long. Now that the American press "assumed as a fact" that the British supplied Indigenous nations with arms and information, he felt it imperative to remind Jefferson of his earlier letter in which he "disclaimed, in the most unequivocal manner" any such imputation. Officers at the posts, he added, had been instructed to maintain the strictest neutrality, and government officials hoped only for restored tranquility between "the Indians and the United States."[40]

The American newspapers piled on Hammond's desk contained a range of opinions concerning American-Indigenous affairs. In January and February 1792, around the time Hammond and Jefferson were exchanging their letters, Americans discussed the cost of fighting Indigenous nations, compared the relative value of treaties against taking land by force, and debated what kind of army would be required to bring the western territory under American control. Hammond likely would have read an article in the *Pennsylvania Gazette* promoting the idea that Indigenous peoples will "be either mildly reduced to the government of laws, or cease to be savage without compulsion." The author argued that "rational conviction" was a better path than "the violence of war or even the refinements of policy," as any warfare against Indigenous nations would be fought in the Indigenous manner. "It must therefore be confessed," the author concluded, "that peace is necessary, lest a certain part of the community should adopt the ferocity of those whom they resist in battle."[41] The concerns facing Indigenous nations and settlers alike tested the authority of Congress and illuminated the differences between military authority and diplomacy. Only after Indigenous nations resisted American expansion and defeated the United States army did Congress dispatch diplomats to treat for peace.[42] Hammond, along with the American literate public, would have read reprints of congressional debates on both the military and diplomatic efforts, including those questioning the need to raise an army and fight an expensive war with Indigenous neighbors.[43] Even if many Americans hoped to extirpate the Indigenous inhabitants to the west, there were those who thought the conflict promised a raft of additional problems.

Hammond likely read Hugh Henry Brackenridge's thoughts on the matter, and he may have been referring to Brackenridge's tracts in his letter to Jefferson. The son of a poor Scottish farmer who emigrated to Pennsylvania before the Seven Years' War, Brackenridge was hard-nosed and well built, with "a wit as ready as his fists."[44] Before he attended the College of New Jersey (later Princeton), where he befriended James Madison, before his brief flirtation with becoming a Presbyterian clergyman, and before he studied law under Samuel Chase (shortly after Chase's return from Montreal), Brackenridge survived attacks from Indigenous warriors in the wake of General Edward Braddock's defeat in 1755. He grew up hating Indigenous peoples and believed ardently that European and later American settlers had the right to take away their lands.[45] His "Thoughts on the present Indian War" appeared first in the *National Gazette* and then, in February 1792, in the *Pennsylvania Gazette*.

Brackenridge dispensed with the idea that Indigenous nations had a legitimate claim to their homelands by arguing that unimproved land was ripe for the taking. "Original right," he scoffed, "is like the claim of the children—it is mine, for I saw it." Even if ancestral rights were legitimate, Indigenous nations had lost their claim to their territories at the close of the War of Independence. They were subservient to the British King— "in his hand, as the tomahawk and scalping knife was in theirs"—and thus their lands were ceded by their British masters at the peace of 1783. And though he hedged on whether the governor of Canada was directly supporting Indigenous nations, Brackenridge was sure British Indian agents were acting "with the knowledge and approbation of the ministry at home." War with the Miami, Shawnee, Iroquois, and other western nations, therefore, was not just an Indigenous war but "a war with the British king under cover."[46] It was a war the United States was duty bound to fight and win.

For men like Brackenridge, the purpose of controlling Indigenous territory was not simply to assert the United States' sovereignty but to reap the benefits of the vast Indigenous trade networks that had long enriched the British provinces. According to one surveyor's report, Canadian merchants supplied Indigenous peoples along the length of the Mississippi, from Natchez to its source. These trade relations enabled the British to exert continuing influence over these Indigenous nations. Any man interested in his country, the surveyor claimed, would want to see that trade's benefits redirected toward the United States.[47] A second option, which Hamilton suggested to George Hammond, was to grant traders from British colonies and American states "a free intercourse of commerce with the Indians" across boundary lines.[48] Montreal merchants had earlier proposed this to John Graves Simcoe, the lieutenant governor of Upper Canada, as a way to soften the blow of surrendering the western posts.[49]

A related question, then, became where this boundary line would be drawn. The British had already realized that the boundary described in the 1783 treaty—drawing a line due west from Lake of the Woods to the Mississippi—was untenable because the Mississippi did not extend far enough north. According to Samuel Kirkland, the British planned to move the boundary south to compensate for the United States' inability to refund property confiscated from Loyalists. The new line would run from the Genesee or Ohio River to the Mississippi, and in return, the British were willing to surrender their western posts. The British government in

Quebec, overestimating American despondency over the failed invasions in 1790 and '91, hoped to mediate an agreement between the United States and the western confederacy over this new boundary.[50] At a March 1792 meeting to discuss this possibility, Jefferson, Hamilton, and Henry Knox voted unanimously "never to admit British mediation," and Washington later informed Gouverneur Morris, the American representative to London, that British mediation in the dispute "not only never will be asked, but would be rejected if offered."[51] American politicians, with much popular support, would rather fight on against their Indigenous neighbors than let the British intervene.

But not all Indigenous nations were in open conflict with the Americans. In a May 1792 letter from the Seven Nations of Canada (a confederacy that lived along the St. Lawrence River), the chiefs wrote that they hoped for "nothing more than peace & harmony among all nations." They promised to meet with New York officials and asked only that "you not to let your people make any advances of settlements upon the lands which we claim, at least until we shall have treated together on the subject."[52] Similar sentiments circulated elsewhere as well. Within a few days, the *Pennsylvania Gazette* reported that a "Stockbridge Indian" had recently returned from Canada with the news that a general meeting would soon be held among leading sachems from the various Indigenous nations "now at variance with the United States," with the ultimate aim of "establishing a permanent peace."[53] But peace would require Congress to rein in unruly settlers. Even as the American government had pivoted to British-style negotiations and treaties with Indigenous nations, politicians had to answer to their constituents' demands to push west. For Congress, land sales were a foundational source of revenue for the new government, and yet many Americans who poured into Indigenous homelands harbored a deep hatred of Indigenous peoples.[54]

If Indigenous nations slowed western expansion, there were fewer barriers for settlers moving north. In the 1780s and '90s, the British provinces in North America took on renewed importance for American citizens and British subjects alike. Each side viewed migration differently, with many British officials hoping to attract settlers to the British side of the boundary while American officials fretted about losing citizens. Phineas Bond, an American Tory who sought asylum in England during the revolution and returned after the peace to serve as both an official consul and representative to British merchants, hoped to exploit the challenges facing

Americans in the 1780s for Canada's benefit. "The wretchedness of the mass of people here," he wrote Lord Carmarthen from Philadelphia shortly after the Constitution was ratified, "occasioned by the reduced and precarious state of all property has inspired a spirit of emigration very detrimental to the consequence and increase of the United States." Given these troubles, "there never was a more favorable period ... to encourage the introduction of settlers into Canada from hence." He had in mind the Quakers, who seemed to have already considered moving to Canada but feared being settled on lands that they could not defend if a new rupture occurred.[55] Even without a rupture, others, such as Thomas Jefferson, saw Canada not as a place for Americans to escape the United States but as one where they might better themselves. Jefferson understood the importance of education. For learning science, Edinburgh had no equal, but to learn French, "unquestionably an important object of education," students should consider Canada. He offered two reasons for this choice: first, "the French of the genteel Canadians is very pure"; and second, living in Canada rather than Paris presented none of the threats to a young man's moral compass, health, or fortune. Moreover, a student in Canada "would be acquiring a knolege of the country and it's [sic] inhabitants which cannot fail to be useful in life to every American." Knowing your neighbor made for better Americans. "On this point I have long ago made up my mind," he concluded, "that Canada is the country to which we should send our children to acquire a knowledge of the French tongue." He saw Canada as a milquetoast France but a place worth understanding.[56]

As either a site for immigrants or a haven for the culturally curious, British Canada continued to influence the way Americans thought of themselves. Newspapers published letters from Britain deriding Canada— "so poor a province in its present state"—and suggesting that "not even national pride would deem it an object worth any great consideration."[57] These depictions became something of a sport. In 1791, London papers republished a 1788 open letter from a resident of Quebec entitled "A State of the Province of Quebec," which was then reprinted in the American press. American editors took great joy in mocking the tract's conclusion, which argued that Britain would retain Canada because, when settled with loyal British subjects, "Great Britain may always hold a rod over the heads of the American states, and keep them in awe."[58] "Alas poor Congress," scoffed the editor of the *Pennsylvania Gazette*, "A ROD from Canada held over your heads, on one side, and a rod from a great state on the other side; beware and tremble!" The sarcastic editor apparently hoped to calm the rattled nerves of his fellow citizens with his assurance that, according to the original tract, no more than three men in any given parish outside Quebec and Montreal could read and write. "This is the province which is to keep the American States in awe," he added. "*Rijum tenaetis!*"[59]

For American officials, however, Canada was hardly a joke. They took note when the British government reorganized the administration of its provinces with the 1791 Constitution Act, which split Quebec into Upper and Lower Canada and assigned each an assembly.[60] The press covered these developments and offered opinions on the new administrative structure, provided outlines of the new constitution, and printed toasts that had been celebrated in Canada after it was enacted.[61] Jefferson, secretary of state at the time, made special requests for Canadian news. He had a good source in Joseph Fay, a Vermont leader with ready access to Canada who had participated in the Allen-Haldimand negotiations, served as the republic's secretary of state, and then became Bennington's postmaster. Jefferson wrote to Fay that he would "be very thankful if you can have the Quebec papers brought to me regularly, to which I would wish to have added those of Montreal, now that they are to be in separate governments. . . . Newspapers show the temper of the country, and it will always be proper for us to have an eye on that of Canada."[62] Fay's reply, when it arrived nearly a year later, included a range of Canadian papers that he described as "begin[ning] to be more liberal, and the spirit of Liberty which rages so Vehemently in Europe begins to kindle in Canada."[63] Jefferson would have already learned from the American press that Upper Canada was developing into a promising settlement and that some in Britain did not think it was worth the cost, arguing that "the loss of Nova Scotia must follow the revolt of Canada; and we shall be fortunate in casting off an expensive and useless appendage to our rickety dominions." That Britain retained Canada at all "can be ascribed to nothing but the moderation of the American Congress."[64] As officials on both sides of the Atlantic negotiated over the western posts and Indigenous alliances, Britain's provinces were developing and, according to some reports, becoming untethered from the empire.

For British officials in London and Quebec, one way to protect provinces and Indigenous homelands from United States encroachment was to create an Indigenous buffer zone that would run along the western and northern limits of the American states.[65] It was a proposal riddled with problems, in part because it depended on both Indigenous

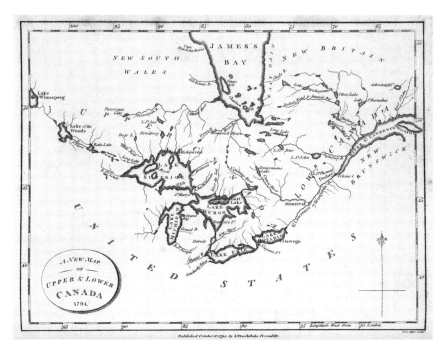

Jedidiah Morse, *A New Map of Upper and Lower Canada, 1794.*
Geographers such as Morse kept United States citizens informed
of political and geographic developments in the British provinces.
Lionel Pincus and Princess Firyal Map Division, The New York
Public Library Digital Collections.

strength and territorial surrender. Lord Dorchester, who initiated the
plan, admitted upon questioning by his superiors in William Pitt's government that the scheme was untenable along the states' northern
boundaries through Iroquoia and east toward the St. Croix. First, the Iroquois were unlikely to surrender any of their lands to create such a
zone; and second, there were too few Indigenous peoples in the lands between Lake Champlain and the St. Croix River to maintain the boundary. Nonetheless, British officials adopted the idea and dispatched
messengers to Philadelphia to inform Hammond, who by then had a better sense of American sentiments than either Dorchester or officials in
London. He used his better judgment and never broached the topic with
the Americans (who would have had to recognize the Indigenous homelands as a buffer between the settler states), effectively killing the plan.[66]

And so a second plan was hatched. This one fit more explicitly into the American narrative that Indigenous warriors and their chiefs were supported and encouraged by the government in Canada, but it relied on the hope that American officials could be persuaded to seek British mediation in their conflict with the Indigenous nations. The crux of this plan was to encourage the Iroquois, Miami, Shawnee, and other nations to demand of American officials that the British participate in settling their differences with the United States. The request must appear "spontaneous," but Hammond encouraged Lieutenant Governor Simcoe to do everything in his power to promote it.[67] This scheme also had problems: the British would never actually support open hostilities against the Americans, and it created the danger that the Americans and the western Indigenous nations might reach a peace without British participation. As Hammond informed Simcoe, American officials knew they could not afford another loss like those of 1790 and '91. They might be prepared for war, but Congress increasingly hoped to negotiate a peace.[68] Rather than provide their Indigenous allies with ammunition for their guns, British officials would supply evidence for their arguments. Simcoe suggested to Alexander McKee that the western nations receive copies of the treaties and deeds they had signed with Britain before American independence. These documents, which American officials would never supply if requested, might support Indigenous territorial claims.[69]

Congress's own tactics, meanwhile, focused on the promise of diplomacy backed by the threat of military intervention. American officials, Washington and Knox included, understood that destroying Indigenous nations could sully the United States' international standing and paint Congress as just another imperial force incapable of making alliances with its neighbors.[70] Administrators thus hoped treaty negotiations would succeed, or at least demonstrate a good-faith attempt at diplomacy, while buying time for military preparations. Convincing the western nations that the United States government believed in peaceful negotiations required just the right messengers. Over the spring and early summer of 1792, Washington and Knox invited Iroquois chiefs to Philadelphia under the premise of discussing a "civilization plan." The idea had originated with Timothy Pickering, who had experience with Indigenous nations and sympathized with their plight at the hands of unscrupulous settlers. Unbeknownst to Pickering, Washington and Knox had a separate goal: to use the Iroquois to mediate a peace with the western confederacy. It took several weeks of careful diplomacy to broach the subject, but eventually Pickering succeeding in convincing several Iroquois delegates, including the Seneca war chief Gyantwachia, or Cornplanter, to undertake the mission.[71] Joseph Brant agreed to serve on the mission even though he had refused the initial invitation to Philadelphia; he traveled to the capital only after receiving a separate invitation.[72] Citizens in Philadelphia and beyond learned almost immediately that "the celebrated Indian Chief from Canada" had been sent "to conciliate the minds of the hostile Indians."[73] By this time, Brant had lost some influence among the western confederacy because he had not immediately joined their battle against the United States. His tenuous position among British, American, and Indigenous forces caused him great stress and drove him to drink.[74] Yet American Indian agents were pleased with developments among the Iroquois and hoped they would be useful in securing peace. Other Indigenous leaders also seemed willing to support the Americans. Indian Agent Israel Chapin reported to Knox that Fish Carrier, the Cayuga chief, had promised to work for peace between the western confederacy and the Americans. "Few Indian chiefs have a more extensive influence than the Fish Carrier," Chapin noted, adding that the chief's assurances "could not but afford me the highest pleasure."[75]

Within weeks, however, Chapin's pleasure was tempered by Brant's reports that the Americans would face a significant challenge in winning over the western confederacy. Writing from Niagara in late July 1792, Brant informed Chapin that members of the western nations were already gathering at the Miami, and they seemed "determined upon a new boundary line, without which I am apprehensive difficulties will be found before a peace will be established." Emboldened by their victories in 1790 and 1791, the western confederacy felt the time was ripe to demand a favorable boundary, and American recognition of Indigenous territorial sovereignty hardened their resolve.[76] The language used by American officials at treaty meetings encouraged Indigenous nations to push for the borders they hoped to secure. The agreement between the United States and the Wabash and Illinois nations, negotiated at Vincennes on the Wabash River in late September 1792, explicitly stated that the United States would take no lands but by fair purchase. Knox instructed General Rufus Putnam to "make it clearly understood, that we want not a foot of their land, and that it is theirs, and theirs only."[77] The settlers who had been pushing into this territory would not have agreed, and the negotiators were aware that a peace treaty itself would not satiate settler demands.[78] In the northwest, the western confederacy clung to the

Ohio River as the boundary between Indigenous homelands and American states. William May, who served as a spy for the American army, reported in October that the western confederacy was organizing and sending representatives south to secure more support for a combined effort against the Americans. It was "common opinion and the common conversation" that "no peace would take place unless the Ohio was established as a boundary."[79] This demand by the western confederacy challenged American desires to open the northwest for settlement. Far from prepared for war, officials in Congress planned to meet with Indigenous diplomats and negotiate while American settlers continued the dirty work of territorial expansion.[80]

Before any such meetings could occur, members of the western nations met with Iroquois delegates at "the Glaize." Located at present-day Defiance, Ohio, where the Auglaize River meets the Maumee, the Glaize was a multicultural, polyglot site, home to British traders, American captives, and Indigenous peoples from several nations. Previously a buffalo wallow, the Glaize in 1792 nourished Indigenous resistance to American encroachment, drawing support and supplies from traders and merchants who worked the commercial routes from Detroit and Montreal. Indigenous, French, and British residents played cards, sang, danced, and maintained a jovial atmosphere. But when matters of importance to the northwestern Indigenous nations arose, the site was reborn as a diplomatic center.[81] In September 1792, representatives of the Shawnee, Wyandot, Delaware, Munsee, Miami, Connoy, Nanticoke, Mahigan, Ottawa, Chippewa, Potawatomi, Cherokee, Creek, Sauk, Fox, Ouiatenon, Six Nations, and Seven Nations of Canada convened to discuss how to defend their territories and to reaffirm their commitment to protecting themselves and each other against American invasion.

It was a large meeting, attended by perhaps 3,600 warriors.[82] One of the chiefs of the Seven Nations of Canada, remarking on the meeting's importance, noted that they had undertaken "a long journey to see you and talk to you and have lost several of our people since we began our journey."[83] The Delaware chief Buckongahelas reaffirmed the importance of a unified response to American influence. He recalled a previous council at which all the assembled nations agreed "that if any one of us were struck, we should consider it as if the whole of the Nations had received a blow and that the whole should join in revenging it."[84]

C. B. King, *Red Jacket. Seneca War Chief*, 1792. Red Jacket,
or Sagoyewatha, is wearing a medallion featuring his meeting
with George Washington in 1792. Library of Congress,
Prints and Photographs Division.

Cornplanter attended but left the speaking to another Seneca, Red
Jacket, or Cow Killer, who reminded his listeners that "the White People
are now looking at us . . . they were always the instigators of our quarrels" and encouraged the councillors and warriors to "let us now unite &

consider what will be the best for us our women & children to lengthen our days & be in peace." Cow Killer's various names speak to his allegiances, his faults, and his strengths. His more common name, Red Jacket, referred to the overcoat given him by the British, which he wore constantly. He was a masterful orator whose speeches kept his audience enthralled, evidenced by another name, Sagoyewatha, that translates to He-Keeps-Them-Awake. His less flattering name, Cow Killer, was assigned him by Iroquois warriors as a form of punishment and humiliation for tending to a cow he had slaughtered rather than joining other warriors in a battle.[85] In his speech at the Glaize, which he offered along with a belt of wampum (a decorative bead and leather belt meant to symbolize and record the message), Sagoyewatha recounted the Indigenous contribution to the American War for Independence, after which the British king "desired us to speak to the Americans for as advantageous a peace as we would get for ourselves."[86] The conference held at the Glaize was part of that process.

Many speakers at the conference were inspired by their relations with the British. Cochenawaga, one of the Seven Nations chiefs, spoke of "our Father the King" who "has always desired us to be of one mind and have but one heart and to unite ourselves firmly together for our general interests & safety." The Americans, by contrast, "want to take our country from us."[87] Suspicion of the Americans also led delegates to chastise the members of the Six Nations who visited Philadelphia and who had come to the council with "a bundle of American speeches under your arm."[88] The Iroquois, Sagoyewatha among them, reassured the assembled delegates that their meetings with United States officials had not altered their dedication to a unified Indigenous cause. "Whatever you may determine on, with regard to a Boundary line, as we have now united ourselves with you, we shall join you heartily in representing to the United States."[89] If this statement was meant to reassure the western confederacy, it did not.

The reply given the Iroquois by other nations was simple, logical, and cutting. A Shawnee chief, Messquakenoe, or Painted Pole, collected the wampum that Red Jacket had spoken over and threw them back at the Seneca's feet.[90] How could the Iroquois have heard nothing from officials in Philadelphia but concern for Indigenous peoples when two armies had been sent to decimate the western confederacy? Had the Americans' speeches "so much intoxicated and blinded you, that your sight could not reach so far as where we are now sitting?" The delegates refused to surrender any additional lands to the Americans, given that the Great Spirit "who governs all things on this Earth" looked "on us with as much or perhaps more compassion than those of a fairer complexion." In the matter of protecting their homelands, the chiefs of the western confederacy were adamant. "You know very well the boundary that was made between us and the English & Americans when they were as one people," said one chief. "It was the Ohio River." The Iroquois, he continued, must return to the Americans and inform them "that the boundary line then fixed on is what we now want and that is the determination of all the Nations present, yours as well as ours." The Iroquois delegates thanked the western nations for their speeches and promised them that the Iroquois joined them in putting "our heads together" and removing American settlers from Indigenous homelands.[91] As American forces regrouped and planned a new attempt to take territory beyond the Ohio, dozens of Indigenous nations hoped to build on their victories of 1790 and 1791 to reclaim lands lost to the United States—by diplomacy if possible, by war if necessary.

The conference at the Glaize concluded with the western confederacy agreeing to meet with United States' delegates the following spring at the Sandusky River, which flowed into Lake Erie. These negotiations were an opportunity for the Americans to treat with the Indigenous nations, avoid war, and establish a peaceful coexistence. The Iroquois delegates complicated matters, however, when they later summarized the Glaize meeting to American officials. The report that made its way to Philadelphia did not clearly indicate the western confederacy's insistence on the Ohio River as the boundary of white expansion.[92] By another channel, Cornplanter informed Anthony Wayne, a general whom Washington had tasked with leading a campaign against the western nations, that he and other delegates hoped to persuade the western nations to come to a peace. Cornplanter emphasized that while the Americans might consider themselves the fathers of their Indigenous neighbors, the familial relations were reversed in the minds of the Miamis and their allies. The western nations, he explained, "wish it to be considered that they were the first people the Great Spirit seated on this island, for which reason [they] look on the Americans as children."[93] The western confederacy was not prepared to accept a subservient position.

As the months passed, Indigenous and American forces prepared for a meeting but increasingly expected a war. In an August 1792 letter published in the *Pennsylvania Gazette*, a trader just back from Canada said he expected that "another battle with the hostile Indians will inevitably take place soon." He had encountered "several Indians from the hostile tribes," including members of the Shawnee, who were "exasperated at the insults offered by some of those out-lawed vagrants who have fled from justice and took up their abode on the frontiers."[94] A western confederacy that demanded a boundary on the Ohio River, was enraged by settler encroachment, and remained convinced that Americans were but the younger siblings in North America did not portend well for a peaceful resolution to the negotiations.

With peace hanging in the balance, British officials worked to maintain their influence among Indigenous nations while limiting that of the Americans. Though the Washington administration had rejected Lieutenant Governor Simcoe's offers to mediate negotiations with the western confederacy, Congress hoped to secure supplies and gifts in Canada that they might more easily ship to the northwest in preparation for the conference. Henry Knox wrote to the western confederacy, "The United States will endeavour to furnish by the way of Canada and the Lakes, a full supply of provisions during the Treaty."[95] On the advice of Joseph Brant and Colonel Butler, one of his Indian agents, Simcoe wrote to George Hammond that he "must decline the giving permission to the Agents of the States, to purchase Provisions in this Colony for the supply of the Indian meeting." Not only had Simcoe already ordered supplies to be sent to the western nations, but there was, according to Brant, a concern that if the Americans provided supplies for the meeting, the western nations "would feel themselves less independent."[96] For Simcoe, provisioning the Indigenous peoples was a worthwhile expense if it kept those nations allied more closely to the British than the Americans.[97] Though Congress certainly viewed Simcoe's refusal as a setback, the president's cabinet voted to forge ahead with the negotiations.[98]

Simcoe was not totally unwilling to help the Americans, but his actions often frustrated officials in Washington and fueled their belief that the British controlled Indigenous policy. He agreed to send British agents to help explain Congress's offers to the western confederacy when they next met in the early summer of 1793 at the Sandusky River, though Henry Knox foresaw problems with such an arrangement.[99] In May 1793, the United States commissioners—Benjamin Lincoln, Timothy Pickering, and Beverley Randolph, accompanied by a large retinue—arrived at Navy Hall (now Niagara, Ontario) en route to the conference. Two commissioners had some experience in Indigenous diplomacy. Pickering had spent three months with the Seneca in New York in 1790, and Lincoln had been part of a peace commission sent to the Creeks in 1789.[100] During their sojourn at Navy Hall, where the Americans spent weeks as Simcoe's "guests" but felt more like his prisoners, Simcoe and the commissioners learned about a meeting between Joseph Brant and members of the western confederacy who were en route to the Sandusky, held at the rapids of the Maumee River in the late spring of 1793. What the commissioners heard did not augur well for the upcoming negotiations. Although Brant and the Iroquois had lost influence with the western confederacy, members who lived closer to Upper Canada—the Ojibwa, Ottawa, and Potawatomi—supported Brant's push for a negotiated boundary with the United States north of the Ohio River. The more militant Shawnee, likely encouraged by the British, did not. A split in the confederacy was emerging, but there was no indication that the western nations would budge from their demand for a boundary on the Ohio River.[101] The United States officials once again saw Simcoe's hand in this development. There had been rumblings by at least one Mohawk resident at the Grand River reserve "that Governor Simcoe advised the Indians to make Peace; 'but not to give up any of their lands.'" The Americans reiterated to Simcoe that they genuinely wanted peace with the western confederacy and that they would offer ample compensation for the lands where their citizens had settled. But the Ohio as a boundary was a nonstarter.[102] The British goal, Simcoe informed the commissioners, had always been to unite the Indigenous nations so that "the real wishes of the several tribes may be fully expressed." He warned that Indigenous "jealousy of a contrary conduct in the agents of the United States, appears . . . to have been deeply impressed upon the minds of the confederacy."[103] As to the Mohawk claim that Simcoe had cautioned them not to sell their lands, "that cannot be true, the Indians not having as yet applied for his advice on the subject;—and it being a point of all others on which they are the least likely to consult a British officer."[104] It was a half answer and partial denial at best.

When Joseph Brant and an Indigenous delegation arrived at Niagara to begin preliminary discussions with Lincoln, Pickering, and Randolph, they downplayed their attachment to the Ohio boundary. Claiming to speak on behalf of the confederacy, Brant raised other concerns. First, he wanted to know why there was "so much the appearance of war" within a day's trek from the Lower Sandusky. General Anthony Wayne was clearing roads and constructing forts in preparation for his campaign in the northwest, and this had not gone unnoticed. Second, Brant asked if the commissioners were "properly authorized to run and establish a new boundary line between the lands of the United States, and of the Indian nations."[105] When the commissioners replied the following day, they began by repeating what Brant had said to them, a tradition of Indigenous diplomacy that ensured each side understood the other. They also offered their response using Indigenous terms and symbolism, showing their understanding that the form of diplomacy mattered. Their "Great Chief" (Washington) and "Great Council" (Congress) would never order "their warriors" to make war while treaty negotiations were underway. They assured the delegates that they were authorized to create a border, and they emphasized that both sides would have to make concessions to come to a mutually satisfactory agreement.[106] Both sides expressed an interest in settling matters at their next meeting.

The American commissioners left Navy Hall for Detroit (en route to the Sandusky) and met with a new delegation on 30 July. It was an inauspicious meeting. The delegates, revealing the cracks in the confederacy, informed the American commissioners that Brant and the others sent to Niagara had not fully explained the western confederacy's position. To clear up any misunderstanding, the delegates gave the Americans a written communication:

> Brothers: you know very well that the boundary line, which was run between the white people and us, at the treaty of fort Stanwix, was the river Ohio. Brothers: If you seriously design to make a firm and lasting peace, you will immediately remove all your people from our side of that river. Brothers: we therefore ask you, are you fully authorized by the United States to continue, and firmly fix on the Ohio river, as the boundary line, between your people and ours?[107]

It was the beginning of the end. The commissioners tried to explain that they could never agree to maintain the Ohio boundary. They outlined the sizeable payments Congress was willing to offer the western confederacy to secure rights to the lands north of the river, where settlers had pushed into homelands. The western delegates turned the economics of the situation against the Americans. "We know these settlers are poor, or they would never have ventured to live in a country which has been in continued trouble ever since they crossed the Ohio," one delegate said. He continued, "Divide, therefore, this large sum of money, which you have offered us, among these people, and we are persuaded, they would most readily accept of it, in lieu of the lands you have sold them."[108] While this option might appease the settlers, it would never satisfy an American government intent on pushing west to the Mississippi.

It didn't take long after the failure of this conference for American officials to begin insinuating that Simcoe and the British were working to derail the negotiations. They simply couldn't comprehend that the western confederacy had its own aims and that British influence was the result of overlapping goals, not unilateral instructions. George Hammond tried to nip these claims in the bud, but to little avail. He complained to Jefferson of "those assertions, which have been lately disseminated with more than usual industry through the public prints in this country, that the Western posts have been used by the government of Canada as the medium of supplying military stores to the Indians now engaged in war with the United States."[109] By late summer 1793, some in the United States seemed resigned to the idea that the Indigenous alliance with the British could be weakened only through war. "No people under heaven," wrote the Connecticut surveyor Medad Mitchell, "are so capable of Trading with Savages, as those Canadians," who have "more influence with the Savages, than any other people or Government whatever."[110] Connections with traders and the British government had emboldened the western confederacy to stick to their demand for a boundary at the Ohio. "Consequently," Jefferson reported to Thomas Pinckney, the United States representative to Britain, "the war goes on, and we may expect very shortly to hear of General Wayne's advance towards them."[111] Several weeks later, Jefferson informed Pinckney that the negotiations with the western confederacy had completely failed. "We expected nothing else," he continued, "and had gone into the negociations only to prove to all our Citizens that peace was unattainable on terms which any one of them would admit."[112] Unable or unwilling to view Indigenous nations as sovereign actors, United States diplomats gave way to the hawks. Around the American hearth, the embers of conflict were set to reignite into war.

By early 1794, Lord Dorchester, the governor of Canada, also believed that only a war could settle the boundaries between British colonies and American states. In a letter to Indigenous delegates from Canada and the Great Lakes region, he lamented the failures of the Lower Sandusky conference by recalling that he had promised to help his Indigenous allies satisfy their desire for an acceptable boundary. He had hoped that Britain and the United States could settle this issue, but he informed his "Children" that "I have waited long and listened with great attention but I have not heard a word from them." In a more ominous declaration— which would catch the attention of American politicians and citizens— Dorchester told the Seven Nations that given the Americans' behavior, "I shall not be surprised if we are at war with them in the course of the present year and if we are, a line ought then be drawn by the warriors." If that happened, American settlers would not be tolerated on Indigenous lands. "The people must all be gone who do not obtain leave to become the King's subjects," the governor assured his allies, continuing, "What belongs to the Indians will of course be confirmed and secured to them."[113] Such statements could not fail to raise the ire of American officials. In May, Washington sent to Congress "sundry papers" that he believed would explain the poor relations between the United States and the Six Nations. Among these papers was a report from Israel Chapin, the United States agent to the Six Nations, to Henry Knox, in which Chapin complained that "the inflammatory speech of Lord Dorchester" to the Six Nations had "induced them to give up" friendly intentions toward the Americans. In Chapin's reading of events, British representatives "took pains, on all occasions, to represent a war between [the British] government and ours, as inevitable."[114]

It wasn't long before Dorchester's speech to Indigenous representatives appeared in the American press. Over two weeks in late May and early June, Edmund Randolph and George Hammond engaged in a testy exchange over its context and content. "If it was a part of the American character to indulge in suspicion," Randolph wrote to the British representative, "what might not be conjectured as to the influence, by which our treaty was defeated in the last year, from the assembling of deputies from almost all the nations, who were at the late general council on the Miami; and whose enmity against us cannot be doubtful?" Randolph quoted Dorchester's declaration that war might come within a year and that a new boundary would be drawn by warriors, a sentiment, he charged, that "only forebodes hostility." Reports that Simcoe had gone to the foot of the rapids on the Miami to build a fort, moreover, were "if true, hostility itself."[115] Randolph concluded his letter with assurances that Americans desired peace but that an invasion would be repelled by force. Hammond was not pleased, either with Randolph's tone or his choice of evidence. Putting aside the affront of Randolph's style, Hammond illuminated the American secretary of state on the substance of Dorchester's message. "But in order to ascertain the precise sense of the only passage of that speech, to which you have referred, and of which you have given merely a partial citation," he chided, "I shall quote the passage at length."[116] Which he did.

Readers of the *Pennsylvania Gazette* were thus informed "that Lord Dorchester was persuaded, that the aggression which might eventually lead to a state of hostility, had proceeded from the United States."[117] As to Randolph's claim that Simcoe was headed to the Miami, Hammond had "no intelligence that such an event had actually occurred." And if it had, context and the location of the fort would determine whether such an act was hostile. If Simcoe was protecting His Majesty's residents at Detroit, or if he was preventing "that fortress from being straitened by the approach of an American army," the principle of "the status quo . . . will strictly apply."[118] The astute American reader would surely have noted that local tensions were shaping international affairs.

A few weeks later, the press reported that even Congress's Indigenous allies were relocating to Upper Canada, which was hardly a promising sign. The *Pennsylvania Gazette* described how "the British lions of the north" had persuaded the "tawny sons of cruelty" to quit their country. As the Onondaga were preparing to leave for Canada, Major Moses De-Witt, a twenty-eight-year-old soldier, offered a speech that he thought might change their minds. DeWitt, who admitted that he was "a young man, not much used to speaking in public," told the Onondaga, "You are misled, and about to destroy your nation." Why would they want to leave their homelands? He presumed "some birds of false report must have passed through your country, and disturbed your minds" and cautioned the Onondaga not to listen to rumors. He then promised that he would help right any wrongs and supply desired provisions. Kyadatagh, a chief of the Onondaga, offered pleasantries, reassured DeWitt that he and his people were merely traveling to visit relations, and promised they would return in a month. DeWitt might have wondered why, if the trip was to visit kin, the Onondaga were bringing "all their heavy kettles" and "moveable property."[119] The answer came soon enough. A second letter accompanied DeWitt's plea, this one from Oneida chief Skenandoa, outlining what had caused the Onondaga removal. Fish Carrier, the Cayuga chief who two years earlier had promised Israel Chapin he would work for American peace, had sent letters to the Six Nations and requested

GENERAL WAYNE.

Edward Savage, *General Wayne* (Anthony), 1796. Mezzotint engraving,
black and white, 37.6 × 27 cm (14 13/16 × 10 5/8 in.), Mabel Brady
Garvan Collection, 1946.9.914. Yale University Art Gallery. Unlike Harmar
(1790) and St. Clair (1791), Wayne's forces succeeding in defeating the
western confederacy and facilitating American western expansion.

that they relocate to Buffalo Creek (present-day Erie County, New York). He warned the Iroquois that "trouble would soon come upon them if they continued there any longer."[120] While Americans were planning their attack in the northwest, many of the Iroquois were preparing for conflict to spread to their homelands. For both Indigenous nations and the Americans, the enemy was hydra-like, and so were the theaters of conflict.

As the Iroquois removed themselves to Buffalo Creek, American officials grew concerned that the British would join the western confederacy in resisting the United States army in the northwest. In a letter to John Jay, Edmund Randolph lamented that "the reports of a determination in the British to abet the Indians grow daily more and more serious." The Indigenous nations in the northwest still insisted on the Ohio River as the boundary between homeland and American territory, and they were willing to fight for it. "There is great reason to apprehend," Randolph continued, "that British troops will be found mixed with the Savages, who are prepared to meet General Wayne."[121] By the summer of 1794, however, the British were fighting a new European war against France and were loath to confront the Americans directly. The western nations, aware that an attack was coming, prepared by sending away women, the elderly, and children. Chief Open Heart, an Ottawa, remembered the scene after the fact: "Canoes were loaded to descend the river; ponies were laden with packs and the smaller children were hastily conducted over the trails . . . old women, burdened with immense packs strapped to their shoulders, followed their retreating families with all the haste their aged limbs would permit."[122] In late August, when General Wayne's troops engaged the western confederacy at Fallen Timbers, the only British troops in the vicinity remained inside Fort Miami, and when the battle turned against the confederacy they refused to open the gates to admit their Indigenous allies.[123] Wayne's victory opened the lands northwest of the Ohio River to American expansion. It was a stinging defeat for the western confederacy and for the promise of American domestic diplomacy.

In the twelve months between the United States' victory at Fallen Timbers and the Treaty of Greenville, signed in August 1795, American officials remained wary that the British in Canada were working to prevent the western confederacy from signing any new agreements. Winning a battle was not the same as securing rights, and it was the land that the

Americans needed.[124] Two months after the battle, Anthony Wayne was busily improving his fortifications on the Miami, which would become Fort Wayne. The British surrendered Fort Miami in 1796. A Canadian prisoner taken at Fallen Timbers swore under oath that Simcoe, Colonel McKee, and "the famous Captain Brandt" were "tampering" with the chiefs of the western confederacy to deter them from signing an agreement. Wayne hoped to counteract these measures by sending agents of his own, but he also knew that the United States must appear as though it were ready for a broader war.[125] News improved for the Americans as the weeks went by. In early November, reports arriving on Wayne's desk informed him that many of the "hostile Indians" were crossing the Mississippi. The British hadn't been seen near any of the American advanced posts, but they had occasionally dropped handbills calling on "all Loyal and Gallant Subjects" to join the Queen's Rangers, which had caused some desertions among U.S. troops.[126] But Simcoe and Brant had been busy, at least according to a Wyandot who informed Wayne that his nation had been prepared to sign a treaty with the Americans until the British lieutenant governor and Mohawk chief convinced his people to treat with the British at Detroit instead. At this meeting, Brant encouraged the chiefs to launch one last attack against the Americans, this time with Iroquois support. In November, when Wayne received this testimony, the Wyandot were weighing their options: peace with the Americans or an alliance with the British and the Iroquois.[127] As 1794 drew to a close, the Americans could take comfort in having defeated their Indigenous enemies in battle, but their efforts to secure a diplomatic peace were thwarted at every turn by British officials, who could still influence the Iroquois and the western nations to keep fighting for their homelands.

A major thorn in the American side was Edmund Burke, not the politician and essayist but a priest. An Irish Catholic who arrived in Canada in 1786, Burke taught mathematics and astronomy at the Seminary of Quebec, but he much preferred the pulpit to the ivory tower. In 1791 he received a pastoral charge, and by 1794 he was the vicar general and superior of the Missions of Upper Canada.[128] He worked assiduously to repress any republican sentiments in the Fort Miami region, a task that included keeping Britain's Indigenous allies from getting too close to the Americans. "This caitiff renegade Irish Priest," Wayne fumed to Pickering, "has lately been appointed Vicar General of Upper Canada, & was sent from Quebec, late last fall in order to try the effect, or trick of priest craft, in poisoning the minds of the Indians . . . to dissuade them from

*Indian Treaty of Greenville*, 1795. Inv. No. 1914.1. Chicago History
Museum, ICHi-064806.

treating with the United States."[129] He suggested that Pickering send a
letter to Lord Dorchester asking the governor "to co-operate in every
proper measure to promote a lasting & good understanding between
Great Britain & the United States of America."

What Wayne really meant was that Dorchester should give "the
most pointed orders to Colo McKee, to Father Edmd. Burke &c to for-
bear in future the nefarious measures they are now practiceing to stimulate the Savages to continue the War."[130] By May 1795, Secretary of State
Randolph was pressing George Hammond on the issue. He sent Hammond a copy of Burke's letter to the Wyandot and asked him to bring it
to Dorchester's attention. Randolph hoped it would be made clear to
Dorchester that "an attempt to dissuade those Indians from treating with
the United States, is not conformable with the views, which he has pro-
fessed."[131] The western confederacy could make up their own minds. The
defeat at Fallen Timbers and the British refusal to offer shelter at Fort
Miami were clear indications that the resistance would have to enter a

new phase. For the moment, they could not continue fighting the Americans. By summer 1795, the dispirited members of the confederacy had all entered into separate agreements with the United States. At the Treaty of Greenville, members of the western confederacy surrendered 25,000 square miles of their homelands in return for $25,000 and no more than $1,000 a year for each nation.[132] The Americans had crossed the Ohio and intended to keep going.

In charge of a weak country hoping to enjoy the benefits of Indigenous trade that had so long flowed to the French and then the British, American officials found themselves unable to imagine a world in which negotiation and fair dealings could avert the horrors and expenses of military engagement. It is thus ironic that General Wayne's campaign against the western confederacy came just months before John Jay signed the Treaty of Amity, Commerce, and Navigation (the Jay Treaty), which signaled the United States' arrival as a nation worthy of international repute. By the treaty, the British agreed to surrender their western posts by 1796, and traders from both British colonies and the United States were allowed to cross the border to trade with Indigenous peoples. Yet by their inability to master Indigenous diplomacy, Congress had made enemies of the very nations with which they hoped to trade.

# CHAPTER SIX

# Portage

THE TREATY OF GREENVILLE hardly resolved the issues with Indigenous nations, but it gave United States officials enough breathing room to consider their own nation's identity generally and its relationship to the British provinces more specifically. In March 1794, President Washington enlisted the help of George Clinton in New York. "It appears important to me," Washington wrote, "to know the present state of things in upper and lower Canada." He requested information on demographics, Canadians' sentiment toward their government, and perhaps most important, "what part they would be disposed to act if a rupture between this Country & G. Britain should take place."[1] Clinton replied within a week with details about the defenses in Lower Canada, his uncertainty about troop numbers in Upper Canada, the poor state of that province's defenses, and the construction of a new fortress at "Torronto (now called the City of York)."[2] Washington might have learned about French Canadian sentiments from the American press, which often was overly enthusiastic about a war. The *Pennsylvania Gazette* reported that residents in Lower Canada were armed, ready to rebel against their government, and only waiting for assistance from the United States.[3] These public reports were supported by private letters sent to Washington. Secretary of State Edmund Randolph, relying on information gathered from his connections in Vermont, wrote Washington that "the great body of the people are nearly ripe for a revolution, and that the Government is in fear of them."[4]

YORK, on LAKE ONTARIO.

York, Upper Canada, later Toronto, as it appeared in the early nineteenth century. Library of Congress, Prints and Photographs Division.

It was a line of argument taken from 1774, and it had not aged well. In the final decade of the eighteenth century, as some in the United States worked to formulate a shared identity among the country's citizens, Great Britain and France fought wars that only indirectly involved North America but that had an outsized influence on how Americans and British North Americans understood their broader connections. For Americans, the creation of a national character faced significant challenges from the revolution in France and from the persistence of British North America. As citizens and officials in the United States came to terms with the revolution in France, old concerns about European territorial interests in North America reemerged. Foreign intrigue and domestic legislation positioned British Canada as both a target and resource. To complicate matters, many Americans, especially in the northern states, saw the British provinces as an opportunity for a new life or as a standard against which the American character could be measured. Imperial wars ensured that Americans paid close attention to their northern neighbors, while turmoil at home and abroad hindered the growth of a specifically American identity so long as British North America offered an alternative.

Well before the Battle of Fallen Timbers secured the Ohio River Valley
for the United States, Jedidiah Morse was trying to secure an income
that would help him promote the idea of an American nation. The son of
a Connecticut Congregationalist deacon, Morse graduated from Yale
College in 1783, just as Great Britain and the united States were finaliz-
ing their peace treaty. In 1784, teaching at a New Haven school for girls,
he found himself without a suitable geography textbook for his students.
So he wrote one, *Geography Made Easy*, intended for students dealing
with Connecticut's transition from imperial colony to independent state.[5]
Like many geographers, Morse hoped that maps and a sense of place
would inspire students and citizens to believe in a political project. There
was not yet a United States in 1784, but rather a union of sovereign
states hoping that a federation would help them deal effectively with European monarchies and Indigenous confederations.[6] Morse's efforts
helped Americans think more clearly about what connected the newly
independent states and what common traits might help craft a national
ethos. *Geography Made Easy* included Amos Doolittle's *A Map of the
United States of America* for reference. Doolittle's map, one of the first to
depict the independent states after the peace of 1783, is an uneven effort
that shows more than the putative "United States of America."[7] Canada,
Nova Scotia, and labels indicating Indigenous homelands dominate its
top third. In details, fonts, size, and coloring, these British provinces are
indistinguishable from the American states. And the title is a misnomer:
this was a map of the united States and British provinces, not the United
States.

While *Geography Made Easy* eventually brought him wealth, the book
initially didn't do much to pay Morse's bills.[8] In letters to his father, he
expressed both pleasure at his textbook's brisk sales and anxiety that
these sales were not bringing in enough money. "My geographies sell beyond my most sanguine expectations," he wrote in early 1785, noting
that purchasers had snapped up over three hundred copies in less than a
month. In fact, "they could not bind them so fast as they were wanted
here."[9] By spring, however, Morse's excitement over sales was tempered
by his difficulties collecting payment. He sold over seventy books in one
day but took only partial payment for them. "If I had the money for all I
have sold I believe I should have nearly enough to pay all my debts," he
lamented, "but money is very scarce."[10] Three weeks later he repeated his
complaints and noted that his creditors were calling but his debtors were
quiet. He asked his father, "Do you sell any books or is there no

Amos Doolittle, *Map of the United States of America*, 1784. Published in
Jedidiah Morse's *Geography Made Easy*, this map of "the United States"
includes Canada and Nova Scotia, largely indistinguishable from the
independent American states. Beinecke Rare Book and Manuscript Library,
Yale University.

money?"[11] These money concerns only added to his anxiety over the
book's reception. He confided to his father that "a prophet, & probably a
geographer, is not without honor [save] in his own country & among his
own kindred," and he was happy to have not yet "had the mortification to
hear any remarks of the unfriendly or depreciating kind."[12]

The actual geography of the united States remained a hotly contested topic. Perhaps the best example of this uncertainty was the dis-

puted boundary between Massachusetts and New Brunswick, a subject that stymied British and American officials as they attempted to craft a post-revolutionary relationship that balanced territory, Indigenous relations, and trading rights. At all points of the compass, American states faced territorial challenges. Down east, where the Maine settlements bled into Indigenous homelands—which were threatened equally by British settlements and American expansion—the problem was focused on the location of the St. Croix River. There were several rivers that might be considered the St. Croix because geographers before Morse hadn't been very exact.[13] The governor of New Brunswick, Thomas Carleton, asserted that the actual boundary was the Schoodic River because Loyalists had built a settlement there.[14] It was the southernmost limit of the British province, in other words, because it was the southernmost limit of British settlements. No fan of such tautologies, John Jay reported to Thomas Jefferson, "The English give us some trouble on our eastern borders . . . and they wish to extend their jurisdiction to lands actually held by Massachusetts."[15] Morse's inclusion of British provinces in his American geographies (including Doolittle's map) encouraged his readers to think continentally, but his lack of detail on subjects like the location of the St. Croix River did little to help officials draw enforceable borders.

Geographic confusion abounded in the 1780s, as British and American officials attempted to draw lines on maps that would delineate possessions on the ground. Such experiments had rarely worked in the past, and men like Morse took it upon themselves to chart borders that could clarify arguments about American territory that was often controlled by Indigenous nations. That the officials attempting to delimit imperial or American space were often ignorant of the relevant geography only increased the challenge. In 1786, for example, W. S. Smith, the American interim chargé d'affaires in London, talked with the commanding officer of the palace guards about the fur trade, the western limits of the united States, and the boundaries set at the peace of 1783. At one point the guard exclaimed, "Dam it I don't know anything about it, only that the gentleman who made that peace, is said to be a fool, & . . . totally unacquainted with the geography of the country he gave away."[16] Morse, hoping to rectify this ignorance among his readers, took his time revising his textbook. "I have determined not to publish a second edition of my geography this fall," he wrote in 1786, complaining that money to complete the project was scarce and emphasizing his desire that the second book improve on the first.[17]

When the second edition of *Geography Made Easy* was published, in the summer of 1788, Morse made sure to write those who had contacted him with corrections or suggestions, including Jeremy Belknap. Belknap and Morse led parallel lives. Each had received a fine education (at Harvard and Yale, respectively), followed the call of religious ministry, and become an evangelist for American identity. Belknap, from Boston, devoted the final decades of his life to collecting early American maps, letters, diaries, and newspapers, establishing and supporting institutions aimed at creating and preserving an American culture (he founded the Massachusetts Historical Society in 1791), and promoting a strong central government led by the educated class.[18] As an expert on the history and geography of New Hampshire, Belknap contacted Morse with corrections and suggestions for *Geography Made Easy*. As he prepared the second edition, Morse assured Belknap that he traveled extensively collecting information on the American states and "have been in some good degree successful." He sent Belknap the new sections on New Hampshire, offering an apology for its physical state: "it is mangled and blotted," he warned, "but I believe it is legible."[19] In June 1788, Morse wrote again to inform Belknap that the second edition had gone to press and also to announce a bigger project. "I have written, or shall write, it entirely over again," he promised, "and scarcely anything contained in the first edition will be republished but the title."[20]

The result of this new effort was Morse's 1789 *The American Geography*. This text sold well and went through several editions, leading George Washington to comment that the book would encourage "a better understanding between the remote citizens of our States."[21] *The American Geography* took its readers on a geographic tour of the United States, which in 1789 was an infant country without a strong national character. Morse, like others in the northeast, considered New England the nation's only coherent region, and he believed that the long-term project of creating a national character was a matter of "New Englandizing" the republic.[22] Even with this view, Morse was careful in his new volume not to ignore the provinces around the United States. Each state received a chapter, with sections on physical geography, demographics, and intellectual life as well as religious influence, commerce, and government. After 470-plus pages, readers reached the British dominions. New Britain, Canada, and Nova Scotia each received a one-page entry (faring only slightly better was Vermont, which, because not yet a state, was relegated to just over three pages). Morse began with New Britain—what today is essentially northern Quebec and Labrador. "To speak generally," he wrote, "this is a mountainous, frozen, barren country," though it possessed abundant fish and a collection of hearty Indigenous peoples.[23] The entry on Canada described the province's boundaries, primary rivers, chief towns, population, and constitution. Readers learned that Quebec was "built on the bank of the St. Lawrence river, on a rock, in two divisions" and that the province was governed by the Quebec Act of 1774, meaning that all legislative power "is vested in the governor and the legislative council," whose members were appointed by the king.[24] This summary was an important reminder that things were different in the British colony. What had been understood as British rights—such as voting for representatives and the right to a jury trial—now helped define the differences between the United States and Canada. The entry on Nova Scotia included sections on climate and history as well as a note that in 1784 the province had been divided to create New Brunswick, "which lies bordering on the United States," and that "since the conclusion of the war, there have been large emigrations of the refugees from the United States to this province."[25] *The American Geography* showed that the British colonies were physically close but ideologically distant, though the boundary between American states and imperial provinces was not so forceful as to prevent migrants from wandering north.

United States officials helped Morse by launching projects meant to determine the limits of American territory. Administrators looking north had to follow diplomatic protocol if they wished to send official representatives across a border that regular citizens largely ignored. With the promise of westward expansion came the necessity to record and chart new territories claimed by American and British powers (but largely under Indigenous control). In late summer 1789, Americans read about British efforts to set out from the St. Lawrence, explore the western part of the continent, and thus provide "a large and valuable addition" to the general understanding of North America.[26] John Jay understood the necessity of recording boundaries and limits, and that September he wrote to Lord Dorchester, the governor of British North America, requesting permission for Andrew Ellicott, an American surveyor, to travel through Canada in order to survey the western limit of Lake Ontario and the strait of Niagara.[27] Dorchester's secretary replied "that his Lordship considers the elucidation of the geographical points in the vicinity of Niagara … as a desirable acquisition of science" and would provide all necessary directions to assure Ellicott's success. Included in this response was a copy of a letter addressed to an officer at Fort Niagara informing him of the project and requesting that he keep the Indigenous nations apprised to prevent any undue alarm—a subtle reminder that it was easier for British and American officials to make territorial claims than to exercise authority.[28]

Piecemeal surveying trips like Ellicott's produced information that could be incorporated into the larger project of mapping the new nation, and it is no surprise that citizens and officials tasked with purchasing or measuring land shared their findings with Morse.[29] In the summer of 1789, Morse received a letter from Samuel Latham Mitchill, a New Yorker with a medical degree from the University of Edinburgh. Upon receiving the degree, Mitchill had completed a European grand tour before returning to New York, and in 1788 he was selected to serve on a commission charged with exploring the purchase of Iroquois homelands in what is now New York State.[30] It was likely on the way to or from Iroquoia that Mitchill took a detour into British Quebec and gathered the information he later shared with Morse. "I have been much pleased," he wrote in his letter, "with your *American Geography*, which is undoubtedly an useful and instructive work. The publication of your book, which contains an account of the United States, written and compiled by an American, wipes away one of the spots upon our national character; for it was truly reproachful that we should be indebted to Europeans for the history of our own country."[31]

Morse's project deserved to be widely read, Mitchill went on, but also to contain the most up-to-date knowledge, and he hoped his remarks might help with a second edition. While in Quebec, Mitchill had made the acquaintance of John Collins, the deputy surveyor general and a member of the provincial council, who invited Mitchill into the council chambers "to see a map of some late surveys made by himself on the north of Lake Ontario." Collins had been charged in 1783 with laying out townships around Cataraqui (now Kingston, Ontario) as well as establishing a communication route between that region and Lake Huron. His travels enabled him to complete a series of surveys of the province.[32] This geographic knowledge was exciting enough, but Mitchill in his later correspondence with Morse had more than simple maps and plans to share. He hoped Morse might improve and expand the flora and fauna described in his book and went on to say that while in Quebec he had seen a two-headed snake shown him by "an industrious collector of objects of natural history." Mitchill also had more general information to share. He closed his letter, "permit me just to add that British America to the northward consists of four provinces, Quebec, Nova Scotia, New Brunswick, and Gaspee, & that the term Canada is almost wholly out of use among the English."[33] As much as *The American Geography* could do for Americans, its author was encouraged not to lose sight of developments north of the states.

The compliments kept coming. Just before Christmas 1789, John Wheelock, the president of Dartmouth College (which his father, Eleazar, had founded in 1769) wrote to say he hoped Morse "would accept of my sincere gratitude for the very valuable present" of the new geography text, which Wheelock considered the very best of its kind that had appeared in the United States. "Such a performance was much needed," Wheelock added; "it communicates useful light, and will strengthen the mirror between the remote citizens of our States."[34]

After the critical success of *The American Geography*, Morse brought out a second edition, with several notable changes, in 1793 under the title *The American Universal Geography* and the claim of "comprehending a complete and improved system of modern geography" that was "Calculated for Americans." Morse recognized that Indigenous nations inhabited most of the western parts of North America, and he showed the continent as peopled from sea to sea. Yet his maps often could not accurately reflect the Indigenous control of lands claimed by the United States, in part because he did not provide enough detailed information to those compiling the maps for his books.[35] Consequently the book transformed Indigenous homelands into American states or British provinces. Moreover, the book's organization had changed: it now included opening chapters on geographic and celestial observations, an overview of how different parts of the world measure time, and observations on weather, winds, tides, and calendars. Only then did Morse turn to geography, beginning with an overview of the history and European discovery of North America and followed by a survey, from north to south, of the countries, provinces, and states on the continent. Readers were expected to follow Morse through an expanded tour of the British colonies before they encountered the American states.

Morse had clearly kept abreast of developments in British North America since the publication of his first edition, a period during which Loyalists had made demands on the British government that reflected the revolutionary spirit they brought into new provinces.[36] He described the new British provinces of Upper and Lower Canada, "constituted by act of

Parliament in 1791, comprehending the territory heretofore called Canada, or the Province of Quebec."[37] Montreal had become "a delightful spot" that "produced every thing that could administer the conveniences of life." Even the government had improved: the Constitutional Act of 1791 had not only divided Canada in two but also given each new province an assembly.[38] The division of other provinces received attention, and Morse included Osgoode Carleton's map of the northeast featuring New Brunswick (with a boundary quite favorable to Massachusetts).[39] While much of what Morse described was well-known general information, he also provided details from his informants, including Latham Mitchill. In his description of waterways in Upper and Lower Canada, Morse copied nearly word for word from Mitchill's account of the portage route from Cataraqui to Lake Huron.[40] Depending on the season, such a voyage could be quite enjoyable. Morse reminded his readers that winters bring "such severity, from December to April," but the deep snows and clear air made the season "neither unhealthy nor unpleasant." Spring arrived quickly and "the summer is delightful."[41] According to *The American Universal Geography*, Upper and Lower Canada were provinces on the up, a fact not lost on (and reinforced by) the thousands of "late Loyalists" moving north in those years.[42] The borders between British provinces and American states were more political than cultural, and it often was easier to find affinities across the national boundary than between northern and southern states. Like Doolittle's map from Morse's first publication, *The American Universal Geography* offered a continental view.

Borders did exist, of course, but they were enforced inconsistently, which resulted in confusion. The lines dividing the British provinces and American states were constantly crossed by subjects moving south and citizens pushing north, resulting in jurisdictional confusion around towns and forts near the border. George Clinton, the governor of New York, found himself fielding complaints from counties along the new Canada-US border. Merchants hoping to transport goods from the United States into the Canadas sometimes found themselves at the mercy of British revenue agents who confiscated goods as contraband before they had even crossed the border. In desperation, these traders turned to their government for aid. Merchants hoped Clinton would suggest to the president and cabinet to take action that "will at once put an end to such authorised insults and show to the government of Upper Canada that however insignificant they may suppose the County of Ontario," the citizens of that place are free and protected by a free government.[43] But these free citizens themselves often pushed against the limits set by international agreements. George Hammond, the British representative to the United States, complained in the spring of 1794 that the people of Vermont continued to settle in territories under British authority, as did citizens of New York. These actions, even in regions where exact borders were uncertain, violated the "harmony and good neighborhood, which ought to subsist between the subjects and citizens of friendly nations living in the vicinity of each other."[44]

Without clear and enforceable borders, officials in the British and American governments could each claim territories inhabited by the other's citizens or subjects. John Graves Simcoe, the lieutenant governor of Upper Canada, certainly kept American officials busy complaining to British representatives. His efforts to establish settlements and police settler-Indigenous relations along the Miami River in 1793 had caused many Americans to believe the British were hindering their negotiations with Indigenous nations. Now his moves to restrict American settlement on the south side of Lake Ontario renewed American distrust. One issue was the settlement at Great Sodus Bay, New York. Simcoe argued that the settlers there had encroached on Indigenous territory and thus violated "his Britannic Majesty's rights, as they unquestionably existed before the treaty."[45] Secretary of State Edmund Randolph remained unconvinced, and in September 1794 he informed George Hammond that Great Sodus Bay was well within the United States, seventy miles from the border. Unable to temper his pen, Randolph fumed that "while peace is sought by us through every channel, which honor permits, the Governor of Upper Canada is accumulating irritation upon irritation."[46] He simply could not comprehend Simcoe's actions and demanded to know "where is the limit of the sentiment, which gave birth to these intrusions? Where is the limit of the principle, which Governor Simcoe avows?"[47] Americans reading press accounts of Simcoe's orders later that month likely asked themselves the same question.[48]

An answer arrived on Randolph's desk in November in the form of a letter from Simcoe to Hammond, which the British representative forwarded to the secretary of state. In response to Randolph's criticisms of both the Miami and Great Sodus actions, Simcoe replied that he was simply following orders he had received from Lord Dorchester. Simcoe suggested Randolph was "anxious to consider every transaction of the King's Government, in its mode, as well as in its substance, as Hostility."

Had he not held such suspicion, Randolph might have been able to see in Upper Canada's concerns regarding the Great Sodus Bay settlement "a spirit of Conciliation, explanatory of the just principle, on which the settlement in question is termed an aggression."[49] The issue, according to Simcoe, was a difference in the way the British and the Americans understood Indigenous sovereignty. Somewhat disingenuously, he rejected Randolph's position (argued to Hammond in an earlier letter) that "the affairs of the Indians within the boundaries of any Nation exclusively belong to that Nation" and wondered how Randolph could have reached such a conclusion. The United States had not always followed this principle, nor was any precedent for it to be found in previous treaties. Such an argument was "incompatible with the natural rights; and injurious to the acknowledged independency of the Indian Americans." It was for exactly this reason, Simcoe noted, that Indigenous diplomats had asked British officials to attend their meetings with United States officers.[50] In contested regions along the proposed British and American border in Vermont, New York, and elsewhere, attempts to delineate possessions and regulate settlement efforts ran up against the continued existence of Indigenous homelands that refused to succumb to settler ideals of sovereignty or to administrators such as Simcoe who saw in Upper Canada a chance to reinvigorate the British empire.[51]

When American officials negotiated the Treaty of Greenville with Indigenous nations, they were engaging in international diplomacy. The very act of treaty making implicitly recognized Indigenous sovereignty over their homelands. Government representatives might have thought these agreements simply formalized the slow march west, but British officials warned their American counterparts that agreements with Indigenous peoples must be understood as international treaties. When officials in London learned in 1796 that the United States had signed the 1795 Treaty of Greenville with "certain tribes of Indians, living on the northewestern frontier of those States," the king and his government grew alarmed that the new agreement contained "certain stipulations repugnant to the due execution" of the Jay Treaty, signed by the Americans and Britain just a year earlier. The Greenville Treaty required traders to have a license before they could reside among or trade with the western confederacy, directly contradicting the third article of the Jay Treaty, which allowed British subjects, American citizens, and Indigenous peoples to "freely pass and repass, by land or inland navigation, into the respective territories and countries of the two parties on the continent of America," with the Hudson's Bay Company lands excepted. To endanger the Jay Treaty was to threaten the Anglo-American peace it helped establish.[52]

Right after the Jay Treaty was signed, Washington had objected to this exact article, arguing that it would have been better for all involved if British and American traders stayed on their respective sides of the border and Indigenous nations could trade with whomever offered the best terms.[53] Now that the Jay Treaty and the Treaty of Greenville contradicted each other, it fell to the British to elevate members of the western confederacy to the status of nations for the purpose of legal agreements. Phineas Bond, the interim British chargé d'affaires in Philadelphia, argued that the Americans must have entered into a treaty with the western confederacy before they had learned the specifics of the Jay Treaty, as "the universal law of nations" prohibited an existing treaty to "be superseded by any engagements subsequently concluded by one of the parties with another State or nation."[54] To remedy this problem, the Jay Treaty would need an additional article to reaffirm the rights of British and American traders to pass freely into the territories claimed by either power. Timothy Pickering, who had succeeded Edmund Randolph as the American secretary of state in August 1795, responded to Rufus King (the U.S. ambassador at London) with a different interpretation. That citizens and subjects could move freely across the border, he wrote, did not "exempt either from the cognizance of laws of the respective jurisdictions." Such an understanding was particularly important when traders met "in the Indian Territories, to which the jurisdiction of neither power extends." The best solution, he suggested, would be that disputes over trespass and other offenses "shall be congizable by us, when they happen on our side of the line, and by the British Government when they happen on their side of the line."[55]

Pickering was working a delicate balance. He had to respect the agreements his government had struck with the British and address the rights of Indigenous nations in territories claimed by the United States while recognizing that state and federal officials encouraged the expansion of settler legal frameworks into US-Indigenous relations.[56]

As the 1790s came to a close, American concerns about Indigenous allegiance to the British in Canada had hardly abated, but proximity to the British gave Americans a model for behavior that might appease Indigenous concerns. Especially in regions where the Americans and British lived in close proximity, such as Detroit and Niagara, each side kept a watchful eye on the other and worked to establish good relations when possible. For John Jacob Ulrich Rivardi, a military engineer stationed temporarily at Niagara in 1799, encounters with the British were both pleasant and helpful. He wrote in a letter to Alexander Hamilton that the simple act of dining with Canadian officials, as Rivardi did when he supped with Edmund Burke, the "great Vicar of Canada & a man perfectly acquainted with this country" (whose attempts to dissuade the Indigenous nations from signing the Treaty of Greenville had raised the ire of American officials), gave him important insights into the rumors that many Indigenous nations were planning a war. Burke told Rivardi that the cause of the unrest was a visit a few years earlier by a French expedition sent to survey the Ohio and Mississippi Rivers with the ultimate goal of reconquering Louisiana.[57] The plan never materialized, but Indigenous nations in and around Detroit complained about the potential loss of their territories to the French and other speculators, and they turned to the Americans for help. A speech delivered at Detroit by chiefs of the Ottawas and Potawatomis implored the Americans to help stop illegal speculators from taking Indigenous lands, especially after the western nations had "given certain Tracts of Land to the Canadians, whom we conceive to be our Brothers and also to many Englishmen in this place, and are determined to make good their title to those Lands." Not wanting to go back on the agreements they had struck and unwilling to have their land taken illegally, these chiefs reminded the Americans that they would uphold the agreements they had made and that they expected Congress to protect Indigenous lands. James McHenry, the secretary of war, responded by suggesting that the Americans would do what the British had done in the past: oversee the sales of Indigenous lands "at public open treaties in the presence of an agent," adding, "We find that the British Government always exercised a power of superintending the sales of Indian lands within their limits."[58]

Even as they tried to model some of their behavior on British precedent, American officials looked for ways to drive a wedge between the British and their Indigenous allies. By late 1799, they had received assurances that British officials would be instructed to stop encouraging Indigenous groups, particularly the Shawnee, to use threats of violence against the United States to "obtain some modifications of the Greenville Treaty." Robert Liston, Britain's ambassador to the United States, reported to Pickering that any such actions were undertaken without Lieutenant Governor Simcoe's "authority or knowledge."[59] Yet threats from aggrieved Indigenous nations were not the only problems Americans faced. At Detroit, officials complained of drunkenness among Indigenous peoples living near the settlement, and administrators tried to solve the problem through legislation. John F. Hamtramck, a commander at Detroit, supported ordinances for the northwest "similar to the Canadian act of March 29, 1777," which prohibited "the sale of liquor to the Indians without written permission from" a leading colonial official.[60] Hamtramck was likely familiar with this law because he had been born in Quebec as Jean François and had Anglicized his name to John Francis when he joined the Patriot cause in 1775.[61] In cases such as these, British relations with Indigenous peoples could be both a cause of and solution to American problems.

One radical idea for bringing Indigenous nations into the American orbit was to give them a representative in Congress. William Duane, a staunch Democratic-Republican and an admirer of Thomas Jefferson, saw such representation as a way to separate the Indigenous nations from their allegiance to the British in Canada. As a spectator on 2 January, he had heard Indigenous chiefs Little Turtle (Mihšihkinaahkwa) and Five Medals (Wonongaseah) address Congress about their concerns over the Greenville Treaty, and he wrote President Jefferson to suggest allowing "each of the Indian Nations, a Representative in the Congress of the United States, under such limitations and conditions as would give them a due sense of their consequence to the American nation." At a time when most women could not vote and African Americans were not considered citizens, this proposal illuminated Duane's concern about the British-Indigenous alliance.[62] He offered no details on how to enact such a plan but was confident it would be neither complicated nor expensive. To make the idea even more attractive, he added "that this subject being mentioned a considerable time since to a Canadian Englishman, he deprecated the idea, and solicited earnestly that it might not be mentioned as it would destroy the British influence for ever, and throw the Fur trade wholly into the States."[63] To win over Indigenous peoples, simply give them a voice in government. There is no record of Jefferson's having replied to Duane's suggestion.

Radical ideas like Duane's could easily divide American politicians and citizens. When the French Revolutionary Wars of 1792–1802 came to dominate international concerns, Americans were forced to pick sides. Initially most supported the uprising, as it was easy to find common ground with men and women pushing to overthrow the rule of an absolute monarch. But as the French Revolution progressed and the violence increased, Federalist support waned while Democratic-Republicans remained largely committed to the cause. British Canadians, who received most of their news from the almost uniformly anti-revolutionary British papers, were more united in their views. American papers were more likely to include reports from French papers or from people who had been in France.[64] One traveler from France reawakened American insecurities about Canada almost as soon as he landed in the United States. Edmund Charles Genêt arrived in Charleston, South Carolina, on 8 April 1793 as the French minister to the United States and immediately caused an uproar. By that time, the French Revolution had become an imperial war, with Britain and other powers fighting to support monarchy throughout Europe.[65] Swept up in the south's support for the French, Genêt took it upon himself to spread the revolutionary movement in North America. He offered a privateering commission to any ship willing to seize British merchant vessels and take their cargo, a plan that threatened President Washington's goal of remaining neutral in the European war.

Genêt's approach to disturbing the British also included encouraging their French subjects to overthrow the government of Canada. In 1793 he published *Les Français libres à leurs frères les Canadiens*, which served as both an apology on behalf of French citizens for ignoring the plight of their Canadian brethren and a call for Canadians to join the French in their revolution against tyrannical kings. Genêt's appeal was not entirely original: he drew heavily on a memorial published by a Canadian newspaper editor, Henri-Antoine Mézière, who had recently moved from Quebec to the United States. Genêt promised the French in Quebec that they could be as free as the French in France and the Americans in the United States. "Imitate their example and ours," he exhorted readers; "the path is paved."[66] In an echo of the letters Congress sent to Quebec two decades earlier, Genêt reminded the Canadians that "the country you inhabit was conquered by your fathers . . . this land belongs to you, it must be independent."[67] He listed myriad reasons why French Canadians should embrace the republican spirit, arm themselves, and ask their Indigenous allies and American neighbors to help them "obtain what energetic men never claim in vain, liberty and independence."[68] As during the American Revolution, French Canadians remained unmoved.

If Genêt's remonstrance did not awaken their revolutionary spirit, he did remind wary Americans of France's territorial interests in North America. At the request of the Washington administration, Genêt was recalled only three months after his arrival in Philadelphia. But during his absence, the Jacobins had seized control of the French government, replacing the more moderate Girondists, and Genêt faced certain execution should he return to France. So he was allowed to remain in the United States.[69] Meanwhile, his replacement, the Jacobin Jean-Antoine-Joseph Fauchet, focused on repairing the Franco-American relations that Genêt had strained. For a time, plans respecting a Canadian uprising were abandoned. When the Jacobins fell in turn, and a five-man committee called the Directory took power in 1795, French eyes once again looked to their former colonies. The Directory replaced Fauchet with Pierre-Auguste Adet and also drafted several plans to retake territory in North America, including both British Canada and Louisiana, which was then under Spanish control. These schemes, if successful, would have surrounded the United States with puppet regimes under the control of the Directory.[70]

United States officials stationed in Europe kept a watchful eye on military movements and other developments that might affect American neutrality. In the summer of 1796, James Monroe, the U.S. ambassador to France, wrote to Timothy Pickering, "It is even whispered that an attempt on Canada is to be made, and which is to be united with Louisiana and the Floridas." Any Americans willing to move into those territories would be welcomed by the French. "This is worthy your attention," Monroe continued, but "it may be mere report."[71] The prospect that France might act against the United States so concerned him that he held two informal meetings with members of the Directory to clarify the matter. In the first meeting, Monroe could only hint at his concerns, but the Directory members told him they had no plans for Canada and none related to Louisiana that should concern the Americans.[72] Monroe pushed the issue in a second meeting, asking what might happen if France came into possession of Canada, Louisiana, and the Floridas. Did the Directory intend "to invite our western people to a junction with them, and thus eventually dismember us"? The reply was explicit: the Directory did not want Canada "but wished it separated from England."[73] These reassuring words hardly quieted American concerns. In late fall, Rufus King warned Washington that a French attack on Quebec via the Mississippi might be unlikely, but "it may be the part of prudence to consider it as possible, in order to guard against its mischiefs."[74] Once an object of American expansion, Canada now became a possible threat.

Some officials, however, thought the United States might combine France's historical ties to Canada with the American goal of expanding north. David McLane was a native of Massachusetts who described himself as an agent of France and sometimes went by the name Jacob Felt. In 1796 he was in his thirties, handsome, and just desperate enough to fancy himself an actor on the world stage. His investment in a Providence Exchange Coffee House (a tavern and gaming establishment) had failed, leaving him heavily in debt, and he fled Massachusetts claiming he might become a highwayman and "collect such duties from travellers as his wants might require."[75] Rather than turn to outright robbery, however, McLane offered his services to France. With a commission from Pierre-Auguste Adet, he pointed himself north.

That summer he styled himself a horse trader and went to Quebec to meet with sympathetic Canadiens and American expatriates who might help him make Canada independent. He first called on Charles Frichet, a farmer living just outside Montreal, and asked him if he was an honest man who could swear an oath and keep a secret. Frichet obliged, at which point McLane asked him to "procure me certificates signed by six persons of Canada to shew that the Canadians are dissatisfied with the British Government and desired the re-establishment of the French Government." If Frichet could provide such documents, McLane would take him to France, pay him generously, and ensure that he never wanted for anything. Frichet declined the offer, and when McLane proposed meeting two weeks later to discuss matters further, Frichet demurred.[76] McLane (who, for a covert agent, told far too many people of his plans) then attempted to win the trust of Elmer Cushing, an American who owned a tavern in Montreal. Cushing wasted no time in using what he learned from McLane for his own benefit. He approached British officials, swore a deposition against McLane in November 1796, and in return was granted the rights to an entire township.[77] The authorities now knew about McLane.

With his plan exposed, McLane returned to his first mark. In March 1797, a messenger arrived at Frichet's door and requested that he meet McLane at the province's border, which Frichet did. When Frichet asked McLane what he was doing, McLane replied that "it was none of your business," but he encouraged Frichet to tell people he was buying horses.[78] Eventually he revealed his intention to lead an invasion of the province, and the pair traveled together toward Quebec City, staying with Frichet's relations when they could. During an evening at St. Nicolas, a parish on the southern shore of the St. Lawrence just west of Quebec City, McLane decided to outline his plans more broadly. "You don't know me yet," he told Frichet and assembled family members. "I am sent by the French government to excite an Insurrection in Canada and to deliver your brothers and relations from slavery." Claiming to be the second-in-command of the army poised to invade the province, he asked the family's help in finding five hundred men to fight with them. Frichet argued that even if McLane could take Quebec, his force could never hold it. "You are mistaken," McLane replied, claiming there were ten thousand men in America ready to join the uprising. Frichet and his family refused to spread the message.[79]

Not ready to give up, McLane then asked Frichet to call upon a Mr. John Black, a ship carpenter in Quebec who had suffered greatly under the British, and bring him to a spot where McLane would be hiding. Black had been imprisoned in 1794 as a suspected agent of France, a charge that had nearly ruined his business and made him a social pariah. By the time McLane took an interest in him, Black was more concerned with rehabilitating his reputation than stirring up revolution.[80] He saw in McLane not a chance to overthrow the British but an opportunity to demonstrate his loyalty. When Frichet arrived at Black's house, the carpenter agreed to a meeting just past the Plains of Abraham. Black's setup of McLane began by his agreeing to participate in an attack and using his connections to help sedate the sentries. "You Mr. Black, can greatly facilitate the Execution of our plan," McLane assured him; "you are well known to the soldiers in garrison, the sentinels will receive liquor from you, and in that you can mix laudanum."[81] Black took these instructions straight to the Quebec authorities. He then invited McLane to spend the night at his house, where, just before midnight, McLane was arrested by the governor's civil secretary and a number of soldiers.[82] He was a French agent but an incompetent one, and while some in Canada were willing to humor him, nobody was prepared to engage in espionage or an attempted revolt. McLane was arrested, tried, and sentenced to the particularly cruel death reserved for high treason: hanging but not until dead, disembowelment while alive, decapitation, and quartering. On 21 July, after an executioner demanded $600 to carry out the sentence, McLane was hanged in front of a huge crowd. As was increasingly the custom, he was hanged until dead before being cut down. The executioner then demanded an additional $300 to complete the more gruesome element of the sentence.[83]

As reports of McLane's activities, capture, and execution circulated in American newspapers, administrators considered the implications of France's interest in the province. Secretary of State Timothy Pickering wrote to Rufus King outlining what he had read of the affair, noting that McLane was apprehended "upon something more than a suspicion of treasonable practices" and that McLane allegedly possessed a commission from the French Republic, that he was being paid by France, that "for about two years [he] had been faithfully employed whispering sedition in the ears of the French Canadians," and that the operation was part of a larger plan that included the arrival of a French fleet, the explosion of British magazines, and an uprising by the Canadiens themselves. The entire ordeal, Pickering continued, "corresponds with prior facts and circumstances indicating the designs of France to repossess Canada" using Canadiens, French troops, and sympathetic Americans. While he doubted Americans would help in such an effort, he expressed concern that France would attempt to regain Louisiana and eventually encircle "what now constitute the Atlantic States." It was a plan "so dangerous to our union and peace, every real American must be firmly opposed."[84] The French design on Canada was perhaps a stalking horse, but few Americans could ignore its implications.

As Franco-American relations grew more strained over the fate of Canada, a new British minister to the United States arrived in Philadelphia and began cultivating friendly relations with the Adams administration. Sir Robert Liston was a Scot who had served in various diplomatic positions, most recently as Britain's ambassador-extraordinary in Constantinople. In March 1796 he accepted, with much apprehension, the position of British minister to the United States. He would face a dizzying array of problems, few of which could be resolved easily: British-Indigenous affairs, American debts, the Anglo-American boundary issues, and Franco-American tensions.[85] After George Hammond's acrimonious tenure as minister to the United States, American officials warmly welcomed Liston and his wife and hoped their arrival signaled improved relations with Great Britain.[86] Liston was in regular contact with Canada's governor and passed along any information he collected respecting both American and French affairs.

As soon as he took up his post, Liston had to deal with renegade plots between American citizens and the French state to invade Canada. While McLane was "whispering sedition" in Canada, Ira Allen was plotting an independent future for Vermont and Quebec. Though Vermont had joined the union as the fourteenth state in 1791, Allen had never surrendered his hopes for an independent republic. In 1795 he traveled to London to lobby for the creation of a canal that would connect northern

Vermont with Montreal, a project that would greatly improve his fortunes given that he owned vast tracts of land along the proposed route. The British, fearing that such a canal would facilitate an American invasion of Canada, rejected the idea. In 1796, Allen began the second phase of his project: the creation of a new democratic republic, "United Columbia," that would incorporate Vermont and Quebec. He hoped to rally the Green Mountain Boys and frustrated French Canadians, and with arms and naval support from France (and possibly the forces that McLane hoped to organize), he would lead an invasion to liberate Canada.[87]

Allen arrived in Paris in the spring of 1796 and reinvented himself as a friend of revolutionary France. After a series of meetings with members of the Directory, and under the cover of purchasing arms for the Vermont militia, he signed an agreement with Claude Louis Petiet, the secretary of war, in July 1796. France agreed to provide arms for an invasion of Canada, which both sides hoped would lead to the creation of "United Columbia," weakening Great Britain while keeping the United States allied with France. Allen had even sewn together a flag, which combined the French Tricolor with the green of Vermont. He intended to sail for New York in the fall of 1796 and launch his attack in August 1797.[88]

In January 1797, French and American officials in the United States learned that Ira Allen was awaiting trial in England. Three months earlier, a British warship had captured him in his vessel, *The Olive Branch*, carrying thousands of French-supplied muskets and other arms. Though they had not yet captured him, British officials in Quebec had known of McLane's plot for two months, so after taking *The Olive Branch* and discovering the French guns, they assumed an attack was in the offing. The arms were considered French contraband, and Allen was put on trial. He argued that the guns were for the Vermont militia, but when he returned to Paris to secure additional documents that might prove this claim, the Directory had him imprisoned for a year on suspicion that he was now a spy for the British. After a lengthy trial and eventual acquittal, Allen returned to the United States in 1801 and lived out the rest of his life in poverty.[89]

In January 1797, Liston wrote to Robert Prescott, who had replaced Lord Dorchester as governor general of the Canadas, to tell him that the French Embassy in Philadelphia was in an anxious state. In addition to the capture of Allen and McLane's disappointing efforts, the French Embassy had learned of uprisings in Montreal over legislation that forced inhabitants to work on road construction. These disturbances had nothing to do with the Directory's invasion plans, and for the French, that was the problem. There was, Liston wrote, "great anxiety discovered [revealed] by Mr. Adet and his Associates here, lest an insurrection should break out before their plans were brought to maturity."[90] Adet wanted French Canadians angry but at the right time and for the right reasons. Allen's capture had been a significant setback. By that summer, the Directory's plan of using Americans to invade Canada ended as McLane swung from the Montreal gallows.

James McHenry, Adams's secretary of war, watched Europe closely, calculating the possible outcomes of France's Revolutionary Wars. In June 1797, he warned Washington that England might have to accept terms of peace. Yet it was also possible that France would become "inebriated with victory" and make unacceptable demands. "Should Canada be among her demands and yielded," McHenry warned, "our situation would become extremely critical."[91] He didn't know that Britain had no intention of surrendering Canada to France, but he could see that France and its allies were capturing territory and redrawing borders all over Europe. The War of the Second Coalition (1798–1802) would lead the Adams administration into a "Quasi-War" with France and push American officials even closer to Robert Liston. This undeclared war resulted from a combination of factors: the United States' refusal to repay debts to a new French regime; the Directory's problems financing its war effort; France's anger at the Jay Treaty; what became known as the XYZ Affair: the French administration's mistreatment of American envoys sent to address these issues. Philadelphia buzzed with these developments, which forced even the staunchest Democratic-Republicans to reconsider their position. In letters to her uncle in the spring of 1798, Henrietta Liston, the British minister's wife, noted that tensions between France and the United States were "too strong for the French party here to swallow" and that "war or peace will now depend on the French themselves."[92]

Behind the bluster of the Quasi-War lay the concern that as the War of the Second Coalition remade borders in Europe, states and powers on the losing end of the struggles might try to offset those losses by taking territory in North America. In March 1798, John Adams's youngest son, Thomas Boylston Adams, wrote to his father from Berlin, where he was acting as secretary to his brother John Quincy, to warn that "by way of indemnity to the princes & States thus despoiled, they may possibly be invited to join with the French emigrants in the enterprize of reconquering Canada."[93] Though troubled by the prospect of a French invasion of

Canada, most Americans thought it natural that certain peoples were destined to control others. The practice of slavery was one example; so too was France's invasion of Egypt. A Boston newspaper published an editorial in late 1799 mocking those who took umbrage at French expansionism. One might ask such people, "What right had Columbus, Pizarro, Cortez to subjugate the people of America? . . . But let us come nearer home, thou most accomplished logician; and enquire by what right the first Congress attempted to annex the whole province of Canada to the United States, by sending a military force under that gallant 'wild Irishman' that accompanied Montgomery, to reduce that British province to the power of this country?"[94] There was no question that Canada could fall to a conquering party. The American objection was that they believed they had right of first refusal.

Robert Liston had waded directly into the United States' fraught relationship with revolutionary France, but he saw an opportunity. He believed Anglo-American relations could be strengthened at the expense of the Directory, and he became the subject of a minor political affair when some of his private letters were captured and printed in William Duane's *Aurora*. For Duane and his ardently Democratic-Republican readers, Adams and the Federalists were edging far too close to the British. On 6 and 23 May 1799, Liston wrote letters to Peter Russell, the acting lieutenant governor of Upper Canada, and gave them, signed and sealed, to Isaac Sweezy [Swayze] for delivery. Unfortunately for Liston, Sweezy was arrested as a horse thief, the letters were confiscated, and eventually the official correspondence made its way to Duane at the *Aurora*.[95] "The letters from Robert Liston to president Russell are enclosed," the paper informed its readers on 13 July 1799, and "from them, among other things, the people will learn, the extreme, not to say improper intimacy subsisting between a foreign minister and the directors of American affairs. If the British minister is to be believed, intentional provocations have been given to France 'in conjunction with the British government,'—For what purpose the world will judge."[96]

Liston's first letter suggested that Franco-American relations could be weakened if the United States administration gave "a new subject of provocation to France, by encouraging (in conjunction with us) the Negro Chief Toussaint," then leading an uprising of enslaved people on the Caribbean island of Saint Domingue (Haiti), in ways that might "tend to a separation of the Island of St. Domingo from the mother country."[97] The United States was already holding informal meetings

Louis Rigaud, *Toussaint L'Ouverture*, 1877. Oil on canvas, 26 1/2 × 21 in. (67.31 × 53.34 cm). Lent by Yale Peabody Museum of Natural History, ILE2012.25.1. Digital image: Yale Center for British Art. There are no portraits of L'Ouverture, the leader of the Haitian Revolution, produced during his life. This is the first known portrait by a Haitian artist.

with representatives of Toussaint, but American officials struggled to incorporate into their domestic and foreign diplomacy an island of the formerly enslaved who were in the process of violently overthrowing French rule. The revolution understandably terrified American slaveholders.[98] Other local uprisings also drew Liston's attention. In a letter sent at the end of May, he had harsh words for the participants in Fries's Rebellion, an uprising in eastern Pennsylvania over a tax issued by the Adams administration to help cover the costs of the Quasi-War. A "number of poor ignorant wretches," Liston wrote, had been led astray by the "democratic faction" on whether the government had the right to levy the tax.[99] Liston applauded the government's response to the uprising and saw little threat of its turning into a wider armed conflict. He thought the United States in 1799 was more likely to defend Canada against a French invasion than to fall into civil conflict over taxes.

While the Adams administration was dealing with Democratic-Republican backlash raised by the *Aurora*'s publication of Liston's two letters, rumors of a third letter emerged. This one seemed to hint at a military alliance between the United States and Great Britain.[100] "There is a third letter of the British minister, of which we have not been able to obtain a copy, because it is in the hands of the administration," the *Aurora* reported in late July 1799, and added a troubling claim: "It states to the British government of Canada, that in the event of that British province being attacked by any foreign power, the government of the United States *stood pledged* to supply a military force adequate to defend that colony, and to preserve it to the British government."[101] These reports did little to increase the Federalists' popularity with voters. Elijah Griffiths, a Philadelphia physician, wrote to Vice President Thomas Jefferson that "Mr. Liston's recent dispatches" indicated a "want of policy" among the Federalists, "as it has very sensibly lessen'd the popularity of the party in Pennsylvania & New Jersey, it may probably have that effect elsewhere."[102]

Jefferson gained more insight into the Liston letters, particularly the apparent Anglo-American defense strategy, in early January 1800. Meeting with Tench Coxe—a wealthy merchant, speculator, former Loyalist, and Federalist who had recently come to support the Democratic-Republicans—Jefferson learned that Liston's frank communications with Timothy Pickering had revealed more than the British minister perhaps intended. In this instance, Coxe benefited from his past political allegiances. He maintained good relations with Federalists, including one of Pickering's closest friends, a Mr. Hodgden of New Jersey. According to

Jefferson's notes of the conversation, Coxe explained to him that the topic of the letters came up during a discussion with Hodgden. It turned out Pickering had shown Hodgden the letters. Coxe observed that the second letter, in which Liston criticized the Pennsylvania rebels and applauded the government response, might be the most serious. Hodgden replied that he thought the third letter was much worse. Coxe, "not betraying his ignorance of a 3rd letter," casually asked him which part of it he found most damaging, to which Hodgden replied "that wherein [Liston] assured the Govr. of Canada that if the French invaded Canada, an army would be marched from these states to his assistance."[103] While this third letter was never published, rumors of its existence demonstrated that while men such as Allen and McLane might hope for a French invasion of Canada, Adams and his government were unlikely to approve or assist it.

Newspaper reports also outlined the variety of connections between states, provinces, and the officials who governed them. Liston's letters provided additional ammunition for Republicans to criticize Adams, most notably in the *Aurora*, which remained the ideal medium for such attacks. Adams himself had long been vilified in the public papers, prompting Abigail Adams to say of one editor that he had "the true spirit of Satan."[104] It was exactly these kinds of attacks that led the Federalists to introduce and pass the Sedition Act in 1798, which made it illegal "to write, print, utter or publish, or cause it to be done, or assist in it, any false, scandalous, and malicious writing against the government of the United States, or either House of Congress, or the President." The maximum punishment was $2,000 and two years in prison.[105] There can be little doubt that in passing the legislation, the Federalists hoped to silence men like Benjamin Franklin Bache, the grandson of Benjamin Franklin and the founder of the *Aurora*, but he evaded government reprimand by dying in the yellow fever epidemic of 1798. William Duane, who took over as publisher, continued to launch attacks against the government even after being beaten unconscious by Federalist supporters and then charged under the Sedition Act.[106] Much to the frustration of Adams and the Federalists, American newspaper publishers refused to be intimidated by laws they thought contrary to the idea of liberty and a free press.

As the presses continued to churn out newspapers large and small, Americans read not only diatribes against political figures but news and opinions about the United States' northern neighbors. For all the ink spilled over Liston's letters or Federalist policies, Americans could also read stories that let them view their internal arguments in the context of a wide range of opinions on Canadian-American relations. *Greenleaf's New York Journal* ran two stories relating to Canada in September 1799. The first, "A State of the Province of Quebec," which readers might have remembered from its initial publication nearly a decade earlier, argued that Britain would retain Canada and "always hold a rod over the heads of American states, and keep them in awe."[107] However dated it was, this description offered a direct challenge to Liston's claim that the United States "stood pledged" to defend Canada. Later in the month, a response to "A State of the Province," published in the same journal, called on Americans to recall British attempts to oppress America, ruin its trade, enslave its people, and influence its politics. The British continued to harass Americans on land and at sea, the author argued; British ships captured American vessels on open waters, and Indian agents were sent "to hover on the rear of our southern states" while Joseph Brant worked against American interests in the north. The article also encouraged Americans to remember Andrew Allen, a Philadelphia Loyalist whose property was confiscated during the revolution. Allen's attempt at securing compensation for his losses brought the case in July 1799 before the Anglo-American commission created to adjudicate claims under Article 6 of the Jay Treaty.[108] He was unsuccessful, but in support of his claim, the British commissioners argued that there had "been no such unconditional submission, or acknowledgement of the independence of the United States on the part of Great Britain but a recognition by solemn treaty, containing reciprocal stipulations, as the price of peace."[109] Americans could hardly be expected to rally to Canada's defense when British officials suggested that "the independence of the United States was a matter of contingency and not of right."[110]

Not everything Americans read depicted tension between the United States and the Canadas. Especially for people living along the northern border, the British provinces were home to friends, business partners, and family. It is not surprising, then, that newspapers in the United States reported on both larger political issues and daily life in the provinces that might interest American citizens. In the fall of 1799, the *New Hampshire Sentinel* reported on the departure of Lieutenant Governor Simcoe, who had left Upper Canada over three years earlier, just before the British surrendered Fort Niagara to the Americans under the terms of the Jay Treaty. "He was saluted by the garrison, on embarking, and by

William Strickland, *Fort Niagara taken from the British side of the River at Newark*, 1814. Library of Congress, Prints and Photographs Division.

the American flag on passing Fort Niagara," read the story, which added that a Canadian newspaper had described the American salute as an acknowledgment of Simcoe's performance in his post: " 'Merit,' says the Canada *Constellation*, 'is respected by all countries.' "[111] Political articles were often paired with lighter fare, such as the account in the *Pennsylvania Gazette* of how a married couple and their dog fought off an angry bear in St. John, New Brunswick.[112]

Some writers, such as John Ogden, dabbled in both political propaganda and descriptive narratives of the British provinces. Ogden made enemies easily. He spent some time as an itinerant missionary, traveling through Vermont, New Hampshire, and Canada, but his inability to find a position as a Protestant Episcopal minister in Congregationalist New England quickly soured him on most of the region's religious leaders. When Matthew Lyon, a Vermont congressman who shared Ogden's political and religious views, was jailed under the Sedition Act for publishing a work critical of John Adams in 1798, Ogden carried a petition to the president himself. His meeting with Adams only pushed him closer to the Democratic-Republicans. He found a welcoming outlet for his tirades at the *Aurora*, where he began making regular (but unsigned) contributions about Federalist misdeeds, especially those in New England.[113] Yet his interests extended north of New England, and he shared those with his readers as well.

At the same time he was writing for the *Aurora*, Ogden published *A Tour through Upper and Lower Canada*. He surely hoped to make some money from his account, but the very act of publishing it was costly. When he traveled to Litchfield, Connecticut, to supervise the book's printing, he was arrested and jailed. Officially, the charge was failure to pay debts from earlier in his life, but he was likely targeted for his published writing.[114] When his travel narrative appeared in print, it included none of Ogden's typically emotional and polemical style. He seemed sorrowful that many Americans saw in Canada a vestige of the supposedly tyrannical British government that the colonies had overthrown a generation earlier. In a view likely shaped by his Episcopalian faith, he saw both Catholic Lower Canada and Protestant Upper Canada as good neighbors connected by loyalties and alliances. Alongside his descriptions of towns, rivers, and people, Ogden offered a general assessment of the Canadas as a society. "Lower Canada appears upon examination, to enjoy as many of the blessings of life, as are needful to make man happy," including a "mild and energetic" government.[115] In Lower Canada, women were generally better educated than men because while there were few schools or colleges, there were many convents where Ursuline nuns educated young girls and women.[116] Far from the Catholic menace that Congregationalists like Ezra Stiles found so threatening during the revolution, Ogden saw in Lower Canada the benefits of France's work with Indigenous peoples and its support of intermarriage among settlers and the land's original inhabitants. "Was this virtuous and rational matrimonial alliance encouraged, by the European emigrants into the American regions north and south," Ogden wrote, "many confusions and outrages would be prevented."[117] While the United States government struggled to win and keep Indigenous allies, he saw in Canada the benefits of a different approach.

In Upper Canada, the American traveler saw that Indigenous peoples could be considered better inhabitants than many Americans. In Kingston, Ogden attended a church service where he saw Molly Brant (Gonwatsijayenni), Joseph Brant's sister and widow of Sir William Johnson. She would have been approximately sixty and very near the end of her life. While Ogden refers to her as "the relict of Sir William Johnson," his description of her activities demonstrated Gonwatsijayenni's skills at diplomacy. She dined at Lieutenant Governor Simcoe's house with Indigenous delegations, and during her time in New York with Johnson "she often persuaded the obstinate chiefs into a compliance with the proposals for peace."[118] Readers could compare this description of Molly Brant to Ogden's claim that authorities in Upper Canada were "cautious in receiving Republicans from the states," and that they preferred husbandmen and laborers over lawyers and merchants.[119] Indigenous peoples loyal to the British cause were preferred over Patriots, who might bring revolution. But Ogden concluded by noting the Canadians' peaceful nature. Earlier in the decade they had celebrated Washington's proclamation of neutrality, and they were unmoved by agents of France who attempted to stir up revolution. "Publications had been issued through the news-papers in Philadelphia, to sound the public opinion, as to a war with Canada," Ogden reminded his readers, adding, "every misrepresentation, as to the state of the popular opinion was sought for, and a great encouragement was given by many in the states." And yet "at this time, the people of Canada, were not projecting trouble for the States, but as far as possible, encouraging a friendly intercourse, and reciprocal good offices."[120] Although a polemicist himself, Ogden wanted his readers to understand the nature of the Canadian inhabitants rather than follow the arguments of those most interested in sowing division.

Through stories and reports about British Canada, American citizens and administrators could learn about themselves. Ogden's work echoed certain American ideas about Canada but also forced readers to examine their own country and government more closely. Like the United States, Upper and Lower Canada had developed a newspaper culture, with papers published in the major settlements of Quebec, Montreal, and Newark (later Niagara). But "they are carefully guarded against every thing that may excite discontents among the inhabitants, or encourage assaults upon religion and government."[121]

At least two of these newspapers had American roots. Fleury Mesplet, a printer and publisher who began his career in France before moving to England, had met Benjamin Franklin in London and in 1774 decided to move to Philadelphia. He published Congress's first letter to the inhabitants of Quebec in 1774, and then traveled to Montreal with Franklin and the commission to Canada, where he stayed and established the province's first newspaper, *La Gazette de Montréal*.[122] In Upper Canada, the brothers Gideon and Silvester Tiffany, who immigrated from

New York around 1795, immediately took over publication of the *Upper Canada Gazette*, which had been established in 1793. The paper was nothing like their previous effort, New York's *American Spy*, but they nevertheless found themselves in the government's crosshairs.[123] Stories of government actions to limit the press had long fueled American criticisms of the British in Canada as anti-democratic, but the Sedition Act forced many Americans to realize their country was not immune to such accusations. "A Revolution! It may be very well called a revolution," bellowed Boston's *Constitutional Telegraph*, "when the British colonies of Canada, point at the republican freemen of the United-States of America, and laughing with scorn, compare their condition with ours." "Some time ago a Canada paper exhibited a contrast of the British with the American liberty of the press, under our sedition law," the paper continued, "in a paper from the same province . . . we find a comparison, which unhappily, is but too true, too just, and irrefutable."[124] Looking north provided some Americans with new ammunition for arguments against their own government.

Many, including the Tiffany brothers, found the Canadas an increasingly attractive option for relocation. Ogden's travel narrative raved about fertile lands, easy navigation, and, importantly, low taxes. In dividing Quebec into two provinces in 1791, British authorities had given each a "liberal and disinterested" constitution that provided inhabitants with all the rights enjoyed in the American colonies before the revolution "and with many additions, the British parliament having renounced forever the right of taxation."[125] Americans in New York paid more for land and suffered much higher taxes than settlers in Upper Canada, and some found the burden simply too much. Even understanding that elections in Canada were less frequent, the franchise more restricted, and political participation less robust, thousands of Americans left for the British provinces and the promise of good lands.[126] A Kentucky newspaper went so far as to republish an article from Philadelphia noting the alarming number of wagons passing through the city en route to Canada. The piece included passages from a Canadian paper, the *Constellation*, which promised that nothing would tempt emigrants to return. "It is an extraordinary revolution indeed," the Philadelphia editor commented, "to hear the British government extolled for its mildness and ours for its oppression." A second passage from the *Constellation* warned Americans, "Your terror and discouragements are articles of your own manufacture, and heaven grant they may be solely for home consumption." Though such oppressive legislation as the Alien and Sedition Acts "may run well across the river Styx, they will not cross the Niagara." The Philadelphia editor was loath to admit that the Canadian paper was correct: "Unfortunately our infamous alien and sedition laws, direct tax, and stamp act, standing army, and the conduct of some abandoned Judges render these severe reflections on us too just, to be controverted, even coming as they do from the country of your greatest enemy."[127] Unlike Ogden, many Americans still saw British Canada as a threat. Increasingly, however, the Canadas became populated by Americans who put opportunity above citizenship.

As the French Revolutionary Wars ended, Americans once again were forced to define their international position in relation to Britain and France. Any hopes that revolutionary France might stir the republican spirit in Canada had been dashed, in no small part because French Canadians were appalled by the attacks on the Catholic church in France. Rather than becoming more democratic, the British provinces were, to American eyes, more monarchical than before. "A general survey of the British Dominions & governments will convince us," Tench Coxe informed James Madison, "that their government & affairs have recd. no infusion of republicanism since the meeting of the French Notables." Quite the contrary, the power of monarchy, aristocracy, and hierarchy had "become more ostentatious & more coercive."[128] If the question was whether the character of the British provinces would repel or attract Americans, the answer seemed to be both. In the spring of 1802, newspapers both reported and criticized reports that a group "of the northern federalists" were working "to dissolve the Union, in order to become allies or 'subjects' of the Province of Canada!!"[129] While northern Federalists, led by Timothy Pickering, had considered secession from the United States because of their disgust and distrust of Jeffersonian Republicanism, they were more likely to believe that British Canada might join their new union rather than vice versa.[130]

The press continued to comment on how the United States might suffer or benefit from the British provinces to the north. In the spring of 1803, newspapers in Pennsylvania and Baltimore published a letter from a gentleman in York, Upper Canada, to his friend in Halifax, Nova Scotia, in which he depicted the growth of his province as "almost beyond description. Last week fourteen wagons, each drawn by six horses, most of them seventeen hands high, arrived in this town from Pennsylvania, eight hundred miles by land, round the head of Lake Ontario, and have gone to settle near Lake Simcoe." The towns were now full of livestock and wagons, each of which could carry more than a dozen people. "Report says," he concluded, "there are 100 waggons more on their way to the Province with similar cargoes."[131] Another report, which claimed to be based on information from the European papers, noted in May 1803 that Spain had granted Louisiana to France. Of additional concern was the fact that the grant "very explicitly connects the claim to Canada, with that to Louisiana and asserts the rights of France to both of those colonies."[132] This development raised the possibility that the United States might hold the balance of power in North America between Britain and France and could use that power to extend its boundaries. Should another war commence, the United States could ally with France and "her armies will occupy, and peace will confirm to her, the British territories of Canada." Should Congress prefer an alliance with Britain, the United States would most likely possess Louisiana.[133] In an unsolicited letter to Thomas Jefferson, a "friend" in Paris urged the president simply to buy Canada from the British to prevent an invasion from the north. Canada was the "only door for redoutable hostile intrance in your country," and it was better to take that door by peaceful means "in order to be not obliged to take or Shut him, the arms in hand, with expensive, uncertain, and sanguinary success" by war.[134]

Any attempt at constructing an American identity during the turbulent final decades of the eighteenth century ran headlong into the revolutions, imperial wars, and local realities that divided American opinions about themselves and their northern neighbors. The end of the Revolutionary Wars in Europe had done little to ease American concerns over the British provinces, which seemed to threaten and beckon in equal measure.

# CHAPTER SEVEN

# Land of Talk

THE FINAL PAGES OF Ogden's *Tour through Upper and Lower Canada* revealed some important news. "For many years past adventurers have attempted without success to cross to the Pacific Ocean," Ogden wrote, adding that "the honor of this arduous task was left to Mr. Alexander Mac Kenzie, a partner in the north-west fur company, who lately returned by the way of the lakes, having fully accomplished the object of his undertaking in the course of two years, by traversing the continent of America."[1] This remarkable achievement, completed in 1793, made Mackenzie one of the most famous explorers in the world. It also alarmed many American citizens and politicians who kept an eye on westward British expansion. Expansion was a commercial interest for the British, but almost an existential one for Americans. Acquiring territory and exploring it forced American politicians and citizens to understand their position relative to British subjects and traders. British North Americans also began defining themselves in contrast to what they saw in the American experience. As the War of 1812 approached, neither side yet had a coherent sense of identity, but their interactions with each other illuminated divergent characteristics that open hostilities would only harden.

While Americans had long looked west, and settlers had increasingly pushed deeper into Indigenous homelands toward the Mississippi, the secret Third Treaty of San Ildefonso (1800), by which Spain ceded control of Louisiana to Napoleon, forced the United States to think about its future and act to make it real. Concerned that they might be caught between Britain and France in some future imperial conflict, American officials also realized that the British were in a precarious position given Canada's largely undefined border with northern Louisiana and the western Indigenous nations' deep ties to France.[2] The near west had been instrumental in driving American actions after the American Revolution, but the early nineteenth century put the far west at the heart of the United States' national development.

In the decades before the War of 1812, the United States became a continental project. The country looked toward the Pacific—with the Louisiana Purchase and the Corps of Discovery meant to explore and claim it before the British did—but faced its biggest threat from English ships in the Atlantic and redcoats and militiamen along the St. Lawrence River. In addition, Congress's difficulty forging Indigenous alliances made the threat of renewed conflict in the homelands very real. Competition with Great Britain over claims to Indigenous homelands to the west was unavoidable, but war in the eastern part of the continent was never inevitable. Initially the idea of another conflict with Britain was unpopular, as many Americans failed to understand the specific maritime grievances with England. To win public support for a renewed campaign to take Canada, American politicians had to harness enthusiasm for western expansion and direct it toward a northern invasion. The administration needed a smoking gun, and when they thought they had found one, they used it to convince the nation that the United States must push the British out of North America altogether. How the young nation dealt with these challenges, and how the British provinces responded to American actions, makes clear that for British America and the United States this was both an ending and a beginning. Certain revolutionary goals remained—prominently including the American capture of Canada—but citizens and subjects on both sides of the border began understanding themselves by recognizing differences as much as by valuing similarities. As it became increasingly clear that the United States would not subsume British America, Americans had to reimagine what their country should look like.

Robert R. Livingston, the United States' representative in Paris, faced a stream of obstacles in his efforts to raise American concerns about French imperial policies. He found it especially frustrating that Napoleon, who served as First Consul of France before declaring himself emperor in 1804, liked to form his own ideas. "It is a rule here," Livingston complained to Secretary of State James Madison in March 1802, "that no person intrudes an idea on the first Consul unless he asks their opinion or the conversation naturally leads to it." France's acquisition of Louisiana and the impact of this move on the United States were an especially tricky subject to introduce, in part because "they believe us to be certainly hostile to this measure and they mean to take possession of it as early as possible and with as little notice to us as they can." The best hope for the United States was to turn Britain against the treaty. Livingston had not "failed to shew in the strongest light to the minister of Britain the dangers that will result to them from the extension of the French possessions into Mexico and the probable loss of Canada if they are suffered to possess it."[3]

In a letter to British officials, Rufus King, the American ambassador in London, reminded them of the 1778 Franco-American peace (in which France promised to renounce all claims east of the Mississippi River) and the British-American peace of 1783 (which stipulated that the Mississippi River would always be free and open to British subjects and American citizens). King asked British officials if their country would stand behind these agreements and if they had been given any prior warning about Louisiana's cession to France.[4] Lord Hawkesbury, the secretary of state for foreign affairs, replied in clear but not terribly reassuring terms: first, if France secured Louisiana, the Law of Nations would require that it keep the Mississippi open to Britons and Americans; and second, the king had received no information about the cession and had not sanctioned it.[5] If British officials were worried about France's territorial aspirations, they gave no hint to American representatives.

The British had also been looking west. In 1801, Alexander Mackenzie's *Voyages from Montreal, on the River St. Laurence, through the Continent of North America, to the Frozen and Pacific Oceans* was published in London. After the death of his mother in 1774, Mackenzie, then just ten years old, moved to the United States from Scotland to join his father and uncle. As Loyalists, in 1778 they made their way to Montreal. Alexander received a brief education in Montreal before entering the fur trade, which by the 1770s was pushing into the western reaches of North America. Traders organized into companies, and those companies competed with each other for access to communication networks and for Indigenous alliances. The North West Company, established in 1779 and then re-formed in 1783, became a dominant force in the western trade and thus the target for reprisals by other Montreal outfits. One such rival was the firm of

*North West Company coat of arms*, ca. 1800–1820. The North West Company, founded in 1779, became the Hudson's Bay Company's primary trade rival. Simon Fraser, David Thompson, and Alexander Mackenzie were all Nor'westers. The outfits competed for furs and influence until they merged in 1821. Library and Archives Canada.

Gregory, McLeod, which employed Alexander Mackenzie. In their efforts to gain an advantage, competing traders resorted to violence and even murder. In 1787, a North West Company trader named Peter Pond shot and killed John Ross, a trader working for Gregory, McLeod. Pond was suspected to have killed another trader in 1782, and to prevent future violence the two companies merged.[6] Pond became a mentor to Alexander Mackenzie, with whom he shared an insatiable desire to explore the northwest.

Over two trips in 1789 and 1793, Mackenzie first reached the Arctic Ocean and then, on the second trip, the Pacific. His arrival at the Arctic Ocean was a mistake caused by following one of Peter Pond's maps, which had imagined a river running north from Lake Athabasca and curving west to a nonexistent inlet that led to the Pacific. After over a month of travel along the river that now bears his name, Mackenzie confided to his journal. "I am at a loss here how to act. . . . It is evident that these waters must empty themselves into the Northern Ocean." But he decided it was worth continuing, in order to satisfy "peoples curiosity tho' not their intentions."[7] He set out on his second attempt to reach the Pacific in the fall of 1792. Over the next ten months he traversed the expanse of the northwest, relying heavily on the geographic knowledge of Indigenous nations he encountered. He reached what is now Bella Coola, British Columbia, on an inlet of the Pacific Ocean, where the Heiltsuk people prevented him from traveling to the coast itself. On the morning of 22 July 1793, he used a mixture of vermillion and grease to write on a large rock: "Alexander Mackenzie, from Canada, by land, the twenty-second of July, one thousand seven hundred and ninety-three." The words themselves were ephemeral, the chosen medium incapable of withstanding the elements, but their impact reverberated from the Pacific Northwest to Montreal to London and eventually to a neoclassical plantation house just outside Charlottesville, Virginia.

Mackenzie's *Voyages from Montreal* appeared in the United States in 1802, published in Philadelphia by John Morgan.[8] Thomas Jefferson, who thought often about western exploration while enjoying the views from Monticello, must have felt robbed. It had been his dream to craft a nation extending from the Atlantic to the Pacific, and he now faced competition from the British and their indefatigable Canadian traders.[9] "Have you seen Mckenzie's account of his journeys across the Continent," Caspar Wistar, a Philadelphia physician, asked Jefferson. He "had very peculiar advantages for such an enterprize, & happily availed himself of them."[10] Reports of Mackenzie's achievements were not news to everyone in Washington. Alexander Hamilton had learned of the voyage in late 1794, just months after Mackenzie returned to Montreal, apparently because he had contacted the explorer for an update. "Agreeable to

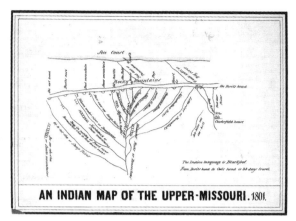

AN INDIAN MAP OF THE UPPER-MISSOURI. 1801.

*An Indian map of the Upper-Missouri, 1801,* ca. 1850. Created by Siksika chief Ackomokki and Peter Fidler, a Hudson's Bay trader, this map shows much of what would become Montana as Indigenous spatial territory. For an interpretive essay, see Jennifer Andrella's www.mappingtheuppermissouri. com. Library of Congress, Geography and Map Division.

your request," Mackenzie wrote to Hamilton, "I will give you Some few remarks on my last expedition." In a brief letter, Mackenzie described his journey and recounted the momentous occasion of reaching the Pacific in humble, unembellished prose: "here I left my Canoe and the greatest part of what we had in her; Latitude 53°. North Longitude 122°. 43 West travelled fifteen days to get to the sea coast."[11] He had reached the Pacific overland and returned to Montreal. It was up to the British and the Americans to decide what came next.

These western concerns were triangulated with northern variables. Mackenzie's voyage focused attention on the Pacific, but for American citizens and politicians, the near west was more pressing. Robert Livingston hoped to ensure that American aspirations were not hindered by British and French interests in North America. In a letter to Charles Maurice Talleyrand, the French minister of foreign affairs, Livingston requested that France cede to the United States "so much of Louisiana as lays above the mouth of the River Arkansa," which would then form a protective barrier between the French colony and British Canada. France would be left with a territory that could easily fit 15 million people, but New Orleans would have a buffer between itself and the British, who otherwise could "without the smallest difficulty attack New Orleans from Canada with 15 or 20,000 men & a host of savages."[12] A month later, Livingston made a similar argument to Napoleon himself, this time adding the importance of the Franco-American friendship into the equation. After asking rhetorically what advantage France might gain from Louisiana, especially given the region's limited development over the past century, Livingston assured the Citizen First Consul that "I could shew that her true interest would lead her to make such cessions out of them to the United States as would at once afford supplies to her Islands without draining the money of France, & rivet the friendship of the United States by removing all ground of jealousy relative to a country of little value in itself." He reminded Napoleon that his new American territory "will be perpetually exposed to the attacks of her natural ennemy as well from Canada as by sea."[13] Few things could be worse for Livingston and American officials than having additional European conflicts brought to their back door.

Others imagined new threats, including that France might keep Louisiana and gain Canada. In March 1803, a handful of newspapers published an editorial entitled "A Democratic Prophecy of the year 1797, partly fulfilled." In it, the author reminded his readers of an article published in 1797, which argued that France would never strike a peace with Britain without first possessing both Canada and Louisiana: "The first the British must grant to her; and the second the Spaniards will sell to her for a valuable consideration." Canada must be returned to France because "it was taken from them unjustly," and republics must correct such errors. And if Americans believed that Upper Canada was mostly inhabited by Americans, they also knew that Lower Canada was traditionally French "and ought to be as free as their brethren in the Commonwealth."[14] When word reached the American press in early 1803 that Spain had ceded Louisiana to France, concerns immediately turned to Canada. "An American" wrote in the *Republican; or, Anti-Democrat* that such a transfer of territory "very explicitly connects the claim to Canada, with that to Louisiana and asserts the rights of France to both of those colonies. This circumstance, no less than the author's name, and the time of publication, is of material import to the US."[15]

Yet by the time these concerns circulated, Napoleon no longer needed Louisiana. The French colony of Saint Domingue, the site of unimaginable suffering for countless enslaved Africans who were worked to death producing sugar, had witnessed a revolution in the truest sense: the enslaved, the formerly enslaved, and free Blacks (known as *gens de cou-leur*) had waged a bloody and horrific battle against Napoleon's troops, and won. Saint Domingue was reborn as Haiti, a free Black republic. This revolution held immediate consequences for the United States. On one hand, enlightened slaveholders like Thomas Jefferson might have hoped to end the practice of slavery, but they believed they could control the process of emancipation. That enslaved peoples in the United States might take matters into their own hands was a terrifying prospect. On the other hand, without enslaved Africans to feed, Napoleon no longer needed Louisiana to grow food.[16]

American politicians thought long and hard about Canada before they acquired Louisiana. Initially, Thomas Jefferson didn't necessarily want all of it. Traders and merchants certainly demanded access to the Mississippi River, and access to that river made sense only if they could use New Orleans as a port. Both before and after his election as president in 1800, Jefferson was an expansionist who envisioned a country of farmers stretching well beyond the Virginia Piedmont, fired by the American ideals that he had expressed in the Declaration of Independence. But expansion raised practical questions. There were constitutional debates over the issue, particularly whether Congress had the power to acquire new territory.[17] In a discussion over the possible acquisition of East and West Florida from France, Jefferson's attorney general, Levi Lincoln, suggested that the safest way to acquire new land would be to extend the boundaries of existing states. This would avoid increasing the number of southern states that depended on a slave economy, and thus prevent a confrontation with northern politicians who were slowly abolishing slavery.[18] Albert Gallatin reminded Jefferson that Article IV, Section 3 of the Constitution states that Congress can admit new states into the union, and noted that if Lincoln thought Congress could not acquire new territory, then surely states faced the same restrictions. The real strength behind Gallatin's argument, however, came not from the Constitution but rather the Articles of Confederation. "It may be further observed in relation to the power of admitting new States in the Union," he argued, "that this section was substituted to the 11th Art. of confederation which was in these words 'Canada acceding &c. shall be admitted into &c. this Union: but no other colony shall be admitted into the same, unless such admission be agreed to by nine states.' " If nine states of the Confederation had the power to admit new colonies (other than Canada, which required no approval to join), and if the powers of those states

were transferred by the Constitution to Congress, then there was no reason to think Congress now lacked any authority to add new territory.[19]

By the spring of 1803, the question had to be applied to much more
than Florida, but Canada remained important in the constitutional reasoning. In April, when Talleyrand and Marquis François Barbé-Marbois,
the French treasury minister, approached Livingston with the idea of
purchasing all of Louisiana, the American replied that the United States
was mostly focused on creating a buffer state between the French colony
and Canada.[20] By the end of the month, however, the United States had
secured rights to all of Louisiana for fifteen million dollars.[21] Questions
remained about the constitutionality of the transfer, but in the fall of
1803, Thomas Paine echoed Gallatin's arguments while making a direct
comparison between Louisiana and Canada. "I do not suppose that the
framers of the Constitution thought anything about the acquisition of
new territory," he wrote to Jefferson, "and even if they did it was prudent
to say nothing about it, as it might have suggested to foreign Nations the
Idea that we contemplated foreign Conquest." As far as Paine was concerned, the Constitution could not foresee future events and thus could
not say how Americans should act. But expansion, he noted, "only extends the principles of [the Constitution] over a larger territory," an action that certainly fell "within the Morality of the Constitution." That
"the Idea of extending the territory of the United States was always contemplated, whenever the opportunity offered itself, is, I think, evident
from the opinion that has existed from the Commencement of the Revolution that Canada would, at some time or other, become a part of the
United States." Paine also reminded Jefferson that the Franco-American
alliance struck during the revolution included a provision that if Canada
was conquered by joint Franco-American forces, it would become part of
the United States. There were important parallels between the Canadian
example (which never came to fruition) and that of Louisiana: "the first,
that of Canada, was generous; and the stipulation, that the Louisianians
shall come into our Union was politic." But in constitutional terms, both
cases could be considered in the same light.[22]

When news of the Louisiana Purchase reached British and French
officials, both sides found something appealing. Pierre Samuel du Pont
de Nemours was a leading French *physiocrat* (an economist who saw agri-
culture as the source of all real wealth) and close confident of Thomas
Jefferson who emigrated to the United States during the French Revolution and facilitated back-channel diplomacy during the Louisiana negoti-

ations. He saw in the purchase an opportunity for the United States to weaken Great Britain in North America. Du Pont, who habitually cautioned against war with Britain, wrote Jefferson from Paris in May 1803, using the revolutionary calendar date of 22 Floreal Year 11, "Allow me to congratulate you and the United States for the wisdom with which you resisted a war that would have thrown your country into the arms of a formidable ally; as a result acquired, without bloodshed, a country ten times larger and richer than the one you wished for." Possessing Louisiana meant that the United States had access to the entire Mississippi and would never be surrounded by another power. Even better, Louisiana "will draw inhabitants away from Canada because of its milder weather and the political climate they will find when their population is sufficiently large to allow them to create a free state in your confederation."[23] British officials seemed less threatened by the purchase than they were relieved that the Americans would guarantee them access to the Mississippi.[24] The thought of French Canadians flocking to Louisiana does not seem to have concerned them. Settlers had thrived in the Quebec winters since 1608, and there was no reason to think they would suddenly flee.

Jefferson may have taken Mackenzie's plea at the close of *Voyages from Montreal* as a personal challenge. Seeing the potential in the Pacific Northwest, Mackenzie encouraged British administrators to act:

> But whatever course may be taken from the Atlantic, the Columbia is the line of communication from the Pacific Ocean, pointed out by nature, as it is the only navigable river in the whole extent of Vancouver's minute survey of that coast: its banks also form the first level country in all the Southern extent of continental coast from Cook's entry, and, consequently, the most Northern situation fit for colonization, and suitable to the residence of a civilized people. By opening this intercourse between the Atlantic and Pacific Oceans, and forming regular establishments through the interior, and at both extremes, as well as along the coasts and islands, the entire command of the fur trade of North America might be obtained, from latitude 48. North to the pole, except that portion of it which the Russians have in the Pacific. To this may be added the fishing in both seas, and the markets of the four quarters of the globe.[25]

The Louisiana Purchase put Jefferson in an excellent position to take up this challenge. Even before he secured the transfer of Louisiana, he had been planning a quasi-scientific exploration of the western part of the continent, and the purchase served to legitimate his larger vision of the United States as a continent-wide power.[26] He had selected the men to lead the expedition as early as 1802. The first was his private secretary, Meriwether Lewis, who in turn asked William Clark to join him. Clark had served with Lewis in the Continental Army and was the younger brother of the infamous "Indian fighter" George Rogers Clark. Both men required training in the finer arts of exploration, including map-making, navigation, and ethnology.

Just as MacKenzie had given Jefferson the impetus to launch the project, other British traders and explorers would help Lewis and Clark as they traversed the continent. They needed reliable maps, and British explorers had created dozens. "You will recieve herewith inclosed some sketches taken from Vancouver's survey of the Western Coast of North America," Lewis wrote to Jefferson in May 1803, while he was in Philadelphia preparing for his departure, adding, "They were taken in a haisty manner, but I believe they will be found sufficiently accurate to be of service in composing the map, which Mr. Gallatin was so good as to promise he would have projected and compleated for me."[27] George Vancouver, a British naval officer and hydrographer who trained under Captain James Cook before commanding his own ship, is credited with mapping much of the Pacific Northwest, including charting Vancouver Island and confirming that the Juan de Fuca Strait was simply a passage among islands and did not feed into an inland sea.[28] If the goal was to reach the Pacific, his maps were just what Lewis and Clark would need. Fortunately for the adventurers, Albert Gallatin, the Swiss emigré who settled in western Pennsylvania and went on to serve as Jefferson's secretary of the Treasury, turned out to be something of a geographer. He helped compile the maps, drawn from Vancouver's and Alexander Mackenzie's charts, that would guide the explorers.

In addition to those Gallatin created, some extant maps were important enough to aid Lewis and Clark on their expedition. One, likely drawn from Jefferson's personal library, was made by David Thompson in 1798 after he visited the Mandans in present-day North Dakota.[29] Thompson personified the British fur trade. He was born into poverty in London and died a pauper in Montreal, but in between he left a mark on North American history. He was apprenticed to the Hudson's Bay

David Thompson commemorative stamp. Canada Post,
1957. David Thompson and his Indigenous wife,
Charlotte Small, traveled through much of western
North America in the early nineteenth century.

Company in 1784 at age fourteen and spent much of his life exploring
North America. He learned the arts of surveying, astronomy, and map-
making in 1789 and 1790 while he recovered from a fractured leg that,
due to severe swelling, couldn't be set properly and thus took several
months to heal. In the spring of 1790, before his leg had fully healed, he
lost sight in his right eye but was determined to continue his training.
Sometime in the mid-1790s, after several promotions and for reasons
that are not entirely clear, Thompson left the Hudson's Bay Company
for one of its rivals, the North West Company. His years in their employ
would be his most prolific. In 1797, as British and American officials
struggled to place the border between the two territories, Thompson set
out to map the forty-ninth parallel, which many on both sides thought
would be the eventual boundary. After 1799, he traveled with his Métis
(of mixed Indigenous and European parents) wife, Charlotte Small,
whom he had married *à la façon du pays* (according to the custom of the
country) and who, like many Indigenous women in the fur trade, greatly
facilitated his encounters.[30] Thompson and Charlotte Small spent years
exploring and surveying the northwest, including the length of the Columbia River—lands that Jefferson hoped would fall into the United
States' political or at least economic orbit.

In the depiction of the Pacific Northwest that had so inspired Jefferson, Mackenzie ignored a central fact: like the rest of North America, it was and is inhabited by Indigenous peoples with deep histories. The Haisla, Bella Coola, Coast Salish, Nootkans, Makah, Chinookans, and other nations lived in their ancestral homelands, but settler aspirations, including Jefferson's, focused not on what the place was but on how they might remake it.[31] Jefferson, who doubted that Indigenous nations held true sovereignty over their homelands, at least foresaw the necessity of securing Indigenous allies. He instructed Lewis, "In all your intercourse with the natives treat them in the most friendly & conciliatory manner which their own conduct will admit; allay all jealousies as to the object of your journey, satisfy them of it's innocence, make them acquainted with the position, extent, character, peaceable & commercial dispositions of the US. of our wish to be neighborly, friendly & useful to them, & of our dispositions to a commercial intercourse with them."[32] A gentle approach to Indigenous peoples would prevent too much alarm and enable Lewis and Clark to collect as much information about these nations as possible. Jefferson wanted to learn about the peoples whose homelands he hoped to transform into America.[33] The Indigenous peoples in North America never agreed that European powers could control or sell their lands, and the Canadian merchants operating throughout the region reminded Americans that trade networks were often more important than international agreements.

Lewis and Clark set out to traverse the Louisiana Purchase in May 1804. They led a fifty-person unit specially created for the expedition, the Corps of Discovery, consisting primarily of U.S. military men, along with some civilians, several *engagés* (contract workers), and Clark's enslaved Black servant, York. The American ideals that the Corps carried across the continent included slavery, a concept not foreign to the Indigenous peoples they would meet.[34] The lands they passed through were ancestral homelands that European empires claimed but as yet could seldom control. When the Corps of Discovery reached the Mandan, who lived along the Missouri River, a homeland they called "the heart of the world," they stopped for the winter. During the months that followed they were frequently visited by members of other Indigenous nations as well as traders from the Hudson's Bay and North West Companies.[35] Not all the traders spoke fondly of the Corps or its mission. Lewis and Clark faced the additional challenge of reminding the Mandan peoples that, as far as the Corps was concerned, they were now under American

*Mih-Tutta-Hangkusch: A Mandan village*, after Karl Bodmer, ca. 1839. The
Mandan hosted fur traders and explorers, including Lewis and Clark.
Aquatint, 44 × 57.5 cm (17 5/16 × 22 5/8 in.), Mabel Brady Garvan
Collection, 1946.9.525. Yale University Art Gallery.

jurisdiction. In late November, traders from the North West Company
gifted the Mandans medallions and flags, leading Clark to ask the chiefs
"to impress it on the minds of their nations that those [symbols] were
not to be received by any of them, without they wished to incur the displeasure of their Great American Father."[36] The Mandans, who understood that gifts went hand in hand with trade, were not easily persuaded
to change their practices.

   One Canadian trader, Toussaint Charbonneau, had been living along
the Missouri River for about eight years when Lewis and Clark arrived.
Charbonneau was a Métis born near Montreal who had been employed
by the North West Company as a trader on the Assiniboine River in
what is now Manitoba, Canada.[37] He was by most accounts an unsavory

character, variously accused of cowardice and, at least once when he was a younger man, rape.[38] At the time the Corps of Discovery arrived at the Heart of the World, Charbonneau had two wives. Polygyny was not uncommon among Indigenous nations, but it is unclear whether Charbonneau had captured his wives or purchased them. In early November 1804, Clark recorded his meeting with "a french man by Name Chabonah, who Speaks the Big Belley language . . . he wished to hire & informed us his 2 Squars were Snake Indians, we engau him to go on with us and take one of his wives to interpet the Snake language."[39] One of Charbonneau's wives was the Otter Woman, and the other was Sacagawea, a young Shoshone woman who had been captured several years earlier by the Hidatsa, who lived along the Knife River in what is now North Dakota. Charbonneau decided to bring Sacagawea as the Corps's interpreter, perhaps because she was well suited for the job or perhaps because she was pregnant with the couple's first child. She would give birth by the time they set off, in spring 1805. While she certainly helped navigate through the regions she knew, and her facility with Indigenous languages aided Lewis and Clark just as Charlotte Small's helped David Thompson, her greatest value came from being a young woman with an infant. For Indigenous nations who might assume that the approaching Corps of Discovery posed a military threat, the inclusion of a young Indigenous mother and her baby was a reassuring sign. "The wife of Shabono our interpetr we find reconsiles all the Indians, as to our friendly intentions," Clark noted in October 1805, adding that "a woman with a party of men is a token of peace."[40]

British traders along the Missouri River were often a cause for concern among the Corps of Discovery. During their stay with the Mandans, Lewis and Clark encountered traders from both the Hudson's Bay Company and the North West Company, some of whom would inquire about the nature of the American expedition or ask about recent changes in the United States government.[41] In early 1805, Charbonneau reported to Clark that a certain clerk of the Hudson's Bay Company was speaking unfavorably about the American outfit, and that the North West Company intended to build a fort in the region.[42] Some British traders asked if they could travel with the Corps. Knowing that British trade companies would be in direct competition with American interests, Clark informed François-Antoine Larocque, a clerk with the North West Company, that under no circumstances could he participate in the expedition to the Pacific.[43] What if, instead of using it to their benefit, the British attempted to sabotage the expedition? This was not an irrational fear given that Charbonneau had once worked for the North West Company.

In March 1805, in reference to Charbonneau's loyalty, Clark noted that "we have every reason to believe that our Menetarre interpreter (whome we intended to take with his wife) . . . has been corupted by the [blank] Companeys." As proof, Clark recorded only that "some explenation has taken place which Clearly proves to us the fact." They gave Charbonneau one night to decide "whether or not he intends to go with us under the regulations stated." The North West and Hudson's Bay Company clerks operating in the region left no indication that they hoped to harm the American expedition, and they were likely too busy competing with each other to make common cause against the Americans.[44] So Lewis and Clark, Sacagawea with Charbonneau and child, and the Corps of Discovery set out from Mandan territory. Over the next several months they made their way to the Pacific, guided in part by their British maps and Indigenous interpreters. On 3 December 1805, twelve years after Mackenzie reached the Pacific, William Clark imitated the British explorer: "I marked my name & the day of the month and year on a large Pine tree on this Peninsella & by land 'Capt William Clark, December 3rd 1805. By Land. U States in 1804 & 1805.' "[45] American explorers, like the British traders before them, had crossed the continent, extending economic and territorial competition from one ocean to the other, in lands that settler powers might claim but Indigenous nations controlled.

While Lewis and Clark were making their voyage, American officials were struggling to triangulate their relationships with British traders, Indigenous neighbors, and escaped enslaved peoples. In places far from the border, Americans hoped to strengthen their position at the expense of the British, while in border towns like Detroit they aimed for peaceful coexistence. Writing from St. Louis, the governor of the Louisiana Territory, James Wilkinson, complained about the influence of Montreal traders on the region's Indigenous peoples. "Engageés are now daily arriving here," Wilkinson lamented, "from Montreal via Michilimackanack and the Ouisconsin, with merchandise not only for the Indians of the Missouri, but the Inhabitants of this Territory." As much as he wanted to prevent Canadian traders from coming to St. Louis, he knew that without them there would not be enough supplies. He suggested, however, that the federal government inform the British representative of its intent "to interdict this intercourse after a given period," that the warning be made public, and that forts with customs officers be built along the waterways leading to St. Louis.[46] But in Detroit, where British settlements lay just across the river, American officials were more interested in maintaining good relations with their neighbors, partly to facilitate trade but also because citizenship in the region was blurry. Upon arriving in Detroit to take up his appointment as governor of the Michigan Territory, William Hull wrote to Madison that he had issued an address "to a numerous assembly of the people," which had "been translated into the french language, read in churches, and communicated in various ways."[47] Hull told his listeners that "the United States and [Great Britain] are in peace and friendship, God grant it may forever continue! It will be our duty and our interest to cultivate harmony and friendship with our respectable neighbors."[48] It was a promising message in a region with a long history of citizens and subjects trading, marrying, and settling on either side of the border.

Even in Detroit, the border meant more to some than to others. The Michigan Territory was slave free, but some settlers in Upper Canada still held people in slavery. Lieutenant Governor Simcoe, even before arriving in Upper Canada in 1791, had argued that the practice of slavery went against Christianity and the British constitution. He had an opportunity to address the issue in 1793, when his council heard the case of Chloe Cooley, an enslaved woman living in Queenston who was forcibly taken across the Niagara River and sold to an American. This was a practice that many Upper Canadians pursued for profit. Simcoe wanted the slave owner punished, but the council ruled that he had broken no laws. So Simcoe instructed his attorney general to introduce a bill for the gradual abolition of slavery, which became law in the summer of 1793. The act freed no slaves. Those held in bondage would remain slaves until their death, but any children born to slaves after 1793 would be freed at age twenty-five. It was a compromise that favored Upper Canadian slaveholders at the expense of those, like Chloe Cooley, who could take little solace in the end of slavery for their descendants.[49]

For William Hull, the challenge was what to do with slaves escaping to Detroit from Canada. In the years before 1833, when Great Britain abolished slavery outright, fleeing to an American territory or state was a way for slaves to attain their freedom. "Much sensibility in upper Canada is excited on account of their slaves," Hull wrote to Madison in July 1806; "some of them have recently left their Masters, and come into this Territory." Canadian slave owners, angered by the prospect of their slaves escaping across the border, had applied to the authorities in Michigan, requesting that their slaves be captured and returned, but Hull considered himself unauthorized to perform such a task.[50] A month later, he was relieved to report that "the agitation respecting the Slaves in Upper Canada has subsided, and I hope nothing in future will take place to revive the subject."[51] But this local issue had national implications that required attention.

Jacob Wagner, the chief clerk of the Department of State, reminded Secretary Madison that the United States didn't seem to have a uniform policy for dealing with fugitive slaves.[52] Resolving the issue in the Michigan Territory fell to Augustus Woodward, whom President Jefferson had named chief justice of the territory's supreme court. Woodward, like Simcoe, abhorred slavery but struggled with the blurred lines between slave and free. Although slavery was outlawed in Michigan, British and French residents who had held slaves before the United States acquired the territory were allowed to keep them. As for the escaped slaves from Canada, Woodward argued that since no treaty required their return, these men and women could stay and enjoy their freedom.[53] It was an inelegant solution, but it seemed to satisfy everyone but the slaveholders of Upper Canada.

To the various tensions affecting British-American relations in North America must be added the looming threat of war. While Jefferson's Corps of Discovery were traversing the continent, British ships on the Atlantic were targeting American vessels in search of deserters. Great Britain needed seamen, especially as its war with Napoleonic France spilled out of Europe and across the Atlantic, but too often English sailors abandoned their ships to work on American vessels, where they received better treatment and remuneration. In the eyes of British officials, these men could not simply take on American citizenship. It was impossible to renounce your status as a Briton or your duties to the nation, and thus the British navy began impressing men who had fled the service. They checked ships—usually private vessels, so as to avoid infringing on the sovereignty of the American naval fleet—and sent impressment crews on shore to ferret out deserters on the wharves, taverns, and anywhere else they might find them.[54] Fear of "Press gangs" was common in harbor towns, exacerbated by widely circulated tales of roving men with clubs out hunting for potential sailors, but there were rules that press gangs had to follow, and the process was much more orderly than most tended to believe.[55] Still, by targeting American vessels and impressing men who believed they were American citizens, the British navy earned the ire of officials and citizens alike.

Two other issues pushed the United States to consider declaring war on Great Britain. The first was the perennial concern over British support for the Indigenous nations whose homelands were claimed by American states, especially those living along the Great Lakes. It was easy for Congress to assume the British were encouraging the Indigenous nations to push back against the United States expansion, but neither the British nor the Americans fully realized how Indigenous nations created a pan-Indigenous resistance to the Americans in the wake of the Louisiana Purchase and unrelenting settler incursions.[56] A second important moment in the road to war was the efforts by Great Britain and Napoleonic France to limit American shipping rights by blockading trade and refusing to acknowledge neutral vessels. A series of British orders in council in 1807 required vessels that wished to trade with France to first dock at British ports and pay duties. In response, Napoleon issued his Milan Decree, which made any ship abiding by the British orders liable to search and seizure.[57] Frustrated by its treatment as a pawn in European affairs, and largely unable to respond effectively in ways that would damage the economic interests of either Britain or France, the American officials increasingly saw war against Great Britain as their only opportunity to gain international respect.

As the cultural, political, and legal differences separating British subjects and American citizens became more evident, both sides developed a keen interest in learning more about each other. American officials such as Madison and Jefferson looked north with both genuine interest and stereotypical assumptions. On one hand, as secretary of state, Madison understood the need to keep his staff informed of doings in other nations, both hostile and friendly. To that end he ordered books. In one order, which included treaties on public law and other tomes on European affairs, Madison requested "A History of Canada by George Heriot," one of the first histories of the region to appear in English. Heriot, a well-educated Scot who served as deputy postmaster general in Canada, based his book on Pierre Charlevoix's 1744 *Histoire et description générale de la Nouvelle France*. If Madison was hoping to understand the Canadian character, he would have been disappointed: Hariot (like Charlevoix) ended his account in 1731.[58] Madison benefited more from men such as Augustus Woodward, who lived on the Canadian border and was required to understand his neighbors. A former clerk at the State Department who had relocated to Detroit, Woodward sent Madison "the map which I promised to procure of, his Britannic Majesty's province of Upper Canada, accompanied by a small pamphlet of statistical information." He noted that Upper Canada was "by no means unimportant" and blamed southern prejudices for the general belief that "these northern countries are cold, sterile, and unprofitable." While he thought New Brunswick and Nova Scotia might be considered barren, the scene grew drastically different as one traveled away from the ocean and along the St. Lawrence. The river's shores were dotted with "fertile, pleasant, and even opulent" settlements, presenting "along the whole line, a scene of activity little imagined in the United States."[59] Settlers who had moved into the region north of the Ohio River were quickly running out of land, which made northern territories even more attractive. A war with Great Britain would again justify the attempt to annex Canada.

Jefferson, who spent considerable time imagining settlements in North America and who, like Madison, collected information about Canada, did occasionally fall into what Woodward called "southern prejudices." Jefferson had a famously grand and eclectic library (which would later become the core holdings of the Library of Congress), including dozens of books detailing Canada's history, geography, and "discovery" by Europeans. Yet he often fell back on simple stereotypes to describe Canadians themselves. In a letter about the impact of climate on identity, Jefferson looked north for the perfect example: "The Canadian glows with delight in his sleigh & snow, the very idea of which gives me the shivers."[60]

Benjamin Rush also shivered when he thought of Canada, but his reasons were more personal. As tensions between Britain and the United States augured for war, Rush's thoughts turned not to his country but to his family. In February 1805 he wrote to his friend John Adams about his predicament: "My eldest daughter is still happy with an excellent husband at Montreal." At her wedding, in March 1799, Rush went so far as to propose a toast to the king of Great Britain, noting that His Majesty had gained another subject. One daughter in Canada was a challenge, but things got worse. "My second daughter visited her in 1803 where she was addressed by a Captain in the British army," which displeased Rush and his wife. But after his eldest daughter and her husband spoke fondly on behalf of the suitor, "we reluctantly submitted to his taking her from us" in February 1804. Rush now had a daughter in Montreal and another "at a remote post in Upper Canada," and while both claimed to be happy, the doctor feared they were "lost to us—for life."[61] Adams responded with words of encouragement about grooms and geography. "Many of those officers are worthy men," he reassured his friend, and his daughters

James Akin, Dr. Benjamin Rush, after Jeremiah Paul,
1800. Etching and engraving, 27.3 × 20 cm (10 3/4 × 7
7/8 in.), Mabel Brady Garvan Collection, 1946.9.837.
Yale University Art Gallery. Two of Rush's daughters
married British soldiers and lived in Canada.

were far from lost forever: "Neither Upper Canada nor England are so
far off, but you may often hear from her, and much of her happiness."[62]
Despite Adams's calming sentiments, Rush and his children would join
the countless examples of how loyalty could divide family.

As war approached, Rush's problems might have been remedied if
Upper Canada simply became part of the United States. As newspapers
reported that the governor of British Canada was demanding all resi-

dents swear an oath or leave the provinces, armchair (and former) generals discussed how the United States might best acquire Upper Canada and why such an endeavor was important.[63] John Nicholas a retired Republican congressman who had recently moved to Geneva, New York, suggested to Jefferson that militia volunteers would easily capture Canada, where the residents were "prepared for revolt." Such an expedition might even be bloodless, but if not, it would be worth the expense to win over Indigenous allies, prevent Great Britain from invading New York, and be relieved of having to maintain military forts along the border.[64]

Nicholas's attitude was echoed by no less a military mind than the Marquis de Lafayette, who had certainly not forgotten his failure to capture Canada and encouraged others to renew the effort. Anglo-American animosities had increased after June 1807, when the HMS *Leopard* approached the USS *Chesapeake*, which was not far from Virginia en route to the Mediterranean, and demanded to board and search for deserters. When the American captain refused, the *Leopard* fired on the ship, killing three Americans, and took an additional four men as "deserters," only one of whom was British.[65] "I Hope the United States may still Avoid a War," Lafayette cautioned Jefferson in the aftermath of the *Chesapeake* affair, "but Should they be obliged to it, dont you think Canada ought to be possessed so as to have this large door shut against every possible attack or machinations? The more America is, at home, free from European Contact, the better for Herself and for Liberty at large."[66] Another revolutionary figure with ties to Canada offered to do the heavy lifting. In letters to James Madison in late 1807 and early 1808, Ira Allen declared, "Should the United States be Necessitated to go to War with Great Britain I offer my Servises (being Duly Authorised) to take the Canada's and Unite them to the Government of the United States." By this time Allen was out of Vermont and living in Philadelphia, having declared bankruptcy after his failed United Columbia scheme. A third attempt to take Canada would have enabled him to return to Vermont, which he had fled in 1804 to avoid debtors' prison. He even suggested new boundaries and reminded Madison that Great Britain might be eager to relieve itself of the expense of supporting military posts and Indigenous allies.[67] Canada, it seemed, was there for the taking.

Even if they thought Canadians themselves might remain neutral or perhaps support an American invasion, Lafayette, Allen, and others recognized that Britain remained a formidable opponent with easy access into American territory. There were some rumblings about the rebellious spirit of Upper Canadians. Reports circulated in the American press of an Upper Canadian newspaper editor, Joseph Willcocks, who dared to criticize the provincial government. "The fate of this independent man, under such a government, was anticipated," railed the *Democratic Press* of Philadelphia, adding, "His press will be destroyed and he no doubt made to linger out a great part of his life in prison."[68] Officials in Canada took offense at Willcocks's newspaper, a four-page sheet he called the *Upper Canada Guardian; or, Freeman's Journal*, griping that there was a copy in nearly every house and that Willcocks was trying to radicalize Upper Canadians.[69] But he was not sent to prison; even after his troubles with officials in Upper Canada, Willcocks was elected to provincial parliament. "This looks like a willingness to cast off the yoke of the crown of England," one Philadelphia paper enthused.[70] The very presence of an opposition newspaper in Upper Canada encouraged some Americans to hope the province had finally seen the light.

Barnabas Bidwell, a Yale-educated author, educator, and lawyer, argued that "the people must judge from impressions, communicated through Newspapers principally."[71] It is likely that Bidwell himself knew how the American press was presenting Canadian sentiments. He certainly considered himself sufficiently expert on the topic to advise James Madison. "I yesterday learned, from a source of information to be relied on," he informed the secretary of state from Vermont in February 1808, "that a considerable number of inhabitants of Canada, having removed from the United States into a range of Towns bordering upon the north line of this State are extremely anxious respecting the critical state of affairs between the United States & Great Britain." Although many of these inhabitants, he added, had sworn oaths of allegiance to the Crown, they had done so purely for access to land and patronage, and "in case of a rupture, they would not willingly oppose the United States, their native country; but on the contrary wish to join us."[72] Bidwell had the chance to determine whether this was the case in 1810, when he joined the ranks of ex-patriot Americans living in Upper Canada, having fled accusations of financial mismanagement during his tenure as a treasurer in Berkshire County, Massachusetts.[73] Yet in his new home he would have also heard arguments against war. One line of reasoning was that only Great Britain and its navy could protect Europe and the United States from Bonaparte, and thus it was better for the northern provinces to remain British. Great Britain had little interest in expanding into American territory, but it was folly to assume that Napoleon would limit his aspirations to Europe.[74]

It was one thing for Congress to consider launching a war against Great Britain and quite another to convince Americans that it was a good idea. The revolution had causes around which Patriots could rally: the demand to be treated like British subjects and, after 1776, the desire to be independent altogether. In the years before the War of 1812, the "war hawks" needed a narrative to inspire a largely divided nation—Federalists and Democratic-Republicans, northern states and southern—to act in concert. A conspiracy theory would do, and John Henry had one to sell: it wasn't entirely true that the British in Canada were uninterested in taking American territory. Henry, a British subject who had lived in the United States for years, hoped to persuade New Englanders to separate from the United States. He was a handsome Irish immigrant who had arrived in the United States in 1796, when he was twenty-one. He used family connections—primarily his wealthy uncle, who lived in New York—to secure a position in the American army. Looking to make his fortune in Philadelphia, he accumulated some money through a string of business ventures and one fortunate marriage. He lived for a time in Boston, where his marriage and connections gained him access to the most refined social circles. It also didn't hurt that he was an ardent Federalist. After about ten years in the United States, at which point he was running a farm in Vermont (his wife having died), he decided that life in the republic no longer suited him. In 1807 he packed his belongings and moved to Montreal, hoping for more luck as a passionate monarchist than he had had as a fervent Federalist.[75]

In Montreal, Henry relied on his charm, looks, and worldliness to ingratiate himself with the fur trading and business elites. He attended dinners at the Beaver Club, an association formed in 1785 that usually met at the Montreal Hotel, where he rubbed elbows with the city's most prominent denizens—the McGills, Frobishers, and McGillivrays, as well as visiting government officials—always with an eye to advancing his career, perhaps as a judge or justice of the peace. He surely enjoyed the fine dining, admired the gold medals inscribed with the club's motto—"Fortune in Distress"—and marveled at the games played by members, including paddling an imaginary canoe, an exercise that was no doubt much more enjoyable after several bottles of wine.[76] His status grew and his connections improved. Though his new friends wrote on his behalf, some in the Canadian administration were less impressed. The lieutenant governor of Upper Canada, Francis Gore, described Henry as "an Irish Adventurer—not even called to the Bar" and, worse, "a citizen of the United States."[77] To raise his profile, Henry took it upon himself to become an asset to the British government. He began documenting his sense of public opinion in New England and forwarded those musings to Herman W. Ryland, the secretary of Lower Canada. Ryland in turn forwarded Henry's letters to Sir James Craig, the governor of Canada, who sent them along to the colonial secretary, Lord Castlereagh, in London. There was a reason British administrators liked what Henry had to say. He argued that the Democratic-Republicans were acting in the French interest, that they "talk openly of the necessity of making Jefferson president for life," and most important, that "the rancorous hostility of the two parties in the States towards each other may be turned to good account; and in the opinion of some of their wisest men, will, should war take place, produce a dissolution of the Confederation."[78] He seemed poised to add "spy" to his long list of occupations.

Ryland encouraged this espionage. Aware that Henry wanted a government job and knowing that militia posts and legal positions were scarce in Upper Canada, he wrote Henry that providing information about the United States "appears to me to afford the most eligible grounds for your immediate introduction to Office in this Country." Then Ryland pushed a little harder. It is true, he noted, that a war with Great Britain might lead to a breakup of the United States, especially "if men of adequate Information and Ability will zealously exert their Talents to bring about this 'Consummation devoutly to be wished.' It is time to cry down these Mob Governments."[79] Henry, taking the hint, used a business trip to Boston in late 1807 and early 1808 to further plumb the attitudes of frustrated Federalists. It was a presidential election year, with James Madison running against the Federalist Charles Cotesworth Pinckney, and Henry listened attentively to public and private conversations. Traveling through Vermont, he learned of "the clamour against the Government" in response to a new law that prohibited merchants from sending goods to Canada, and he noted that if the United States allied with Bonaparte, many citizens in Vermont would favor leaving the union and joining the British colonies. One editorial in a Boston newspaper, he reported, suggested that "the people of the New England States will be ready to withdraw from the confederacy, establish a separate government and adopt a policy congenial with their interest and happiness." Finally,

Henry suggested he might be able to get his hands on some letters written by Jefferson during the revolution that would, if released publicly, "lessen his influence at the coming election of president."[80] Ryland collected the letters from Henry and sent them along to Craig, who increasingly saw value in Henry's sleuthing and reporting.

In February 1809, Sir James Craig sent Henry a letter. The governor instructed him to continue his work in New England "to obtain the most accurate information of the true state of affairs in that part of the Union." Craig was most interested in the Federalists, whose presidential candidate had won only the New England states and lost badly to Madison everywhere else. Henry was charged with sending "the earliest intelligence if his party should contemplate a separation from the Union." Should the Federalists seem interested in British help, Henry was authorized "to insinuate that he will forward communications." Craig provided his spy with the necessary credentials, though Henry was to keep them secret until they might prove necessary.[81] Ryland echoed Craig's sentiments: "The extraordinary situation of things at this time in the neighbouring States has suggested to the Governor in Chief the idea of employing you as a secret and confidential mission to Boston provided an arrangement can be made to meet the important end in view, without throwing an absolute obstacle in the way of your professional pursuits." Henry, excited by the opportunity, didn't think to ask for money, so sure was he that this work would lead to a government position.[82]

Henry toured the New England states and dutifully reported what he learned from new acquaintances and old: the 1807 embargo laws—Jefferson's feeble and ineffective response to Britain's orders in council and Napoleon's Milan Decree, which prevented trade with either power—continued to infuriate Vermont businessmen; Democratic-Republicans in the region argued Canada could be taken with only five thousand men; and a junto in Boston was weighing its options should war be declared, including "an application to the Governor General of British America for aid."[83] Henry collected his information from public rumors, published newspapers, and lips loosened by long dinners. His comfort among the Federalist elite meant that he was invited to social gatherings and multicourse meals, where the diners could say in private things they might not share in public. Perhaps they referred to "that Jacobin in the White House" or half joked that the return of Hanover was preferable to Jefferson or Madison.[84] Henry hoped his reports would make him invaluable, but his efforts brought him no closer to a government post. The government had other spies in different parts of the United States who offered the same or better information.[85] To improve his prospects, Henry would have to get creative. Fortunately, he had made copies of his letters.

As Henry charmed his way through Boston society on behalf of the governor of Canada, officials in James Madison's administration wondered how they could win public support for a looming war with Britain. To convince American citizens that war was necessary, the Democratic-Republicans could suggest that Canadians would welcome an invasion if they had assurances that their churches and property would be protected.[86] There were more popular arguments for war, including the issue of British impressment, the fear of Anglo-Indigenous alliances, and Britain's refusal to recognize American trade sovereignty. The Federalists rebutted these arguments by calling them exaggerations and pointing out that France had also ignored the United States' trade rights. In addition, Federalists questioned whether the United States, with its limited army and navy, was prepared to fight a war.[87]

Democratic-Republican officials had heard the same rumors John Henry did: that some in the New England states might see war as an opportunity to strengthen relations with the British colonies rather than fight for the American republic.[88] At the very least, many leading Federalists were cautioning against war. In 1811, American newspapers published Timothy Pickering's letters "addressed to the people of the United States of America," in which he argued that the country was unprepared for war and that the Madison administration would never defy its southern roots by supporting a conquest of Canada, "which will add to the population and power of the northern states." Congress had banned the importation of slaves in 1808, and thus each new state added to the union was a battle between slavery and abolition—the moral question at the heart of American expansion in the early nineteenth century. It would be much better, Pickering argued, to keep Canada in British hands so as to prevent its being captured by France.[89]

It was increasingly obvious to both Federalists and Republicans that the country was divided as to the reasons for and benefits from a war with Great Britain. Few Americans were happy with the fact that Britain stopped American ships to look for British sailors, and many were concerned that Britain and France refused to recognize American neutrality at sea.[90] But frustration with British practices was not the same as wishing to launch headlong into a conflict with a global superpower, especially given that an attack on Britain would certainly play into Napoleon's favor.

Democratic-Republican officials wanted war, and they wanted to crush the Federalists who stood in their way. Evidence that suggested Great Britain was actively meddling in the affairs of the United States, and, worse, that Federalists welcomed such an intervention, would be worth its weight in gold. John Henry was ready to collect.

In the summer of 1810, Henry followed Ryland to England in the hope that the secretary would finally offer him a government position. To bolster his status, Henry curried favor with London merchants by contributing to a pamphlet extolling the importance of the North West Company and advocating a trade monopoly in the area of the Columbia River. His efforts came to nothing, and in late 1811 he caught one of the last ships of the season back to Quebec.[91] During this voyage, Henry met a man who called himself Count Edward de Crillon—a grifter and confidence man who saw in Henry either a kindred spirit or a target, or possibly both. Henry confided in Crillon about his espionage and the letters he had copied and showed him some pages. Crillon suggested that Henry consider selling the papers, perhaps to the French ambassador in Washington or perhaps to the Americans themselves. The self-proclaimed count assured the English spy that he could help make the necessary connections, and the two could then split the profits and return to France.[92] Having gained nothing from his work for the British, Henry apparently figured he had little to lose.

Crillon and Henry arrived in the United States just before Christmas 1811 to capitalize on the rising British-American tensions. Attacks by an Indigenous confederacy over the course of 1811 (known as Tecumseh's War) against American settlers around the Great Lakes had led to a widespread belief that the British were instigating their Indigenous allies. The Indigenous nations, however, needed no encouragement, and the British were walking a fine line: preparing their Indigenous allies to fight while also cautioning restraint to prevent a war in North America that would distract from British efforts to defeat Napoleon in Europe. During the first decade of the nineteenth century, Indigenous leaders emerged—Tecumseh and Tenskwatawa (the Prophet) being two of the most prominent—to assemble pan-Indigenous alliances that could challenge settler expansion into their homelands. These alliances had to be reconstituted after the Treaty of Greenville, which had caused various confederacies to splinter and pursue their own interests. As president, Thomas Jefferson encouraged state and territorial governors, primarily William Hull of Michigan and William Henry Harrison of Indiana, to continue the work of dispossession. While Indigenous leaders realized they were increasingly outnumbered, they began fighting to keep their lands. Though Harrison had persuaded older leaders to sign treaties surrendering hundreds of thousands of acres, younger warriors rejected these agreements. Flocking to Tecumseh and Tenskwatawa, these warriors organized at Prophetstown in the Wabash Valley. In early November 1811, having pushed into the northern Indiana Territory, Harrison and his troops were set upon by warriors at Tippecanoe Creek. The surprised Americans suffered initially but rallied, and eventually the warriors fled just before the Americans retreated to Vincennes. Harrison, in his recounting of the action, transformed the relatively indecisive battle into a great American victory against the warriors and, more important, against the dastardly British who had supported them.[93]

British officials denied any involvement in the Indigenous attacks, but trust was eroding on both sides.[94] British subjects and American citizens grew tired of each other's insults. A *New York Herald* editorial recognized that Canadians could "manage the bayonet, pike and gun" as well as any American army, and they were "very little inferior to our bravest spouters" in the "wordy war" raging across the border. As evidence, the editorial republished an article from the *Quebec Mercury* that included a litany of complaints against Americans who disparaged Great Britain and its North American colonies. The *Mercury* lamented that Americans could think British people capable of arming Indigenous allies and setting them against American settlers, a claim found not only in American papers but also "roundly asserted in the speeches of their legislators." Englishmen, the *Mercury* declared, would never forgive the insult to the honor of England.[95] But one insulted Englishman and his new French friend had returned to the United States with a stack of letters that put Britain's honor in question. John Henry hoped that the war hawks in the White House would see their value.

They persuaded Massachusetts Governor Elbridge Gerry to make the introduction. On Christmas Eve, Henry and "Count" de Crillon presented themselves to Gerry in Boston and briefly outlined their intentions. A few days later, Gerry wrote to Madison. "The Count de Crillon, son of the celebrated Duke, who beseiged Gibralter, & was famous as a great mi[li]tary character, arrived here a day or two past, & proposes to go on to Washington," Gerry informed President Madison, taking Crillon's fabricated past as authentic. He described Henry as someone Madison likely knew and "also a great military character, & in every point, truly respectable."[96] The following day, perhaps having talked with some people who knew Henry, Gerry sent Madison a clarifying message. "I addressed, at the request of some Gentlemen, a line to you yesterday, introducing the Count de Crillon to your Excellency," he noted, "and think it expedient to inform you, that I am in every respect uninformed in regard to the politicks of that nobleman, he being to me an entire stranger."[97] Others were more suspicious. The French minister to the United States, who himself had received a letter from Crillon, wrote to his superiors that while Crillon had a very fine French name, "it might cover a trap." But given that the papers could "produce an immediate explosion between America and Great Britain," the minister was content to see how matters developed.[98]

With introductions made, Henry and Crillon began working their connections and hinting at the value of Henry's papers. Crillon operated as Henry had done in Boston: he attended dinner parties, made the rounds of social events, and generally worked to ingratiate himself with important people. Henry had a meeting with Madison in which he convinced the president of his letters' value: they would persuade the American public to support a war against Great Britain. He then moved into an apartment in Georgetown and waited.

The negotiations between Crillon, representing Henry, and Secretary of State James Monroe, on behalf of Madison, lasted for weeks. Henry wanted assurances that no word of the letters or the negotiations would be released until he and Crillon had sailed for Europe, and he demanded the princely sum of £25,000 before a single American had even seen the papers. American officials offered $50,000, well short of Henry's request. Outraged, Henry threatened to burn the papers, while Crillon, playing his role to perfection, promised to talk some sense into his partner. They settled on a price of $90,000, with $50,000 to be paid up front. To ensure that Henry went for the deal and that Crillon got his cut of the profits, the count turned the con on his partner: to make up for the remaining $40,000, Crillon promised Henry title to his fictional family estate in Gascony, and, in addition, he made Henry his squire.[99] Henry was thrilled. He exclaimed, "My name will be rescued from oblivion by living near Crillon, the habitation of your ancestors, and of a man who has been my best friend."[100] It was a bad deal all around: the money was a promissory note, the estate was imaginary, the letters largely worthless. When the agreement was finalized, however, each party thought it had come out on top. Henry was so pleased that he gave Crillon a gift of $1,000 and a loan of $6,000.

Henry was particularly talented at convincing himself that all his hard work had paid off. He went so far as to write Monroe to suggest how he might get the most value from the letters. Monroe, he wrote, now had "it in your power at any time or upon any emergency, to extinguish every thing worth the name of opposition to the government." While the Democratic-Republican majority in Congress was strong, he advised, the Federalists would abandon the nation as soon as the government pushed for a declaration of war against Great Britain. Only at that point should the papers be circulated, as "the production of them will confound, astonish and alarm the opposition, as well as rouse the spirit of their constituents; and the unanimous voice of all classes and of all parties, will be with you in any measures of retaliation upon Your enemy."[101] Henry then sailed for France. Not until he landed did he learn he was a dupe. There was an heir to the Crillon family, but only one, and he lived in Paris. The "count" turned out to be a known con man named Soubiran, and the estate Henry was promised did not exist. When Soubiran himself reached France in the summer of 1812, he was arrested for impersonation.[102]

Madison, meanwhile, attempted to put the letters—which Henry had edited and embellished—to work. In March 1812 he sent them to Congress and argued that they "prove that at a recent period" the government of Great Britain worked to foment "disaffection to the constituted authorities of the nation," even though none of the correspondence named any Americans or outlined any nefarious British plot.[103] Madison then wrote to his fellow Virginians, John G. Jackson and Thomas Jefferson, sending them copies of the letters in advance of their publication.[104] Augustus Foster, the British minister to the United States, assured Monroe that he had had no knowledge of Henry's work, that he doubted the government in Canada would advance "any schemes hostile to the internal tranquility of the United States," and that American officials should consider Henry's character when evaluating the letters' contents.[105] That March and April, American newspapers published extracts of Henry's letters. They provided ammunition for hawks—those who were not bothered by their lack of substance—who saw Great Britain as a perfidious power whose influence in North America had to be checked.[106] Democratic-Republicans saw in the letters evidence that the British and the Federalists were not to be trusted, and that a sufficient response would be war against Great Britain and an invasion of Canada to root out the source of the trouble. It was 1775 all over again. While Henry's letters did not include a smoking gun, he dealt in the kind of conspiracy theories that enraged those who already held anti-British sentiments. His efforts brought him nothing, but they revived the American calls for war and further divided Democratic-Republicans from Federalists.[107]

Over the winter and spring of 1812, war fever whipped the nation and attention turned to the northern British colonies and their Indigenous allies, which many saw as obstacles to American expansion. There was a market for information about Canada, especially travel narratives and maps, and people stepped in to fill it. John Melish, a Scottish-born merchant turned mapmaker who arrived in the United States in 1806, undertook an extensive tour of the western part of the nation that included crossing over into Canada.[108] The object of his narrative was "to render a service to the Inhabitants" of both the United States and the British provinces.[109] *Travels through the United States of America* appeared in 1812 and included an entire chapter on his trip to Upper Canada. Melish was unimpressed by Canadians. Whereas Americans were fired by a spirit of independence and equality, the Canadians he encountered seemed either obsequious (guides, for instance, did not demand a price but rather accepted whatever their client would pay) or rude (particularly the soldiers, who often drank to excess). The government was run by the military, and according to one Yankee from New Hampshire whom Melish encountered, settlers need only accuse their neighbors of disloyalty to have them thrown in jail.[110] Melish echoed what others had surmised about Canadian loyalty: it was broad but not deep. "Were 5000 men to be sent into the province with a proclamation of independence," he wrote, "the great mass of the people would join the American government."[111] The man who issued one of the first maps of the United States—a map that Jefferson hung in the entrance to Monticello—and several maps of the war itself, understood that Americans should focus on territorial growth. If war was necessary, then so be it. Melish would map it all.

In the Canadas, British subjects responded to American threats of invasion by demonstrating a nascent nationalism that paralleled the growth of American identity. Like their southern neighbors, Upper and Lower Canadians took to the press to express their frustrations and concerns, and newspapers in New York, Maryland, and Pennsylvania republished these articles for their readers. In a piece entitled "From Canada. To the Editor of the *Quebec Mercury*," a Canadian addressed "the inhabitants of these provinces, upon the critical state of our political relations with the

U. States." The author cautioned that in the coming war, Canadians would be forced to defend all they held dear "against a system of warfare grounded upon the avowed principles of plunder and rapine." A simple perusal of the American papers, the author continued, would demonstrate that Canada was being offered up to soldiers of the conquering army; even the highest politicians in America supported the plan, but Americans should not count on an easy victory. Canadians, drawing upon the strength of their ancestors, must be prepared to meet any such invasion and defend their lands against "the corrupt and venal political speculations in the United States." In encouraging his fellow subjects to defend themselves, the Canadian author turned some of the American rhetoric on its head: "We have real liberty, grounded upon the most wise and equitable laws; we have property ... transmitted to us by our ancestors, or acquired by our own industry, arising out of the happy connexion subsisting between us and the parent state. ... The husbandman cultivates his farm with the comfortable assurance, that what he sows with hope, he will reap in safety." This life stood in stark relief against the American example, where "the heads of that party are the avowed patrons of slavery and dealers in human blood and traffic which has a natural tendency to eradicate from their minds every feeling of humanity."[112]

Until the war broke out in 1812, Americans had looked to expand. While Jefferson's focus had been on the west, the conquest of Canada had been a driving feature of United States policy from shortly after the first shots were fired at Lexington and Concord. As a new conflict grew closer, those living in British provinces—French Canadians, British immigrants, Loyalists and late Loyalists, and Indigenous peoples who themselves challenged British sovereignty in their homelands—recognized that they would once again be forced to defend their lands. The invaders would look like them and often share last names or commercial connections, and some would be kin. But the differences were beginning to matter. Like the Americans during the revolution, the subjects living in the British colonies could rally against a shared threat to their way of life. British subjects increasingly realized that, whatever they were, they were not American. And despite their hopes of conquest, citizens of the United States were beginning to feel the same way about the provinces: they were not, and would never be, one people.

# Epilogue

I N LATE 1812, after the United States had declared war against Great Britain and suffered early defeats at the hands of British, Canadian, and Indigenous forces, a pamphlet appeared in New York satirizing the Republican obsession with taking Canada. *The Wars of the Gulls; An Historical Romance* opens with James Madison, drunk on mint juleps in his sitting room in Montpelier, gazing at a map of British America. The map has been filled in with future American successes: there is an American viceroy of Labrador, a collector of customs along the Mackenzie River, a military general controlling what is left of Quebec. Madison flops back in his lolling chair and muses, "Who can like me put his thumb on a whole continent at once?"[1] The narrative continues by describing the ease with which naval commanders control ships that don't exist and how Republican newspapers transform every American loss at sea into an impressive victory. But a central question remains: how to take Canada? Madison receives a flurry of suggestions: place the God of War in the stomach of a wooden horse and send it into the heart of Quebec; dry up the St. Lawrence River; march a fleet of ships across the continent to the Columbia River and then descend from the west. Madison, however, "was resolved to take Canada *by Proclamation*."[2] The government then decides, for the sake of appearances, that the proclamation should be attended by a regiment or two. And if they run into any trouble, they "should call for advice and direction upon their trusty cidevant cabineteer Barnabas Bidwell, and other confidential friends of the great Mo-gul, resident in that country."[3]

The actual march to war was a less inebriated affair.[4] But attention did quickly turn to Canada. Jonathan Russell, the American chargé d'affaires

THE

# WARS OF THE GULLS;

AN

## HISTORICAL ROMANCE.

### IN THREE CHAPTERS.

CHAP. I. *Shewing how, and why, and with whom the Gulls went to war.*

CHAP. II. *Shewing how the Gulls make the deep to boil like a pot.*

CHAP. III. *Shewing how a certain doughty General of the Gulls goes forth to play the game of* HULL-GULL *in Upper Canada.*

" And from the pinnacle of glory,
" Falls headlong into purgatory."

*NEW-YORK:*
PUBLISHED AT THE DRAMATIC REPOSITORY,
*Shakespeare Gallery.*

1812.

Title page for Jacob Bigelow, *The Wars of the Gulls; an Historical Romance*, published in 1812.
Library of Congress.

at London, was looking forward to the war. As soon as it was declared, he suggested that "we ought rather to leave if possible nothing to chance" and immediately demonstrate to Great Britain "our strength & spirit." The best method, he argued, would involve rallying "the energies of the nation

& pouring over Canada & Nova Scotia like a torrent." Americans had it in their power "to finish in a single campaign the war on our continent."[5] For John Adams, taking Canada was both a distraction and an inevitability. Adams well remembered the failed Canadian campaign during the revolution, when the best military efforts of Montgomery and Arnold, and even the diplomatic contingent led by Benjamin Franklin, could not persuade the people of Quebec to join the American cause. The prospect of yet another war with Britain did not shake the idea of taking Canada from Adams's mind, but he wished others had their priorities in line. He took great satisfaction from the belief that all of the policies enacted during his presidency—his taxes, his immigration laws, and his attention to the navy—were proving useful. But he saw shortcomings in the preparations for war, particularly in the lack of ships and defenses. "It would have been more conformable to my wishes," he noted, "if less had been said, and done, about Canada, and more about floating castles and wooden walls."[6] But men preferred joining the army—with its promises of large tracts of land when the fighting was done—over the roaring storms encountered by seamen. For Adams, however, it was a question of priorities; winning the war at sea would ensure victories on land. Britain had employed this strategy for much of the eighteenth century and used it to become the most powerful empire in the world.[7] "Canada must be ours, to be sure," Adams argued, "and will be ours [or] we should be dunces indeed, to leave such a nest for conspiracies against us, in the hands of England."[8]

Fighting on water would at least put some distance between American forces and Great Britain's Indigenous allies.[9] A newspaper in Schenectady, New York, ran a letter from Detroit suggesting that British Indian agents at Amherstburg were providing arms to their Indigenous neighbors. Much worse, according to the article, members of the Canadian Parliament seemed to take satisfaction when those arms were used against Americans. Even if the British government itself might disavow Indigenous attacks, the editorial suggested, "yet perhaps there are certain 'persons' in the employment of that Government, whose hands are not so clear of the blood of our citizens."[10] It was hard for many Americans to understand that Indigenous nations operated with their own agendas. Many settlers, American and British, saw Indigenous peoples only as pawns or subjects, subservient to whatever power claimed their ancestral homelands.

Yet on the eve of the war, Thomas Jefferson, perhaps by accident, gave a more accurate depiction of Indigenous-American relations. In a May 1812 letter to the American businessman and fur trader John Jacob

Astor, Jefferson explained the reach of the trade embargo against Britain and France he had introduced in the waning years of his presidency, a policy meant to assert American trade strength and avoid a war but which caused more harm to the American economy than to European merchants.[11] The embargo could only "have in view the consumption of our own citizens . . . we certainly did not mean to interfere with the consumption of nations foreign to us, as the Indians of the Columbia and Missouri are."[12] On one hand, Jefferson envisioned a future in which Indigenous inhabitants were "civilized" and lived much like other rural Americans, and in which those who refused were so reduced in numbers as to be largely irrelevant. He had even proposed an interdiction of trade with recalcitrant nations in 1808, a year after Congress passed the Embargo Act.[13] Yet on the other hand, Jefferson seemed to recognize, at least when writing to Astor, that Indigenous affairs were international relations. A country does not generally strike treaties with its own citizens.

Madison, however, never quite believed that Indigenous violence was not incited by British agents, or even the government itself.[14] Augustus Foster, the British representative to the United States, adamantly rejected the suggestion and forwarded to American officials copies of letters from British administrators throughout the western parts of British North America that documented their attempts to calm Indigenous anger.[15] For their part, Indigenous nations friendly with the United States worked toward securing their position as allies for the upcoming war against the British. Leading Oneida chiefs and warriors, who had sided with the Patriots during the revolution, requested military commissions and expressed some concern that members of their nation might be tempted to side with the British. "We find our people will not rest at ease if there is war," the chiefs argued in a June letter to Madison, "and if we have our commitions soon our Brethren will Stay with us and be faithful and true to your honor and the united States."[16] American officials understood that, despite promises from the Oneida, a war against Britain would also be a war against thousands of Indigenous peoples allied to the British. What was less clear to many in the United States government was that Indigenous nations on both sides of the conflict fought for themselves, their homelands, and their future.

It was easy for Americans to imagine a future without Indigenous peoples, or at least a future in which Indigenous peoples were simply dark-skinned Americans. Over the late eighteenth and early nineteenth centuries, "civilization" replaced eradication as the policy goal, a project that required transforming "savages" into citizens rather than simply wiping them off the continent. Jefferson, whose Monticello estate was decorated with Indigenous cultural items—some given by chiefs as presents, some stolen by settlers as trinkets—was concerned that the coming war with Great Britain would slow and possibly reverse the civilization project. The Cherokee, he wrote to John Adams in June 1812, served as an example of a successful transformation: "They have good Cabins, inclosed fields, large herds of cattle & hogs, spin & weave their own clothes of cotton, have smiths & other of the most necessary tradesmen, write & read, are on the increase in numbers, & a branch of the Cherokees is now instituting a regular representative government." All of these "advances," however, did little to protect the Cherokee from ultimate removal in the 1830s. In Jefferson's estimation, among the less advanced nations "the backward will yield" and "relapse into barbarism & misery," at which point the United States "shall be obliged to drive them, with the beasts of the forest into the Stony mountains." But the present war could prevent future attacks from Indigenous nations in Canada. When the United States removed the British from Canada, as Jefferson was sure it would, American women and children would be protected forever "from the tomahawk & the scalping knife, by removing those who excite them."[17]

John Adams could recall a time when Indigenous peoples were both friends and foe. Chiefs and sachems had been regular visitors to his father's house, and a large Indigenous family had lived not a mile from Adams's childhood home. He used to visit their wigwam regularly, where he enjoyed a traditionally warm welcome. But over the years, he lamented, "the girls went out to service and the boys to sea till not a soul is left." He also remembered Indigenous violence, which as a settler he understood as "murders, scalpings, depredations," but which, on Indigenous terms, were instances of sovereign nations defending their territories and families from settlers set on aggressive expansion. Like Jefferson, he saw the conquest of Canada as a way to prevent Indigenous attacks in the west. The British capture of Canada from the French in 1763 had ended many of the Indigenous attacks in and around the northeast, and Adams shared Jefferson's belief "that another Conquest of Canada will quiet the Indians forever and be as great a Blessing to them as to Us."[18] Not surprisingly, Indigenous nations, as well as the Canadians, saw things differently.

Whether to declare war, and how to proceed if a war began, remained central topics of debate in early June 1812. These discussions

often revolved around Canada's relations with the various Indigenous nations that would inevitably be pulled into the conflict. As the House and
Senate deliberated and then passed a declaration of war, officials received
letters and newspapers issued editorials expressing their concerns.

There were balances of power to consider. While the United States
clearly wanted to strengthen its position relative to Great Britain, other
dynamics also required attention. An anonymous correspondent urged
President Madison to consider the relative value of Canada: "By the Conquest of Canada, you may injure the Commerce of England, but the object will cost more than it is worth." The United States had a weak navy
and not enough money to fund a successful war. And taking Canada, a
place not yet free of slavery but certainly not defined by it, would add
power to the north and anger slaveholders in the south.[19] Yet many
southerners disagreed. An editorial in Charleston's *City Gazette and Commercial Advertiser* asked why war hadn't already been declared. The revolution itself was begun when the states weren't fully prepared militarily or
financially, and that was a success. "Instead of receiving the enemy on our
own shores, we will march to Canada: the way is open." It was time to
finish the work of the revolution and take Quebec, "the American Gibral-
tar." Though Montgomery failed in 1775, a British general had succeeded
in 1759. "Shall American valor," the paper demanded, "shrink from obstacles over which British courage has triumphed?"[20] This sentiment was
echoed by many in the north, including a group of Republican delegates
from Essex county in Massachusetts. Put simply, Canada mattered too
much, and the threat that Britain and its Indigenous allies posed from
there was too great to ignore.[21] Should Canada fall to the United States,
there could be no returning it at the negotiating table. The American
people wouldn't stand for it.[22]

Given that their country lacked enough men for land or naval forces,
American officials were oddly optimistic about their chances. For Jefferson, it was never a question of if Canada would fall, but when. Taking
Quebec, he thought, would "be a mere matter of marching."[23] British
Canadians had a different idea: a Vermont newspaper published a letter
from Montreal boasting about Quebec's preparedness for conflict. "The
inhabitants here from the age of sixteen to sixty are all soldiers," and
British regulars were arriving from the West Indies, "two thousand of
which were blacks."[24] Madison, as a southern slaveholder, was unwilling
to recruit Black soldiers to fight against the British, even though the
United States desperately needed men. The British, in contrast, offered

enslaved Americans land and freedom should they flee their plantations and join the Royal Navy.[25] In the aftermath of the war, when Black soldiers and sailors found new homes in Nova Scotia, these "Refugee Negroes" learned that even if slavery in the British provinces was waning, racism was alive and well.[26]

Ideas, ideologies, and even identities crossed the border separating British colonies from American states. Like the American Revolution, the War of 1812 was in many ways a civil war, especially in the border regions.[27] But it was also regional, with the more hawkish states found in the south and many settlers in British North America prepared to define their way of life in opposition to the southern United States. In Kentucky, readers were treated to a letter from Montreal arguing Canadians were prepared for war but hoped for peace.[28] Within the American government, the author noted, "the conquest of the Canadas has long been a favorite object" that was linked to "their revolutionary struggle." United States officials would rely on "every possible artifice," egged on by "their corrupt and mercenary presses," to invade and conquer Canada. And yet "we wage no war on them—we wish and have asked for peace," but all overtures had been refused. The American vanguard should come "at their peril . . . and they may learn by its fate that, tho' resolved to defend ourselves with every means which God and nature has placed in our hands, we omit no opportunity of shewing our foe, that the glory of a British warrior is to 'conquer or to save.' "[29]

War mania had infected subjects and citizens on both sides of the border; a doctor was hardly necessary to diagnose it. Benjamin Rush, who admitted that the United States had just cause to declare war against Great Britain, compared the "party men" in the American government to the poor souls—"mad people"—he visited in hospital yards. Such mania could tear families apart, as Rush knew only too well. His daughters and their children planned to stay in Philadelphia "while the husbands of the former, and the fathers of the latter are in Arms against our Country."[30]

The war's first months looked promising for Rush's sons-in-law in Montreal but caused great distress for the American government. The United States army was modest, the militias disorganized and spread across the states, the navy essentially nonexistent, and military leadership a mixed bag of generals with various levels of experience.[31] But many of those making the decisions believed such men as Barnabas Bidwell, who had argued that much of Canada was populated by Americans (including, by 1810, Bidwell himself) and thus sympathetic to the cause. The administration decided on an ambitious invasion plan: a three-pronged assault on Montreal, Niagara, and Amherstburg. General William Hull was tasked with taking Fort Malden, just across the Detroit River in Amherstburg, and he led a two-thousand-man militia from the Ohio River to the Canadian border. Their march helped inspire *The Wars of the Gulls:* Hull planted an American flag in Canadian soil, issued a proclamation encouraging the Canadians to flock to the American cause, and exaggerated the size of his forces.[32] He gained little respect from his subordinates, who quarreled among themselves and openly criticized Hull for his lack of leadership. When his troops reached the border, more than two hundred men argued that as members of the militia they would not fight outside of the United States. It was a sign of things to come. After a number of false starts on Fort Malden, Hull declared the operation impossible and retreated to Fort Detroit. When British General Isaac Brock and his Indigenous ally Tecumseh organized a force of two hundred to march on Detroit, they employed an ingenious bit of theater to play on Hull's fear of Indigenous warriors. They had their men walk in view of the fort, then circle back to the end of the line and walk past again, giving those peering nervously from the ramparts the illusion of thousands of warriors planning an attack. Hull surrendered the fort without firing a shot.[33]

In *The Wars of the Gulls*, Hull's fateful march on Fort Malden is undertaken not with a militia but with "Michigan racoon catchers and a band of music." The "Procession of the Proclamation" does not make it to Fort Malden any more than the real Hull did. The fictional Hull, confident that it was unfair to drive the proclamation by force into the undefended Fort Malden, turns back. But that does not stop backwoods Republicans from declaring a victory. More "victories" follow: a force of four hundred wins against twice as many sheep; and, later, an entire regiment flees into the woods, finds itself outnumbered by trees, and yet retreats without losing a man.[34] Hull, wondering how the Gulls will transform this retreat into a victory, takes solace in the thought "that when a fight becomes a chase, those win the day that win the race."[35] He then retires to his "dung hill" at Detroit and surrenders the fort when threatened by Brock and Tecumseh. The Gulls, forced to reevaluate their position, "lustily cry 'build a navy and man it; and if we must *be gulls*, O let us be sea-gulls, and give up our conquests to Bidwell and Gannett.' "[36]

The authors of *Wars of the Gulls* were satirizing both the Republican obsession with taking Canada and the United States' poor preparation for war, themes that appeared regularly in the American press. Even Republicans questioned the strategy of attacking Great Britain. In the summer of 1813, an "Old Republican" published a letter in the *Albany Register* that seemed to echo many of the criticisms leveled in *Wars of the Gulls*, arguing, "In the first place, the manner in which the war is carried on, renders it very doubtful whether the managers of it really intend to conquer the Canadas." Moreover, the war was expensive and could ruin American credit.[37] But having started, the American government could not simply surrender its efforts.

As during the American Revolution, the government named three commissioners—Albert Gallatin, John Quincy Adams, and James A. Bayard—to prepare for peace negotiations. There were certain demands that the United States saw as nonnegotiable. First, British traders would no longer be allowed to travel across the border into the United States to work among Indigenous nations, a right provided by the Jay Treaty that had had "pernicious effects . . . by the influence which it gave to the traders over the Indians."[38] The British relationship with Indigenous allies living in territory claimed by or adjacent to the United States had been a constant concern despite British assurances that they were not encouraging or facilitating attacks against American settlers. The best way to remove this threat was for Britain to surrender all or part of the Canadas. The challenge facing the commissioners was to convince their British counterparts that such a surrender would be good for both sides: Great Britain would derive the same economic benefits but would no longer have the burden of supporting the territory. Such a transfer would also greatly reduce the chance of future conflict between the two powers.[39]

As the war continued through 1813 and 1814, the increasingly violent battles began to test the unwritten rules of war. Soldiers on both sides took aim at civilians by burning entire towns: the Americans put York (Toronto) to flames, and the British ravaged Niagara and Buffalo before eventually setting fire to the White House and the Capitol in Washington.[40] The British recognized that the Americans were becoming better soldiers, and pitched battles in places such as Lundy's Lane and Queenston Heights in Upper Canada demonstrated that there would be no easy victory for either side. In late 1813, the Americans captured a cache of letters from British General Henry Proctor, which were then laid before Congress. The letters suggested not only that the British had set Indigenous warriors against Americans before the war began, but also that Britain was sanctioning and supporting Indigenous raids during the war. Secretary of State Monroe wrote the commissioners, "These facts will, it is presumed, give great support, in case a negotiation is entered into, to the considerations urged in my Letter to you of the 23rd June last in favor of the cession of the Canadas to the United States, or at least of that portion lying between the western end of Lake Ontario, and the Eastern end of Lake Huron." It would be impossible, he added, echoing the complaints from the revolution, for British officials to think a durable peace could exist with the United States so long as Canada remained British.[41] A few weeks later, Monroe wrote the commissioners again with yet more reasons why Great Britain must surrender Canada. The most pressing issue was that settlers were pushing west, and should the British remain in Canada and maintain claims to and navigation through the Great Lakes, there would be no way to prevent conflict between Americans and British traders. There would soon be a line of continuous settlement all the way to Detroit, and beyond. The pressure these settlers would put on British inhabitants would force the latter to "feel their strength, and assert independence."[42] To avoid these conflicts and guarantee a lasting peace, Canada must be American.

In late summer of 1814, the American commissioners met with delegates from Great Britain in the city of Ghent, United Netherlands. By that time, the war had turned in Britain's favor. Napoleon's abdication in April meant the British could turn all of their attention to North America. The British commissioners listed the topics that they felt were central to any lasting peace. Eager to take advantage of the weakened American negotiating position, and cautious to avoid the mistakes they had made at the conclusion of the American Revolution, they demanded that their Indigenous allies be included in the peace "and a definite boundary to be settled for their territory. . . . An arrangement upon this point," the American commissioners reported to Monroe, "was a *sine qua non.*"[43] As they had done in the Royal Proclamation of 1763 and the Quebec Act of 1774, British officials were using their Indigenous allies to prevent American expansion. Yet if Indigenous territory was not fully British, it was certainly not American. To secure this territory for their Indigenous allies, British boots needed to remain firmly planted on American necks.

The gods of war had other plans. In early September 1814, British General George Prevost's bungled attack on Plattsburgh, New York, ended any hopes that Britain might capture enough American territory to be traded away at the negotiating table for an Indigenous state.[44] By the fall of 1814, both sides had had enough, and Monroe authorized the commissioners to push for the status quo ante as a negotiating position.[45] The war ended with no winner but one obvious loser: Indigenous nations were unquestionably worse off in 1815 than they had been in 1812. The Treaty of Ghent restricted Indigenous movement across the U.S.-Canadian border, and perhaps more important, the British in Canada had fewer reasons to accommodate their Indigenous allies when their warriors were no longer needed to protect against an American invasion.[46]

The conclusion of the War of 1812 did not sever ties between British subjects and American citizens, but it did mark both an ending and a beginning.[47] The elite in Upper Canada still felt an affinity for New England Federalists, the Six Nations and other Indigenous peoples maintained (and maintain) transnational communities, and Blacks in Canada and the United States (in various forms of freedom and unfreedom) worked to build relations across a border that represented much more than a national dividing line.[48] For many of these people, however, the border became increasingly national. Family members could live on either side, ideas could move across with relative ease, and commerce (legal and illegal) persisted. But citizens of the United States now had to accept that the British provinces would never become American states— not by war, not by will, and not by wishing. Neither a threat nor an ambition, the regions north of America—British colonies and, after 1867, Canadian provinces—developed in parallel to the republic to the south, an example of the path not taken and a constant reminder that the failure to incorporate Canada during the Age of Revolutions shaped the creation of the United States.

The promise of a continental nation was dead, and thus the United States would forever be limited both in its territorial and its conceptual identity.[49] As Alan Taylor has argued, "The United States was far from united before 1850."[50] But after the War of 1812, American citizens and British subjects dealt with similar issues in different ways. Slavery— though not racism—was largely legislated away in the colonies by politicians and judges, even before Great Britain officially ended slavery in 1833.[51] Tragically, the United States would nearly come apart over the question of abolition. The process of settler-colonialism and violence against Indigenous peoples would also vary on either side of the border. The United States launched wars against Indigenous nations, and after fierce resistance, most nations were forced onto reserves, from which they have continued to fight for their ancestral rights within the United States.[52] In the British colonies, and then Canada, Indigenous nations were denied even the limited independence granted to nations in the United States and were forced into the status of wards of the state under the Indian Act of 1876. Like their kin south of the border, Indigenous nations in Canada have never stopped fighting against the state for recognition and reconciliation.[53] As the United States and Canada developed over the nineteenth and twentieth centuries, the gaze from one side to the other has reversed, as citizens in the provinces have been unable to ignore the states beneath them. Yet in the eighteenth and nineteenth centuries, American citizens looked beyond their borders, at times because they were greedy but as often because they were inquisitive.[54] The founding generation's relationships to Indigenous peoples whose homelands they hoped to transform and to the British provinces along their northern borders illustrate that forging a nation was an international exercise, shaped from both without and within.

# Notes

## Abbreviations

*AA*: *American Archives*. Ed. Peter Force. Online edition: http://amarch.lib.niu.edu/.

*ANB*: *American National Biography Online*. http://www.anb.org.

*ASPIA*: *American State Papers, vol. 4: Indian Affairs*, vol. 1.
    Washington, DC: Published by Gales and Seaton, 1832.

*DCB*: *Dictionary of Canadian Biography*. www.biographi.ca.

*DCCR*: *Diplomatic Correspondence of the United States: Canadian Relations,
    1784–1860*, vol. 1: 1784–1820. Ed. William R. Manning. Washington, DC:
    Carnegie Endowment for International Peace, 1940.

*DHRC*: *Documentary History of the Ratification of the Constitution*, Digital Edition.
    https://rotunda.upress.virginia.edu/founders/RNCN.html.

*DHSM*: *Documentary History of the State of Maine*. Published by the Maine Historical
    Society. Portland: Bailey and Noyes, 1869–1916.

*DRCHC*: *Documents Relating to the Constitutional History of Canada, 1759–1791*.
    1st and 2nd editions. Ed. Adam Shortt and Arthur G. Doughty. Ottawa:
    Printed by S. E. Dawson, Printer to the King's Most Excellent Majesty,
    1907, 1918.

*DRSNY*: *Documents Relative to the Colonial History of the State of New-York: Procured
    in Holland, England, and France*. E. B. (Edmund Bailey) O'Callaghan, Berthold
    Fernow, John Romeyn Brodhead, and New York (State) Legislature. Albany:
    Weed, Parsons, 1853–87.

*Emerging Nation*: *Documents of the Emerging Nation: U.S. Foreign Relations,
    1775–1789*. Ed. Mary A. Giunta and J. Dane Hartgrove. Wilmington, DE:
    Scholarly Resources, 1998.

FONA: Founders Online, National Archives. www.founders.archives.gov.

*JCC*: *Journals of the Continental Congress, 1774–1789*. Edited from the Original
    Records in the Library of Congress by Worthington Chauncey Ford, Chief,
    Division of Manuscripts. Washington, DC: Government Printing Office,
    1904.

*JLCE: Journals of the Lewis and Clark Expedition*. https://lewisandclarkjournals. unl.edu/.

LAC: Library and Archives Canada. Online at Library and Archives of Canada.

LOC: Library of Congress. http://www.loc.gov.

*LOD: Letters of Delegates to Congress, 1774–1789*. Ed. Paul Hubert Smith. Washington, DC: Library of Congress, 1976.

MFP: Morse Family Papers. Yale University, Manuscript Collections, MS 358.

NSARM: Nova Scotia Archives and Records Management.

*ODNB: Oxford Dictionary of National Biography*. http://www.oxforddnb.com.

*PAH: The Papers of Alexander Hamilton, vol. 1, 1768–1778*. Ed. Harold C. Syrett. New York: Columbia University Press, 1961.

*PBF: The Papers of Benjamin Franklin*. http://www.franklinpapers.org.

*PGWRWS: Papers of George Washington, Revolutionary War Series*, vol. 3, 1 January 1776–31 March 1776. Ed. Philander D. Chase. Charlottesville: University Press of Virginia, 1988.

*PJA: Papers of John Adams*, vol. 2, "Founding Families: Digital Editions of the Papers of the Winthrops and Adamses." Ed. James Taylor. Boston: Massachusetts Historical Society, 2007. Available at http://www.masshist.org/ff/.

PWD: Papers of the War Department, 1784–1800. https://wardepartmentpapers.org/.

RCA: Report on the Canadian Archives, 1891, 1893. Ottawa: 1892 and 1894.

*RGCSV: Records of the Governor and Council of the State of Vermont*, vol. 2. Montpelier: J. & J. M. Poland, 1874.

*Simcoe: The Correspondence of Lieut. Governor John Graves Simcoe with Allied Documents [. . .]*, vol. 1. Ed. E. A. Cruikshank. Toronto: Ontario Historical Society, 1923.

*Writings: The Writings of Benjamin Franklin*. Ed. Albert H. Smyth. New York: Macmillan, 1907.

# Prologue

1. *The Literary Diary of Ezra Stiles, D.D., LL.D.*, vol. 1, ed. Franklin Bowditch Dexter (New York: Charles Scribner's Sons, 1901), 455.

2. For an overview of the negotiations required after 1713, see John G. Reid et al., *The "Conquest" of Acadia, 1710: Imperial, Colonial, and Aboriginal Constructions* (Toronto: University of Toronto Press, 2004); Jeffers Lennox, *Homelands and Empires: Indigenous Spaces, Imperial Fictions, and Competition for Territory in Northeastern North America, 1690–1763* (Toronto: University of Toronto Press, 2017).

3. Administrative officials worked from at least seven reports concerning how to govern Quebec drafted in the 1760s and 1770s by officials in Quebec and London. See Hilda Neatby, *Quebec: The Revolutionary Age, 1760–1791* (Toronto: McClelland and Stewart, 1966), 126.

4. While it was possible for British Americans, especially those with Patriot leanings, to see the hand of the king in the creation of the Quebec Act, it

was a bill influenced as much by colonists and administrators in Quebec as by officials in London. Many Patriots certainly did blame the king, however. See Vernon P. Creviston, " 'No King Unless It Be a Constitutional King': Rethinking the Place of the Quebec Act in the Coming of the American Revolution," *Historian* 73, no. 3 (2011): 463–79.

5. Stephen Hornsby, *British Atlantic, American Frontier: Spaces of Power in Early Modern British America* (Hanover, NH: University Press of New England, 2005), especially chap. 6.

6. David Hackett Fischer, *Champlain's Dream* (New York: Simon & Schuster, 2008), 294–96.

7. Ibid. The post-1763 challenges facing British-Indigenous relations are thoroughly discussed in a number of excellent monographs. A few selections include S. Max Edelson, *The New Map of Empire: How Britain Imagined America before Independence* (Cambridge: Harvard University Press, 2017), chap. 4; Colin G. Calloway, *The Scratch of a Pen: 1763 and the Transformation of North America* (New York: Oxford University Press, 2006); Daniel K. Richter, *Facing East from Indian Country: A Native History of Early America* (Cambridge: Harvard University Press, 2001); Colin G. Calloway, *New Worlds for All: Indians, Europeans, and the Remaking of Early America* (Baltimore: Johns Hopkins University Press, 1998); Richard White, *The Middle Ground: Indians, Empires, and Republics in the Great Lakes Region, 1650–1815* (Cambridge: Cambridge University Press, 1991).

8. See *A Narrative of the Captivity and Restoration of Mrs. Mary Rowlandson* (1682), https://www.gutenberg.org/files/851/851-h/851-h.htm. Captivity was both an abstract idea that concerned Britons surveying their growing empire and a very real fear facing colonial settlers. For an overview, see Linda Colley, *Captives: Britain, Empire and the World, 1600–1850* (London: Jonathan Cape, 2002); John Demos, *The Unredeemed Captive: A Family Story from Early America* (New York: Knopf, 1994).

9. Donald William Meinig, *The Shaping of America: A Geographical Perspective on 500 Years of History*, vol. 1, *Atlantic America, 1492–1800* (New Haven: Yale University Press, 1986), 284–86.

10. Calloway, *New Worlds for All*, 195.

11. Colin G. Calloway, *The Indian World of George Washington: The First President, the First Americans, and the Birth of the Nation* (Oxford: Oxford University Press, 2018), 184–90.

12. Johnson and Stuart faced a formidable challenge, as their attempts to limit expansion and negotiate acceptable boundaries were ignored by settlers and speculators, especially from Virginia, which hoped to lay claim to territory around the Ohio River. See Matthew L. Rhoades, "Blood and Boundaries: Virginia Backcountry Violence and the Origins of the Quebec Act, 1758–1775," *West Virginia History: A Journal of Regional Studies* 3, no. 2 (2009): 1–22.

13. Johnson was particularly adept at engaging with Indigenous leaders, and he was not above using his diplomatic skills for personal gain. See "Johnson, Sir

William," *DCB*; Calloway, *New Worlds for All,* 195; Fintan O'Toole, *White Savage: William Johnson and the Invention of America* (New York: Excelsior Editions, 2005).

14. "Johnson, Sir William," *DCB*. See also O'Toole, *White Savage*.

15. "Claus, Christian Daniel," *DCB*.

16. *The Papers of Sir William Johnson,* vol. 13, ed. Milton W. Hamilton (Albany: University of the State of New York, 1962), 625.

17. Ibid., 628–29.

18. *DRCHC* (1908), 339.

19. Ibid., 338.

20. Philip Lawson, *The Imperial Challenge: Quebec and Britain in the Age of the American Revolution* (Montreal and Kingston: McGill-Queen's University Press, 1989), 109–10.

21. For an overview of merchant interests, see Stanley Brice Frost, *James McGill of Montreal* (Montreal and Kingston: McGill-Queen's University Press, 1995), chaps. 2 and 3.

22. *DRCHC* (1908), 351.

23. Ibid., 355–56.

24. Ibid., 358.

25. Ibid., 359.

26. Francis Maseres to the English Merchants of Quebec, Inner Temple, 22 August 1774, in Francis Maseres, *An Account of the Proceedings of the British, and other Protestant Inhabitants, of the Province of Quebeck, in North America, in order to obtain an House of Assembly in that Province* (London, 1775), 224.

27. Jack M. Sosin, *Whitehall and the Wilderness: The Middle West in British Colonial Policy, 1760–1775* (Lincoln: University of Nebraska Press, 1961), 238.

28. Sosin, *Whitehall and the Wilderness,* 244–49.

29. Lawson, *Imperial Challenge,* 108–45; Jeffers Lennox, "Seeing Red: The Quebec Act and Its Geographic Implications," in Hubert and Furstenberg, eds., *Entangling the Quebec Act: Transnational Contexts, Meanings, and Legacies in North America and the British Empire* (Montreal and Kingston: McGill-Queen's University Press, 2020), 267–303.

30. Pauline Maier, *From Resistance to Revolution: Colonial Radicals and the Development of American Opposition to Britain, 1765–1776* (New York: W. W. Norton, 1991), 11–12.

31. Edmund S. Morgan, *Benjamin Franklin* (New Haven: Yale University Press, 2002), 189–204; "Franklin, Benjamin," *ANB*. Also Bernard Bailyn, *The Ordeal of Thomas Hutchinson* (Cambridge: Harvard University Press, 1974).

32. Benjamin L. Carp, *Defiance of the Patriots: The Boston Tea Party and the Making of America* (New Haven: Yale University Press, 2010).

33. Stiles, *Literary Diary,* 470, entry for 5 November 1774; Kathleen Wilson, *The Sense of the People: Politics, Culture, and Imperialism in England, 1715–1785* (Cambridge: Cambridge University Press, 1995), 244; David Wald-

streicher, *In the Midst of Perpetual Fetes: The Making of American Nationalism, 1776–1820* (Chapel Hill: Published for the Omohundro Institute of Early American History and Culture, University of North Carolina Press, 1997), 17–52.

34. Fols. 356–57, B-1, MG21-Add.MSS, Haldimand Papers, LAC.

35. Geoffrey Gilbert Plank, *An Unsettled Conquest: The British Campaign against the Peoples of Acadia* (Philadelphia: University of Pennsylvania Press, 2001); N. E. S. Griffiths, *From Migrant to Acadian: A North American Border People, 1604–1755* (Montreal: McGill-Queen's University Press, 2005); William Craig Wicken, *Mi'kmaq Treaties on Trial: History, Land and Donald Marshall Junior* (Toronto: University of Toronto Press, 2002); Jeffers Lennox, "Nova Scotia Lost and Found: The Acadian Boundary Negotiation and Imperial Envisioning, 1750–1755," *Acadiensis* 40, no. 2 (2011): 3–31; Jeffers Lennox, "A Time and a Place: The Geography of British, French, and Aboriginal Interactions in Early Nova Scotia, 1726–44," *William and Mary Quarterly* 72, no. 3 (2015): 423–60.

36. See Hannah Weiss Muller, "As May Consist with Their Allegiance to His Majesty: Redefining Loyal Subjects in 1774," in *Entangling*. Also Hannah Weiss Muller, *Subjects and Sovereign: Bonds of Belonging in the Eighteenth-Century British Empire* (Oxford: Oxford University Press, 2017), 122–65.

37. Maier, *From Resistance to Revolution*, 185.

38. The English had long defined themselves in relation to the French. See Linda Colley, *Britons: Forging the Nation, 1707–1837* (New Haven: Yale University Press, 1992).

39. Many thanks to Matthew Edney for pointing me toward Stiles's map. See "The Irony of Imperial Mapping," in James R. Akerman, ed., *The Imperial Map: Cartography and the Mastery of Empire* (Chicago: University of Chicago Press, 2009), 11–45.

40. *JCC*, vol. 1, 34.

41. Notes of Debates in the Continental Congress, [17?] October 1774, *PJA*.

42. *JCC*, vol. 1, 87–88.

43. Ibid.

44. Brett Rushforth, *Bonds of Alliance: Indigenous and Atlantic Slaveries in New France* (Chapel Hill: Published for the Omohundro Institute of Early American History and Culture, University of North Carolina Press, 2012); Robin W. Winks, *Blacks in Canada: A History* (Montreal and Kingston: McGill-Queen's University Press, 1997), 24–60.

45. *JCC*, vol. 1, 87–88.

46. Robert Emmett Curran, *Papist Devils: Catholics in British America, 1574–1783* (Washington, DC: Catholic University of America Press, 2014); Maura Jane Farrelly, *Papist Patriots: The Making of an American Catholic Identity* (New York: Oxford University Press, 2012).

47. Paul Langston, " 'Tyrant and Oppressor!': Colonial Press Reaction to the Quebec Act," *Historical Journal of Massachusetts* 34, no. 1 (2006): 1–17.

48. Jürgen Habermas, *The Structural Transformation of the Public Sphere: An Inquiry into a Category of Bourgeois Society* (Cambridge: MIT Press, 1989); Benedict R. Anderson, *Imagined Communities: Reflections on the Origin and Spread of Nationalism* (London: Verso, 2006); Mark Kamrath, ed., *Periodical Literature in Eighteenth-Century America* (Knoxville: University of Tennessee Press, 2005); Martin Brückner, *The Geographic Revolution in Early America: Maps, Literacy, and National Identity* (Chapel Hill: Published for the Omohundro Institute of Early American History and Culture by University of North Carolina Press, 2006).

49. *Pennsylvania Gazette*, 27 July 1774.

50. Ibid., 31 August 1774.

51. Ibid., 12 October 1774.

52. *South Carolina Gazette*, 1 November 1774.

53. Samuel Sherwood, *A Sermon, Containing Scriptural Instructions to Civil Rulers, and all Free-Born Subjects* (New Haven, 1774), 48.

54. Ibid., 56.

55. Ibid., 67.

56. Elizabeth Fenton argues that anti-Catholicism in the British American colonies was a central element of developing an American national identity. She writes, "In imagining Canadian Catholics as subjects whose private lives were entirely dictated by papal rule, Anglo-Protestant colonists constructed themselves as freely private subjects capable of shaping a religiously plural—and therefore 'liberal'—nation that could accommodate diversity because it was 'not Catholic.' " See Elizabeth Fenton, "Birth of a Protestant Nation: Catholic Canadians, Religious Pluralism, and National Unity in the Early U.S. Republic," *Early American Literature* 41, no. 1 (2006): 30.

57. David Morgan, *The Devious Dr. Franklin, Colonial Agent: Benjamin Franklin's Years in London* (Macon, GA: Mercer University Press, 1999), 241–42.

58. Benjamin Franklin, *Memoirs of the Life and Writings of Benjamin Franklin*, vol. 1 (Philadelphia: T. S. Manning, 1818), 284.

59. *PBF*, vol. 21, 467–68. Sosin argues that any suggestion that the boundaries might be changed was a misunderstanding of imperial desires. Dartmouth was unwilling to alter Quebec's limits. Sosin, *Whitehall and the Wilderness*, 249n21; Morgan, *Devious Dr. Franklin*, 242–45.

60. *PBF*, vol. 21, 540.

61. Max M. Edling, *Perfecting the Union: National and State Authority in the US Constitution* (New York: Oxford University Press, 2021); Kathleen DuVal, *Independence Lost: Lives on the Edge of the American Revolution* (New York: Random House Trade, 2015); Max M. Edling, *A Revolution in Favor of Government: Origins of the US Constitution and the Making of the American State* (New York: Oxford University Press, 2003).

62. Recently, see "Forum: Situating the United States in Vast Early America," *William and Mary Quarterly* 78, no. 2 (2021): 187–280; Alan Taylor, *American Republics: A Continental History of the United States, 1783–1850* (New York:

W. W. Norton, 2021); Alan Taylor, *American Revolutions: A Continental History, 1750–1804* (New York: W. W. Norton, 2016); Lawrence B. A. Hatter, *Citizens of Convenience: The Imperial Origins of American Nationhood on the U.S.-Canadian Border* (Charlottesville: University of Virginia Press, 2016); Harvey Amani Whitfield, *North to Bondage: Loyalist Slavery in the Maritimes* (Vancouver: University of British Columbia Press, 2016); Lawrence B. A. Hatter, "The Narcissism of Petty Differences? Thomas Jefferson, John Graves Simcoe and the Reformation of Empire in the Early United States and British-Canada," *American Review of Canadian Studies* 42, no. 2 (2012); Maya Jasanoff, *Liberty's Exiles: American Loyalists in the Revolutionary World* (New York: Knopf, 2011); Alan Taylor, *The Civil War of 1812: American Citizens, British Subjects, Irish Rebels, and Indian Allies* (New York: Vintage, 2010); Fischer, *Champlain's Dream*; Alan Taylor, *The Divided Ground: Indians, Settlers, and the Northern Borderland of the American Revolution* (New York: Vintage, 2007); John Mack Faragher, *A Great and Noble Scheme: The Tragic Story of the Expulsion of the French Acadians from their American Homeland* (New York: W. W Norton, 2005); Alan Taylor, "The Late Loyalists: Northern Reflections of the Early American Republic," *Journal of the Early Republic* 27, no. 1 (2007).

63. Maya Jasanoff, "The Other Side of Revolution: Loyalists in the British Empire," *William and Mary Quarterly* 65, no. 2 (April 2008): 205–32.

## Chapter One. Of Montreal

1. Walter Isaacson, *Benjamin Franklin: An American Life* (New York: Simon & Schuster, 2004), 28, 306.

2. For a broad interpretation of the Declaration's influence, see David Armitage, *The Declaration of Independence: A Global History* (Cambridge: Harvard University Press, 2007).

3. This is, as Eliga H. Gould suggests, American history from "the outside in." Eliga H. Gould, *Among the Powers of the Earth: The American Revolution and the Making of a New World Empire* (Cambridge: Harvard University Press, 2012), 13. "Canada" and "Quebec" were used interchangeably at the time.

4. It is also important to understand the Loyalist responses to Thomas Paine, which have been too easily discounted by historians. See Philip Gould, "Loyalists Respond to *Common Sense:* The Politics of Authorship in Revolutionary America," in Jerry Bannister and Liam Riordam, eds., *The Loyal Atlantic: Remaking the British Atlantic in the Revolutionary Era* (Toronto: University of Toronto Press, 2012), 105–27.

5. P. J. Marshall, *The Making and Unmaking of Empires: Britain, India, and America, c. 1750–1783* (Oxford: Oxford University Press, 2005), 353.

6. James Drake, *The Nation's Nature: How Continental Presumptions Gave Rise to the United States of America* (Charlottesville: University of Virginia Press, 2011), 179–93.

7. Gordon S. Wood, *The Radicalism of the American Revolution* (New York: Vintage Books, 1993).

8. Edmund S. Morgan put it a little more bluntly. When discussing the failed Canadian expedition, "Americans reassured one another that no such thing could occur among themselves. If the Canadians lacked the noble urge to be free, if they would not help themselves, then they deserved slavery. Meanwhile American patriots would establish their rights on battlefields closer to home." See Edmund S. Morgan, *The Birth of the Republic, 1763–89*, 3rd ed. (Chicago: University of Chicago Press, 1992), 77–78. Morgan also discounts the impact of neutrals, claiming that "the war itself sooner or later obliged men to get off the fence on one side or the other" (78).

9. Alberto Lena, "Benjamin Franklin's Canada Pamphlet or The Ravings of a Mad Prophet: Nationalism, Ethnicity and Imperialism," *European Journal of American Culture* 20, no. 1 (2001): 36–49.

10. Charles-Guillaume-Frédéric Dumas to Benjamin Franklin (hereafter BF), La Haie, 30 June 1775, *PBF*.

11. Ibid. "Cela n'est pas de moi: je ne suis pas assez instruit pour un pareil ouvrage."

12. BF to Charles-Guillaume-Frédéric Dumas, 9 December 1775, FONA.

13. Pierre Monette, *Rendez-vous manqué avec la evolution américaine* (Montreal: Québec Amérique, 2007), 60–61.

14. "Letter to the Inhabitants of the Province of Quebec," 26 October 1774, http://en.wikisource.org/wiki/Letter_to_the_Inhabitants_of_the_Province_of_Quebec; "Address to the People of Great Britain," 21 October 1774, https://en.wikisource.org/wiki/Address_to_the_People_of_Great_Britain.

15. "Letter to the Oppressed Inhabitants of Canada," 29 May 1775, http://avalon.law.yale.edu/18th_century/contcong_05-29-75.asp.

16. George Washington (hereafter GW) to the Massachusetts General Court, 12 August 1775, FONA; Andrew Jackson O'Shaughnessy, *The Men Who Lost America: British Leadership, the American Revolution, and the Fate of the Empire* (New Haven: Yale University Press, 2013), 17–82; Wilson, *Sense of the People*, 237–53; Eliga H. Gould, *The Persistence of Empire: British Political Culture in the Age of the American Revolution* (Chapel Hill: Published for the Omohundro Institute of Early American History and Culture, Williamsburg, Virginia, by the University of North Carolina Press, 2000), 148–80.

17. GW to Samuel Washington, 30 September 1775, FONA.

18. Ibid.

19. *DRSNY*, vol. 8, 658–60.

20. *JCC*, 16 June 1775, vol. 2, 93.

21. *JCC*, 30 June 1775, vol. 2, 123.

22. *JCC*, 1 July 1775, vol. 2, 123. Mohawk leaders also favored neutrality, though they did not believe that was the same as nonengagement. See Caitlin A. Fitz, " 'Suspected on Both Sides': Little Abraham, Iroquois Neutrality, and the American Revolution," *Journal of the Early Republic* 28, no. 3 (2008): 299–335.

23. *DRSNY*, vol. 8, 592. Indigenous peoples were just as divided as Britons and Americans over what role to play in the war. But when the war reached "Indian country," Indigenous nations applied their own strategies to decide which side to support. See Colin G. Calloway, *The American Revolution in Indian Country* (New York: Cambridge University Press, 1995), 26–64; Taylor, *Divided Ground*.

24. *DRSNY*, vol. 8, 596.

25. Indigenous alliances varied from region to region. In central and southern New England, many Indigenous peoples openly supported the Americans, even after suffering numerous losses. Some Delaware also supported the Americans, in part to secure some independence from the Iroquois. The Six Nations Confederacy itself was split, with the majority of the Oneida and Tuscarora siding with the rebels, while most of the Mohawk, Seneca, Onondaga, and Cayuga fought for the British or strove to remain neutral. Calloway, *American Revolution in Indian Country*, 30–35.

26. *DRSNY*, vol. 8, 605–7. As a general policy, the Seven Nations of Canada had revived the pre-1763 policy of playing one power off the other, hoping to win for themselves a strong position regardless of the outcome. Calloway, *American Revolution in Indian Country*, 35.

27. "Campbell, John," *DCB*.

28. "Walker, Thomas," *DCB*; A. L. Burt, "The Mystery of Walker's Sar," *Canadian Historical Review* 3, no. 3 (1922): 233–55; Jacqueline Reynoso, "(Dis)placing the American Revolution: The British Province of Quebec in the Greater Colonial Struggle, 1759–1783" (PhD diss., Cornell University, 2017), 37–39.

29. "Campbell, John," *DCB*.

30. "Johnson, Guy," *DCB*.

31. Joan R. Gundersen, *To Be Useful to the World: Women in Revolutionary America, 1740–1790* (Chapel Hill: University of North Carolina Press, 2006), 47, 134; Lois M. Huey and Bonnie Pulis, *Molly Brant: A Legacy of Her Own* (Youngstown: Old Fort Niagara Association, 1997), 21–23.

32. Susan M. Hill, *The Clay We Are Made Of: Haudenosaunee Land Tenure on the Grand River* (Winnipeg: University of Manitoba Press, 2017); Daniel K. Richter, *The Ordeal of the Longhouse: The Peoples of the Iroquois League in the Era of European Colonization* (Chapel Hill: Published for the Institute of Early American History and Culture, Williamsburg, Virginia, by the University of North Carolina Press, 1992); William N. Fenton, *The Great Law and the Longhouse: A Political History of the Iroquois Confederacy* (Norman: University of Oklahoma Press, 1998), 517–601.

33. *DRSNY*, vol. 8, 670–71; Taylor, *Divided Ground*, 87–89.

34. "Brant, Joseph (Thayendanegea)," *DCB*.

35. Lawson, *Imperial Challenge*, 109.

36. *DRCHC*, vol. 2, 664–65.

37. Ibid., 668–72; Reynoso, "(Dis)placing the American Revolution," 77–79.

38. *DRCHC*, vol. 2, 667.

39. I draw the narrative in this section from Neatby, *Quebec: The Revolutionary Age*, 145–54. Also Gustave Lanctot, *Canada and the American Revolution, 1774–1783*, trans. Margaret M. Cameron (London: George G. Harrap, 1967), 93–106.

40. GW to John Hancock, 28 November 1775, FONA.

41. *LOD*, vol. 3, 18.

42. *LOD*, vol. 3, 58.

43. *LOD*, vol. 3, 85; *LOD*, vol. 3, 105.

44. "Letter to the Inhabitants of the Province of Canada," 24 January 1776, http://en.wikisource.org/wiki/Letter_to_the_Inhabitants_of_the_Province_of_Canada.

45. *LOD*, vol. 3, 118.

46. *DRSNY*, vol. 8, 665.

47. GW to Richard Henry Lee, 4 April 1776, FONA.

48. John Hancock to GW, 23 April 1776, FONA.

49. John Adams (hereafter JA) to Horatio Gates, 27 April 1776, FONA.

50. O'Shaughnessy, *Men Who Lost America*, 59.

51. *LOD*, vol. 3, 125.

52. Kate Davies, *Catharine Macaulay and Mercy Otis Warren: The Revolutionary Atlantic and the Politics of Gender* (New York: Oxford University Press, 2005), 203–4; Linda K. Kerber, *Women of the Republic: Intellect and Ideology in Revolutionary America* (Chapel Hill: Published for the Omohundro Institute of Early American History and Culture, University of North Carolina Press, 2000), 35–67.

53. Drake, *Nation's Nature*, 186–87.

54. Thomas Paine, *Common Sense*, https://oll.libertyfund.org/page/1776-paine-common-sense-pamphlet.

55. *AA*, 4th series, vol. 4, 1191.

56. To the Author of Common Sense, 26 February 1776, ibid., 1496; Drake, *Nation's Nature*, 188.

57. Amy Noel Ellison, "Montgomery's Misfortune: The American Defeat at Quebec and the March toward Independence, 1775–1776," *Early American Studies* 15, no. 3 (2017): 591–616.

58. "A DIALOGUE between the GHOST of general MONTGOMERY and a DELEGATE, in a wood near Philadelphia," 8 March 1776, *Virginia Gazette*. This was a reprint of Thomas Paine's *A Dialogue between the Ghost of General Montgomery Just Arrived from the Elysian Fields; and an American Delegate, in a Wood Near Philadelphia* (Philadelphia: R. Bell, 1776); Ellison, "Montgomery's Misfortune," 613–14.

59. "A DIALOGUE."

60. Lanctot, *Canada and the American Revolution*, 126–27; Mark R. Anderson, *The Battle for the Fourteenth Colony: America's War of Liberation in Canada, 1774–1776* (Hanover, NH: University Press of New England, 2013), 229.

61. See Curran, *Papist Devils*; Farrelly, *Papist Patriots*. The Carrolls' participation in the commission helped Catholics win increased participation in the early United States. See Mitchell Edward Oxford, " 'This Very Important and Almost Unbounded Trust': The Commission to Canada and the Place of Catholics in Revolutionary America," *US Catholic Historian* 36, no. 4 (2018): 1–24.

62. John Carroll, *The John Carroll Papers*, vol. 1, ed. Thomas O'Brien Hanley and the American Catholic Historical Association (Notre Dame: University of Notre Dame Press, 1976), 46.

63. *LOD*, vol. 3, 178–79.

64. *LOD*, vol. 3, 232; Carol Berkin, *Revolutionary Mothers: Women in the Struggle for America's Independence* (New York: Vintage, 2007); Mary Beth Norton, *Liberty's Daughters: The Revolutionary Experience of American Women, 1750–1800* (Cornell: Cornell University Press, 1996), 155–227.

65. BF to General Schuyler, 11 March 1776, FONA. In early March, Richard Smith noted in his diary that a discussion over part of the instructions for commissioners going to Canada took up three or four hours. The debate over whether Canadians should form a constitution and government for themselves led to "much Argumt. On this Ground." *LOD*, vol. 3, 364.

66. *LOD*, vol. 3, 272.

67. Ibid., 275.

68. *JCC*, vol. 4, 215–16.

69. Anderson, *Battle for the Fourteenth Colony*, 294; Jonathan Israel, *The Expanding Blaze: How the American Revolution Ignited the World, 1775–1848* (Princeton: Princeton University Press, 2017), 191–200.

70. *JCC*, vol. 4, 217–18.

71. Mark R. Anderson does an excellent job of detailing the commissioners' daily activities in Anderson, *Battle for the Fourteenth Colony*, 290–332.

72. David Ramsay, *The History of the American Revolution in Two Volumes*, vol. 1, ed. Lester H. Cohen (Indianapolis: Liberty Classics, 1990 [1789]), 251.

73. BF to Anthony Todd, 29 March 1776, FONA.

74. *Journal of Charles Carroll of Carrollton, during His Visit to Canada in 1776, as One of the Commissioners from Congress* (Baltimore: Maryland Historical Society, 1876), 51.

75. BF to Josiah Quincy Sr., 15 April 1776, *PBF*, vol. 22.

76. BF to John Hancock, 13 April 1776, *PBF*, vol. 22.

77. *Journal of Charles Carroll of Carrollton*, 88.

78. Ibid., 92.

79. Calloway, *Indian World*, 40–41, 225; Taylor, *Divided Ground*, 3.

80. Karim M. Tiro, "James Dean in Iroquoia," *New York History* 80, no. 4 (October 1999): 397.

81. Taylor, *Divided Ground*, 62, 81.

82. Tiro, "James Dean in Iroquoia," 401.

83. Ibid.

84. *AA*, 4th series, vol. 5, 1100.

85. Ibid; Fenton, *Great Law*, 594–98.

86. *AA*, 4th series, vol. 5, 1101.

87. Ibid. Settlers were often confused or annoyed by the ceremonies involved in negotiating with Indigenous nations, but the ceremonial aspects of these meetings were a central element of Indigenous diplomacy. See Richter, *Facing East*.

88. "Butler, John," *DCB*.

89. Letter from the Oneida Chiefs to Philip Schuyler, 22 May 1776, Kirkland Papers; Taylor, *Divided Ground*, 85.

90. *AA*, 4th series, vol. 5, 1100.

91. Letter from the Oneida Chiefs to Philip Schuyler, 22 May 1776, Kirkland Papers.

92. *AA*, 4th series, vol. 5, 1103.

93. Samuel Chase to JA, 18 April 1776, FONA.

94. GW to Major General Philip Schuyler, 19 April 1776, FONA.

95. Major General Philip Schuyler to GW, 27 April 1776, FONA.

96. R. Cole Harris, ed., *Historical Atlas of Canada*, vol. 1: *From the Beginning to 1800* (Toronto: University of Toronto Press, 1987), plates 47 and 49.

97. Afua Cooper, *The Hanging of Angelique: The Untold Story of Canadian Slavery and the Burning of Old Montreal* (Athens: University of Georgia Press, 2007); Rushforth, *Bonds of Alliance*.

98. Commissioners to Canada to [John Hancock], 6 May 1776, FONA.

99. Ibid.

100. Ibid.

101. Commissioners to Canada to [John Hancock], 8 May 1776, FONA.

102. *Violence, Order, and Unrest: A History of British North America, 1749–1876*, ed. Elizabeth Mancke et al. (Toronto: University of Toronto Press, 2019), 36–77; Israel, *Expanding Blaze*, 195.

103. Anderson, *Battle for the Fourteenth Colony*, 305–15.

104. Commissioners to Canada to Schuyler, 11 May 1776, FONA.

105. BF to Charles Carroll and Samuel Chase, 27 May 1776, FONA.

106. *LOD*, vol. 4, 4; *Journal of Charles Carroll of Carrollton*, 93–100.

107. GW to Major General Philip Schuyler, 17 May 1776, FONA.

108. Brigadier General John Sullivan to GW, 8–12 June 1776, FONA.

109. *Virginia Gazette*, 8 June 1776.

110. Anderson, *Battle for the Fourteenth Colony*, 320.

111. *Virginia Gazette*, 14 June 1776.

112. *Virginia Gazette*, 15 June 1776.

113. GW to Major General Philip Schuyler, 22 May 1776, FONA.

114. Brigadier General John Sullivan to GW, 5–6 June 1776, FONA.

115. Brigadier General John Sullivan to GW, 7 June 1776, FONA.

116. JA to James Warren, 18 May 1776, FONA.

117. Ibid.

118. *LOD*, vol. 3, 655.
119. General Philip Schuyler to GW, 21 May 1776, FONA.
120. Commissioners to Canada to [John Hancock], 8 May 1776, FONA.
121. John Hancock to the Commissioners of Canada, 24 May 1776, FONA.
122. Brigadier General William Thompson to GW, 2 June 1776, FONA.
123. Lanctot, *Canada and the American Revolution*, 150–53.
124. *LOD*, vol. 4, 118.
125. *LOD*, vol. 4, 147.
126. John Hancock to GW, 7 June 1776, FONA.
127. GW to Philip Schuyler, 7 June 1776, FONA.
128. *LOD*, vol. 4, 140.
129. Mercy Otis Warren to Abigail Adams, 27 May 1776, FONA.
130. Jane Mecom to Catharine Greene, 1 June 1776, FONA. On Mecom's life and her letters, see Jill Lepore, *Book of Ages: The Life and Opinions of Jane Franklin* (New York: Knopf, 2013).
131. *LOD*, vol. 4, 228–29.
132. *LOD*, vol. 4, 335.
133. General Benedict Arnold to General John Sullivan, Chambly, 13 June 1776, in *Correspondence of the American Revolution*, ed. Jared Sparks, vol. 1 (Boston: Little, Brown, 1853), 528–29.
134. *AA*, 4th series, vol. 5, 1139.
135. *AA*, 4th series, vol. 6, 1029.
136. Robert Middlekauff, *The Glorious Cause: The American Revolution, 1763–1789* (New York: Oxford University Press, 2005), 620–24; Edling, *Perfecting*, 36–43; Justin du Rivage, *Revolution against Empire: Taxes, Politics, and the Origins of American Independence* (New Haven: Yale University Press, 2017), 221–24.
137. LOC, http://hdl.loc.gov/loc.mss/mtj.mtjbib000104.
138. The Articles of Confederation adopted by Congress in November 1777 included the same stipulation, now as Article 11. Canada was unique among the loyal British provinces in North America in this regard. *DHRC*, vol. 1, 85, 93, 126.
139. Drake, *Nation's Nature*, 190.
140. Pauline Maier, *American Scripture: Making the Declaration of Independence* (New York: Vintage, 1997), 41–45.
141. Ibid., 99–103.
142. Robert G. Parkinson, *The Common Cause: Creating Race and Nation in the American Revolution* (Chapel Hill: University of North Carolina Press, 2016), 235–41. Quote from 241.
143. *LOD*, vol. 4, 353–54; Israel, *Expanding Blaze*, 201.
144. *AA*, 4th series, vol. 6, 1193–94.
145. Ibid.
146. *LOD*, vol. 4, 335.
147. *AA*, 4th series, vol. 6, 1194.
148. Declaration of Independence, 1776.

149. *LOD*, vol. 4, 375.
150. Ellison, "Montgomery's Misfortune."
151. *LOD*, vol. 4, 378.
152. *LOD*, vol. 4, 474.

# Chapter Two. Sea Power

1. Christopher Hodson, *The Acadian Diaspora: An Eighteenth-Century History* (Oxford: Oxford University Press, 2012), 9; Faragher, *Great and Noble*, 254–55.
2. Lennox, *Homelands and Empires*.
3. John Bartlet Brebner, *New England's Outpost: Acadia before the Conquest of Canada* (New York: Columbia University Press, 1927); George A. Rawlyk, *Nova Scotia's Massachusetts: A Study of Massachusetts-Nova Scotia Relations, 1630–1784* (Montreal: McGill-Queen's University Press, 1973); John J. McCusker and Russell R. Menard, *The Economy of British America, 1607–1789* (Chapel Hill: Published for the Institute of Early American History and Culture by the University of North Carolina Press, 1985), 91–117. More recent scholarship has demonstrated the important distinctions between Maine and Nova Scotia. See Elizabeth Mancke, *The Fault Lines of Empire: Political Differentiation in Massachusetts and Nova Scotia, ca. 1760–1830* (New York: Routledge, 2005).
4. *Handbook of North American Indians*, ed. William C. Sturtevant and Bruce G. Trigger (volume editor), vol. 15 (Washington, DC: Smithsonian Institution, 1978), 110–38.
5. Bruce J. Bourque, Steven L. Cox, and Ruth Holmes Whitehead, *Twelve Thousand Years: American Indians in Maine* (Lincoln: University of Nebraska Press, 2001).
6. John G. Reid, *Essays on Northeastern North America, Seventeenth and Eighteenth centuries* (Toronto: University of Toronto Press, 2008); William C. Wicken, "Encounters with Tall Sails and Tall Tales: Mi'kmaq Society, 1500–1760" (PhD diss., McGill University, 1994); Colin G. Calloway, *Dawnland Encounters: Indians and Europeans in Northern New England* (Hanover, NH: University Press of New England, 1991); Bruce J. Bourque, "Ethnicity on the Maritime Peninsula, 1600–1759," *Ethnohistory* 36, no. 3 (1989); Charles A. Martijn, *Les Micmacs et la mer* (Quebec: Recherches amérindiennes au Québec, 1986).
7. See *New England and the Maritime Provinces: Connections and Comparisons*, ed. Stephen J. Hornsby and John G. Reid (Montreal and Kingston: McGill-Queen's University Press, 2005), 32–49, 74–93; *The Northeastern Borderlands: Four Centuries of Interaction*, ed. Stephen Hornsby, Victor A. Konrad, and James Herlan (Fredericton: Acadiensis Press, 1989); Reginald C. Stuart, *United States Expansionism and British North America, 1775–1871* (Chapel Hill: University of North Carolina Press, 1988), 8–27.
8. GW to the Massachusetts General Court, 12 August 1775, FONA.

9. *JCC*, vol. 3, 316; *DHSM*, vol. 14, 322; *PGWRWS*, vol. 3, 95–97; Ernest Clarke, *Siege of Fort Cumberland, 1776: An Episode in the American Revolution* (Montreal and Kingston: McGill-Queen's University Press, 1995), 10–12.

10. James Lyon to GW, 25 December 1775, FONA. See note 4 for Washington's response. On Lyon's Nova Scotia roots, see Mancke, *Fault Lines of Empire*, 100.

11. James Lyon to GW, 25 December 1775, FONA.

12. Kerber, *Women of the Republic*, 48–49.

13. *JCC*, vol. 3, 348. See also Instructions to Aaron Willard and Moses Child, 24 November 1775, FONA.

14. *Early American Imprints*, series 1, no. 14449.

15. GW to John Hancock, 30–31 January 1776, FONA.

16. Report of Aaron Willard and Moses Child, 14 February 1776, enclosed in GW to John Hancock, Cambridge, 14 February 1776, FONA.

17. Ibid.

18. Citizen of Nova Scotia to GW, 8 February 1776, FONA.

19. *Extract from the Votes of the House of Assembly of the Province of Nova Scotia* (Boston, 1775), 10–11.

20. Citizens of Nova Scotia to GW, Cumberland, NS, 8 February 1776, FONA; *JCC*, vol. 4, 314; Mancke, *Fault Lines of Empire*, 66–81.

21. *JCC*, vol. 4, 155; GW to John Hancock, 1 April 1776, FONA; *JCC*, vol. 4, 314.

22. Alexander Cluny, *The American Traveller: or, Observations on the Present State, Culture and Commerce of the British Colonies in America* [. . .] (London, 1769), 51–2; John Robinson, Farmer, *A journey through Nova-Scotia, containing, a particular account of the country and its inhabitants* [. . .] (London: 1774), 37–38. See also Barbara DeWolfe, *Discoveries of America: Personal Accounts of British Emigrants to North America during the Revolutionary Era* (Cambridge: Cambridge University Press, 1997), 51–52.

23. Emerson W. Baker and John G. Reid, "Amerindian Power in the Early Modern Northeast: A Reappraisal," *William and Mary Quarterly* 61, no. 1 (2004): 77–106.

24. *DHSM*, vol. 14, 254–55.

25. *DHSM*, vol. 14, 355; Colin G. Calloway, *The American Revolution in Indian Country: Crisis and Diversity in Native American Communities* (Cambridge: Cambridge University Press, 1995), 65–85.

26. *JCC*, vol. 5, 527.

27. GW to John Hancock, 4–5 July 1776, FONA; Calloway, *Indian World*, 228–29.

28. Calloway, *Indian World*, 218–19.

29. GW to the Massachusetts General Court, New York, 11 July 1776, FONA.

30. Questions for the Committee, 18 October 1775, FONA; Speeches of the Caughnawaga, St. Johns, and Passamaquoddy Indians, Cambridge, 31 January 1776, FONA.

31. The Mi'kmaq signed similar treaties in 1760–61. An overview of this treaty and its implications is in Wicken, *Mi'kmaq Treaties on Trial,* 191–209.

32. *AA,* 4th series, vol. 3, 1464–65. The General Court informed the Mi'kmaq and Wulstukwiuk, "We shall be always ready to help you, and stand firm together with you in opposing the wicked people of *Old England,* who are fighting against us, and who are seeking to take your and our lands and liberties from us, and make us their servants."

33. *AA,* 5th series, vol. 1, 839. George Washington's February 1776 letter has not been found. A letter he sent to the St. John natives in December 1776 stated, "It gave me great Pleasure to hear by Major Shaw, that you kept the Chain of Friendship, which I sent you in February last from Cambridge bright & unbroken." See James Bowdoin to GW, 30 July 1776, note 1, FONA.

34. Historians debate the influence of these treaties. See John G. Reid, "*Pax Britannica* or *Pax Indigena?* Planter Nova Scotia (1760–1782) and Competing Strategies of Pacification," *Canadian Historical Review* 85, no. 4 (December 2004): 669–92; Reid, "Empire, the Maritime Colonies, and the Supplanting of Mi'kma'ki/Wulstukwik, 1780–1820," *Acadiensis* 38, no. 2 (Summer/Autumn 2009): 78–97. Stephen E. Patterson, "Indian-White Relations in Nova Scotia, 1749–61: A Study in Political Interaction," *Acadiensis* 23, no. 1 (Autumn 1993): 23–59; Patterson, "Anatomy of a Treaty: Nova Scotia's First Native Treaty in Historical Context," *University of New Brunswick Law Journal* 48 (1999): 41–64; Patterson, "Eighteenth-Century Treaties: The Mi'kmaq, Maliseet, and Passamaquoddy Experience," *Native Studies Review* 18, no. 1 (2009): 25–52. Wicken, "Mi'kmaq Decisions: Antoine Tecouenemac, the Conquest, and the Treaty of Utrecht," in *The "Conquest" of Acadia, 1710: Imperial, Colonial, and Aboriginal Constructions,* by John G. Reid et al. (Toronto: University of Toronto Press, 2004), 86–100.

35. *AA,* 5th series, vol. 1, 839; Francis Cogliano, "No King, No Popery: Anti-Popery and Revolution in New England, 1745–1791" (PhD diss., Boston University, 1993), 142.

36. Cogliano, "No King, No Popery," 144–46.

37. *AA,* 5th series, vol. 1, 840.

38. Euro-Indigenous diplomacy in the northeast and much of North America followed Indigenous protocol, which serves as an example of their political power. For examples, see Baker and Reid, "Amerindian Power," 77–107; Daniel K. Richter, *Before the Revolution: America's Ancient Pasts* (Cambridge: Harvard University Press, 2011), 43, 133–35; Wicken, "Encounters with Tall Sails," 403–8.

39. *AA,* 5th series, vol. 1, 840–41.

40. Ibid., 841. See Laura M. Chmielewski, *The Spice of Popery: Converging Christianities on an Early American Frontier* (Notre Dame: University of Notre Dame Press, 2012); Tracy Neal Leavelle, *The Catholic Calumet: Colonial Con-*

*versions in French and Indian North America* (Philadelphia: University of Pennsylvania Press, 2011).

41. *AA*, 5th series, vol. 1, 841–46.

42. Michael Witgen, *An Infinity of Nations: How the Native New World Shaped Early North America* (Philadelphia: University of Pennsylvania Press, 2011); Francis Jennings, *Ambiguous Iroquois Empire: The Covenant Chain Confederation of Indian Tribes with English Colonies from Its Beginnings to the Lancaster Treaty of 1744*, 1st ed. (New York: W. W. Norton, 1984).

43. *AA*, 5th series, vol. 1, 848.

44. John G. Reid, "Imperial-Aboriginal Friendship in Eighteenth-Century Mi'kma'ki/Wulstukwik," in Bannister and Riordam, *Loyal Atlantic*, 75–102.

45. James Bowdoin to GW, 30 July 1776, FONA.

46. Taylor, *American Revolutions*, 163–65.

47. Calloway, *Indian Country*, 36.

48. *DHSM*, vol. 4, 398–99; "Eddy, Jonathan," *DCB*; Régis Brun, A. J. B. Johnston, and Ernest Clarke, *Fort Beauséjour—Fort Cumberland: Une Histoire/A History* (Memracook, NB: 1991), 17–21; Clarke, *Siege of Fort Cumberland, 1776: An Episode in the American Revolution*; James S. Leamon, *Revolution Downeast: The War for American Independence in Maine* (Amherst: University of Massachusetts Press, 1995), 89–90; Mancke, *Fault Lines of Empire*, 83–107.

49. Leamon, *Revolution Downeast*, 82–85.

50. *AA*, 5th series, vol. 3, 800.

51. Ibid., 802.

52. Ibid., 803.

53. Ibid., 804; Calloway, *Indian World*, 231.

54. *AA*, 5th series, vol. 3, 805–6.

55. *JCC*, vol. 7, 18, 20, 30. See also "Allan, John," *DCB*.

56. Ibid., 38; Cogliano, "No King, No Popery," 153–56.

57. Several responses from men chosen to participate in the campaign indicate that they wished someone more capable than they might have been appointed. For examples, see *DHSM*, vol. 14, 436, 437, 438.

58. "Allan, John," *DCB*; Leamon, *Revolution Downeast*, 90–93; Rawlyk, *Nova Scotia's Massachusetts*, 244–46.

59. "Francklin [Franklin], Michael," *DCB*.

60. Leamon, *Revolution Downeast*, 96–97.

61. Larrie D. Ferreiro, *Brothers at Arms: American Independence and the Men of France and Spain Who Saved It* (New York: Knopf, 2017).

62. Leamon, *Revolution Downeast*, 96–97; Cogliano, "No King, No Popery," 158–61. "Francklin [Franklin], Michael," *DCB*.

63. See Calloway, *Indian Country*, 65–85; Fitz, " 'Suspected on Both Sides,' " 299–335.

64. John G. Reid, "*Pax Britannica* or *Pax Indigena*? Planter Nova Scotia (1760–1782) and Competing Strategies of Pacification," *Canadian Historical Review* 85, no. 4 (2004): 669–92; Reid, "Empire, the Maritime Colonies," 78–97.

65. Scott Weidensaul, *The First Frontier: The Forgotten History of Struggle, Savagery, and Endurance in Early America* (New York: Houghton Mifflin Harcourt, 2012), 77; *American Beginnings: Exploration, Culture, and Cartography in the Land of Norumbega*, ed. Emerson W. Baker (Lincoln: University of Nebraska Press, 1994). "Ingram, David," *DCB*. Ingram published his account, *A true discourse of the adventures and travailes of David Ingram*, in 1583. No copies survive.

66. Lennox, "Time and a Place," 431–35.

67. *Handbook of North American Indians*, 15, 123–60; Thomas M. Wickman, *Snowshoe Country: An Environmental and Cultural History of Winter in the Early American Northeast* (Cambridge: Cambridge University Press, 2018); Andrew Hill Clark, *Acadia; the Geography of Early Nova Scotia to 1760* (Madison: University of Wisconsin Press, 1968); Bourque, Cox, and Whitehead, *Twelve Thousand Years*; Calloway, *Dawnland Encounters*.

68. *JCC*, vol. 11, 518.

69. Robert W. Sloan, "New Ireland: Loyalists in Eastern Maine during the American Revolution" (PhD diss., Michigan State University, 1971), 10–39.

70. Samuel Francis Batchelder, *The Life and Surprising Adventures of John Nutting, Cambridge Loyalists, and His Strange Connection with The Penobscot Expedition of 1779*. Reprinted from the Proceedings of the Cambridge Historical Society (Cambridge, MA, 1912), 55–68.

71. Sloan, "New Ireland," 19.

72. Leamon, *Revolution Downeast*, 174–75.

73. *The Diary and Letters of His Excellency Thomas Hutchinson, Esq.*, vol. 2, ed. Peter Orlando Hutchinson (London, 1883), 217–18, cited in Sloan, "New Ireland," 16–17. See also, Joseph Williamson, "The Proposed Province of New Ireland," *Collections of the Maine Historical Society*, 3rd series, vol. 1. (Portland: Published by the Society, 1904), 147–57.

74. Batchelder, *Life and Surprising Adventures*, 68–74. See also, John Caleff, "The Seige of Penobscot by the Rebels [. . .]," in *Magazine of History*, Extra Number, no. 11. (New York: William Abbatt, 1910), 7.

75. Ibid., 76–77.

76. "McLean, Francis," *DCB*; George E. Buker, *The Penobscot Expedition: Commodore Saltonstall and the Massachusetts Conspiracy of 1779* (Annapolis: Naval Institute Press, 2002), 6.

77. Robert W. Sloan, "New Ireland: Men in Pursuit of a Forlorn Hope, 1779–1784," *Maine Historical Quarterly* 19 (1979): 73–74. "Caleff, John," *DCB*.

78. Caleff, "Siege of Penobscot," 33–36.

79. Report of Mr. Button and Mr. Capon, 3 January 1714, 19, vol. 6, RG 1, NSARM.

80. Caleff, "Siege of Penobscot," 15.

81. Buker, *Penobscot Expedition*, 12.

82. Leamon, *Revolution Downeast*, 106–7.

83. *LOD*, vol. 13, 238; Leamon, *Revolution Downeast*, 107.

84. *LOD*, vol. 13, 267.

85. *LOD*, vol. 13, 269.

86. Caleff, "Siege of Penobscot," 16.

87. "Lovell, Solomon," *ANB*; Buker, *Penobscot Expedition*, 19.

88. "Saltonstall, Dudley," *ANB*; Buker, *Penobscot Expedition*, 22. For many men in New England, seafaring was a stage of life rather than an enduring vocation. See Daniel Vickers and Vince Walsh, *Young Men and the Sea: Yankee Seafarers in the Age of Sail* (New Haven: Yale University Press, 2005).

89. Massachusetts Historical Society, *Collections* (Boston: Massachusetts Historical Society, 1904), series 7, pt. 2, 4:319; and Massachusetts Archives Collection, 145: 199. Both cited in Buker, *Penobscot Expedition*, 29–31.

90. "Lovell, Solomon," *ANB*. In 2022 dollars, the amount would be around $300,000,000.

91. Caleff, "Siege of Penobscot," 17–18.

92. "Saltonstall, Dudley," *ANB*.

93. Caleff, "Siege of Penobscot," 23; Buker, *Penobscot Expedition*, 55.

94. *LOD*, vol. 13, 323.

95. Cited in Buker, *Penobscot Expedition*, 55.

96. Andrew Jackson O'Shaughnessy, *An Empire Divided: The American Revolution and the British Caribbean* (Philadelphia: University of Pennsylvania Press, 2000), 169–70; Ferreiro, *Brothers at Arms*, 165–206.

97. *LOD*, vol. 13, 341.

98. *LOD*, vol. 13, 354. Washington had informed the Massachusetts Council on 3 August 1779 that British ships had left from Sandy Hook to reinforce the Penobscot expedition. George Washington to the Massachusetts Council, West Point, 3 August 1779, FONA.

99. Leamon, *Revolution Downeast*, 114–19; Buker, *Penobscot Expedition*, 77–97.

100. *Pennsylvania Gazette*, 18 August 1779.

101. *Virginia Gazette*, 28 August 1779.

102. *LOD*, vol. 13, 408.

103. Ibid., 429.

104. Ibid., 434.

105. *Pennsylvania Journal*, 22 September 1779.

106. Leamon, *Revolution Downeast*, 118. George E. Buker offers an insightful defense of Saltonstall, suggesting that his actions were restricted by the technical limits of his ships. Buker, *Penobscot Expedition*.

107. Buker, *Penobscot Expedition*, 136–37; Leamon, *Revolution Downeast*, 116.

108. Buker, *Penobscot Expedition*, 140–48; Michael M. Greenburg, *The Court-Martial of Paul Revere* (Lebanon, NH: Fore Edge, 2014).

109. Quoted in "McNutt, Alexander," *DCB*.

110. McNutt, *To the inhabitants of the state of New Ireland, and all others on both sides of the Atlantic, who are interested in the great and important contest between*

*the rising empire of North America and the island of Great Britain* (Philadel-phia, 1780); *Pennsylvania Gazette,* 14 February 1781.

111. Alexander McNutt, *The constitution and frame of government of the free and independent state and commonwealth of New Ireland: as prepared by the special direction of the people, for the consideration of their convention, when met. Composed by those who are invested with proper authority for that purpose* (Philadel-phia, 1780), 4–6. Connecticut and Rhode Island did not draft new constitutions but instead removed all references to the king in their colo-nial charters. Akhil Reed Amar, *America's Constitution: A Biography* (New York: Random House, 2006).

112. Steve Pincus, *The Heart of the Declaration: The Founders' Case for an Activist Government* (New Haven: Yale University Press, 2016), 34–36.

113. McNutt, *Constitution and Frame of Government,* 7–12;

114. Ibid., 13–16.

115. Ibid., 16–18.

116. Ibid., "Advertisement"; Alan Taylor, *Liberty Men and Great Proprietors: The Revolutionary Settlement on the Maine Frontier, 1760–1820* (Chapel Hill: Published for the Omohundro Institute of Early American History and Culture, The University of North Carolina Press, 1990), 4–11.

117. Sloan, "New Ireland," 36–38, 84, 93–95; Sloan, "New Ireland: Men in Pur-suit of a Forlorn Hope, 1779–1784," 79–83.

118. Alexander McNutt to BF, 9 April 1782, FONA.

119. Alexander McNutt, *Considerations on the Sovereignty, Independence, Trade and Fisheries of New-Ireland, Formerly known by the Name of Nova-Scotia and the Adjacent Islands: Submitted to the European Powers, That may be engaged in set-tling the Terms of* PEACE, *among the* NATIONS AT WAR [Philadelphia?], [1781?], 3–5.

## Chapter Three. A Northern Chorus

1. Samuel Flagg Bemis, *The Diplomacy of the American Revolution* (Bloomington: Indiana University Press, 1957 [1935]), 197, 201n34.

2. *JCC,* vol. 6, 1054–56; Elbridge Gerry to JA, 8 January 1777, FONA.

3. Olaf U. Janzen, *War and Trade in Eighteenth-Century Newfoundland* (Liver-pool: Liverpool University Press, 2013), 194–95.

4. William James Newbigging, "The Cession of Canada and French Public Opinion," *Proceedings of the Meeting of the French Colonial Historical Society* 22 (1998): 164; Helen Dewar, "Canada or Guadeloupe? French and British Perceptions of Empire, 1760–1763," *Canadian Historical Review* 91, no. 4 (2010): 637–60.

5. Middlekauff, *Glorious Cause,* 402–3; James Stewart Pritchard, *In Search of Empire: The French in the Americas, 1670–1730* (Cambridge: Cambridge University Press, 2004).

6. Bemis, *Diplomacy,* 17–22.

7. Ibid., 24–25.
8. Bemis, *Diplomacy*, 27.
9. Thomas J. Schaeper, *Edward Bancroft: Scientist, Author, Spy* (New Haven: Yale University Press, 2011), 107–8.
10. Morgan, *Birth of the Republic: 1763–89*, 81–84; Schaeper, *Edward Bancroft*, 114–25; Paul Mapp, "The Revolutionary War and Europe's Great Powers," in Edward G. Gray and Jane Kamensky, eds., *The Oxford Handbook of the American Revolution* (Oxford: Oxford University Press, 2012), 316–18.
11. BF to James Hutton, 1 February 1778, FONA.
12. "Lafayette, Marquis de," *ANB;* Lloyd S. Kramer, "America's Lafayette and Lafayette's America: A European and the American Revolution," *William and Mary Quarterly* 38, no. 2 (1981): 228–41.
13. Lafayette to GW, 20 January 1778, FONA.
14. *JCC*, vol. 9, 985–87.
15. *JCC*, vol. 10, 84–96; *JCC*, vol. 10, 193.
16. The details of Lafayette's instructions are found in note 1, Major General Horatio Gates to GW, 24 January 1778, FONA.
17. Lafayette to GW, 19 February 1778, FONA.
18. Ibid.
19. GW to Brigadier General Thomas Nelson, 8 February 1778, FONA.
20. GW to Lafayette, 10 March 1778, FONA.
21. *JCC*, vol. 10, 216.
22. JA to James Warren, 26 July 1778, FONA.
23. O'Shaughnessy, *Men Who Lost America*, 62–63; Anthony Gregory, " 'Formed for Empire': The Continental Congress Responds to the Carlisle Peace Commission," *Journal of the Early Republic* 38, no. 4 (2018): 643–72.
24. JA to Samuel Adams, 28 July 1778, FONA.
25. *JCC*, vol. 12, 1039–41.
26. Ibid., 1042–48.
27. Ibid., 1053.
28. Bemis, *Diplomacy*, 67–68, 198.
29. *JCC*, vol. 12, 1060. Bemis, *Diplomacy*, 199.
30. "d'Estaing, Comte," *ANB*.
31. *DRSNY*, vol. 10, 1165–67. His letter was published in several colonial newspapers. See, for one example, the *South Carolina Gazette*, 17 February 1779.
32. *JCC*, vol. 12, 1190. George M. Wrong, *Canada and the American Revolution: The Disruption of the First British Empire* (New York: Macmillan, 1935), 345–46; Marcel Trudel, "La servitude de l'Église catholique du Canada français sous le régime anglais," *Rapport—Société canadienne d'histoire de l'Église catholique* 30 (1963): 11–33.
33. GW to Henry Laurens, FONA.
34. *PAH*, vol. 1, 579. See also Bemis, *Diplomacy*, 199.
35. *JCC*, vol. 13, 11–14.
36. *LOD*, vol. 12, 42.

37. Ibid., 103.

38. *JCC*, vol. 13, 239–42; *LOD*, vol. 12, 186.

39. *Pennsylvania Gazette*, 10 March 1779; *The Parliamentary Register*, vol. 11 (London, 1779), 30–44.

40. "Morris, Gouverneur," *ANB*.

41. *LOD*, vol. 12, 146–51. The original manuscript has never been found, but the letter was reprinted in the *Pennsylvania Packet; or the General Advertiser*, 11 March 1779.

42. *LOD*, vol. 12, 355.

43. Ibid., 401–2; Gerald S. Graham, *Empire of the North Atlantic: The Maritime Struggle for North America* (Toronto: University of Toronto Press, 1958), 193–216.

44. Richard B. Morris, *The Peacemakers: The Great Powers and American Independence* (New York: Harper & Row, 1965), 2.

45. Ibid., 21–25.

46. Morgan, *Benjamin Franklin*, 243.

47. Ibid., 245–47.

48. JA to President of Congress, 4 August 1779, FONA.

49. 7 April 1779, *Pennsylvania Gazette*.

50. 5 May 1779, *South Carolina Gazette*.

51. 15 September 1779, *South Carolina Gazette*.

52. Taylor, *Divided Ground*, 206.

53. Calloway, *Indian Country*, 49–51; Barbara Graymont, *The Iroquois in the American Revolution* (Syracuse, NY: Syracuse University Press, 1972), 193–222.

54. Many of the Iroquois had fled to Fort Niagara, from which they would later launch campaigns against those Six Nations who had supported the Americans. Fenton, *Great Law*, 601; Calloway, *Indian World*, 235–60; Taylor, *Divided Ground*, 97–100.

55. Calloway, *Indian Country*, 50.

56. Lauren Duval, "Mastering Charleston: Property and Patriarchy in British-Occupied Charleston, 1780–82," *William and Mary Quarterly* 75, no. 4 (2018): 589–622; Martha Condray Searcy, "1779: The First Year of the British Occupation of Georgia," *Georgia Historical Quarterly* 67, no. 2 (1983): 168–88.

57. GW to Lafayette, 19 May 1780, FONA.

58. *A Catalogue of the Washington Collection in the Boston Athenaeum*, ed. Appleton P. C. Griffin (Boston Athenaeum, 1897), 374; *The Writings of George Washington*, vol. 7, ed. Jared Sparks (Boston, 1853), 44–45; "Arnold, Benedict," *DCB*.

59. "Rochambeau, Comte de," *ANB*.

60. Comte Rochambeau to GW (with enclosure from Schuyler), 31 August 1780, FONA.

61. Taylor, *Divided Ground*, 206–7; Calloway, *Indian World*, 224.

62. *The True Interest of Great-Britain set forth in Regard to the Colonies* (London, 1774) and *Dispassionate Thoughts on the American War Addressed to Moderates of All Parties* (London, 1780).

63. JA to President of Congress, no. 62, 9 May 1780, FONA.

64. JA to Edmé Genêt, 9 May 1780, FONA.

65. JA to Edmé Jacques Genêt, 17 May 1780, FONA.

66. JA to Edmund Jenings, 11 June 1780, FONA. Jenings had previously argued that "immediate peace is necessary for the welfare and safety of the nation, and that peace cannot be had but by the acknowledgment of the independancy of America, in which all Europe, and indeed the whole universe are interested." Edmund Jenings, *Considerations on the Mode and Terms of a Treaty of Peace with America* (London, 1779), 3.

67. Antoine-Marie Cerisier to JA, 17 October 1780, FONA.

68. Gould, *Persistence*, 166.

69. 11 August 1779, *Pennsylvania Gazette*; Mapp, "Revolutionary War and Europe's Great Powers."

70. 18 August 1779, *Pennsylvania Gazette*.

71. 23 February 1780, *Pennsylvania Gazette*.

72. Reid et al., *"Conquest,"* 3–24; Faragher, *Great and Noble*, 1–34; Griffiths, *Migrant*, 224–83. See also Plank, *Unsettled*. The text of the Treaty of Utrecht is in *The Consolidated Treaty Series XXVII*, ed. Clive Parry (Dobbs Ferry, NY: Oceana Publications, 1969), 481.

73. See Jeffers Lennox, "An Empire on Paper: The Founding of Halifax and Conceptions of Imperial Space, 1744–55," *Canadian Historical Review* 88, no. 3 (2007): 373–412.

74. Lennox, "Nova Scotia Lost and Found," 3–31. See also Lennox, *Homelands and Empires*.

75. The boundary memorials can be found in *The Memorials of the English and French Commissaries Concerning the Limits of Nova Scotia or Acadia*, vol. 1 (London: n.p., 1755).

76. *The Examination of Doctor Benjamin Franklin, Before an August Assembly, Relating to the Repeal of the Stamp-Act, etc.* (Philadelphia: 1766) in Gordon S. Wood, ed., *The American Revolution: Writings from the Pamphlet Debate, I: 1764–1772* (New York: Library of America, 2015), 354.

77. 23 February 1780, *Pennsylvania Gazette*.

78. O'Shaughnessy, *Men Who Lost America*, 334–37.

79. Taylor, *American Revolutions*, 302–4.

80. "Adams, John," *ANB*.

81. [September and October 1779], FONA. Also "John Adams' Instructions Respecting a Peace Treaty with Great Britain," 16 October 1779, FONA.

82. 3 January 1781, *Pennsylvania Journal*; 3 January 1781, *Providence Gazette*; 27 February 1781, *Connecticut Courant*; 27 March 1781, *Pennsylvania Packet*; 28 June 1781, *Pennsylvania Packet*; 11 July 1781, *Freeman's Journal*; 11 November 1781, *Norwich Packet*.

83. O'Shaughnessy, *Men Who Lost America*, 238–40.
84. Ibid., 242–43. See also "Cornwallis, Charles, First Marquess of Cornwallis," *ODNB.*
85. Morris, *Peacemakers*, 251.
86. Taylor, *American Revolutions*, 296–97; O'Shaughnessy, *Empire Divided*, 232–38.
87. O'Shaughnessy, *Men Who Lost America*, 76–78.
88. "Wentworth, Charles-Watson," *ODNB.*
89. Bemis, *Diplomacy*, 192–93; Morris, *Peacemakers*, 257.
90. "Oswald, Richard," *ODNB.*
91. *Writings*, vol. 8, 461–62.
92. Ibid., 428.
93. Esmond Wright, "The British Objectives, 1780–1783: 'If Not Dominion Then Trade,' " in Ronald Hoffman and Peter J. Albert, eds., *Peace and the Peacemakers: The Treaty of 1783* (Charlottesville: University Press of Virginia for the United States Capitol Historical Society, 1986), 15.
94. Morris, *Peacemakers*, 261–62. *Writings*, vol. 8, 465.
95. *Writings*, vol. 8, 469–70.
96. Ibid., 471–72; Marcus Gallo, "Property Rights, Citizenship, Corruption, and Inequality: Confiscating Loyalist Estates during the American Revolution," *Pennsylvania History: A Journal of Mid-Atlantic Studies* 86, no. 4 (2019); Brett Palfreyman, "The Loyalists and the Federal Constitution: The Origins of the Bill of Attainder Clause," *Journal of the Early Republic* 35, no. 3 (2015): 451–73.
97. *Writings*, vol. 8, 473.
98. Morris, *Peacemakers*, 263–64.
99. *Writings*, vol. 8, 465–66.
100. Morris, *Peacemakers*, 265–66.
101. *Writings*, vol. 8, 477–78; Charles R. Ritcheson, "Britain's Peacemakers, 1782–1783," in Hoffman and Albert, *Peace and the Peacemakers*, 70–71.
102. *Writings*, vol. 8, 474; Morris, *Peacemakers*, 263.
103. *Writings*, vol. 8, 430.
104. Ibid., 480.
105. Wright, "British Objectives," in Hoffman and Albert, *Peace and the Peacemakers*, 13, 18.
106. Ibid., 18.
107. *Writings*, vol. 8, 487.
108. Ibid., 485.
109. Morris, *Peacemakers*, 270.
110. Ritcheson, "Britain's Peacemakers," in Hoffman and Albert, *Peace and the Peacemakers*, 83–87.
111. *Writings*, vol. 8, 490–91; Wright, "British Objectives," in Hoffman and Albert, *Peace and the Peacemakers*, 19.
112. *Writings*, vol. 8, 491.
113. Ibid.

114. Edward E. Hale and Edward E. Hale Jr., *Franklin in France*, vol. 2 (Boston: Roberts Brothers, 1888), 56–58.

115. Vickers and Walsh, *Young Men and the Sea: Yankee Seafarers in the Age of Sail*; Daniel Vickers, *Farmers and Fishermen: Two Centuries of Work in Essex County, Massachusetts, 1630–1850* (Chapel Hill: University of North Carolina Press, 1994).

116. https://malegislature.gov/VirtualTour/Artifact/64.

117. Hale and Hale Jr., *Franklin in France*, 2:166.

118. Wright, "British Objectives," in Hoffman and Albert, *Peace and the Peacemakers*, 22; Morris, *Peacemakers*, 280.

119. JA to BF, 24 May 1782, FONA.

120. Francis Dana to JA, 11/22 July 1782, FONA. King James's grant to William Alexander is significant because it provided a historical British claim to Nova Scotia. James was king of England and Scotland, and though the grant was made to a Scot (giving rise to the name New Scotland, or Nova Scotia), the 1707 union of England and Scotland strengthened the British claim to Nova Scotia. See John G. Reid, "The Conquest of 'Nova Scotia': Cartographic Imperialism and the Echoes of a Scottish Past," in Ned C. Landsman, ed., *Nation and Province in the First British Empire: Scotland and the Americas, 1600–1800* (Lewisburg, PA: Bucknell University Press, 2001), 39–59.

121. On the post-revolution boundary negotiations, see Francis M. Carroll, *A Good and Wise Measure: The Search for the Canadian-American Boundary, 1783–1842* (Toronto: University of Toronto Press, 2001), 264–86; Howard Jones, *To the Webster-Ashburton Treaty: A Study in Anglo-American Relations, 1783–1843* (Chapel Hill: University of North Carolina Press, 2017 [1977]).

122. Hale and Hale Jr., *Franklin in France*, 2:115.

123. Edmund Pendleton to James Madison (hereafter JM), 26 August 1782, in *Proceedings of the Massachusetts Historical Society*, 2nd ser., vol. 19 (Boston, 1905), 161.

124. Thomas Paine, *Letter addressed to the abbe Raynal on the affairs of North-America: In which the mistakes in the abbe's account of the revolution of America are corrected and cleared up* (Philadelphia, 1782).

125. Ibid., 64–65.

126. Ibid., 66.

127. An excerpt from Paine's pamphlet was published on 23 August 1782 in the *Pennsylvania Evening Post*, and it was republished in various other newspapers in the fall of 1782.

128. *Independent Gazetteer*, 31 August 1782.

129. *New York Gazetteer*, 16 September 1782.

130. *Philadelphia Journal*, 19 October 1782.

131. *Pennsylvania Gazette*, 27 November 1782.

132. William Gordon to JA, 7 September 1782, FONA.

133. Hale and Hale Jr., *Franklin in France*, 2:148.

134. Ibid., 169.

135. Taylor, *American Revolutions*, 306–7.
136. Hale and Hale Jr., *Franklin in France*, 2:171.
137. Ibid., 173.
138. Bemis, *Diplomacy*, 230.
139. Preliminary Articles of Peace: First Draft Treaty [5–7 October 1782], FONA.
140. Preliminary Articles of Peace: Second Draft [4–7 November 1782]; Draft Peace Treaty Agreed to by the American Peace Commissioners and Richard Oswald, 4 November 1782; British Counterproposal to the Second Draft Treaty: Selected Articles [19 November 1782]; Henry Strachey's Remarks to the American Peace Commissioners, Paris (?) (unclear), 25 November 1782, FONA.
141. *Diary and Autobiography of John Adams*, ed. L. H. Butterfied, vol. 3 (Cambridge: The Belknap Press of Harvard University Press, 1962), 79.
142. Bemis, *Diplomacy*, 232–3; Ritcheson, "Britain's Peacemakers," 96–97.
143. Middlekauff, *The Glorious Cause*; Morris, *Peacemakers*, 341–85.
144. Quoted in Drake, *Nation's Nature*, 180.
145. Proposed Articles for the Definitive Peace Treaty [ca. 10–13 December 1782], FONA.
146. *PBF*, vol. 38, 433–35.
147. *New York Gazetteer*, 2 December 1782; reprinted *Providence Gazette*, 27 January 1783.
148. *Pennsylvania Journal*, 18 January 1783.
149. *Independent Chronicle*, 23 January 1783.
150. *Freeman's Journal*, 5 March 1783.
151. *Pennsylvania Journal*, 15 March 1783.

## Chapter Four. The National

1. "Du Calvet, Pierre," *DCB*.
2. *Writings*, vol. 9, 112–13.
3. Jedidah Morse, *The American Geography* (London, 1792), 470.
4. Chilton Williamson, *Vermont in Quandary: 1763–1825*, vol. 4 (Barre: Vermont Historical Society, 1949), 10–11; Peter S. Onuf, *The Origins of the Federal Republic: Jurisdictional Controversies in the United States, 1775–1787* (Philadelphia: University of Pennsylvania Press, 1983), 127.
5. Onuf, *Origins*, 127. As Willard Sterne Randall argues, Vermont thus "was the first republic in the new world." Willard Sterne Randall, *Ethan Allen: His Life and Times* (New York: W. W. Norton, 2011), 441.
6. Onuf, *Origins*, 127–28.
7. *RGCSV*, 396.
8. Ibid., 397.
9. Ibid.

10. "Allen, Ethan," *ANB*. See also Randall, *Ethan Allen;* Taylor, *Liberty Men and Great Proprietors,* 100–103.

11. "Allen, Ethan," *ANB*. Allen published an account of his captivity shortly after his release. See Ethan Allen, *A Narrative of Colonel Ethan Allen's Captivity* (Philadelphia: Robert Bell, 1779).

12. Randall, *Ethan Allen,* 479–80.

13. Ibid., 480.

14. "Chittenden, Thomas," *ANB*.

15. Loyalism in New York was both an ideological position and a reflection of the state of the war. See Christopher F. Minty, " 'Of One Hart and One Mind': Local Institutions and Allegiance during the American Revolution," *Early American Studies* 15, no. 1 (2017): 99–132.

16. *RGCSV,* 397–98.

17. *JCC,* vol. 18, 839–40; JM to Joseph Jones, 19 September 1780, FONA.

18. Randall, *Ethan Allen,* 484–85.

19. Schuyler to GW, 31 October 1780, FONA.

20. Warren to JA, 22 November 1780, FONA.

21. *RGCSV,* 401.

22. Ibid., 402.

23. Onuf, *Origins,* 130.

24. Chittenden to GW, 15 January 1781, FONA.

25. Jacob Bayley to GW, 26 February 1781, FONA.

26. *RGCSV,* 407.

27. Ibid., 409.

28. Ibid., 410–11.

29. Samuel Holden Parsons to GW, 30 April 1781, FONA.

30. *RGCSV,* 408.

31. Ibid., 417.

32. JM to Edmund Pendleton, 14 August 1781, FONA.

33. *RGCSV,* 438–39.

34. Ibid., 445–51.

35. Ibid., 458.

36. Robert. R. Livingston to BF, 13 February 1782, FONA.

37. *RGCSV,* 479.

38. Onuf, *Origins,* 145.

39. *Pennsylvania Gazette,* 22 January 1783.

40. *Pennsylvania Gazette,* 12 March 1783.

41. *LOD,* vol. 20, 206–7.

42. Ibid., 208.

43. Winks, *Blacks in Canada,* 31–32.

44. James W. St. G. Walker, *The Black Loyalists: The Search for a Promised Land in Nova Scotia and Sierra Leone, 1783–1870* (New York: Africana and Dalhousie University Press, 1976), 18–145.

45. Washington's Sentiments on a Peace Establishment, 1 May 1783, FONA.

46. Hatter, *Citizens of Convenience*, 1–13.

47. http://avalon.law.yale.edu/18th_century/paris.asp.

48. Stephen Higgens to Samuel Adams, 20 May 1783, FONA.

49. *Pennsylvania Gazette*, 18 June 1783.

50. Margaret Conrad and Barry Moody, eds., *Planter Links: Community and Culture in Colonial Nova Scotia* (Fredericton: Acadiensis Press, 2001); Margaret Conrad, ed., *They Planted Well: New England Planters in Maritime Canada* (Fredericton: Acadiensis Press, 1988); Reid, "*Pax Britannica* or *Pax Indigena?*," 669–92; Hornsby and Reid, *New England and the Maritime Provinces*.

51. AH to George Clinton, 1 June 1783, FONA.

52. JA to Robert R. Livingstone, 23 June 1783, FONA.

53. *Pennsylvania Gazette*, 18 June 1783; Jasanoff, *Liberty's Exiles*, 147–76; Reid, "Empire, the Maritime Colonies," 78–97.

54. *Pennsylvania Gazette*, 9 July 1783.

55. Christopher Boucher, " 'The land God gave to Cain': Jacques Cartier Encounters the Mythological Wild Man in Labrador," *Terrae Incognitae* 35, no. 1 (June 2003): 28–42.

56. Canadian Officers to GW, 14 July 1783, FONA.

57. GW to Elias Boudinot, 16 July 1783, FONA.

58. *LOD*, vol. 20, 580–81.

59. *Pennsylvania Gazette*, 19 November 1783 and 31 March 1784.

60. *Vermont Gazette*, 5 July 1784.

61. *Emerging Nation*, vol. 2, 483–84.

62. *Massachusetts Centinel*, 22 December 1784.

63. *Pennsylvania Gazette*, 5 January 1785; Michel Ducharme, *The Idea of Liberty in Canada during the Age of Atlantic Revolutions, 1776–1838*, trans. Peter Feldstein (Montreal and Kingston: McGill-Queen's University Press, 2014), 38–42; Mason Wade, *The French Canadians, 1760–1967*, vol. 1 (Toronto: Macmillan Company of Canada, 1968), 81.

64. *DCCR*, 302.

65. Ibid., 162; Allan S. Everest, *Moses Hazen and the Canadian Refugees in the American Revolution* (Syracuse: Syracuse University Press, 1976), 113–14.

66. "Hazen, Moses," *ANB*.

67. *DCCR*, 356.

68. Ibid., 357–58.

69. *Emerging Nation*, vol. 3, 702.

70. Everest, *Moses Hazen and the Canadian Refugees*, 113–41; Jasanoff, "Other Side of Revolution," 205–32; Neil MacKinnon, *This Unfriendly Soil: The Loyalist Experience in Nova Scotia, 1783–1791* (Montreal and Kingston: McGill-Queen's University Press, 1986).

71. Friedrich Kapp, *Life of Frederick William von Steuben, Major General in the Revolutionary Army* (New York: Mason Brothers, 1859), 520.

72. Steuben to GW, Saratoga, 23 August 1783, www.rotunda.upress.virginia.edu/founders.

73. *LOD*, vol. 20, 644.

74. *LOD*, vol. 21, 119.

75. James Monroe to TJ, 1 November 1784, FONA.

76. Ibid.; Bethel Saler, *The Settlers' Empire: Colonialism and State Formation in America's Old Northwest* (Philadelphia: University of Pennsylvania Press, 2014), 13–14.

77. Ann Gorman Condon, "1783–1800: Loyalist Arrival, Acadian Return, Imperial Reform," in *The Atlantic Region to Confederation: A History*, ed. Phillip A. Buckner and John G. Reid (Toronto: University of Toronto Press, 1994), 184–209.

78. *Pennsylvania Gazette*, 18 May 1785.

79. *Pennsylvania Gazette*, 15 June 1785.

80. *Pennsylvania Gazette*, 29 June 1785.

81. Gordon S. Wood, *The Creation of the American Republic, 1776–1787* (Chapel Hill: Published for the Omohundro Institute of Early American History and Culture, University of North Carolina Press, 1998 [1969]), 411–13; Woody Holton, "An 'Excess of Democracy,' Or a Shortage? The Federalists' Earliest Adversaries," *Journal of the Early Republic* 25, no. 3 (2005): 339–82.

82. Woody Holton, "Did Democracy Cause the Recession That Led to the Constitution?," *Journal of American History* 92, no. 2 (2005): 442–69.

83. Leonard L. Richards, *Shays's Rebellion: The American Revolution's Final Battle* (Philadelphia: University of Pennsylvania Press, 2002), 4–42.

84. Eric Nellis, *The Long Road to Change: America's Revolution, 1750–1820* (Toronto: Broadview Press, 2007), 180–81.

85. "Shays, Daniel," *ANB*.

86. Taylor, *American Revolutions*, 366–69.

87. Henry Lee to GW, 17 October 1786, FONA.

88. Henry Lee to St. George Tucker, 20 October 1786, FONA.

89. *Massachusetts Spy*, 26 October 1786; David Armitage, *Civil Wars: A History in Ideas* (New York: Knopf, 2017), 134–47.

90. *New Hampshire Spy*, 31 October 1786.

91. John Jay (hereafter JJ) to JA, 1 November 1786, FONA.

92. William Grayson to JM, 22 November 1786, FONA.

93. *DCCR*, 33.

94. *Pennsylvania Gazette*, 14 February 1787.

95. *Pennsylvania Gazette*, 28 February 1787. For additional reports, see *New York Packet*, 23 February 1787; *Pennsylvania Gazette*, 7 March, 14 March, 28 March 1787.

96. *DHRC*, vol. 13, 141–42. This particular piece was also published in the *New York Daily Advertiser* and an additional thirteen times by mid-July in newspapers from Massachusetts to Virginia.

97. *Pennsylvania Packet*, 19 June 1787.

98. *DHRC*, vol. 13, 308–9.

99. Richards, *Shays's Rebellion*, 118–24.

100. Linda Colley, *The Gun, the Ship, and the Pen: Warfare, Constitutions, and the Making of the Modern World* (New York: Liveright Publishing, 2021).

101. Wood, *Creation of the American Republic*, 469–519; Woody Holton, *Unruly Americans and the Origins of the Constitution* (New York: Hill and Wang, 2008); Saul Cornell, *The Other Founders: Anti-federalism and the Dissenting Tradition in America, 1788–1828* (Chapel Hill: Published for the Omohundro Institute of Early American History and Culture, University of North Carolina Press, 2012).

102. *LOD*, vol. 21, 30.

103. Arthur Campbell to JM, 28 October 1785, FONA.

104. *LOD*, vol. 23, 100.

105. *DHRC*, vol. 13, 73.

106. Ibid.

107. Ibid., 71–73.

108. Alfred LeRoy Burt, *The United States, Great Britain, and British North America from the Revolution to the Establishment of Peace after the War of 1812* (New York: Russell & Russell, 1961), 103–5.

109. *Emerging Nation*, vol. 3, 443; Gabriel Paquette and Gonzalo M. Quintero Saravia, eds., *Spain and the American Revolution: New Approaches and Perspectives* (New York: Routledge, 2019), 192.

110. *Emerging Nation*, vol. 3, 443–44.

111. JM to GW, 18 March 1787, FONA.

112. New York Assembly. Remarks on an Act Acknowledging the Independence of Vermont [28 March 1787], FONA; Taylor, *American Revolutions*, 344–47.

113. *DHRC*, vol. 13, 152–54.

114. Ibid., 105–11.

115. *DHRC*, vol. 3, 481–82.

116. *DHRC*, vol. 19, 438–39.

117. *DHRC*, vol. 8, 340–41; Lorri Glover, *The Fate of the Revolution: Virginians Debate the Constitution* (Baltimore: Johns Hopkins University Press, 2016).

118. *DHRC*, vol. 16, 304–6.

119. "Clinton, De Witt," *ANB*.

120. *DHRC*, vol. 19, 374–75.

121. *DHRC*, vol. 5, 636, 638.

# Chapter Five. Oneida

1. Richter, *Facing East*, 134–35, 43.

2. *Emerging Nation*, vol. 2, 472.

3. Calloway, *Indian World*, 301–2; Leonard J. Sadosky, *Revolutionary Negotiations: Indians, Empires, and Diplomats in the Founding of America* (Charlottesville: University of Virginia Press, 2009), 128–38; Reginald Horsman, *Expansion and American Indian Policy, 1783–1812* (Norman: University of Oklahoma Press, 1992 [1967]), 18–21.

4. *Emerging Nation*, vol. 2, 474.

5. Gould, *Among the Powers of the Earth*; Edling, *Revolution*, 3–12.

6. Gregory Ablavsky, "Species of Sovereignty: Native Nationhood, the United States, and International Law, 1783–1795," *Journal of American History* 106, no. 3 (2019): 591–613; Saliha Belmessous, *Native Claims: Indigenous Law Against Empire, 1500–1920* (New York: Oxford University Press, 2011), 3–16.

7. Stuart Banner, *How the Indians Lost Their Land: Law and Power on the Frontier* (Cambridge: Harvard University Press, 2007), 122–23.

8. Ibid., 135.

9. *LOD*, vol. 21, 807.

10. Ibid., 808.

11. *LOD*, vol. 22, 192.

12. *DCCR*, 312.

13. *Pennsylvania Gazette*, 3 August 1785; *Emerging Nation*, vol. 2, 864.

14. *DCCR*, 323–24; Whitfield, *North to Bondage*, 31–32.

15. *Emerging Nation*, vol. 2, 874–76.

16. *LOD*, vol. 22, 588.

17. Peter Silver, *Our Savage Neighbors: How Indian War Transformed Early America* (New York: W. W. Norton, 2008), 227–93.

18. Banner, *How the Indians*, 128–29; Fenton, *Great Law*, 601–21.

19. Timothy D. Willig, *Restoring the Chain of Friendship: British Policy and the Indians of the Great Lakes, 1783–1815* (Lincoln: University of Nebraska Press, 2008), 13–14.

20. Isabel Thompson Kelsay, *Joseph Brant, 1743–1807: Man of Two Worlds* (Syracuse: Syracuse University Press, 1984), 360–64; Hill, *Clay We Are Made Of*, 132–85.

21. *DCCR*, 339–40.

22. Josiah Harmar to Henry Knox, Fort Pitt, 3 July 1786, PWD.

23. David Humphreys to GW, 16 November 1786, FONA.

24. *DCCR*, 353; Kelsay, *Joseph Brant*, 379–94.

25. Knox to Kirkland, 11 May 1791, Samuel Kirkland Correspondence, 136c (a,e,g), Hamilton College; Jeffrey Ostler, *Surviving Genocide: Native Nations and the United States from the American Revolution to Bleeding Kansas* (New Haven: Yale University Press, 2019), 93–94.

26. Gregory Ablavsky, *Federal Ground: Governing Property and Violence in the First US Territories* (New York: Oxford University Press, 2021), 4; Banner, *How the Indians*, 130–32; Sadosky, *Revolutionary Negotiations*, 156–60; Burt, *United States*, 107; Gould, *Among the Powers of the Earth*, 133–34.

27. Ablavsky, *Federal*, 1–15.

28. *Emerging Nation*, vol. 3, 774.

29. Calloway, *Indian Country*; Richter, *Facing East*; Fenton, *Great Law*.

30. Gilles Havard, *The Great Peace of Montreal of 1701: French-Native Diplomacy in the Seventeenth Century*, trans. Phyllis Aronoff and Howard Scott (Montreal and Kingston: McGill-Queen's University Press, 2001); Baker and Reid, "Amerindian Power," 77–106.

31. Willig, *Restoring*, 16–18; Jennings, *Ambiguous Iroquois Empire*.

32. Saler, *Settlers' Empire*, 19–22.

33. Banner, *How the Indians*, 134.

34. Quoted in Banner, *How the Indians*, 133. See also Taylor, *American Revolutions*, 340–42.

35. Arthur St. Clair to Henry Knox, 23 August 1790, PWD; *ASPIA*, 98.

36. Burt, *United States*, 114–17; Colin G. Calloway, *The Victory with No Name: The Native American Defeat of the First American Army* (Oxford: Oxford University Press, 2014); Taylor, *American Revolutions*, 403–4.

37. GW to TJ, Mount Vernon, 4 April 1791, FONA.

38. *DCCR*, 387.

39. Ibid., 47–48.

40. Ibid., 389–90.

41. *Pennsylvania Gazette*, 18 January 1792.

42. Gould, *Among the Powers of the Earth*, 134–35; Carol Berkin, *A Sovereign People: The Crises of the 1790s and the Birth of American Nationalism* (New York: Basic Books, 2017), 7–80.

43. *General Advertiser*, 31 January 1792.

44. Alexander Leitch, *A Princeton Companion* (Princeton: Princeton University Press, 2015), 63.

45. "Brackenridge, Hugh Henry," *ANB*.

46. *Pennsylvania Gazette*, 8 February 1792; Ellen Holmes Pearson, *Remaking Custom: Law and Identity in the Early American Republic* (Charlottesville: University of Virginia Press, 2011), 160–65.

47. Medad Mitchell to AH, 9 February 1792, FONA.

48. Conversation with George Hammond [April 30–July 3, 1792], FONA.

49. *Simcoe*, 91–94, 133–37.

50. GW to TJ, [7 March 1792], FONA; Burt, *United States*, 120.

51. Memorandum of Consultation on Indian Policy, 9 March 1792, Papers of Thomas Jefferson, Digital Edition, ed. James P. McClure and J. Jefferson Looney (Charlottesville: University of Virginia Press, Rotunda, 2008–2022); *Simcoe*, 127–29, 130–31, 168; Taylor, *Divided Ground*, 268–69.

52. Tobias Lear to Timothy Pickering, [Philadelphia, 3 May 1792], FONA.

53. *Pennsylvania Gazette*, 9 May 1792.

54. Banner, *How the Indians*, 139.

55. *Emerging Nation*, vol. 3, 809; Joanne Loewe Neel, *Phineas Bond: A Study in Anglo-American Relations, 1786–1812* (Philadelphia: University of Pennsylvania Press, 1968), 39–81.

56. TJ to Dugald Stewart, 21 June 1789, FONA; Alan Taylor, *Thomas Jefferson's Education* (New York: W. W. Norton, 2019), 1–2.

57. *Pennsylvania Gazette*, 4 August 1790.

58. *The Literary Magazine and British Review* 6 (May 1791): 336; Michael Eamon, " 'An Extensive Collection of Useful and Entertaining Books': The

Quebec Library and the Transatlantic Enlightenment in Canada," *Journal of the Canadian Historical Association* 23, no. 1 (2012): 1–38.

59. *Pennsylvania Gazette*, 21 September 1791. The Latin translates to "Can you help laughing?"

60. Robert Bothwell, *Your Country, My Country: A Unified History of the United States and Canada* (New York: Oxford University Press, 2015), 59–89; Jeffrey L. McNairn, *The Capacity to Judge: Public Opinion and Deliberative Democracy in Upper Canada, 1791–1854* (Toronto: University of Toronto Press, 2000); Jane Errington, *The Lion, the Eagle, and Upper Canada: A Developing Colonial Ideology* (Montreal and Kingston: McGill-Queen's University Press, 1987), 35–54.

61. *Pennsylvania Gazette*, 6 July 1791; *Albany Gazette*, 21 November 1791; *General Advertiser*, 2 February 1792.

62. TJ to Joseph Fay, 24 June 1792, FONA.

63. Joseph Fay to TJ, 12 March 1793, FONA.

64. *Philadelphia Daily Advertiser*, 15 March 1793; *Pennsylvania Gazette*, 15 August 1792.

65. Notes for a Conversation with George Hammond, [ca. 10 December 1792], FONA; Willig, *Restoring*, 39.

66. Burt, *United States*, 119–21.

67. *Simcoe*, 176–77.

68. Ibid; Burt, *United States*, 124–25; Horsman, *Expansion*, 95.

69. *Simcoe*, 207–9.

70. Kelsay, *Joseph Brant*, 468.

71. Gerard H. Clarfield, *Timothy Pickering and the American Republic* (Pittsburgh: University of Pittsburgh Press, 1980), 134–36; Kelsay, *Joseph Brant*, 453–57.

72. Horsman, *Expansion*, 90–92; Calloway, *Indian World*, 408–10.

73. *Pennsylvania Gazette*, 11 July 1792.

74. Taylor, *Divided Ground*, 259–60; Willig, *Restoring*, 44–47.

75. *ASPIA*, vol. 1, 242.

76. Ibid., 243; Joseph Brant to Henry Knox, 26 July 1792, PWD.

77. *ASPIA*, 235; Banner, *How the Indians*, 135; Horsman, *Expansion*, 93–49. The wording of this agreement was unacceptable to American officials and thus the treaty was never ratified.

78. Patrick Griffin, *American Leviathan: Empire, Nation, and Revolutionary Frontier* (New York: Hill and Wang, 2008), 216–17.

79. Extracts of Correspondence on Indian Affairs, [October 1792], FONA; *ASPIA*, 243–44.

80. As Patrick Griffin argues, settlers' relentless intrusion into homelands and administrative efforts at diplomacy worked "as an act of co-creation," resulting in the United States western expansion and the displacement of Indigenous nations. Griffin, *American Leviathan*, 240–43.

81. Helen Hornbeck Tanner, "The Glaize in 1792: A Composite Indian Community," *Ethnohistory* (1978): 15, 25, 27, 32.

82. William H. Bergmann, *The American National State and the Early West* (Cambridge: Cambridge University Press, 2012), 74–76.
83. *Simcoe*, 218.
84. Ibid., 220.
85. Calloway, *Victory*, 145; Anthony Wallace, *The Death and Rebirth of the Seneca* (New York: Vintage, 1972), 24–25.
86. *Simcoe*, 221–22.
87. Ibid., 223.
88. Ibid., 224.
89. Ibid., 225.
90. Calloway, *Victory*, 146; Kelsay, *Joseph Brant*, 477–82.
91. *Simcoe*, 226–28.
92. Burt, *United States*, 126–27.
93. Cornplanter and New Arrow to Anthony Wayne, 25 December 1792, PWD.
94. *Pennsylvania Gazette*, 15 August 1792.
95. *Simcoe*, 270; AH to William Edgar, 17 January 1793, FONA; William Hull to Alexander Hamilton (hereafter AH), Niagara, 6 February 1793, FONA.
96. *Simcoe*, 277.
97. Ibid., 297.
98. Cabinet Meeting, 25 February 1793, FONA.
99. Henry Knox to William Hull, 28 February 1793, PWD.
100. "Lincoln, Benjamin," *ANB;* Richard P. Guidorizzi, "Timothy Pickering: Opposition Politics in the Early Years of the Republic" (PhD diss., St. John's University, 1968), 25.
101. Clarfield, *Pickering*, 139–40; Willig, *Restoring*, 47–50; Burt, *United States*, 128–29.
102. Lt. Col. Edward Baker Littlehales to Simcoe, 7 June 1793, PWD.
103. *ASPIA*, 347.
104. Simcoe to General Clarke (Commissioners of the US to make peace with the Western Indians), 7 June 1793, PWD.
105. *ASPIA*, 349; Clarfield, *Pickering*, 141.
106. *ASPIA*, 350.
107. Ibid., 352.
108. Quoted in Calloway, *Victory*, 147.
109. Hammond to TJ, 20 June 1793, FONA.
110. Medad Mitchell to AH, 27 August 1793, FONA.
111. *DCCR*, 58.
112. Ibid., 60.
113. Dorchester to Chiefs and Warriors of the Indian Nations, 10 February 1794, PWD.
114. *ASPIA*, 480.
115. *DCCR*, 67. Printed in the *Pennsylvania Gazette*, 28 May 1794.
116. Ibid., 411.

117. *Pennsylvania Gazette*, 28 May 1794.

118. *DCCR*, 412.

119. *Pennsylvania Gazette*, 9 July 1794.

120. Ibid.

121. *DCCR*, 77.

122. Quoted in Ostler, *Surviving Genocide*, 109.

123. Gordon S. Wood, *Empire of Liberty: A History of the Early Republic, 1789–1815* (Oxford: Oxford University Press, 2009), 130–31.

124. Saler, *Settlers' Empire*, 13–28.

125. *ASPIA*, 525.

126. Ibid., 550.

127. Ibid., 529.

128. "Burke, Edmund," *DCB*.

129. Wayne to Pickering, Greenville, 8 March 1795, in Richard C. Knopf, *Anthony Wayne: A Name in Arms* (Pittsburgh: University of Pittsburgh Press, 1959), 387.

130. Wayne to Pickering, Greenville, 7 April 1795, in Knopf, *Wayne*, 391–92.

131. *DCCR*, 90.

132. Taylor, *American Revolutions*, 406; Ostler, *Surviving Genocide*, 109–11.

## Chapter Six. Portage

1. GW to Clinton, 31 March 1794, FONA.

2. Clinton to GW, 7 April 1794, FONA.

3. *Pennsylvania Gazette*, 25 June 1794, 9 July 1794.

4. Edmund Randolph to GW, 2–3 October 1794, FONA.

5. "Morse, Jedidiah," *ANB*.

6. Edling, *Pefecting*, 1–35; Taylor, *American Republics*, 1–17.

7. Brückner, *Geographic Revolution*, 116.

8. Geoffrey J. Martin, "The Emergence and Development of Geographic Thought in New England," *Economic Geography* 74, no. 1 (1998): 2.

9. Jedidiah Morse to his father, 8 January 1785, MFP, box 1, np.

10. Ibid., box 1, fol. 7.

11. Ibid., box 1, fol. 5.

12. Ibid., box 1, fol. 9.

13. David Demeritt, "Representing the 'True' St. Croix: Knowledge and Power in the Partition of the Northeast," *William and Mary Quarterly* 54, no. 3 (1997): 515–48; Carroll, *Good and Wise*, 264–86.

14. *DCCR*, 18.

15. Ibid., 19.

16. Ibid., 354.

17. Jedidiah Morse to his father, 20 September 1786, MFP, box 1, np.

18. "Belknap, Jeremy," *ANB*; Ralph H. Brown, "The American Geographies of Jedidiah Morse," *Annals of the Association of American Geographers* 31, no. 3 (1941): 153.

19. Jedidiah Morse to Jeremy Belknap, 18 January 1788, MFP, box 1, np.

20. Jedidiah Morse to Jeremy Belknap, 3 June 1788, MFP, box 1, np.

21. Quoted in "Morse, Jedidiah," *ANB*.

22. Joseph A. Conforti, *Imagining New England: Explorations of Regional Identity from the Pilgrims to the Mid-Twentieth Century* (Chapel Hill: University of North Carolina Press, 2001), 83–85; Benjamin Park, "The Bonds of Union: Benjamin Rush, Noah Webster, and Defining the Nation in the Early Republic," *Early American Studies* 15, no. 2 (2017): 382–408.

23. Jedidiah Morse, *The American Geography; or, A View of the Present Situation of the United States of America*, 1st ed. (Elizabeth Town: Shepard Kollock, for the author, 1789), 473.

24. Ibid., 475.

25. Ibid., 476; Brown, "American Geographies of Jedidiah Morse," 174–76.

26. *Pennsylvania Gazette*, 26 August 1789.

27. *DCCR*, 38.

28. Ibid., 365.

29. Brückner, *Geographic Revolution*; Martin Brückner, *The Social Life of Maps in America, 1750–1860* (Chapel Hill: Omohundro Institute and University of North Carolina Press, 2017); Juliana Barr, "Geographies of Power: Mapping Indian Borders in the 'Borderlands' of the Early Southwest," *William and Mary Quarterly* 68, no. 1 (2011): 5–46; Matthew H. Edney, *Mapping an Empire: The Geographical Construction of British India, 1765–1843* (Chicago: University of Chicago Press, 1997); J. B. Harley, Barbara Bartz Petchenik, and Lawrence W. Towner, *Mapping the American Revolutionary War*; Kenneth Nebenzahl Jr. Lectures in the History of Cartography (Chicago: University of Chicago Press, 1978); Karl H. Offen, "Creating Mosquitia: Mapping Amerindian Spatial Practices in Eastern Central America, 1629–1779," *Journal of Historical Geography* 33, no. 2 (2007): 254–82; Anderson, *Imagined Communities*; John C. Weaver, *The Great Land Rush and the Making of the Modern World, 1650–1900* (Montreal and Kingston: McGill-Queen's University Press, 2003).

30. "Mitchill, Samuel Latham," *ANB*; "Mitchill, Samuel Latham," *Biographical Directory of the United States of Congress*.

31. 4 July 1789, MFP, box 1, np.

32. "Collins, John," *DCB*.

33. 4 July 1789, MFP, box 1, np.

34. 19 December 1789, MFP, box 1, np.

35. Brown, "American Geographies of Jedidiah Morse," 188.

36. Jasanoff, *Liberty's Exiles*, 147–215.

37. Morse, *The American Universal Geography*, 2nd ed. (1793), 135.

38. Ibid., 137.

39. Ibid., 130; Jerry Bannister, *The Rule of the Admirals: Law, Custom, and Naval Government in Newfoundland, 1699–1832* (Toronto: Published for the Osgoode Society for Canadian Legal History by University of Toronto Press, 2003).

40. Morse, *American Universal Geography*, 2nd ed., 136.

41. Ibid.

42. Taylor, "Late Loyalists," 1–34.

43. Charles Williamson to George Clinton, 26 November 1793, FONA.

44. *DCCR*, 409–10.

45. Ibid., 80–81.

46. Ibid., 81.

47. Ibid.

48. *Pennsylvania Gazette*, 3 September 1794.

49. *DCCR*, 448.

50. Ibid., 449.

51. Taylor, *Divided Ground*, 268–70.

52. *DCCR*, 466; Errington, *Lion*, 61.

53. GW to AH, 13 July 1795, FONA.

54. *DCCR*, 466–67.

55. Ibid., 98.

56. Taylor, *Divided Ground*, 17–19, 298–302; Lauren A. Benton, *Law and Colonial Cultures: Legal Regimes in World History, 1400–1900* (Cambridge: Cambridge University Press, 2002), 2–27.

57. J. U. Rivardi to AH, 3 April 1799, FONA; Rivardi to AH, 21 March 1799, FONA, notes 21 and 23.

58. James McHenry to AH, 18 May 1799, FONA, notes 4 and 5.

59. *DCCR*, 517.

60. John F. Hamtramck to AH, 19 September 1799, FONA.

61. https://detroithistorical.org/learn/encyclopedia-of-detroit/hamtramck-captain-john.

62. Jan Lewis, " 'Of Every Age Sex and Condition': The Representation of Women in the Constitution," *Journal of the Early Republic* 15, no. 3 (1995): 359–87; David Waldstreicher, *Slavery's Constitution: From Revolution to Ratification* (New York: Hill and Wang, 2010), 3–19; Rosemarie Zagarri, *Revolutionary Backlash: Women and Politics in the Early American Republic* (Philadelphia: University of Pennsylvania Press, 2007), 60.

63. William Duane to TJ, 7 January 1802, FONA; "Duane, William," *ANB*; Address of Little Turtle, [4 January 1802], FONA.

64. Jordan E. Taylor, "The Reign of Error: North American Information Politics and the French Revolution, 1789–1795," *Journal of the Early Republic* 39, no. 3 (2019): 437–66.

65. Peter McPhee, *Liberty or Death: The French Revolution* (New Haven: Yale University Press, 2016), 367.

66. [Edmund Genêt], *Les Français libres à leur frères les Canadiens* (Philadelphia: [1793]), 2. Author's translation. Ducharme, *Idea of Liberty*, 40–41.

67. Genêt, *Les Français libres*, 3.

68. Ibid., 6.

69. Editorial Note: The Recall of Edmond Charles Genet, FONA; Eugene R. Sheridan, "The Recall of Edmond Charles Genêt: A Study in Transatlantic Politics and Diplomacy," *Diplomatic History* 18, no. 4 (1994): 463–88.

70. Frank Murray Greenwood, *Legacies of Fear: Law and Politics in Quebec in the Era of the French Revolution* (Toronto: University of Toronto Press, 1993), 83–84.

71. *DCCR*, 475.

72. Ibid., 476.

73. Ibid., 477.

74. Rufus King to GW, 12 November 1796, FONA.

75. Cited in Greenwood, *Legacies of Fear,* 141.

76. RCA 1891, 69.

77. Greenwood, *Legacies of Fear,* 142–43.

78. RCA 1891, 69.

79. Ibid., 70.

80. Greenwood, *Legacies of Fear,* 45, 139.

81. RCA 1891, 70.

82. Greenwood, *Legacies of Fear,* 139.

83. Greenwood, *Legacies of Fear,* 164–66; Donald Fyson, *Magistrates, Police, and People: Everyday Criminal Justice in Quebec and Lower Canada, 1764–1837* (Toronto: Published for the Osgoode Society for Canadian Legal History by University of Toronto Press, 2006), 4–5.

84. *DCCR*, 111–12.

85. "Liston, Sir Robert," *ODNB;* George W. Kyte, "The Detention of General Collot: A Sidelight on Anglo-American Relations, 1798–1800," *William and Mary Quarterly* 6, no. 4 (1949): 628–30.

86. Bradford Perkins, "A Diplomat's Wife in Philadelphia: Letters of Henrietta Liston, 1796–1800," *William and Mary Quarterly* 11, no. 4 (1954): 592.

87. J. Kevin Graffagnino, " 'Twenty Thousand Muskets!!!': Ira Allen and the Olive Branch Affair, 1796–1800," *William and Mary Quarterly* 48, no. 3 (1991): 409–31.

88. Jeanne A. Ojala, "Ira Allen and the French Directory, 1796: Plans for the Creation of the Republic of United Columbia," *William and Mary Quarterly* 36, no. 3 (1979): 436–48.

89. "Allen, Ira," *ANB.*

90. Greenwood, *Legacies of Fear,* 102; Wade, *French Canadians,* 1, 98–99.

91. McHenry to Washington, Philadelphia, 15 June 1797, FONA.

92. Perkins, "Diplomat's Wife," 615.

93. Thomas Boylston Adams to JA, 4 March 1798, FONA.

94. *Independent Chronicle* (Boston), 21 February 1799.

95. Nigel Little, *Transoceanic Radical: William Duane: National Identity and Empire, 1760–1835* (New York: Routledge, 2016), 145–46.

96. *Maryland Herald,* 25 July 1799.

97. Ibid.

98. Ronald Angelo Johnson, "A Revolutionary Dinner: US Diplomacy toward Saint Domingue, 1798–1801," *Early American Studies* (2011): 114–41; Tyson Reeder, "Liberty with the Sword: Jamaican Maroons, Haitian Revolutionaries, and American Liberty," *Journal of the Early Republic* 37, no. 1 (2017): 81–115.

99. *Maryland Herald*, 25 July 1799.

100. Pickering to JA, 12 July 1799, FONA; Berkin, *Sovereign People*, 197.

101. *The Bee* (New London, CT), 24 July 1799; *Carlisle (PA) Gazette*, 31 July 1799.

102. Elijah Griffiths to TJ, 4 August 1799, FONA.

103. Notes on a Conversation with Tench Coxe, 2 January 1800, FONA.

104. Quoted in Berkin, *Sovereign People*, 210–11.

105. An Act in Addition to the Act Entitled, "An Act for the Punishment of Certain Crimes against the United States" (approved 14 July 1798), sec. 2, https://avalon.law.yale.edu/18th_century/sedact.asp.

106. Berkin, *Sovereign People*, 217–25.

107. *Greenleaf's New York Journal*, 4 September 1799.

108. *Greenleaf's New York Journal*, 25 September 1799.

109. John Bassett Moore, *International Adjudications, Ancient and Modern: History and Documents*, vol. 3 (Oxford University Press, 1931), 238–52, quote on 47. Both Patriots and Loyalists used confiscation of property as a way of controlling the opposition during the Revolution. Only after Independence did Americans become wary of the power of assemblies to issue bills of attainder. See Palfreyman, "The Loyalists and the Federal Constitution: The Origins of the Bill of Attainder Clause," 451–73; Duval, "Mastering Charleston," 589–622.

110. *Greenleaf's New York Journal*, 25 September 1799.

111. *New Hampshire Sentinel*, 19 October 1799; Taylor, *Divided Ground*, 328–29.

112. *Pennsylvania Gazette*, 20 November 1799.

113. "Ogden, John Cosens," *ANB*.

114. Ibid.

115. John Ogden, *A Tour through Upper and Lower Canada, By a Citizen of the United States* (Litchfield, 1799), 35.

116. Ibid., 42.

117. Ibid., 50.

118. Ibid., 61–62.

119. Ibid., 55.

120. Ibid., 85–86.

121. Ibid., 84. McNairn, *Capacity to Judge*, 116–75.

122. "Mesplet, Fleury," *DCB*.

123. Taylor, "Late Loyalists," 16–17.

124. *Constitutional Telegraph* (Boston), 14 May 1800.

125. Ogden, *Tour*, 106–7.

126. *Massachusetts Mercury* (Boston), 17 June 1800; *American Citizen* (New York), 12 July 1800; Taylor, "Late Loyalists," 6–7; James Keith Johnson, *In Duty Bound: Men, Women, and the State in Upper Canada, 1783–1841* (Montreal and Kingston: McGill-Queen's University Press, 2013), 11–48.

127. *Stewart Kentucky Herald* (Lexington), 30 September 1800.

128. Tench Coxe to JM, [ca. 22 November 1801], FONA.

129. *Courier of New Hampshire*, 29 April 1802.

130. Kevin M. Gannon, "Escaping 'Mr. Jefferson's Plan of Destruction': New England Federalists and the Idea of a Northern Confederacy, 1803–1804," *Journal of the Early Republic* 21, no. 3 (2001): 434.

131. *Poulson's American Daily Advertiser* (Philadelphia), 29 April 1803; *Carlisle (PA) Gazette*, 4 May 1803; *Federal Gazette* (Baltimore), 4 May 1803.

132. *Republican; or Anti-Democrat* (Baltimore), 4 May 1803.

133. *The Gazetteer* (Boston), 22 June 1803; *Washington Federalist* (Georgetown), 22 June 1803.

134. "A Friend" to TJ, 19 October 1805, FONA.

## Chapter Seven. Land of Talk

1. Ogden, *Tour*, 118.

2. *DCCR*, 155, 530.

3. Robert R. Livingston to JM, 14 March 1802, FONA.

4. *DCCR*, 531.

5. Ibid., 532.

6. "Mackenzie, Alexander," *DBC*; *Documents Relating to the North West Company*, 12; Anne F. Hyde, *Empires, Nations, and Families: A History of the North American West, 1800–1860* (New York: Ecco, 2012), 98–99.

7. Alexander Mackenzie, *The Journals of Alexander Mackenzie: Exploring across Canada in 1789 and 1793*, Historical Adventure and Exploration Series (Santa Barbara, CA: Narrative Press, 2001), 155.

8. John Vaughan to TJ, 8 May 1802, FONA.

9. Eric Jay Dolin, *Fur, Fortune, and Empire: The Epic History of the Fur Trade in America* (New York: W. W. Norton, 2011), 170–71; Jon Meacham, *Thomas Jefferson: The Art of Power* (New York: Random House, 2012), 370–71.

10. Caspar Wistar to TJ, 8 June 1802, FONA; Donald Jackson, *Thomas Jefferson and the Rocky Mountains: Exploring the West from Monticello* (Norman: University of Oklahoma Press, 2002 [1981]), 121.

11. *PAH*, 362–64.

12. *DCCR*, 548.

13. Ibid., 551.

14. *Balance and Columbian Repository* (Hudson, NY), 15 February 1803; *Hampshire Gazette* (Northampton, MA), 2 March 1803; *The Patriot* (Utica, NY), 7 March 1803.

15. *Republican; or, Anti-Democrat* (Baltimore), 4 May 1803.
16. Laurent Dubois, "The Haitian Revolution and the Sale of Louisiana," *Southern Quarterly* 44, no. 3 (2007): 18–41; Annette Gordon-Reed and Peter S. Onuf, *"Most Blessed of the Patriarchs": Thomas Jefferson and the Empire of the Imagination* (New York: W. W. Norton, 2016), 283–84; Laurent Dubois, *Avengers of the New World: The Story of the Haitian Revolution* (Cambridge: Harvard University Press, 2005).
17. Wood, *Empire of Liberty*, 76, 371.
18. Levi Lincoln to TJ, 10 January 1803, FONA.
19. Albert Gallatin to TJ, 13 January 1803, FONA.
20. *DCCR*, 553.
21. Jon Kukla, *A Wilderness So Immense: The Louisiana Purchase and the Destiny of America* (New York: Knopf, 2003), 233–58.
22. Thomas Paine to TJ, 23 September 1803, FONA.
23. Pierre Samuel du Pont de Nemours to TJ, 12 May 1803, FONA; Robert F. Haggard, "The Politics of Friendship: Du Pont, Jefferson, Madison, and the Physiocratic Dream for the New World," *Proceedings of the American Philosophical Society* 153, no. 4 (2009): 419–40.
24. *DCCR*, 558, 560.
25. Mackenzie, *Voyages from Montreal*, 411, quoted in Jackson, *Thomas Jefferson and the Rocky Mountains*, 95.
26. Wood, *Empire of Liberty*, 377; Dolin, *Fur, Fortune, and Empire*, 171.
27. Meriwether Lewis to TJ, 29 May 1803, FONA.
28. "Vancouver, George," *ODNB*; Daniel Wright Clayton, *Islands of Truth: The Imperial Fashioning of Vancouver Island* (Vancouver: University of British Columbia Press, 2000).
29. Jackson, *Thomas Jefferson and the Rocky Mountains*, 132; J. Nisbet, *Sources of the River: Tracking David Thompson across North America*, 2nd ed. (Seattle: Sasquatch Books, 2011), 76.
30. "Thompson, David," *DCB*; D'Arcy Jenish, *Epic Wanderer: David Thompson and the Mapping of the Canadian West* (Toronto: Doubleday, 2003); Sylvia Van Kirk, *Many Tender Ties: Women in Fur-Trade Society, 1670–1870* (Winnipeg: Watson & Dwywer, 1999); David Thompson, *David Thompson's Narrative of His Explorations in Western America, 1784–1812*, ed. Joseph Burr Tyrrell (Toronto: Champlain Society, 1916).
31. Arthur J. Ray, *Illustrated History of Canada's Native People: I Have Lived Here since the World Began* (Montreal and Kingston: McGill-Queen's University Press, 2016), 112–21; Jean Barman, *The West beyond the West: A History of British Columbia*, 3rd ed. (Toronto: University of Toronto Press, 2007), 15–54.
32. Instructions for Meriwether Lewis, 20 June 1803, FONA; Ostler, *Surviving Genocide*, 134–35.
33. Anthony F. C. Wallace, *Jefferson and the Indians: The Tragic Fate of the First Americans* (Cambridge: Harvard University Press, 2009), 96–100.

34. Wood, *Empire of Liberty*, 378; Alan Gallay, *Indian Slavery in Colonial America* (Lincoln: University of Nebraska Press, 2009); Rushforth, *Bonds of Alliance;* Pekka Hämäläinen, *The Comanche Empire* (New Haven: Yale University Press, 2008), chaps. 5 and 6.

35. 8 and 19 November 1804, *JLCE;* Elizabeth A. Fenn, *Encounters at the Heart of the World: A History of the Mandan People* (New York: Hill and Wang, 2014), 177–229.

36. 28–29 November 1804, *JLCE.*

37. Lawrence Barkwell, *The Métis Men of the Lewis and Clark Expedition, 1804–1806* (Winnipeg: Louis Riel Institute, 2011), 2.

38. Susan M. Colby, *Sacagawea's Child: The Life and Times of Jean-Baptiste (Pomp) Charbonneau* (Norman: University of Oklahoma Press, 2014), 34.

39. 4 November 1804, *JLCE.*

40. "Sacagawea," *ANB;* 13 October 1805, *JLCE.*

41. 16 December 1804, *JLCE.*

42. 13 January 1805, *JLCE.*

43. 30 January 1805, *JLCE.* Larocque instead voyaged from the Missouri to the country of the Crows and recounted his experiences in his *Journal of Larocque from the Assiniboine to the Yellowstone, 1805.* See "Larocque, François-Antoine," *DCB.*

44. 11 March 1805, *JLCE.*

45. 3 December 1805, *JLCE.*

46. James Wilkinson to JM, 28 July 1805, FONA.

47. William Hull to JM, 3 August 1805, FONA.

48. *Michigan Pioneer and Historical Collections,* 31 [1902], 533.

49. Winks, *Blacks in Canada,* 96–98.

50. William Hull to JM, 31 July 1806, FONA.

51. William Hull to JM, 28 August 1806, FONA.

52. Jacob Wagner to JM, 5 September 1806, FONA.

53. "Woodward, Augustus Brevoort," *ANB.*

54. Taylor, *Civil War,* 102–3; Nathan Perl-Rosenthal, *Citizen Sailors: Becoming American in the Age of Revolution* (Cambridge: Harvard University Press, 2015).

55. Keith Mercer, "Northern Exposure: Resistance to Naval Impressment in British North America, 1775–1815," *Canadian Historical Review* 91, no. 2 (2010): 199–232; Keith Mercer, "The Murder of Lieutenant Lawry: A Case Study of British Naval Impressment in Newfoundland, 1794," *Newfoundland and Labrador Studies* (2006).

56. Willig, *Restoring,* 199–205; Taylor, *Civil War,* 125–26.

57. Wood, *Empire of Liberty,* 645–47.

58. JM to John Henry Purviance, 24 December 1804, FONA; "Heriot, George," *DCB.*

59. Augustus Woodward to JM, 31 January 1807, FONA.

60. TJ to Constantin François Chasseboeuf Volney, 8 February 1805, FONA.

61. Benjamin Rush to JA, 19 February 1805, FONA; Perkins, "Diplomat's Wife," 623.
62. JA to Benjamin Rush, 27 February 1805, FONA.
63. *Vermont Precursor* (Montpelier), 4 September 1807.
64. John Nicholas to TJ, 2 August 1807, FONA; "The Two John Nicholases: Their Relationship to Washington and Jefferson," *American Historical Review* 45, no. 2 (1940): 338–53.
65. Wood, *Empire of Liberty*, 647.
66. Lafayette to TJ, 10 September 1807, FONA.
67. Ira Allen to JM, 14 December 1807 and 11 January 1808, FONA; Graffagnino, " 'Twenty Thousand Muskets!!!': Ira Allen and the Olive Branch Affair, 1796–1800," 428–29.
68. *Democratic Press* (Philadelphia), 31 December 1807.
69. "Wilcocks, Joseph," *DCB*; McNairn, *Capacity to Judge*, 156–57; Errington, *Lion*, 48–50; Gerald M. Craig, *Upper Canada: The Formative Years, 1784–1841* (Toronto: McClelland & Stewart, 1963), 62–63.
70. *Democratic Press* (Philadelphia), 20 January 1808.
71. "Bidwell, Barnabas," *DCB*.
72. Bidwell to JM, 19 February 1808, FONA; Errington, *Lion*, 35–54.
73. "Bidwell, Barnabas," *DCB*.
74. *North American, and Mercantile Daily Advertiser* (Maryland), 26 April 1808.
75. "Henry, John," *DCB*; Samuel Eliot Morison, "The Henry-Crillon Affair of 1812," *Proceedings of the Massachusetts Historical Society* 69 (1947): 208–9.
76. Hatter, *Citizens of Convenience*, 19–20.
77. "Henry, John," *DCB*.
78. Henry to Ryland, 5 October 1807, in E. A. Cruikshank, *The Political Adventures of John Henry: The Record of an International Imbroglio* (Toronto: Macmillan Company of Canada, 1936), 4; Morison, "Henry-Crillon Affair of 1812," 209.
79. Cruikshank, *Political Adventures*, 5–6, 36.
80. Ibid., 18–22.
81. RCA 1893, 24; Morison, "Henry-Crillon Affair of 1812," 210.
82. Cruikshank, *Political Adventures*, 40–41.
83. RCA 1893, 25–29. Henry usually wrote in cypher, used the initials A.B., and did not name a recipient in his letters sent to Canada.
84. Morison, "Henry-Crillon Affair of 1812," 210.
85. "Secret Reports of John Howe, 1808," *American Historical Review* 17, no. 1 (1911): 70–74.
86. McKinney to JM, 5 April 1809, FONA.
87. Nicole Eustace, *1812: War and the Passions of Patriotism* (Philadelphia: University of Pennsylvania Press, 2012), 25.
88. *The Washingtonian* (Vermont), 20 August 1810.
89. "Mr Pickering, to the People of the United States, no. 18," 26 August 1811, *The Washingtonian*. See also, Timothy Pickering, *Letters Addressed to*

the People of the United States of America, on the Conduct of the Past and Present Administrations of the American Government Towards Great Britain and France (London, 1811); Eustace, *1812*, 25, 78.

90. Paul A. Gilje, *Free Trade and Sailors' Rights in the War of 1812* (Cambridge: Cambridge University Press, 2013); Wood, *Empire of Liberty*, 659–700.

91. "Henry, John," *DCB*.

92. Morison, "Henry-Crillon Affair of 1812," 211–12; Cruikshank, *Political Adventures*, 72–73.

93. Ostler, *Surviving Genocide*, 141–50; Taylor, *Civil War*, 125–27; Willig, *Restoring*, 197–242.

94. *DCCR*, 182.

95. *New York Herald*, 12 February 1812.

96. Gerry to JM, 2 January 1812, FONA.

97. Gerry to JM, 3 January 1812, FONA.

98. Cruikshank, *Political Adventures*, 74–75.

99. "Henry, John," *DCB*.

100. Cruikshank, *Political Adventures*, 78–84; Morison, "Henry-Crillon Affair of 1812," 213–15.

101. Cruikshank, *Political Adventures*, 87.

102. "Henry, John," *DCB*; Augustus Foster, "Notes on America," HM 1732, Huntington Library.

103. *DCCR*, 183–99.

104. JM to John G. Jackson and TJ, 9 March 1812, FONA.

105. *DCCR*, 611.

106. For a few examples, see *Eastern Argus* (Portland, ME), 26 March 1812; *The Supporter* (Chillicothe, OH) 4 April 1812; *The Washingtonian* (Windsor, VT) 6 April 1812; *Georgia Journal* (Milledgeville, GA) 8 April 1812.

107. Taylor, *Civil War*, 130–31.

108. Brückner, *Social Life of Maps in America*, 65–66.

109. John Melish to TJ, 18 January 1812, FONA.

110. John Melish, *Travels through the United States of America*, vol. 2 (Philadelphia, 1812), 323–26.

111. Ibid., 338.

112. *Federal Gazette* (Baltimore, MD), 28 January 1812; *New York Herald*, 1 February 1812; *The Reporter* (Washington, PA), 17 February 1812.

## Epilogue

1. *The Wars of the Gulls; An Historical Romance* (New York, 1812), 3–5.

2. Ibid., 20–22.

3. Ibid., 22.

4. Burt, *United States*, 207–317.

5. *DCCR*, 610.

6. JA to William Cranch, 19 March 1812, FONA.

7. Graham, *Empire of the North Atlantic*, 41–57, 105; Gould, *Persistence*, 37–71.

8. JA to William Cranch, 19 March 1812, FONA.

9. Indigenous peoples were excellent sailors, but they were most effective along riverways and coastlines and became less of a threat farther out to sea. See Matthew R. Bahar, *Storm of the Sea: Indians and Empires in the Atlantic's Age of Sail* (New York: Oxford University Press, 2018); Andrew Lipman, *The Saltwater Frontier: Indians and the Contest for the American Coast* (New Haven: Yale University Press, 2015); Matthew R. Bahar, "People of the Dawn, People of the Door: Indian Pirates and the Violent Theft of an Atlantic World," *Journal of American History* 101, no. 2 (2014); Martijn, *Les Micmacs et la mer.*

10. *Cabinet* (Schenectady, NY), 25 March 1812.

11. Wood, *Empire of Liberty*, 650–56.

12. TJ to Astor, 24 May 1812, FONA.

13. Wallace, *Jefferson and the Indians*, 77–85, 270.

14. *DCCR*, 200.

15. Ibid., 612–14.

16. Chiefs and Warriors of the Oneida Nation to JM, Oneida, 2 June 1812, FONA.

17. TJ to JA, 11 June 1812, FONA; Wallace, *Jefferson and the Indians*, 287–88; John Demos, *The Heathen School: A Story of Hope and Betrayal in the Age of the Early Republic* (New York: Knopf, 2014), 211–18.

18. JA to TJ, 28 June 1812, FONA.

19. Unidentified to JM, 9 June 1812, FONA.

20. *City Gazette and Commercial Advertiser* (Charleston, SC), 10 June 1812.

21. Moses Townsend to JM, 10 June 1812, FONA.

22. *DCCR*, 206–7; TJ to Kosciuszko, 28 June 1812, FONA; *Kline's Weekly Carlisle (PA) Gazette*, 17 July 1812; Nichols to JM, 17 July 1812, FONA.

23. TJ to William Duane, 4 August 1812, FONA.

24. *Vermont Mirror* (Middlebury, VT), 30 September 1812.

25. Taylor, *Civil War*, 326–27.

26. Winks, *Blacks in Canada*, 113–15.

27. Taylor, *Civil War*, 6–10.

28. Errington, *Lion*, 70–77.

29. *The Reporter* (Lexington, KY), 25 November 1812.

30. Benjamin Rush to JA, 30 June 1812, FONA.

31. Taylor, *Civil War*, 319–29.

32. Eustace, *1812*, 47–48.

33. Wood, *Empire of Liberty*, 674–79; Craig, *Upper Canada*, 72–73.

34. Ibid., 27–29.

35. Ibid., 31.

36. Ibid., 36.

37. *Albany (NY) Register*, 6 August 1813.

38. *DCCR*, 212.

39. Ibid., 213–15.

40. Wood, *Empire of Liberty*, 685, 90–91; Craig, *Upper Canada*, 78.

41. *DCCR*, 216.

42. Ibid., 217–18.

43. Ibid., 617–18.

44. Craig, *Upper Canada*, 82–83; Hatter, *Citizens of Convenience*, 163–91.

45. *DCCR*, 221.

46. J. R. Miller, *Skyscrapers Hide the Heavens: A History of Native-Newcomer Relations in Canada* (Toronto: University of Toronto Press, 1991), 92; Cecilia Morgan, *Travellers through Empire: Indigenous Voyages from Early Canada*, vol. 91 (Montreal and Kingston: McGill-Queen's University Press, 2017), 55.

47. See Nicole Eustace and Fredrika J. Teute, eds., *Warring for America: Cultural Contests in the Era of 1812* (Chapel Hill: Omohundro Institute of Early American History and Culture, University of North Carolina Press, 2017).

48. Errington, *Lion*, 83–86; Harvey Amani Whitfield, " 'We Can Do as We Like Here': An Analysis of Self Assertion and Agency among Black Refugees in Halifax, Nova Scotia, 1813–1821," *Acadiensis* 32, no. 1 (Autumn 2002): 29–49.

49. On the continental ideals that shaped early American identity, see Drake, *Nation's Nature*.

50. Taylor, *American Republics*, xxiii.

51. Winks, *Blacks in Canada*, 96–114.

52. See Hämäläinen, *Comanche Empire*; Hämäläinen, *Lakota America: A New History of Indigenous Power* (New Haven: Yale University Press, 2019)

53. Miller, *Skyscrapers*, 211–309.

54. Caitlin Fitz, *Our Sister Republics: The United States in an Age of American Revolutions* (New York: W. W. Norton, 2016).

# Bibliography

Ablavsky, Gregory. *Federal Ground: Governing Property and Violence in the First US Territories*. New York: Oxford University Press, 2021.

———. "Species of Sovereignty: Native Nationhood, the United States, and International Law, 1783–1795." *Journal of American History* 106, no. 3 (2019): 591–613.

Akerman, James R., ed. *The Imperial Map: Cartography and the Mastery of Empire*. Chicago: University of Chicago Press, 2009.

Amar, Akhil Reed. *America's Constitution: A Biography*. New York: Random House, 2006.

*American Beginnings: Exploration, Culture, and Cartography in the Land of Norumbega*. Edited by Emerson W. Baker. Lincoln: University of Nebraska Press, 1994.

Anderson, Benedict R. *Imagined Communities: Reflections on the Origin and Spread of Nationalism*. London: Verso, 2006.

Anderson, Mark R. *The Battle for the Fourteenth Colony: America's War of Liberation in Canada, 1774–1776*. Hanover, NH: University Press of New England, 2013.

Armitage, David. *Civil Wars: A History in Ideas*. New York: Knopf, 2017.

———. *The Declaration of Independence: A Global History*. Cambridge: Harvard University Press, 2007.

*The Atlantic Region to Confederation: A History*. Edited by Phillip A. Buckner and John G. Reid. Toronto: University of Toronto Press, 1994.

Bahar, Matthew R. "People of the Dawn, People of the Door: Indian Pirates and the Violent Theft of an Atlantic World." *Journal of American History* 101, no. 2 (2014): 401–26.

———. *Storm of the Sea: Indians and Empires in the Atlantic's Age of Sail*. New York: Oxford University Press, 2018.

Bailyn, Bernard. *The Ordeal of Thomas Hutchinson*. Cambridge: Harvard University Press, 1974.

Baker, Emerson W., and John G. Reid. "Amerindian Power in the Early Modern Northeast: A Reappraisal." *William and Mary Quarterly* 61, no. 1 (2004): 77–106.

Banner, Stuart. *How the Indians Lost Their Land: Law and Power on the Frontier.* Cambridge: Harvard University Press, 2007.

Bannister, Jerry. *The Rule of the Admirals: Law, Custom, and Naval Government in Newfoundland, 1699–1832.* Toronto: Published for the Osgoode Society for Canadian Legal History by University of Toronto Press, 2003.

Bannister, Jerry, and Liam Riordam, eds. *The Loyal Atlantic: Remaking the British Atlantic in the Revolutionary Era.* Toronto: University of Toronto Press, 2012.

Barkwell, Lawrence. *The Métis Men of the Lewis and Clark Expedition, 1804–1806.* Winnipeg: Louis Riel Institute, 2011.

Barman, Jean. *The West Beyond the West: A History of British Columbia.* 3rd ed. Toronto: University of Toronto Press, 2007.

Barr, Juliana. "Geographies of Power: Mapping Indian Borders in the 'Borderlands' of the Early Southwest." *William and Mary Quarterly* 68, no. 1 (2011): 5–46.

Belmessous, Saliha. *Native Claims: Indigenous Law against Empire, 1500–1920.* Oxford: Oxford University Press, 2011.

Bemis, Samuel Flagg. *The Diplomacy of the American Revolution.* Bloomington: Indiana University Press, 1957 [1935].

Benton, Lauren A. *Law and Colonial Cultures: Legal Regimes in World History, 1400–1900.* Cambridge: Cambridge University Press, 2002.

Bergmann, William H. *The American National State and the Early West.* Cambridge: Cambridge University Press, 2012.

Berkin, Carol. *Revolutionary Mothers: Women in the Struggle for America's Independence.* New York: Vintage, 2007.

———. *A Sovereign People: The Crises of the 1790s and the Birth of American Nationalism.* New York: Basic Books, 2017.

Bothwell, Robert. *Your Country, My Country: A Unified History of the United States and Canada.* New York: Oxford University Press, 2015.

Boucher, Christopher. " 'The land God gave to Cain': Jacques Cartier Encounters the Mythological Wild Man in Labrador." *Terrae Incognitae* 35, no. 1 (June 2003): 28–42.

Bourque, Bruce J. "Ethnicity on the Maritime Peninsula, 1600–1759." *Ethnohistory* 36, no. 3 (1989): 257–84.

Bourque, Bruce J., Steven L. Cox, and Ruth Holmes Whitehead. *Twelve Thousand Years: American Indians in Maine.* Lincoln: University of Nebraska Press, 2001.

Brebner, John Bartlet. *New England's Outpost: Acadia before the Conquest of Canada.* New York: Columbia University Press, 1927.

Brown, Ralph H. "The American Geographies of Jedidiah Morse." *Annals of the Association of American Geographers* 31, no. 3 (1941): 145–217.

Brückner, Martin. *The Geographic Revolution in Early America: Maps, Literacy, and National Identity.* Chapel Hill: Published for the Omohundro Institute of Early American History and Culture by University of North Carolina Press, 2006.

———. *The Social Life of Maps in America, 1750–1860.* Chapel Hill: Omohundro Institute and University of North Carolina Press, 2017.

Brun, Régis, A. J. B. Johnston, and Ernest Clarke. *Fort Beauséjour—Fort Cumberland: Une Histoire/A History.* Memracook, NB, 1991.

Buker, George E. *The Penobscot Expedition: Commodore Saltonstall and the Massachusetts Conspiracy of 1779.* Annapolis: Naval Institute Press, 2002.

Burt, A. L. "The Mystery of Walker's Ear." *Canadian Historical Review* 3, no. 3 (1922): 233–55.

———. *The United States, Great Britain, and British North America from the Revolution to the Establishment of Peace after the War of 1812.* New York: Russell & Russell, 1961.

Calloway, Colin G. *The American Revolution in Indian Country.* New York: Cambridge University Press, 1995.

———. *The American Revolution in Indian Country: Crisis and Diversity in Native American Communities.* Cambridge: Cambridge University Press, 1995.

———. *Dawnland Encounters: Indians and Europeans in Northern New England.* Hanover, NH: The University Press of New England, 1991.

———. *The Indian World of George Washington: The First President, the First Americans, and the Birth of the Nation.* Oxford: Oxford University Press, 2018.

———. *New Worlds for All: Indians, Europeans, and the Remaking of Early America.* Baltimore: Johns Hopkins University Press, 1998.

———. *The Scratch of a Pen: 1763 and the Transformation of North America.* New York: Oxford University Press, 2006.

———. *The Victory with No Name: The Native American Defeat of the First American Army.* Oxford: Oxford University Press, 2014.

Carp, Benjamin L. *Defiance of the Patriots: The Boston Tea Party and the Making of America.* New Haven: Yale University Press, 2010.

Carroll, Francis M. *A Good and Wise Measure: The Search for the Canadian-American Boundary, 1783–1842.* Toronto: University of Toronto Press, 2001.

Carroll, John, *The John Carroll Papers.* Vol. 1. Ed. Thomas O'Brien Hanley and the American Catholic Historical Association. Notre Dame: University of Notre Dame Press, 1976.

Chmielewski, Laura M. *The Spice of Popery: Converging Christianities on an Early American Frontier.* Notre Dame: University of Notre Dame Press, 2012.

Clarfield, Gerard H. *Timothy Pickering and the American Republic.* Pittsburgh: University of Pittsburgh Press, 1980.

Clark, Andrew Hill. *Acadia; the Geography of Early Nova Scotia to 1760.* Madison: University of Wisconsin Press, 1968.

Clarke, Ernest. *Siege of Fort Cumberland, 1776: An Episode in the American Revolution.* Montreal and Kingston: McGill-Queen's University Press, 1995.

Clayton, Daniel Wright. *Islands of Truth: The Imperial Fashioning of Vancouver Island.* Vancouver: University of British Columbia Press, 2000.

Cogliano, Francis. "No King, No Popery: Anti-Popery and Revolution in New England, 1745–1791." PhD diss., Boston University, 1993.

Colby, Susan M. *Sacagawea's Child: The Life and Times of Jean-Baptiste (Pomp) Charbonneau.* Norman: University of Oklahoma Press, 2014.

Colley, Linda. *Britons: Forging the Nation, 1707–1837*. New Haven: Yale University Press, 1992.

———. *Captives: Britain, Empire and the World, 1600–1850*. London: Jonathan Cape, 2002.

———. *The Gun, the Ship, and the Pen: Warfare, Constitutions, and the Making of the Modern World*. New York: Liveright Publishing, 2021.

Conforti, Joseph A. *Imagining New England: Explorations of Regional Identity from the Pilgrims to the Mid-Twentieth Century*. Chapel Hill: University of North Carolina Press, 2001.

Conrad, Margaret, ed. *They Planted Well: New England Planters in Maritime Canada*. Fredericton: Acadiensis Press, 1988.

Conrad, Margaret, and Barry Moody, eds. *Planter Links: Community and Culture in Colonial Nova Scotia*. Fredericton: Acadiensis Press, 2001.

Cooper, Afua. *The Hanging of Angelique: The Untold Story of Canadian Slavery and the Burning of Old Montreal*. Athens: University of Georgia Press, 2007.

Cornell, Saul. *The Other Founders: Anti-Federalism and the Dissenting Tradition in America, 1788–1828*. Chapel Hill: Published for the Omohundro Institute of Early American History and Culture, University of North Carolina Press, 2012.

Craig, Gerald M. *Upper Canada: The Formative Years, 1784–1841*. Toronto: McClelland & Stewart, 1963.

Creviston, Vernon P. " 'No King Unless It Be a Constitutional King': Rethinking the Place of the Quebec Act in the Coming of the American Revolution." *Historian* 73, no. 3 (2011): 463–79.

Cruikshank, E. A. *The Political Adventures of John Henry: The Record of an International Imbroglio*. Toronto: Macmillan Company of Canada, 1936.

Curran, Robert Emmett. *Papist Devils: Catholics in British America, 1574–1783*. Washington, DC: Catholic University of America Press, 2014.

Davies, Kate. *Catharine Macaulay and Mercy Otis Warren: The Revolutionary Atlantic and the Politics of Gender*. New York: Oxford University Press, 2005.

Demeritt, David. "Representing the 'True' St. Croix: Knowledge and Power in the Partition of the Northeast." *William and Mary Quarterly* 54, no. 3 (1997): 515–48.

Demos, John. *The Heathen School: A Story of Hope and Betrayal in the Age of the Early Republic*. New York: Knopf, 2014.

———. *The Unredeemed Captive: A Family Story from Early America*. New York: Knopf, 1994.

Dewar, Helen. "Canada or Guadeloupe? French and British Perceptions of Empire, 1760–1763." *Canadian Historical Review* 91, no. 4 (2010): 637–60.

DeWolfe, Barbara. *Discoveries of America: Personal Accounts of British Emigrants to North America during the Revolutionary Era*. Cambridge: Cambridge University Press, 1997.

Dolin, Eric Jay. *Fur, Fortune, and Empire: The Epic History of the Fur Trade in America*. New York: W. W. Norton, 2011.

Drake, James. *The Nation's Nature: How Continental Presumptions Gave Rise to the United States of America*. Charlottesville: University of Virginia Press, 2011.

du Rivage, Justin. *Revolution against Empire: Taxes, Politics, and the Origins of American Independence*. New Haven: Yale University Press, 2017.

Dubois, Laurent. *Avengers of the New World: The Story of the Haitian Revolution*. Cambridge: Harvard University Press, 2005.

———. "The Haitian Revolution and the Sale of Louisiana." *Southern Quarterly* 44, no. 3 (2007): 18–41.

Ducharme, Michel. *The Idea of Liberty in Canada during the Age of Atlantic Revolutions, 1776–1838*. Translated by Peter Feldstein. Montreal and Kingston: McGill-Queen's University Press, 2014.

DuVal, Kathleen. *Independence Lost: Lives on the Edge of the American Revolution*. New York: Random House Trade, 2015.

Duval, Lauren. "Mastering Charleston: Property and Patriarchy in British-Occupied Charleston, 1780–82." *William and Mary Quarterly* 75, no. 4 (2018): 589–622.

Eamon, Michael. " 'An Extensive Collection of Useful and Entertaining Books': The Quebec Library and the Transatlantic Enlightenment in Canada." *Journal of the Canadian Historical Association* 23, no. 1 (2012): 1–38.

Edelson, S. Max. *The New Map of Empire: How Britain Imagined America before Independence*. Cambridge: Harvard University Press, 2017.

Edling, Max M. *Perfecting the Union: National and State Authority in the US Constitution*. New York: Oxford University Press, 2021.

———. *A Revolution in Favor of Government: Origins of the US Constitution and the Making of the American State*. New York: Oxford University Press, 2003.

Edney, Matthew H. *Mapping an Empire: The Geographical Construction of British India, 1765–1843*. Chicago: University of Chicago Press, 1997.

Ellison, Amy Noel. "Montgomery's Misfortune: The American Defeat at Quebec and the March toward Independence, 1775–1776." *Early American Studies* 15, no. 3 (2017): 591–616.

Errington, Jane. *The Lion, the Eagle, and Upper Canada: A Developing Colonial Ideology*. Montreal and Kingston: McGill-Queen's University Press, 1987.

Eustace, Nicole. *1812: War and the Passions of Patriotism*. Philadelphia: University of Pennsylvania Press, 2012.

Eustace, Nicole, and Fredrika J. Teute, eds. *Warring for America: Cultural Contests in the Era of 1812*. Chapel Hill: Omohundro Institute of Early American History and Culture, University of North Carolina Press, 2017.

Everest, Allan S. *Moses Hazen and the Canadian Refugees in the American Revolution*. Syracuse: Syracuse University Press, 1976.

Faragher, John Mack. *A Great and Noble Scheme: The Tragic Story of the Expulsion of the French Acadians from Their American Homeland*. New York: W. W. Norton, 2005.

Farrelly, Maura Jane. *Papist Patriots: The Making of an American Catholic Identity*. New York: Oxford University Press, 2012.

Fenn, Elizabeth A. *Encounters at the Heart of the World: A History of the Mandan People*. New York: Hill and Wang, 2014.

Fenton, Elizabeth. "Birth of a Protestant Nation: Catholic Canadians, Religious Pluralism, and National Unity in the Early U.S. Republic." *Early American Literature* 41, no. 1 (2006): 29–57.

Fenton, William N. *The Great Law and the Longhouse: A Political History of the Iroquois Confederacy*. Norman: University of Oklahoma Press, 1998.

Ferreiro, Larrie D. *Brothers at Arms: American Independence and the Men of France and Spain Who Saved It*. New York: Knopf, 2017.

Fischer, David Hackett. *Champlain's Dream*. New York: Simon & Schuster, 2008.

Fitz, Caitlin. *Our Sister Republics: The United States in an Age of American Revolutions*. New York: W. W. Norton, 2016.

———. " 'Suspected on Both Sides': Little Abraham, Iroquois Neutrality, and the American Revolution." *Journal of the Early Republic* 28, no. 3 (2008): 299–335.

"Forum: Situating the United States in Vast Early America." *William and Mary Quarterly* 78, no. 2 (2021): 187–280.

Frost, Stanley Brice. *James McGill of Montreal*. Montreal and Kingston: McGill-Queen's University Press, 1995.

Fyson, Donald. *Magistrates, Police, and People: Everyday Criminal Justice in Quebec and Lower Canada, 1764–1837*. Toronto: Published for the Osgoode Society for Canadian Legal History by University of Toronto Press, 2006.

Gallay, Alan. *Indian Slavery in Colonial America*. Lincoln: University of Nebraska Press, 2009.

Gallo, Marcus. "Property Rights, Citizenship, Corruption, and Inequality: Confiscating Loyalist Estates during the American Revolution." *Pennsylvania History: A Journal of Mid-Atlantic Studies* 86, no. 4 (2019): 474–510.

Gannon, Kevin M. "Escaping 'Mr. Jefferson's Plan of Destruction': New England Federalists and the Idea of a Northern Confederacy, 1803–1804." *Journal of the Early Republic* 21, no. 3 (2001): 413–43.

Gilje, Paul A. *Free Trade and Sailors' Rights in the War of 1812*. Cambridge University Press, 2013.

Glover, Lorri. *The Fate of the Revolution: Virginians Debate the Constitution*. Baltimore: Johns Hopkins University Press, 2016.

Gordon-Reed, Annette, and Peter S. Onuf. *"Most Blessed of the Patriarchs": Thomas Jefferson and the Empire of the Imagination*. New York: W. W. Norton, 2016.

Gould, Eliga H. *Among the Powers of the Earth: The American Revolution and the Making of a New World Empire*. Cambridge: Harvard University Press, 2012.

———. *The Persistence of Empire: British Political Culture in the Age of the American Revolution*. Chapel Hill: Published for the Omohundro Institute of Early American History and Culture, Williamsburg, Virginia, by the University of North Carolina Press, 2000.

Graffagnino, J. Kevin. " 'Twenty Thousand Muskets!!!': Ira Allen and the Olive Branch Affair, 1796–1800." *William and Mary Quarterly* 48, no. 3 (1991): 409–31.

Graham, Gerald S. *Empire of the North Atlantic: The Maritime Struggle for North America*. Toronto: University of Toronto Press, 1958.

Gray, Edward G., and Jane Kamensky, eds. *The Oxford Handbook of the American Revolution*. Oxford: Oxford University Press, 2012.

Graymont, Barbara. *The Iroquois in the American Revolution*. Syracuse, NY: Syracuse University Press, 1972.

Greenburg, Michael M. *The Court-Martial of Paul Revere*. Lebanon, NH: Fore Edge, 2014.

Greenwood, Frank Murray. *Legacies of Fear: Law and Politics in Quebec in the Era of the French Revolution*. Toronto: University of Toronto Press, 1993.

Gregory, Anthony. " 'Formed for Empire': The Continental Congress Responds to the Carlisle Peace Commission." *Journal of the Early Republic* 38, no. 4 (2018): 643–72.

Griffin, Patrick. *American Leviathan: Empire, Nation, and Revolutionary Frontier*. New York: Hill and Wang, 2008.

Griffiths, N. E. S. *From Migrant to Acadian: A North American Border People, 1604–1755*. Montreal and Kingston: McGill-Queen's University Press, 2005.

Guidorizzi, Richard P. "Timothy Pickering: Opposition Politics in the Early Years of the Republic." PhD diss., St. John's University, 1968.

Gundersen, Joan R. *To Be Useful to the World: Women in Revolutionary America, 1740–1790*. Chapel Hill: University of North Carolina Press, 2006.

Habermas, Jürgen. *The Structural Transformation of the Public Sphere: An Inquiry into a Category of Bourgeois Society*. Cambridge: MIT Press, 1989.

Haggard, Robert F. "The Politics of Friendship: Du Pont, Jefferson, Madison, and the Physiocratic Dream for the New World." *Proceedings of the American Philosophical Society* 153, no. 4 (2009): 419–40.

Hale, Edward E., and Edward E. Hale Jr. *Franklin in France*. Vol. 2. Boston: Roberts Brothers, 1888.

Hämäläinen, Pekka. *The Comanche Empire*. New Haven: Yale University Press, 2008.

*Handbook of North American Indians*. Edited by William C. Sturtevant and Bruce G. Trigger (volume editor). Vol. 15. Washington, DC: Smithsonian Institution, 1978.

Harley, J. B., Barbara Bartz Petchenik, and Lawrence W. Towner. *Mapping the American Revolutionary War*. Kenneth Nebenzahl Jr. Lectures in the History of Cartography. Chicago: University of Chicago Press, 1978.

Harris, R. Cole, ed. *Historical Atlas of Canada*. Vol. 1, *From the Beginning to 1800*. Toronto: University of Toronto Press, 1987.

Hatter, Lawrence B. A. *Citizens of Convenience: The Imperial Origins of American Nationhood on the U.S.-Canadian Border*. Charlottesville: University of Virginia Press, 2016.

———. "The Narcissism of Petty Differences? Thomas Jefferson, John Graves Simcoe and the Reformation of Empire in the Early United States and British-Canada." *American Review of Canadian Studies* 42, no. 2 (2012): 130–41.

Havard, Gilles. *The Great Peace of Montreal of 1701: French-Native Diplomacy in the Seventeenth Century.* Translated by Phyllis Aronoff and Howard Scott. Montreal and Kingston: McGill-Queen's University Press, 2001.

Hill, Susan M. *The Clay We Are Made Of: Haudenosaunee Land Tenure on the Grand River.* Winnipeg: University of Manitoba Press, 2017.

Hodson, Christopher. *The Acadian Diaspora: An Eighteenth-Century History.* Oxford University Press, 2012.

Hoffman, Ronald, and Peter J. Albert, eds. *Peace and the Peacemakers: The Treaty of 1783.* Charlottesville: University Press of Virginia for the United States Capitol Historical Society, 1986.

Holton, Woody. "Did Democracy Cause the Recession That Led to the Constitution?" *Journal of American History* 92, no. 2 (2005): 442–69.

———. "An 'Excess of Democracy,' or a Shortage? The Federalists' Earliest Adversaries." *Journal of the Early Republic* 25, no. 3 (2005): 339–82.

———. *Unruly Americans and the Origins of the Constitution.* New York: Hill and Wang, 2008.

Hornsby, Stephen. *British Atlantic, American Frontier: Spaces of Power in Early Modern British America.* Hanover, NH: University Press of New England, 2005.

Hornsby, Stephen J., and John G. Reid, eds. *New England and the Maritime Provinces: Connections and Comparisons.* Montreal and Kingston: McGill-Queen's University Press, 2005.

Horsman, Reginald. *Expansion and American Indian Policy, 1783–1812.* Norman: University of Oklahoma Press, 1992 [1967].

Hubert, Ollivier, and François Furstenberg, eds. *Entangling the Quebec Act: Transnational Contexts, Meanings, and Legacies in North America and the British Empire.* Montreal and Kingston: McGill-Queen's University Press, 2020.

Huey, Lois M., and Bonnie Pulis. *Molly Brant: A Legacy of Her Own.* Youngstown, NY: Old Fort Niagara Association, 1997.

Hyde, Anne F. *Empires, Nations, and Families: A History of the North American West, 1800–1860.* New York: Ecco, 2012.

Isaacson, Walter. *Benjamin Franklin: An American Life.* New York: Simon & Schuster, 2004.

Israel, Jonathan. *The Expanding Blaze: How the American Revolution Ignited the World, 1775–1848.* Princeton: Princeton University Press, 2017.

Jackson, Donald. *Thomas Jefferson and the Rocky Mountains: Exploring the West from Monticello.* Norman: University of Oklahoma Press, 2002 (1981).

Janzen, Olaf U. *War and Trade in Eighteenth-Century Newfoundland.* Liverpool: Liverpool University Press, 2013.

Jasanoff, Maya. *Liberty's Exiles: American Loyalists in the Revolutionary World.* New York: Knopf, 2011.

———. "The Other Side of Revolution: Loyalists in the British Empire." *William and Mary Quarterly* 65, no. 2 (April 2008): 205–32.

Jenish, D'Arcy. *Epic Wanderer: David Thompson and the Mapping of the Canadian West.* Toronto: Doubleday, 2003.

Jennings, Francis. *Ambiguous Iroquois Empire: The Covenant Chain Confederation of Indian Tribes with English Colonies from Its Beginnings to the Lancaster Treaty of 1744*. 1st ed. New York: W. W. Norton, 1984.

Johnson, James Keith. *In Duty Bound: Men, Women, and the State in Upper Canada, 1783–1841*. Montreal and Kingston: McGill-Queen's University Press, 2013.

Johnson, Ronald Angelo. "A Revolutionary Dinner: US Diplomacy toward Saint Domingue, 1798–1801." *Early American Studies* 9, no. 1 (Winter 2011): 114–41.

Jones, Howard. *To the Webster-Ashburton Treaty: A Study in Anglo-American Relations, 1783–1843*. Chapel Hill: University of North Carolina Press, 2017 [1977].

Kamrath, Mark, ed. *Periodical Literature in Eighteenth-Century America*. Knoxville: University of Tennessee Press, 2005.

Kapp, Friedrich. *Life of Frederick William von Steuben, Major General in the Revolutionary Army*. New York: Mason Brothers, 1859.

Kelsay, Isabel Thompson. *Joseph Brant, 1743–1807: Man of Two Worlds*. Syracuse: Syracuse University Press, 1984.

Kerber, Linda K. *Women of the Republic: Intellect and Ideology in Revolutionary America*. Chapel Hill: Published for the Omohundro Institute of Early American History and Culture, University of North Carolina Press, 2000.

Knopf, Richard C. *Anthony Wayne: A Name in Arms*. Pittsburgh: University of Pittsburgh Press, 1959.

Kramer, Lloyd S. "America's Lafayette and Lafayette's America: A European and the American Revolution." *William and Mary Quarterly* 38, no. 2 (1981): 228–41.

Kukla, Jon. *A Wilderness So Immense: The Louisiana Purchase and the Destiny of America*. New York: Knopf, 2003.

Kyte, George W. "The Detention of General Collot: A Sidelight on Anglo-American Relations, 1798–1800." *William and Mary Quarterly* 6, no. 4 (1949): 628–30.

Lanctot, Gustave. *Canada and the American Revolution, 1774–1783*. Translated by Margaret M. Cameron. London: George G. Harrap, 1967.

Landsman, Ned C., ed. *Nation and Province in the First British Empire: Scotland and the Americas, 1600–1800*. Lewisburg, PA: Bucknell University Press, 2001.

Langston, Paul. " 'Tyrant and Oppressor!': Colonial Press Reaction to the Quebec Act." *Historical Journal of Massachusetts* 34, no. 1 (2006): 1–17.

Lawson, Philip. *The Imperial Challenge: Quebec and Britain in the Age of the American Revolution*. Montreal and Kingston: McGill-Queen's University Press, 1989.

Leamon, James S. *Revolution Downeast: The War for American Independence in Maine*. Amherst: University of Massachusetts Press, 1995.

Leavelle, Tracy Neal. *The Catholic Calumet: Colonial Conversions in French and Indian North America*. Philadelphia: University of Pennsylvania Press, 2011.

Leitch, Alexander. *A Princeton Companion*. Princeton: Princeton University Press, 2015.

Lena, Alberto. "Benjamin Franklin's Canada Pamphlet or the Ravings of a Mad Prophet: Nationalism, Ethnicity and Imperialism." *European Journal of American Culture* 20, no. 1 (2001): 36–49.

Lennox, Jeffers. "An Empire on Paper: The Founding of Halifax and Conceptions of Imperial Space, 1744–55." *Canadian Historical Review* 88, no. 3 (2007): 373–412.

———. *Homelands and Empires: Indigenous Spaces, Imperial Fictions, and Competition for Territory in Northeastern North America, 1690–1763*. Toronto: University of Toronto Press, 2017.

———. "Nova Scotia Lost and Found: The Acadian Boundary Negotiation and Imperial Envisioning, 1750–1755." *Acadiensis* 40, no. 2 (2011): 3–31.

———. "A Time and a Place: The Geography of British, French, and Aboriginal Interactions in Early Nova Scotia, 1726–44." *William and Mary Quarterly* 72, no. 3 (2015): 423–60.

Lepore, Jill. *Book of Ages: The Life and Opinions of Jane Franklin*. New York: Knopf, 2013.

Lewis, Jan. " 'Of Every Age Sex and Condition': The Representation of Women in the Constitution." *Journal of the Early Republic* 15, no. 3 (1995): 359–87.

Lipman, Andrew. *The Saltwater Frontier: Indians and the Contest for the American Coast*. New Haven: Yale University Press, 2015.

Little, Nigel. *Transoceanic Radical: William Duane: National Identity and Empire, 1760–1835*. New York: Routledge, 2016.

Mackenzie, Alexander. *The Journals of Alexander Mackenzie: Exploring across Canada in 1789 and 1793*. The Historical Adventure and Exploration Series. Santa Barbara, CA: Narrative Press, 2001.

MacKinnon, Neil. *This Unfriendly Soil: The Loyalist Experience in Nova Scotia, 1783–1791*. Montreal and Kingston: McGill-Queen's University Press, 1986.

Maier, Pauline. *American Scripture: Making the Declaration of Independence*. New York: Vintage, 1997.

———. *From Resistance to Revolution: Colonial Radicals and the Development of American Opposition to Britain, 1765–1776*. New York: W. W. Norton, 1991.

Mancke, Elizabeth. *The Fault Lines of Empire: Political Differentiation in Massachusetts and Nova Scotia, Ca. 1760–1830*. New York: Routledge, 2005.

Marshall, P. J. *The Making and Unmaking of Empires: Britain, India, and America c. 1750–1783*. Oxford: Oxford University Press, 2005.

Martijn, Charles A. *Les Micmacs et la mer*. Quebec: Recherches amérindiennes au Québec, 1986.

Martin, Geoffrey J. "The Emergence and Development of Geographic Thought in New England." *Economic Geography* 74, no. 1 (1998): 1–13.

McCusker, John J., and Russell R. Menard. *The Economy of British America, 1607–1789*. Chapel Hill: Published for the Institute of Early American History and Culture by the University of North Carolina Press, 1985.

McNairn, Jeffrey L. *The Capacity to Judge: Public Opinion and Deliberative Democracy in Upper Canada, 1791–1854*. Toronto: University of Toronto Press, 2000.

McPhee, Peter. *Liberty or Death: The French Revolution*. New Haven: Yale University Press, 2016.

Meacham, Jon. *Thomas Jefferson: The Art of Power*. New York: Random House, 2012.

Meinig, Donald William. *The Shaping of America: A Geographical Perspective on 500 Years of History*. Vol. 1, *Atlantic America, 1492–1800*. New Haven: Yale University Press, 1986.

Mercer, Keith. "The Murder of Lieutenant Lawry: A Case Study of British Naval Impressment in Newfoundland, 1794." *Newfoundland and Labrador Studies* (2006).

———. "Northern Exposure: Resistance to Naval Impressment in British North America, 1775–1815." *Canadian Historical Review* 91, no. 2 (2010): 199–232.

Middlekauff, Robert. *The Glorious Cause: The American Revolution, 1763–1789*. New York: Oxford University Press, 2005.

Miller, J. R. *Skyscrapers Hide the Heavens: A History of Native-Newcomer Relations in Canada*. Toronto: University of Toronto Press, 1991.

Minty, Christopher F. " 'Of One Hart and One Mind': Local Institutions and Allegiance during the American Revolution." *Early American Studies* 15, no. 1 (2017): 99–132.

Monette, Pierre. *Rendez-vous manqué avec la Révolution Américaine*. Montreal: Québec Amérique, 2007.

Moore, John Bassett. *International Adjudications, Ancient and Modern: History and Documents*. Vol. 3. Oxford: Oxford University Press, 1931.

Morgan, Cecilia. *Travellers through Empire: Indigenous Voyages from Early Canada*. Vol. 91. Montreal and Kingston: McGill-Queen's University Press, 2017.

Morgan, David. *The Devious Dr. Franklin, Colonial Agent: Benjamin Franklin's Years in London*. Macon, GA: Mercer University Press, 1999.

Morgan, Edmund S. *Benjamin Franklin*. New Haven: Yale University Press, 2002.

———. *The Birth of the Republic: 1763–89*. 3rd ed. Chicago: University of Chicago Press, 1992.

Morison, Samuel Eliot. "The Henry-Crillon Affair of 1812." *Proceedings of the Massachusetts Historical Society* 69 (1947): 207–31.

Morris, Richard B. *The Peacemakers: The Great Powers and American Independence*. New York: Harper & Row, 1965.

Morse, Jedidiah. *The American Geography; or, A View of the Present Situation of the United States of America*. 1st ed. Elizabeth Town: Shepard Kollock, for the author, 1789.

Muller, Hannah Weiss. *Subjects and Sovereign: Bonds of Belonging in the Eighteenth-Century British Empire*. Oxford: Oxford University Press, 2017.

Neatby, Hilda. *Quebec: The Revolutionary Age, 1760–1791*. Toronto: McClelland and Stewart, 1966.

Neel, Joanne Loewe. *Phineas Bond: A Study in Anglo-American Relations: 1786–1812*. Philadelphia: University of Pennsylvania Press, 1968.

Nellis, Eric. *The Long Road to Change: America's Revolution, 1750–1820*. Toronto: Broadview Press, 2007.

Newbigging, William James. "The Cession of Canada and French Public Opinion." *Proceedings of the Meeting of the French Colonial Historical Society* 22 (1998): 163–76.

Nisbet, J. *Sources of the River: Tracking David Thompson across North America*. 2nd ed. Seattle: Sasquatch Books, 2011.

*The Northeastern Borderlands: Four Centuries of Interaction*. Edited by Stephen Hornsby, Victor A. Konrad, and James Herlan. Fredericton: Acadiensis Press, 1989.

Norton, Mary Beth. *Liberty's Daughters: The Revolutionary Experience of American Women, 1750–1800*. Ithaca, NY: Cornell University Press, 1996.

O'Shaughnessy, Andrew Jackson. *An Empire Divided: The American Revolution and the British Caribbean*. Philadelphia: University of Pennsylvania Press, 2000.

———. *The Men Who Lost America: British Leadership, the American Revolution, and the Fate of the Empire*. New Haven: Yale University Press, 2013.

O'Toole, Fintan. *White Savage: William Johnson and the Invention of America*. New York: Excelsior Editions, 2005.

Offen, Karl H. "Creating Mosquitia: Mapping Amerindian Spatial Practices in Eastern Central America, 1629–1779." *Journal of Historical Geography* 33, no. 2 (2007): 254–82.

Ojala, Jeanne A. "Ira Allen and the French Directory, 1796: Plans for the Creation of the Republic of United Columbia." *William and Mary Quarterly* 36, no. 3 (1979): 436–48.

Onuf, Peter S. *The Origins of the Federal Republic: Jurisdictional Controversies in the United States, 1775–1787*. Philadelphia: University of Pennsylvania Press, 1983.

Ostler, Jeffrey. *Surviving Genocide: Native Nations and the United States from the American Revolution to Bleeding Kansas*. New Haven: Yale University Press, 2019.

Oxford, Mitchell Edward. "'This Very Important and Almost Unbounded Trust': The Commission to Canada and the Place of Catholics in Revolutionary America." *US Catholic Historian* 36, no. 4 (2018): 1–24.

Palfreyman, Brett. "The Loyalists and the Federal Constitution: The Origins of the Bill of Attainder Clause." *Journal of the Early Republic* 35, no. 3 (2015): 451–73.

Paquette, Gabriel, and Gonzalo M. Quintero Saravia, eds. *Spain and the American Revolution: New Approaches and Perspectives*. New York: Routledge, 2019.

Park, Benjamin. "The Bonds of Union: Benjamin Rush, Noah Webster, and Defining the Nation in the Early Republic." *Early American Studies* 15, no. 2 (2017): 382–408.

Parkinson, Robert G. *The Common Cause: Creating Race and Nation in the American Revolution*. Chapel Hill: University of North Carolina Press, 2016.

Pearson, Ellen Holmes. *Remaking Custom: Law and Identity in the Early American Republic*. Charlottesville: University of Virginia Press, 2011.

Perkins, Bradford. "A Diplomat's Wife in Philadelphia: Letters of Henrietta Liston, 1796–1800." *William and Mary Quarterly* 11, no. 4 (1954): 592–632.

Perl-Rosenthal, Nathan. *Citizen Sailors: Becoming American in the Age of Revolution.* Cambridge: Harvard University Press, 2015.

Pincus, Steve. *The Heart of the Declaration: The Founders' Case for an Activist Government.* New Haven: Yale University Press, 2016.

Plank, Geoffrey Gilbert. *An Unsettled Conquest: The British Campaign against the Peoples of Acadia.* Philadelphia: University of Pennsylvania Press, 2001.

Pritchard, James Stewart. *In Search of Empire: The French in the Americas, 1670–1730.* Cambridge: Cambridge University Press, 2004.

Randall, Willard Sterne. *Ethan Allen: His Life and Times.* New York: W. W. Norton, 2011.

Rawlyk, George A. *Nova Scotia's Massachusetts: A Study of Massachusetts-Nova Scotia Relations, 1630–1784.* Montreal: McGill-Queen's University Press, 1973.

Ray, Arthur J. *Illustrated History of Canada's Native People: I Have Lived Here since the World Began.* Montreal and Kingston: McGill-Queen's University Press, 2016.

Reeder, Tyson. "Liberty with the Sword: Jamaican Maroons, Haitian Revolutionaries, and American Liberty." *Journal of the Early Republic* 37, no. 1 (2017): 81–115.

Reid, John G. "Empire, the Maritime Colonies, and the Supplanting of Mi'kma'ki/Wulstukwik, 1780–1820." *Acadiensis* 38, no. 2 (Summer 2009): 78–97.

———. *Essays on Northeastern North America, Seventeenth and Eighteenth Centuries.* Toronto: University of Toronto Press, 2008.

———. "*Pax Britannica* or *Pax Indigena?* Planter Nova Scotia (1760–1782) and Competing Strategies of Pacification." *Canadian Historical Review* 85, no. 4 (2004): 669–92.

Reid, John G., Maurice Basque, Elizabeth Mancke, Barry Moody, Geoffrey Plank, and William Wicken. *The "Conquest" of Acadia, 1710: Imperial, Colonial, and Aboriginal Constructions.* Toronto: University of Toronto Press, 2004.

Reynoso, Jacqueline. "(Dis)Placing the American Revolution: The British Province of Quebec in the Greater Colonial Struggle, 1759–1783." PhD diss., Cornell University, 2017.

Rhoades, Matthew L. "Blood and Boundaries: Virginia Backcountry Violence and the Origins of the Quebec Act, 1758–1775." *West Virginia History: A Journal of Regional Studies* 3, no. 2 (2009): 1–22.

Richards, Leonard L. *Shays's Rebellion: The American Revolution's Final Battle.* Philadelphia: University of Pennsylvania Press, 2002.

Richter, Daniel K. *Before the Revolution: America's Ancient Pasts.* Cambridge: Harvard University Press, 2011.

———. *Facing East from Indian Country: A Native History of Early America.* Cambridge: Harvard University Press, 2001.

———. *The Ordeal of the Longhouse: The Peoples of the Iroquois League in the Era of European Colonization.* Chapel Hill: Published for the Institute of Early

American History and Culture, Williamsburg, Virginia, by the University of North Carolina Press, 1992.

Rushforth, Brett. *Bonds of Alliance: Indigenous and Atlantic Slaveries in New France.* Chapel Hill: Published for the Omohundro Institute of Early American History and Culture, University of North Carolina Press, 2012.

Sadosky, Leonard J. *Revolutionary Negotiations: Indians, Empires, and Diplomats in the Founding of America.* Charlottesville: University of Virginia Press, 2009.

Saler, Bethel. *The Settlers' Empire: Colonialism and State Formation in America's Old Northwest.* Philadelphia: University of Pennsylvania Press, 2014.

Schaeper, Thomas J. *Edward Bancroft: Scientist, Author, Spy.* New Haven: Yale University Press, 2011.

Searcy, Martha Condray. "1779: The First Year of the British Occupation of Georgia." *Georgia Historical Quarterly* 67, no. 2 (1983): 168–88.

"Secret Reports of John Howe, 1808." *American Historical Review* 17, no. 1 (1911): 70–74.

Sheridan, Eugene R. "The Recall of Edmond Charles Genet: A Study in Transatlantic Politics and Diplomacy." *Diplomatic History* 18, no. 4 (1994): 463–88.

Silver, Peter. *Our Savage Neighbors: How Indian War Transformed Early America.* New York: W. W. Norton, 2008.

Sloan, Robert W. "New Ireland: Loyalists in Eastern Maine during the American Revolution." PhD diss., Michigan State University, 1971.

———. "New Ireland: Men in Pursuit of a Forlorn Hope, 1779–1784." *Maine Historical Quarterly* 19 (1979): 73–90.

Sosin, Jack M. *Whitehall and the Wilderness: The Middle West in British Colonial Policy, 1760–1775.* Lincoln: University of Nebraska Press, 1961.

Stuart, Reginald C. *United States Expansionism and British North America, 1775–1871.* Chapel Hill: University of North Carolina Press, 1988.

Tanner, Helen Hornbeck. "The Glaize in 1792: A Composite Indian Community." *Ethnohistory* (1978): 15–39.

Taylor, Alan. *American Republics: A Continental History of the United States, 1783–1850.* New York: W. W. Norton, 2021.

———. *American Revolutions: A Continental History, 1750–1804.* New York: W. W. Norton, 2016.

———. *The Civil War of 1812: American Citizens, British Subjects, Irish Rebels, and Indian Allies.* New York: Vintage, 2010.

———. *The Divided Ground: Indians, Settlers, and the Northern Borderland of the American Revolution.* New York: Vintage, 2007.

———. "The Late Loyalists: Northern Reflections of the Early American Republic." *Journal of the Early Republic* 27, no. 1 (2007): 1–34.

———. *Liberty Men and Great Proprietors: The Revolutionary Settlement on the Maine Frontier, 1760–1820.* Chapel Hill: Published for the Omohundro Institute of Early American History and Culture, The University of North Carolina Press, 1990.

———. *Thomas Jefferson's Education.* New York: W. W. Norton, 2019.

Taylor, Jordan E. "The Reign of Error: North American Information Politics and the French Revolution, 1789–1795." *Journal of the Early Republic* 39, no. 3 (2019): 437–66.

Thompson, David. *David Thompson's Narrative of His Explorations in Western America, 1784–1812.* Edited by Joseph Burr Tyrrell. Toronto: Champlain Society, 1916.

Tiro, Karim M. "James Dean in Iroquoia." *New York History* 80, no. 4 (October 1999): 391–422.

Trudel, Marcel. "La servitude de l'Église catholique du Canada Français sous le régime Anglais." *Rapport—Société canadienne d'histoire de l'Église catholique* 30 (1963): 11–33.

"The Two John Nicholases: Their Relationship to Washington and Jefferson." *American Historical Review* 45, no. 2 (1940): 338–53.

Van Kirk, Sylvia. *Many Tender Ties: Women in Fur-Trade Society, 1670–1870.* Winnipeg: Watson & Dwywer, 1999.

Vickers, Daniel. *Farmers and Fishermen: Two Centuries of Work in Essex County, Massachusetts, 1630–1850.* Chapel Hill: University of North Carolina Press, 1994.

Vickers, Daniel, and Vince Walsh. *Young Men and the Sea: Yankee Seafarers in the Age of Sail.* New Haven: Yale University Press, 2005.

*Violence, Order, and Unrest: A History of British North America, 1749–1876.* Edited by Elizabeth Mancke, Jerry Bannister, Denis McKim, and Scott W. See. Toronto: University of Toronto Press, 2019.

Wade, Mason. *The French Canadians, 1760–1967.* Vol. 1. Toronto: Macmillan Company of Canada, 1968.

Waldstreicher, David. *In the Midst of Perpetual Fetes: The Making of American Nationalism, 1776–1820.* Chapel Hill: Published for the Omohundro Institute of Early American History and Culture, University of North Carolina Press, 1997.

———. *Slavery's Constitution: From Revolution to Ratification.* New York: Hill and Wang, 2010.

Walker, James W. St. G. *The Black Loyalists: The Search for a Promised Land in Nova Scotia and Sierra Leone, 1783–1870.* New York: Africana and Dalhousie University Press, 1976.

Wallace, Anthony. *The Death and Rebirth of the Seneca.* New York: Vintage, 1972.

———. *Jefferson and the Indians: The Tragic Fate of the First Americans.* Cambridge: Harvard University Press, 2009.

Weaver, John C. *The Great Land Rush and the Making of the Modern World, 1650–1900.* Montreal and Kingston: McGill-Queen's University Press, 2003.

Weidensaul, Scott. *The First Frontier: The Forgotten History of Struggle, Savagery, and Endurance in Early America.* New York: Houghton Mifflin Harcourt, 2012.

White, Richard. *The Middle Ground: Indians, Empires, and Republics in the Great Lakes Region, 1650–1815.* Cambridge: Cambridge University Press, 1991.

Whitfield, Harvey Amani. *North to Bondage: Loyalist Slavery in the Maritimes.* Vancouver: University of British Columbia Press, 2016.

———. " 'We Can Do as We Like Here': An Analysis of Self Assertion and Agency among Black Refugees in Halifax, Nova Scotia, 1813–1821." *Acadiensis* 32, no. 1 (Autumn 2002): 29–49.

Wicken, William C. "Encounters with Tall Sails and Tall Tales: Mi'kmaq Society, 1500–1760." PhD diss., McGill University, 1994.

———. *Mi'kmaq Treaties on Trial: History, Land and Donald Marshall Junior.* Toronto: University of Toronto Press, 2002.

Wickman, Thomas M. *Snowshoe Country: An Environmental and Cultural History of Winter in the Early American Northeast.* Cambridge: Cambridge University Press, 2018.

Williamson, Chilton. *Vermont in Quandary: 1763–1825.* Vol. 4. Barre: Vermont Historical Society, 1949.

Willig, Timothy D. *Restoring the Chain of Friendship: British Policy and the Indians of the Great Lakes, 1783–1815.* Lincoln: University of Nebraska Press, 2008.

Wilson, Kathleen. *The Sense of the People: Politics, Culture, and Imperialism in England, 1715–1785.* Cambridge: Cambridge University Press, 1995.

Winks, Robin W. *Blacks in Canada: A History.* Montreal and Kingston: McGill-Queen's University Press, 1997.

Witgen, Michael. *An Infinity of Nations: How the Native New World Shaped Early North America.* Philadelphia: University of Pennsylvania Press, 2011.

Wood, Gordon S., ed. *The American Revolution: Writings from the Pamphlet Debate, I: 1764–1772.* New York: Library of America, 2015.

———. *The Creation of the American Republic, 1776–1787.* Chapel Hill: Published for the Omohundro Institute of Early American History and Culture, University of North Carolina Press, 1998 [1969].

———. *Empire of Liberty: A History of the Early Republic, 1789–1815.* Oxford: Oxford University Press, 2009.

———. *The Radicalism of the American Revolution.* New York: Vintage Books, 1993.

Wrong, George M. *Canada and the American Revolution: The Disruption of the First British Empire.* New York: Macmillan, 1935.

Zagarri, Rosemarie. *Revolutionary Backlash: Women and Politics in the Early American Republic.* Philadelphia: University of Pennsylvania Press, 2007.

# Acknowledgments

Acknowledgments are impossible. I'm surely going to forget someone, and for that I apologize in advance. So many people, institutions, and inanimate objects helped make this book; I'll do my best to express my gratitude here.

I didn't travel much for this book. With two young children and an incurable desire to hang out with my wife all the time, I had to get creative. Aside from regular trips from my "home" in Connecticut to my *home* in Canada, most of the traveling I did was from the kitchen to the office upstairs. So big thanks to the internet and the many archives that have digitized their collections. When I did have the pleasure of visiting libraries and archives—at Wesleyan, Yale, Princeton, the University of Virginia, the Huntington, the Library and Archives Canada, Tulane, the New Orleans Public Library, the American Philosophical Society, and the Nova Scotia Archives and Records Management—the archivists and research staff were welcoming and invaluable resources. For all those working in libraries and archives—thank you.

I benefited immensely from thinking through these ideas in classes, at conferences, and over kitchen tables. My students at Wesleyan didn't make a beeline for the door when they learned that their early-American professor was a Canadian (for which I'm grateful). And now they know about Prince Edward Island (for which they are grateful). I was fortunate enough to work with several student research assistants, and I'd like to thank them by name. Kelvin Cuesta and Noa Azulai dug through online archives and helped compile materials to read. And my brain trust, Jacob Singer and Ian Foster, performed all kinds of research tasks, read a few drafts, and even got to know the kids at dinner. My colleagues in the history department at Wesleyan, and Wesleyan University more generally, have been supportive and encouraging through the research and writing of this book.

I am especially thankful for the institutions that sponsored conferences and workshops where I got to test out some of these ideas, including the Omohundro Institute for Early American History and Culture, Duke University's John

Hope Franklin Humanities Institute, University of New Brunswick, Yale Early American History Workshop, Columbia University's International History Workshop, McGill University, Wesleyan University's Indigenous Studies Research Network, and the American Antiquarian Society. My friends and mentors raised pints with me over the years as we shared ideas. I'm especially grateful for Bradley Miller, Jerry Bannister, John G. Reid, and the late Danny Vickers for their friendship and guidance.

Bringing this book into the world was certainly a team effort. My agent, Don Fehr, at Trident Media believed in the project and, even better, convinced others to believe in it too. William Frucht, my editor at Yale University Press, offered both big-picture advice and crucial editing to keep the arguments connected and the prose under control. Karen Olson, Amanda Gerstenfeld, and Joyce Ippolito marshaled the book through production and ensured I knew exactly what I was supposed to do, while Eliza Childs copyedited the text with clarity and consistency. Many thanks to Meridith Murray for compiling the index and to Marnie Wiss for the careful proofreading. Working on the cover (and chatting about good bands) with Will Schmiechen was a really fun way to finish the project. The anonymous reviewers helped me sharpen my arguments and broaden my perspective and saved me from embarrassing errors. Any shortcomings that remain, however, are entirely my own (but don't tell me about them because it's too late to change anything).

This book is dedicated to my family, who are now experts at border crossings. My sisters are the best, my parents' support is unflinching, and we all take pride in each other's successes. That said, I expect each of them to buy a copy at full price (hardcover). My in-laws, Paul and Christine, have been enthusiastic supporters of this book. Paul deserves special thanks, as he read various drafts of each chapter and made sure I didn't lose any threads and accounted for all the ears. He is the platonic ideal of the interested reader.

There is no way to thank my immediate world of Rosemary, Rooke, and Rosalind. It just can't be done. As I said, acknowledgments are impossible.

# Index